J23305

W9-DDI-460

National
Industrial Strategies
and the
World Economy

Other Research Volumes
from The Atlantic Institute for International Affairs

TOWARDS INDUSTRIAL DEMOCRACY: EUROPE,
JAPAN AND THE UNITED STATES
    edited by Benjamin C. Roberts

BANKS AND THE BALANCE OF PAYMENTS:
PRIVATE LENDING IN THE INTERNATIONAL
ADJUSTMENT PROCESS
    by Benjamin J. Cohen
    in collaboration with Fabio Basagni

THE INTERNAL FABRIC OF
WESTERN SECURITY
    by Gregory Flynn
    with Josef Joffe, Yves Laulan,
    Laurence Martin, and Stefano Silvestri

National Industrial Strategies and the World Economy

edited by
JOHN PINDER

An Atlantic Institute for International Affairs
Research Volume

ALLANHELD, OSMUN   Publishers
CROOM HELM   London

198307

337.09
N 277

ALLANHELD, OSMUN & CO. PUBLISHERS, INC.

Published in the United States of America in 1982
by Allanheld, Osmun & Co. Publishers, Inc.
(A Division of Littlefield, Adams & Company)
81 Adams Drive, Totowa, New Jersey   07512

Copyright © 1982 by The Atlantic Institute for International Affairs

All rights reserved. No part of this publication may
be reproduced, stored in a retrieval system, or
transmitted in any form or by any means, electronic,
mechanical, photocopying, recording, or otherwise,
without the prior permission of the publisher.

Library of Congress Cataloging in Publication Data
Main entry under title:

National industrial strategies and the world economy.

(An Atlantic Institute for International Affairs
research volume)
   Includes bibliographical references and index.
   1. Industry and state — Addresses, essays, lectures.
2. International economic relations — Addresses, essays,
lectures.   I. Pinder, John.   II. Series.
HD3611.N37   1981   337'.09'048   81-65010
ISBN 0-86598-040-3   AACR2

Published in 1982 in Great Britain by

Croom Helm Limited
2–10 St. John's Road
London, SW 11

ISBN (U.K.) 0-7099-2010-5

Printed and bound in the United States of America

82 83 84 / 10 9 8 7 6 5 4 3 2 1

Contents

Tables and Charts

Charts

Foreword

Industrial problems in today's world are common concerns of all advanced and developing economies. The structure of industry in many countries has in the last ten years undergone fundamental changes due to a number of internal and external factors. Demography and labor mobility (or immobility) as well as technology, energy, terms of trade, and political factors have all worked to affect and alter the basis of industrial growth. The 1980s will certainly witness as much or more change in the world economy, and will probably prove to be a decade of transition rather than one of stable industrial development. Private and public institutions will continue their efforts to adapt to or, in some cases, to resist changes in international competitiveness, and in this way will either contribute to international cooperation or friction.

This situation in the world economy has been the focus of the two-year project that the Atlantic Institute for International Affairs undertook with the generous support of the Commission of the European Communities in Brussels, building on the basis of a previous preparatory and collaborative effort on the same subject between the Institute and the Trilateral Commission. Several leading experts on the structural problems of industry in key countries have worked together during the course of the project and have made, we believe, a real contribution to the understanding of national industrial strategies, whether private or public. Furthermore, their studies add considerably to our knowledge of the international, often neglected, implications of national actions. The task of integrating individual national situations into their larger regional and world contexts is indeed at the heart of the continuing economic work of the Institute.

We are grateful to the Commission of the European Communities and in particular to Commissioner Étienne Davignon and to Mr. Fernand Braun, Director General for Internal Market and Industrial Affairs, for the financial and intellectual support they have given the project during its course.

Martin J. Hillenbrand
Director General
Atlantic Institute for
International Affairs

National
Industrial Strategies
and the
World Economy

Introduction

As the economic crisis of the Western industrialized countries continues into the 1980s, explanations in terms of macroeconomics alone become less and less convincing. Diagnosis must take account of the evident difficulty of adapting our industrial structures to respond to contemporary needs. But the exact nature of the problem is hard to grasp, because such a diversity of knowledge is required. There are many sectors of industry, each with its own complex structure and difficulties. There are dozens of countries which influence world trade and production, each with its own pattern of industrial behavior based on its peculiar economic, political, and cultural characteristics. There are the interactions among all these sectors and countries in what has irrevocably become an international market for industrial goods.

Inadequate knowledge about these many sides of the problem of adapting and developing the structure of industry may be one reason why it has proved so hard to solve. This book is an attempt to supply this knowledge by assembling the contributions of people who are familiar with a wide range of the more important aspects of the problem. While the authors are not collectively responsible for each other's work, we have endeavored to shape the book into a coherent whole; and it may help the reader if I explain the logic of the successive chapters.

The first chapter, by Saunders, analyzes the development of world production and trade in manufactures and shows the pace of structural change, the emergence of Japan and then of the newly industrializing countries, and the changes that have had to be accommodated in the pattern of international trade. In the next chapter I have tried to explain some of the motives for industrial policy and to relate them to the forms that policy takes. Thus these two chapters provide a statistical background and an analytical framework for problems and policies discussed in the chapters on different sectors and countries.

The following two chapters, by Woolcock and Edwards, examine the recent development of five industrial sectors and policy responses of major governments and international organizations. The steel industry, where national and international reactions to the difficulties of the 1970s have been particularly interesting, has a chapter to itself. This can be compared in the following chapter with the experience of three other troubled sectors—textiles, man-made fibers, and shipbuilding—and set against that of aircraft manufacture, where governments are promoting an industry that is expected to thrive in the 1980s. These chapters put some flesh on the statistical and analytical bones of the first two, and show the intensity of interaction among international market forces, national policies, and international attempts to regulate them.

The four chapters on industrial policies in the four major economies of the advanced industrial part of the world are the heart of the book. The aim is to give some basis for understanding how the different governments are liable to react to industrial circumstances of the types described earlier. Their behavior is strikingly diverse. Hosomi and Okumura show how industrial policy is taken for granted in Japan as constructive and accepted as "a meaningful tool for promotion of the national economy." They trace its evolution from the strong planning needed for postwar reconstruction to the selective support at key points (R & D, energy conservation, small firms, recession cartels) in the highly competitive economy of today. For Diebold, writing on the United States, the task is quite different. For many Americans, abstinence from industrial policy has been almost an article of faith. Diebold examines the history of American policy and finds a variety of experience, which contradicts the belief that the United States is constrained by a tradition of abstinence: "nothing . . . that can be regarded as evidence of why certain things can or cannot be done today." He foresees that "efforts will be made in the United States in the years to come not only to think structurally but to shape at least some measures of industrial policy," and he goes on to analyze the American debate on measures for industries such as automobiles, steel, shoes, and shipbuilding, and for issues such as energy, the environment, technology, investment abroad, protection, and antitrust. Diebold then shows how Canada's doubts concern not the principle of an industrial policy but certain dilemmas regarding its content: capital inflow versus restriction of foreign investment, a more open and specialized economy versus a more protected one with a wider range of industries, and the relationship between primary production, processing, manufacture, and services.

European industrial policy is itself a most complex concept, because of wide differences among the different countries, even within Western Europe, and a certain division of powers between the European Community and its member states. Given only one chapter on the subject, Hager concentrates on establishing that almost all these countries share strong traditions of industrial policy (even if only recently in Britain) and of social democracy; hence there is a tendency to use industrial policy as an instrument of social policy that helps to keep the peace between the social classes. European attachment to what Hager calls "the comfortable industrial society," with its high wages and wealth of social legislation, is a powerful motive for protection against imports from countries where labor is much more pliant or much lower paid. While suggesting that some protection is inevitable, he analyzes measures of industrial policy that the Community and the governments can take to favor international competitiveness without sacrificing the benefits of social welfare.

In the final chapter I draw some conclusions about the implications of industrial policies for the relations between these countries and in the wider international economy. Some of these conclusions concern the types of industrial policy that could help overcome the economic crisis by encouraging adaptation at the same time as creating employment. Others concern the international arrangements, in the European Community, the OECD, and more widely for example in the GATT, that will be required if national policies are not going to undermine the international economic order.

These conclusions are perhaps unfashionable since, instead of lamenting that the time is out of joint, they suggest, in the light of the contents of this book, some things that could be done to set it right. But fashionable pessimism should be resisted. Although most governments and international institutions are ill-prepared to conceive industrial policies that are more than a polite new word for protection, the book contains many examples of measures that promote industrial development without jeopardizing the international trading system, and which thus improve the condition of both the national and international economies. It is tempting to seek more and newer examples and try to make our analysis more complete. But the problems with which industrial policy must deal have continued to mount and it seemed important to publish without delay. The text is therefore confined to what was known by the latter part of 1980.

John Pinder

1 Changes in the Distribution of World Production and Trade

CHRISTOPHER SAUNDERS

Introduction

This chapter is about the transformation of the industrial sectors, or more strictly the manufacturing sectors, of the world economy during the past decade or two. It is intended as a summary record as reflected, mainly, in the statistics, recognizing that statistics are no more than a mirror, sometimes a distorting mirror, of events and human performance. No attempt is made to suggest any new or systematic analysis of the underlying causes of changes or to assess the technological developments, policies, and strategies, social and political forces—or indeed historical accidents—that have brought about the transformations described. The chapter may provide a background for the more detailed studies of particular industries and regions that follow.

Structural change—which we can call transformation—of the world economy can be perceived under many dimensions. Here we deal basically in two: (a) the shift in the economic balance between the national economies, which are still the main determining units of the world economy, but dealing mostly with countries in groups (since an encyclopedia would be needed for a country-by-country approach), with special emphasis on relations between developed and, to the extent that they have entered the industrial sector, developing countries; and (b) the shift in the balance between the various industries and products into which an economic structure is divided for convenient classification.

Further, structural change can be perceived under two headings: production structures, involving continuous change in the distribution of employment and capital (the subject of the next section of this chapter), and the structure of international trade (the final section). The two ways of looking at the international division of labor are obviously interdependent, the nature of the mutual interaction being a matter of controversy not dealt with here. Nor do we deal with the interactions between structural changes in manufacturing and those in the rest of the economy. The account throughout is summary, and aims only to highlight some major features of the transformation process as it actually occurred.

A general remark: it is certainly not suggested that the pattern of structural change in the years covered by this summary record must be repeated in future decades. Indeed, one lesson from the record, as set out here, is that structural change is an intensely complex and variegated process, following no simple rules of historical determinism. It is in many respects a confusing process for those analysts who seek a systematic pattern of international development (in anything except the broadest and most-obvious terms). The process can be interpreted, it is true, by models and equations—but with limited explanatory power and leaving many unresolved residuals and exceptions to average rules. The advantage of an unsatisfactory and sometimes disorderly process, however, is that the opportunities for improvement on past trends, with the help of appropriate policies and social adjustments, need never be closed. History, happily, is full of breaches of supposed laws of economic behavior.

A caution: for convenience in summary accounts, it is necessary to refer to the performance of nations, or industries, as though each represented a homogeneous, single-minded unit impelled by common objectives and common patterns of behavior. In fact, the performance of a national economy, or industry, is of course a weighted average of good, bad, and indifferent units within it.

Changing Manufacturing Structures

Total Manufacturing Production

We may look first, for a very general perspective, at the broad pattern of the location of manufacturing production in the world (see Table 1.1).

These figures, showing the dollar value of manufacturing output in developing countries to be about one-eighth of that in the industrial West, cannot be taken as more than broad orders of magnitude. For two reasons they may somewhat understate the relative importance of the developing countries: first, because comparisons at official exchange rates generally tend to exaggerate differences in real output between countries at different levels of development; and second, because there is always some uncertainty about how far small-scale industry is covered in developing countries. Nevertheless, the main point to be made by the table is the still very small number of developing countries with a manufacturing industry of significant size.

Table 1.1 is confined to market economies, and omits the substantial manufacturing output in the socialist world, because of the difficulties of compiling even approximately comparable valuations of output. Both UNCTAD and UNIDO have attempted tentative comparisons, which suggest a level of manufacturing output in the socialist countries—including the Soviet Union but not China, North Korea, or Vietnam—not very different from that in the European market economies.[1] This seems an overestimate for the socialist countries: the number employed in manufacturing in the Soviet Union and Eastern Europe is probably quite close to the number in the European market economies, but it is difficult to believe that on any reasonable basis of comparison the real output per head could fail to be significantly smaller than in Western Europe.[2]

The other major omission from the distribution of world manufacturing output is the People's Republic of China. A diversity of indirect and speculative estimates reported by UNIDO suggests that China's share in world manufacturing value added (output) might be between 8 and 12 percent of that of the developed market economies.[3]

For comparable employment rates—for which data, although subject to their own uncertainties, may be somewhat more comparable than for value added—we get the results shown in Table 1.2.

If the employment data were to be matched with the value of output (Table 1.1), it would appear that the developing countries, with a larger manufacturing

Table 1.1 Value Added in Manufacturing—Market Economies, 1975

	In U.S. billion $ (1970 prices)	Number of countries
The industrial West		
Industrial Europe	255	13
Southern Europe[a]	26	4
United States and Canada	285	2
Japan	92	1
Australia, New Zealand, South Africa	20	3
Total industrial West	678	23
Developing countries		
Output of more than $5 billion		
Brazil	17	
Mexico	12	
Argentina	9	
India	8	
Total	46	4
Output of $2 to $5 billion		
Iran	4	
South Korea	3	
Turkey	3	
Taiwan	2	
Philippines	2	
Total	15	5
Output of less than $ billion	32	81
Total developing countries	93	90
Total market economies	771	113

[a]Greece, Portugal, Spain, and Yugoslavia. In some analyses by the international organizations, these southern European countries are included in the never formally defined category of "developing countries."

Source: Derived from World Bank, *World Development Report*, 1979, Annex Table 6.

Table 1.2 Employment in Manufacturing, 1975 (in millions)

Developed market economies[a]	74
Developing countries[a]	87
Socialist countries[b]	47
Total	208

[a]Defined as in Table 2.1.
[b]Excluding socialist countries in Asia.

Source: UNCTAD, *Handbook of International Trade and Development Statistics* 1979, Table 6.8. The data include self-employers, family workers, etc.

manpower than the industrial West, produce not much more than one-eighth of the industrial West's manufacturing output. The comparison, again, probably overstates the contrast, especially because employment data based on population censuses can be expected to be more complete in developing countries than their industrial output statistics. But the figures afford some indication of the immense gap in labor productivity. (This gap is not due simply to the greater concentration in developing countries of industries where productivity is everywhere relatively low, although that structural factor plays some part.)

GROWTH RATES IN MANUFACTURING

Fast growth in manufacturing during the 1960s was shared by all the main world regions; the slow-down in the 1970s was not. Despite the fall in manufacturing growth in the industrial West and a certain slackening in the socialist economies, the rate of manufacturing growth in the developing countries as a whole accelerated; while manufacturing increased its weight in the developing economies, the growth of GDP, and of GDP per head, was well maintained (see Table 1.3). In China, too, unofficial and necessarily somewhat speculative estimates show a marked acceleration of growth in the 1970s.[4]

Table 1.3   Growth Rates of Manufacturing and GDP

	Percentage a year					
	Manufacturing output		GDP		GDP per head of population	
	1960–70	1970–76	1960–70	1970–77	1960–70	1970–77
Developed market economies	5.8	3.4	4.9	3.4	3.8	2.5
Centrally planned economies[a]	9.3	8.7	6.6	6.0	5.4	5.1
Developing countries	6.4	7.5	5.3	5.8	2.6	3.2
China (People's Republic)[b]	5.7	9.7	5.7	7.0	3.4	4.3

[a] Excluding socialist countries in Asia.

[b] A. G. Ashbrook, Jr., "China: Shift of Economic Gears" in *Chinese Economy Post-Mao* (Joint Economic Committee of the US Congress, 1978). Estimates relate to total industrial production in 1970–76.

Source: UNCTAD, *Handbook of International Trade and Development Statistics, Supplement 1979*, Tables 6.2 and 6.8 (except for China).

Two comments may be made on the acceleration of growth in developing countries in the 1970s. (a) At first sight it suggests that growth in the developing world is less fragile, and less dependent on growth in the industrial West, than might be expected. It is of course true that the fast rise in commodity prices (other than oil) in the early 1970s considerably weakened the balance-of-payments block to development. Some of the gains were lost by the OPEC action in 1973 and then by recession and inflation in the West; on the other hand, the OPEC surpluses, combined with Western recession, opened up a greatly increased flow of capital funds for the developing countries able and willing to tap them (indeed, Western banks and order-hungry Western exporters became only too ready to lend). (b) It must also be observed, however, that the accelerated growth of the 1970s was by no means universally shared among the developing nations. Among the economies with substantial manufacturing industries, growth of GDP accelerated in Brazil, South Korea, the Philippines, and Turkey. But in as many other semi-industrial countries the growth of manufacturing output was seriously reduced (India, Argentina, Mexico, Iran, and Taiwan); in others, it was no more than maintained.[5] The concentration of manufacturing activity in a few countries in the developing world was probably intensified.[6]

THE CHANGING BRANCH STRUCTURE OF MANUFACTURING

The *tendances lourdes* of structural change in manufacturing production are familiar enough: the transition from food processing, textiles, and clothing to metal using and chemicals, or from consumer goods to capital and intermediate goods (a development sometimes treated as almost analogous to that from herds to crops or from stone to iron). The process of transformation, and its diffusion over the world as industrialization spread and output expanded, has been described historically by Svennilson up to the early years after World War II.[7] It was first systematized in quantitative equations by Chenery, and his cross-section equations were further refined in a United Nations study.[8] A kind of modal or average pattern of national manufacturing output between branches of manufacturing can be constructed from cross-country observations, of which the main statistical determinants appear to be the size of the country (in terms of population) and the level of development (in terms of income per head).

Underlying this overall pattern and its application to individual countries are various factors emanating from both the demand and supply sides. On the demand side are the fairly uniform patterns of consumer demand for the major product groups at given levels of real income per head, moderated by many peculiarities of national habits and ways of living, and by investment levels and foreign demand, so far as these affect domestic manufacturing output. The determining elements on the supply side are more complex and probably carry a greater weight in shaping the pattern of output: they include a nation's natural resource base, its endowment in human and capital resources, its technological capacity, its international competitiveness or comparative advantages – as well as population size, which has its particular significance for branches of industry subject to important economies of scale. The supply factors must include, too, the influence of government and industrial policies shaping both the domestic expenditure pattern and foreign trade (notably whether development policies have been oriented toward import substitution or export promotion); further, the supply pattern is bound to be influenced, especially in developing countries, by the extent of foreign investment and the operations of transnational corporations.

This incomplete inventory of elements contributing to national manufacturing structures and to their pattern of change is listed simply to show that structural change, although subject to some more or less universal influences, cannot be regarded as a wholly deterministic process.

It is best to start with the broad picture, however. For a very general summary, it is common and convenient to follow the UN statisticians by dividing the branches of manufacturing between "heavy" and "light" industry (although it may not be clear in what meaningful sense a ton of steel is "heavier" than a ton of cloth).[9] Table 1.4 provides a measure, in the most summary form possible, of structural change since 1960. We can observe:

a. the convergence between the developed and developing market economies: in 1960, the shares of the two blocks of industries in the developed countries (62

Table 1.4   Structure of Manufacturing Output, 1960-76

	Percentage of value added		
	1960	1970	1976
Developed market economies ("industrial West")			
Heavy	62.0	67.0	67.6
Light	38.0	33.0	32.4
Developing market economies			
Heavy	37.5	47.2	51.1
Light	62.5	52.8	48.9
Socialist economies[a]			
Heavy	58.1	67.0	71.8
Light	41.9	33.0	28.2
World[a]			
Heavy	59.3	65.6	67.7
Light	40.7	34.4	32.3

[a]Other than socialist economies in Asia.

Heavy industry: Paper and products (ISIC 341), chemicals (351 and 352), oil refineries (353), nonmetallic mineral products (354 and 36), basic metals (37) and metal products, machinery, and equipment (38) (see Table 1.5).

Light industry: Food, drink, and tobacco (31), textiles, leather, and clothing (32), wood and wood products (33), printing, publishing, etc. (342), rubber products (355), plastic products (356), and other manufactures (39) (see Table 1.5).

Source: UNIDO, *World Industry since 1960* (1979), Table 3.1

percent heavy, 38 percent light) were almost precisely the reverse of the shares in the developing countries. By 1976, this structural difference between the two groups of countries was greatly reduced: manufacturing in the developing countries was by then almost equally divided between heavy and light industry.

b. that the structural shift from light to heavy industry was marked in both developed and developing countries, but was distinctly greater in the developing countries. In this rather limited sense it was the developing countries which adjusted more rapidly to the trend in world demand (if that can be roughly represented by the trend in "world" production).

c. that the structural shift was temporarily frozen in the developed market economies during the difficult 1970s, when their overall growth slowed down.[10] But the rate of structural change was effectively maintained in the developing countries when, as we have seen, their growth rate of total manufacturing output accelerated. (This is a crude indication, to be developed further below, that structural change tends to be faster in conditions of fast growth.)

d. that the structural pattern in the socialist economies of Europe shows throughout a stronger shift from light to heavy industry than that in the industrial West, again accompanying the faster overall growth rate in the socialist group. Although the differing cost and price structures make difficult any comparison of shares of value added, it seems probable that the difference between the two structures was not very great, and that it lessened during the past 15 years. This similarity of broad manufacturing structures is confirmed by an analysis of branch shares of employment and of the wage and salary bill (both variables which lend themselves to comparison more easily than value added) between the European socialist countries (including the Soviet Union) and the fully industrialized West European countries, for the mid-1960s.[11]

Although, broadly, it is the block of heavy industries that, in total, displays the fastest growth rates, this does not necessarily apply to all the constituent branches. We pass now to a somewhat more disaggregated analysis of branch growth rates and of their relative importance in the developed and developing market economies. (A similarly disaggregated analysis for the socialist economies is not practicable.) This more detailed comparison considerably qualifies the broad picture of structural change presented in terms of heavy and light industries. Table 1.5 sets out, from UNIDO estimates, the rates of growth under 27 branches (following the three-digit International Standard Classification of all economic activities – ISIC). This allows an analysis according to branch growth rates, which appears more relevant to the character of structural change than the too-summary division between heavy and light industries. Hence the branches are ordered according to the growth rates in 1960-74 in the developed market economies; this ordering, in view of the dominance of the developed economies, represents an approximate approach to the relative growth of demand in terms of added values (whether met from domestic production or from imports) in the nonsocialist world as a whole.

The 27 branches are divided into three groups, each accounting for about one-third of the value added in manufacturing in the developed market economies

Table 1.5 Growth Rates (1960-74) and Structure (1970) of Manufacturing Output

		Growth rates % p.a.			Percentage weights (1970)	
ISIC	Branches ranked by growth in developed market economies	Developed market economies	Developing countries (market)	Developed as % of developing	Developed countries	Developing countries
	Fast growth					
356	Plastic products	14.0	10.5	133	1.4	1.2
351	Industrial chemicals	9.8	12.3	84	5.7	3.6
352	Other chemicals	7.9	7.4	107	3.5	4.9
383	Electrical machinery	7.2	12.0	60	9.0	3.9
385	Scientific instruments, etc.	6.9	9.6	72	2.1	0.7
382	Nonelectrical machinery	6.1	10.3	59	12.2	3.6
	Weighted average	7.6	10.3	74	33.9	17.9
	Average growth					
313	Beverages	5.6	7.5	75	1.8	3.6
362	Glass	5.5	8.0	69	0.9	0.9
372	Nonferrous metals	5.5	7.8	71	1.9	2.5
341	Paper	5.4	7.9	68	3.3	2.1
353	Oil refining	5.3	3.7	143	1.5	6.7
384	Transport equipment	5.2	9.8	53	9.9	5.6
381	Metal products (exc. machinery)	5.1	8.7	59	7.4	4.3
355	Rubber products	5.1	7.6	67	1.5	1.8
332	Furniture and fixtures	5.0	3.2	156	1.6	1.1
361	Pottery, china, etc.	4.8	5.1	94	0.4	0.8
369	Other nonmetallic mineral products	4.7	8.7	54	2.7	3.5
	Weighted average	5.2	7.3	71	32.9	32.9
	Slow growth					
371	Iron and steel	4.5	8.4	54	6.4	3.7
331	Wood and cork products	4.0	5.3	75	2.3	2.2
321	Textiles	3.7	3.9	95	4.5	12.5
311/2	Food products	3.7	5.1	73	8.6	15.2
342	Printing and publishing	3.6	7.5	48	4.6	2.7
354	Misc. products of oil and coal	2.5	14.8	17	0.2	0.8
322	Clothing (exc. footwear)	2.4	7.6	31	2.9	4.0
314	Tobacco products	2.0	3.7	54	0.7	3.5
323	Leather and fur products	0.3	3.9	8	0.5	0.9
324	Footwear	-0.1	3.5	0	0.6	2.0
	Weighted average	3.6	5.7	63	31.3	47.5
390	Other manufacturing	...	...		1.8	1.6
	Total	5.2	7.4	70	100	100

Source: Derived from UNIDO, *World Industry since 1960* (1979), Tables 3.2, 3.3, and 2.7. Weights for 1970 based on data for 96 developing and 27 developed market economies. Growth rates based on varying number of countries for each branch.

(and, therefore, on our rough assumption, in total demand): fast growth, average growth, and slow growth branches. In relation to the previous analysis, it can be observed that the grouping of branches by growth does not at all points correspond with the division into heavy and light industries. Thus, the fastest growing branch in Table 1.5 happens to be plastic products, a light industry, and among the slow growth branches is the typically heavy iron and steel industry.[12]

The major differences in branch structures between the two groups of countries can be seen from the difference in the shares of value added (in 1970). While the fast growth branches account for 34 percent of manufacturing output in the developing economies, they represent only 18 percent of output in the developing countries. The shares of the average growth branches are the same—33 percent—in both groups of countries. But the slow growth branches—also nearly one-third of output in the developed contries—account for nearly half of the output in the developing world. Among the *fast growth* branches, the main and not unexpected reason for the dominance of the developed countries is the much higher share in total output (23 percent versus 8 percent in the developing countries) of engineering products (electrical and nonelectrical machinery, scientific instruments, etc.). There is less difference in the combined shares of the two chemical branches (9 percent vs. 8 percent).[13] Among the *average growth* branches, the higher share of transport equipment in the developed countries is offset by their relatively small share in oil refining.

In the *low growth* branches, as could be expected, the shares of total output in the developing countries are nearly all much greater than in the developed economies: textiles, clothing, and footwear make up 18 percent of the value added in manufacturing output in the developing countries, versus 8 percent in the developed countries, and food products 15 percent versus 9 percent. Taken together, these branches represent the biggest differences in structure between the two groups of countries, offsetting the gap in engineering among the fast growth branches.

In nearly all branches, the growth rates in 1960–74 have been faster in the developing countries. In this sense, the developing countries as a group are "catching up" almost all round: the only exceptions are plastic products, chemicals other than industrial chemicals (including some technologically less-advanced products such as paints and soap, as well as pharmaceuticals), oil refining (which was shifting away from the producing countries), and furniture. Overall, the rate of manufacturing growth in developed countries is 70 percent of that in the developing countries. It is true that the developing countries' lead in growth is slightly less marked in the fast growth branches; but in the two most-important fast growth branches, output expansion in the developing countries has run far ahead of that in the industrial West: these branches are electrical machinery, where the 12 percent annual growth rate in developing countries reflects the rapid advance of light electrical and electronic consumer goods and components (especially in Hong Kong and Singapore), and nonelectrical machinery.[14]

The penetration of the developing countries into the fast growth branches is still limited. It can be calculated, however, that the 1960–74 branch growth rates in the developing countries, if extrapolated into the future, would lead by 1990–95 to an equal division of output between fast, average, and slow growth branches, similar to that obtaining in the developed countries in the 1970s.[15] A similar extrapolation for the developed countries would put more than half of their output in the fast growth group by 1990-95. (These are intended not as serious projections nor "targets," but as one way of displaying the rate of convergence between the two branch structures. Whether a lag of 20 years or so is regarded as a long or a short time depends on the historical sense and expectations of the observer.)

Among the branches of average and slow growth rates we note those in the developed countries—the industrial West—that are falling behind by more than their lag in total manufacturing output (i.e., where the developed countries' growth rate is substantially less than 70 percent of that of the developing countries). In the branches of average growth rate, perhaps the most significant example is transport equipment. We have not full data in the same terms as Table 1.5 for the constituents of this heterogeneous group, but the broad picture can be seen from incomplete figures of output in physical units (see Table 1.6).

In the automobile industries of the developing world, the main producer is Brazil, where the transport equipment branch accounts for 8 percent of total manufacturing output (1973)—a proportion not much less than the 10 percent in

Table 1.6 Growth Rate of Output (1967-76) of Some Items of Transport Equipment

	Developed market economies	Developing market economies	World[a]	Share of developing countries in world	
		percentages a year		total	percentage
				1967	1976
Passenger cars	4.6	10.4	5.3	2.2	3.3
Trucks	6.2	14.0	6.6	3.5	6.5
Motor coaches and buses	4.4	8.0	5.8	5.1	6.2
Tractors (10 HP or more)	3.5	19.7	4.5	2.7	9.1
Merchant vessels[b]	6.2	26.1[c]	6.7[b]	1.1	4.9

[a]Excluding socialist countries in Asia.
[b]Excluding also USSR from world total.
[c]Brazil, India, S. Korea, and Peru. NB low base.

Source: United Nations, *Yearbook of Industrial Statistics 1976.*

the industrial West – and has an important impact on other branches of engineering. Other significant centers of automobile production are found in Argentina, Chile, Iran, Mexico, South Korea, and Venezuela, largely resulting from the activities of the transnational companies and to some extent integrated with production in North America, Western Europe, and Japan.

Among the slow growth industries, it is worth noting the almost equal rates of growth, between the two groups of countries, in textiles. But textiles, even in 1970, accounted for less than 5 percent of manufacturing output in the developed countries, versus 12½ percent in the developing world. This industry – the favorite candidate for restructuring to the benefit of the developing countries – now offers only limited opportunities for withdrawal in the industrial West. In clothing and footwear, the shift of production toward the developing countries continues, with growth rates more than three times greater than in the industrial West. Again, the share of these industries in the manufacturing output of the developed countries has sunk to very small proportions.

We can also compare structural changes between the two groups of countries by examining the rank orders of branch growth rates in each area. The rank correlation between them in fact works out at only 0.53; this is statistically significant at the 1 percent level and indicates a certain degree of common response to the general factors that determine structural change. The larger differences in rank order are of some interest, however, and exemplify cases where the different growth paths in developed and developing countries display a certain complementarity. These (taking only gaps in rank order of five or more places) are shown in Table 1.7. Only one of these (chemicals other than industrial chemicals) figures among the fast growth branches, and here the relative advantage lies with the developed countries. Of the seven branches that are higher in the growth hierarchy among developing rather than developed countries, four, of which the most important are iron and steel and clothing, are slow growth industries.[16]

Another test of similarity of the extent of structural change can be gained by comparing the variances between branch growth rates in the two groups of countries. There appears to be slightly more movement between branches in the developing countries: the coefficient of variation between the branch growth rates is 40 percent, versus 37 percent in the developed countries, but the difference is hardly significant.[17]

STRUCTURAL CHANGE IN DEVELOPED AND DEVELOPING COUNTRIES

A few general, and certainly not original, reflections on the process of structural change arise from these comparisions – overaggregated as they are in terms of both production and countries – and some questions also arise.

a. Interaction between the structural patterns of the developed and developing countries has clearly influenced the relative growth patterns, but cannot be traced in much detail. Its dimensions will become clearer when we examine the trade relations. The greater part of the growth in each of the two large groups of countries, although influenced by cross–frontier investment, by the diffusion of technology between them, and by trade, represents the structural transformations resulting from *domestic* demand and supply factors.

Table 1.7 Rank Order of Output Growth Rates, 1960–74

Higher in developed countries	Rank order		Growth group[b]
	Developed	Developing	
Chemicals other than industrial chemicals	3	18	Fast
Beverages	7	16.5	Average
Oil refining	11	24.5	Average
Furniture, etc.	15	27	Average
Higher in developing countries			
Transport equipment	12	6	Average
Metal products (excluding machinery)	13.5	8.5	Average
Other nonmetallic mineral products	17	8.5	Average
Iron and steel	18	10	Slow
Printing and publishing	22	16.5	Slow
Miscellaneous oil and coal products	23	1[a]	Slow[a]
Clothing	24	14.5	Slow

[a]Note very small size of this branch.
[b]From Table 1.5.

b. In the *developed* market economies, structural change through shifts of production into what we have described as the fast growth branches clearly is important. But the differences between branch growth rates, when considered in relation to their relative importance in the existing structure, have not been immense. The areas of really fast growth, at the degree of disaggregation used in our 27-branch classification, are few. Of course, there are individual products and processes within these categories—the various uses of electronics being the most publicized at present—where rates of growth have been, and no doubt will be, far more dramatic. Nevertheless, their contribution to the growth of output in manufacturing industry as a whole in the industrial countries seems to have qualitative rather than quantitative significance. The greater part of industrial progress, measured in statistical terms of value added, has come, and must continue to come, from a broad-based growth in the less-dramatized sectors of the industrial structures. The same must apply to the industrial countries in the socialist area.

c. In the *developing* countries, there is more opportunity, in principle, for industrial progress by shifts into areas of fast growth. Moreover, developing countries' output growth has been slow in the older industries, where world demand advances rather slowly (textiles and processed food products, which make up more than a quarter of their total manufacturing output). It is true that a significant contribution to overall growth in developing countries has been made in newer industries (for example, the 12 percent annual growth rate for electrical machinery), in part as a result of the activities of the transnational corporations. How far can the newer industries continue to support industrial progress in the developing countries?[18] It seems probable that continued industrial progress in developing, as in developed, economies must continue to rely mainly on the wide range of industries of moderate growth in demand (e.g., in general engineering, metal, mineral and wood processing, transport equipment, and perhaps in some chemical branches). For many developing countries which have already achieved a considerable level of industrialization, the era of drastically fast growth through market penetration by the older industries may be coming to an end. The question is whether, and which, other countries now at lower levels of industrialization will take their place in the historical and geographical product cycle.[19]

STRUCTURAL SIMILARITIES AND CONTRASTS IN INDIVIDUAL COUNTRIES

In the previous discussion, we dealt with the market economy world mainly in terms of the oversimplified division between the developed and the developing groups. Examination of the patterns in individual countries throws a much more variegated light on structural similarities and contrasts. Table 1.8 shows, for a selection of countries, the shares in manufacturing output of five major industry groups.

The structural similarity between the more-industrialized market economies has often been observed and is evident from the table. At the level of aggregation in Table 1.8 there is rather little evidence of specialization, especially among the larger countries. We note, however, the (partly) natural resource specialization in food, drink, and tobacco (mainly food products) in Belgium and the Netherlands, contrasting with the small share of these industries in Japan, West Germany, and Sweden; the Italian specialization in textiles and clothing; the Netherlands specialization in chemicals; and the Norwegian specialization, which applies also to Finland and Sweden, in the rag-bag category of other manufacturing (mainly because of natural resource specialization in wood and paper products which are important constituents of this group). But the process of adjustment toward fast-growing products *within* these groups (for example in Japan) does not appear from these summary figures.

The less-industrialized European market economies show a much greater variety of structures. Ireland shows the heaviest European concentration on food processing, Greece on textiles and clothing. In Yugoslavia, the share of engineering, which reflects the emphasis on investment in a fast-growing economy, is not very different from that in Italy or the Netherlands. Among the CMEA countries, Bulgaria and Poland are still heavily involved in food processing, textiles, and clothing, compared with the more-industrialized market economies; but the manufacturing structure of the GDR is not much different from that in the Federal Republic in the importance of engineering and chemicals.

STRUCTURAL CHANGE IN WESTERN EUROPE

Structural trends in manufacturing in Western and Eastern Europe during the 1950s and 1960s have been analyzed in great detail by the Secretariat of the UN

Economic Commission for Europe.[20] The following points, inter alia, emerge from the analysis of ten countries in Western Europe:[21]

a. A high degree of structural similarity between the countries is shown by statistical measures based upon both output (value added) and employment. These measures are derived from disaggregation into 18 branches and are only slightly affected by further disaggregation.

b. Nevertheless, there are important exceptions indicating certain degrees of specialization, (e.g. forest products in the Nordic countries, electrical machinery as well as chemicals in the Netherlands). Apart from the well-known factors of natural resource endowment, level of real income per head and size of country, the most general determinant of differences between countries in the relative importance of particular branches of industry appears to be competitiveness in foreign trade (based on the branch's export/import ratio).

c. The measures of similarity, moreover, show increasing convergence during the 1960s, with few exceptions. A significant exception is the chemicals industry, where inter-country differences widened: growth was faster than elsewhere in the largest national chemical industries (France, FR Germany, Netherlands, Britain) where economies of scale, especially in research and innovation, reinforced competitiveness.

d. The hypothesis is examined that structural change tends to be more rapid when overall growth is fastest. This proposition appears to be confirmed by the exceptionally large shifts between industries in the fast-growing Netherlands and Yugoslavia and by rather small shifts in slow-growing Britain. But among the other West European countries examined, no clear association between overall growth and the degree of structural change is found.

e. Structural change in the ten countries as a whole in the 1960s is summarized as follows: in five branches employment declined by 900,000 or 10 percent, with falls of 550,000 (17 percent) in textiles and 170,000 (6 percent) in clothing and footwear. These declines were equal to about one-quarter of the 3,300,000 (16 percent) expansion of employment in the rest of manufacturing industry, the remaining increase coming from the 7.4 percent increase in total manufacturing employment.

f. A rough attempt is made to compare structural change in the 1960s with earlier periods, by computing similarity coefficients between the shares of six major branches in various years from 1901 to 1955, and from 1958–60 to 1968–70.[22] The conclusion is that the annual rate of structural change in the 1960s was distinctly more rapid than in the previous half-century as a whole—associated with a much more rapid rate of overall growth. However, the rate of structural change in the first 12 years of the century—also a period of quite rapid overall growth in Western Europe, based on the rapid expansion of engineering—seems to have been even faster than in the 1960s. In the inter-war period, overall growth was slow and the main feature of structural change was the beginning of the long decline in textiles. The major change during the 1960s, when food processing and textiles were declining, was the rising share of the chemical industry.

The average Western European manufacturing structure, in terms of the same 18 branches, can also be compared with that in the United States and Japan for

Table 1.8   The Structure of Manufacturing Output – Selected Countries 1975

	(1) Machinery and transport equipment	(2) Chemicals a	(3) Food, drink, and tobacco	(4) Textiles and clothing	(5) Other manufacturing b	(6) Total value added in manufacturing ($ billion)
	Percentage of total manufacturing					
Developed market economies						
United States	31	11	12	8	38	264.2
Japan	36	11	8	7	38	91.8
Federal Republic of Germany	33	11	9	7	40	79.1
France	35	8	13	6	38	49.4
United Kingdom	32	11	13	9	35	35.0
Italy	27	11	12	13	37	31.8
Belgium	29	9	19	10	33	9.9
Netherlands	22	17	21	6	34	10.8
Norway	26	6	13	5	50	2.8
Sweden	35	6	9	5	45	9.9
Finland	25	6	13	10	46	3.4
Ireland	12	9	33	16	30	...
Greece	10	7	15	27	41	2.4
Spain	18	9	22	8	43	15.2
Yugoslavia	24	10	9	14	43	...
Socialist economies						
Bulgaria	25	5	23	15	32	...
Poland	26	10	18	16	30	...
German Democratic Republic	36	11	11	12	30	...

Developing countries

Brazil	30	12	15	10	33	17.3
Mexico	19	14	21	14	32	11.6
Argentina	24	13	16	13	34	8.6
India	12	11	14	30	33	8.3
Pakistan	..	9	40	43	8	1.6
South Korea	23	8	17	24	28	3.4
Iran	26	6	11	26	31	3.2
Philippines	6	17	41	12	24	2.2
Egypt	11	13	17	34	25	1.7
Israel	26	6	11	17	40	1.5
Hong Kong	..	..	..	..c	..	1.0
Malaysia	10	10	30	5	45	0.9
Singapore	46	7	8	5	34	0.6
Kenya	19	8	18	13	42	0.3

aExcluding oil refining (in principle.)
bIncluding basic metals, wood and paper products, etc.
cThe 98 percent concentration of manufacturing on textiles and clothing given by World Bank seems implausible. Statistics of Employment, given in UN, *Growth of World Industry*, show about half of total manufacturing employment in textiles and clothing, about a quarter in machinery and transport equipment.

Source: From World Bank, *World Development Report 1979*, Annex Table 6.

around 1970.[23] Between Western Europe and the United States, differences are very small (textiles are a slightly smaller proportion of manufacturing value added in the United States, and transport equipment slightly greater). Between Western Europe and Japan, the differences are rather more marked: in Japan, chemicals, basic metals, and machinery (especially electrical machinery) all account for somewhat larger shares of manufacturing than in Western Europe, and clothing (but not textiles) for a smaller share.

THE DEVELOPING COUNTRIES

We return to the structural composition of output in selected developing countries in 1975 (Table 1.8). The variety of patterns among these more or less semiindustrialized economies stands in strong contrast with the fair degree of structural similarity among the fully industrialized countries.

Under the broad categories of Table 1.8, each of the five major groups of industries of course masks a wide variety of products and processes. Even in terms of the five groups, however, a clear difference in specialization emerges. If we may take the combined shares of machinery and transport equipment and chemicals as a guide, we find:

— a set of countries where the structural composition of manufacturing is not very different from that in the fully industrialized economies at the top of the table: Brazil, Argentina, and Singapore (the very small share of textiles and clothing in Singapore suggests incomplete coverage of small establishments, but its specialization in light electrical goods is well-known).
— at the other extreme the countries where textiles and clothing or food processing, or both, dominate the industrial structure, and where engineering and chemicals are still relatively underdeveloped: India, the Philippines (but note the extremely high share of chemicals—this figure is suspicious and may indicate some peculiarity of the price structure), Pakistan (the biggest share of textiles and clothing among the countries listed), and Egypt.
— a group intermediate between the other two groups, with a combined engineering and chemicals share of around one third and about the same, or a little more, in food, textiles and clothing: Mexico, South Korea, Iran, Israel, Kenya, and Malaysia.

FACTOR INTENSITIES AND STRUCTURAL CHANGE

We have described structural change broadly in terms of heavy and light industries and of branches of industry classified according to relative growth rates of output. No mention has been made of structural change in terms of the common distinction between industries with differing factor intensities. Yet many analysts have treated this distinction as a main key to the development process, leading to the view that structural transformation consists largely in a shift in the industrial pattern toward capital-intensive, and away from labor-intensive, industries. On this view an optimal international division of labor would indicate a concentration of resources in the more-developed countries, where capital is relatively plentiful, on the more capital-intensive industries; in the less-developed countries, where labor is plentiful and cheap, on the more labor-intensive industries. Empirical studies have applied factor endowment theories, in various forms, mainly to explain the structure of international trade, and some of the findings will be reported below. But a few observations may be made about the relevance of factor intensity distinctions between branches of industry to the pattern of manufacturing growth.

The problem is to find an adequate definition and measure of "capital." Empirical research has swung away from Hecksher-Ohlin explanations of growth and competitiveness in terms of the amount of physical capital (machinery, vehicles, buildings) per worker or per unit of output. Increasing stress has been laid on human skills (which we may or may not like to describe as human capital). Thus one of the first and most-influential analyses of international trade by industries in terms of factor intensities, by Hal Lary, distinguished industries according to value added per worker — a measure intended to combine the input of fixed capital (represented by the profit element in value added) with human skills (represented by the relative pay — compared with the industrial average — per person employed).[24] Later studies added a technological element (measured, for example, by R and D expenditure or R and D staffs).[25] The use of such measures of course involves many bold assumptions: that relative profit rates between branches reflect inputs of physical capital despite monopoly influences, and that relative pay levels reflect skill despite the many obstacles to competition in labor markets.

The study by the Secretariat of the Economic Commission for Europe, already quoted in other connections, investigates differences in factor proportions in European industrial countries, West and East, analyzing 15–16 branches of manufacturing according to physical capital intensity (based both on profit rates and on cumulated investment, because of the absence of sufficient comparable data of capital stocks), labor skill intensity (relative pay), and research intensity (based on R and D inputs for Western Europe only).[26] This study shows the expected positive correlations between growth of branch output and high physical capital intensity, labor skill intensity, and research intensity. But the correlations are weak, sometimes even insignificant, in several countries, and important exceptions appear to the general rule. (For example, basic metals, despite high physical capital intensity, high wages, and high research intensity, exhibited hardly more growth of output or of productivity than the average for all manufacturing.) Partial correlations (based on the unweighted average for nine Western countries) display a closer association of growth with labor skill than of growth with either physical capital intensity or with research intensity.[27]

Further, such associations must be qualified by observing the kind of patterns presented by these measures of factor intensities. Thus physical capital intensity is far above average, in all countries, in a few industries — chemicals, oil refining, basic metals, and paper-making. Chemicals is a fast growth industry but accounts for only 9 percent of manufacturing output; the others are not (see Table 1.5). But the rest of industry, in respect of physical capital intensity, clusters not very far from the average (apart from very low capital intensity in clothing and footwear). For example, according to the ECE measures for Western Europe, the physical capital intensities in electrical machinery and nonelectrical machinery (both fast growth branches), in transport equipment (average growth) and in textiles (slow growth) are all between 70 and 80 percent of the mean for all manufacturing industry.[28] Moreover, a strong structural shift toward industries with high physical capital intensity should result in an increasing ratio of capital stock to output in manufacturing as a whole. Data on capital stock can be treacherous and of doubtful comparability. The figures in Table 1.9 for a few Western countries do not suggest any general tendency for capital-output ratios to increase, however.

R and D activities are also highly concentrated, again in chemicals and oil refining and to a lesser extent in basic metals, but also in electrical machinery (which is not among the high physical capital-intensity branches). In this case also, there is a cluster of branches with little R and D (textiles, clothing, nonelectrical machinery, printing, wood, food and drink) while the rest are scattered around the average.

In skill intensity (i.e. relative wages), chemicals and oil refining again stand out with high relative pay, and textiles, clothing, and leather at the opposite end.[29] The range around the average, however, is much narrower than for the proportions of capital or research inputs.

Thus, although factor proportions cannot be dissociated from the growth process, historical experience in the developed countries does not suggest that factor proportions reflect anything like a deterministic explanation of the pattern of structural change in industry.

Table 1.9   Growth Rates in Manufacturing, 1959 to 1973

| | Percentage per annum (1963 prices) | |
	Value added (factor cost)	Gross capital stock
Austria	5.5	5.3[a]
France	6.6	6.3[a,b]
Federal Republic of Germany	5.7	7.3
Italy	7.0	5.6[c]
Norway	5.1	5.3[d]
Sweden	5.5	4.9
United Kingdom	3.1	3.9
United States	4.8	3.0

[a] Includes mining.
[b] 1959–70.
[c] 1959–72; net capital stock.
[d] 1959–70; includes mining, oil extraction and construction.

Source: UN/ECE, *Structure and Change in European Industry*, Part I, Table 1.1.

EMPLOYMENT AND PRODUCTIVITY TRENDS

How far are these changes in manufacturing output reflected in changes in the structure of employment?

In the *developed market economies* as a whole, the first striking feature has been the modest growth of manufacturing employment in total — only about half of 1 percent a year in OECD Europe (1959-73) and 1½ percent a year in the United States. Almost the whole growth of manufacturing output resulted from the growth of labor productivity (see Table 1.10). Within the manufacturing sector, there have been considerable shifts, reflecting the shifts in output. It appears, however, that on the whole the shifts in employment structures were somewhat less marked than the shifts in output. For example, summary analysis by the ECE for the average of ten Western European countries for the 1960s shows the following: among 18 branches of manufacturing, output increases ranged between 2 and 10½ percent a year; employment changes ranged from a fall of 3 percent to a rise of 3 percent a year.[30] The reason is that greater increases in labor productivity were achieved in the fast growth branches than elsewhere, thus softening somewhat the impact of output changes on employment. The same analysis (in general — subject, as usual, to several exceptions) thus confirmed the "Verdoorn Law," i.e., productivity growth was fastest where output growth was fastest, both between countries and between industries within countries.[31]

Table 1.10 Growth Rates of Output, Employment, and Labor Productivity in Manufacturing, 1960-76

	Percentage a year					
	Output		Employment		Labor productivity	
	1960-70	1970-76	1960-70	1970-76	1960-70	1970-76
Developed market economies	5.8	3.4	1.3	−0.6	4.4	3.9
Centrally planned economies (Europe)	9.3	8.7	3.6	1.9	5.5	6.6
Developing countries	6.4	7.3[b]	3.8	6.2[b]	2.5	1.0[b]
World[a]	6.8	4.7[b]	2.8	2.1[b]	3.9	2.6[b]

[a]Excluding socialist countries in Asia.
[b]1970-75.

Source: UNCTAD, *Handbook of International Trade and Development Statistics 1979*, Table 6.8. Productivity derived from indexes of output divided by indexes of employment.

Yet the differences between branch growth rates of productivity were not very large: among the 18 branches referred to above (again taking the ten-country average), productivity increased in the 1960s by between 4 and 6 percent a year in all except three (8 percent in chemicals, 10 percent in the small petroleum and coal products branches and, at the other extreme, only 2 percent in printing).

The trend in the *developing countries* was very different. Two thirds of the growth in manufcturing output since 1960, according to the UNCTAD estimates (Table 1.10), was associated with increasing employment; the rise in labor productivity, about 2 percent a year, was less than half that in the developed market economies. Moreover, the acceleration of output growth in the 1970s, already noted, was matched by an acceleration of employment growth – but by a slowing down of productivity gains. It must be remembered that these statistics generally relate only to establishments of a certain size (employing more than, say, five or ten persons). They omit the large mass of small workshops, artisan shops, homeworkers, and so on, in the "informal sector," and this omission is likely to be more serious for the employment data used here than for the output data. Some of the striking gains in recorded manufacturing employment may well be offset by displacement of workers in the informal sector.

The labor intensiveness of the growth process in the developing countries is also demonstrated by an UNCTAD estimate. The total manufacturing labor force in developing countries is believed to have risen from about 39 million in 1955 to about 86 million in 1974. This was twice as large as the corresponding increase in the developed market economies. But the increase in manufacturing output in the developing countries was only about one-eighth as large.[32]

Between countries, the rates of growth in manufacturing employment varied immensely: among the more-important NICs, from only 2 percent a year in India to as much as 17 percent a year in South Korea (data for 1970–76).[33] The experience of South Korea illustrates how in favorable circumstances structural change and all-round industrial growth can combine simultaneous increases in both productivity (suggesting a shift toward capital-intensive technologies) and in employment (Table 1.11). The data are a good example, too, of the operation of the Verdoorn Law: the biggest increases in productivity accompany the biggest increases in output.

From the point of view of trading relations between the developed economies and the NICs, it is obviously important to compare the *levels* of labor productivity between the two groups – or, putting it the other way round, to compare the labor requirements for a given amount of output. Detailed comparisons in this area were made for the ILO by Harold Lydall.[34] He shows, on the basis of cross-country comparisons, how labor requirements for a given amount of value added (expressed in dollars) increase as the overall level of development falls. Typically, for a variety of industries representative of the major exports of NICs, labor requirement per dollar of output would be around three to four times as high in the main NICs as in Western Europe or North America. Moreover, Lydall's analysis is derived from data for 1963; after that, labor productivity seems to have grown fastest in the developed countries, so that the contrast by the mid-1970s would have been even greater. These comparisons show how a shift of production from the

Table 1.11   South Korea: Growth of Output, Employment, and Labor Productivity, 1968-74

	Percentage a year		
	Output	Employment	Productivity
Food, drink, and tobacco	14.5	8.0	6.0
Textiles	21.8	7.2	13.6
Clothing, footwear, and leather	38.5	17.7	17.7
Wood and products	7.0	3.3	3.6
Paper and products	10.3	5.4	4.7
Chemicals	15.8	10.3	5.0
Nonmetallic minerals	11.9	3.2	8.4
Basic metals	30.1	8.9	19.5
Metal products and engineering	34.3	17.0	14.8

Source: UNIDO, *World Industry since 1960* (1979), from Table 7.4.

industrial West to the NICs, of the kinds of goods which the NICs produce (and export), creates much more employment in the latter countries than it displaces in the former.

Changing Patterns of
International Trade In Manufactures

The changing structures of manufacturing output described above are reflected in, and respond to, changing structures in world trade. In all countries, developed and developing, capitalist and (nowadays) socialist, foreign trade plays an essential part in economic policy and development strategy; this is true even in the largest countries, such as the United States or the Soviet Union, where foreign trade is a statistically small proportion of the economy. Foreign trade is one of the instruments (if not always the "engine") of growth. But the instrument can be used in two ways, to push import substitution or to stimulate exports, and for both it can be used negatively (by protection against imports) or positively (by encouraging or creating import substitution or export capacity, with or without financial or fiscal aid). The story of industrialization in the developing world exhibits both methods: in the recent history of industrial development, the most-frequent approach has been import-substitution as a first stage, followed, as the industrial base expands, by export stimulation. The difficulties of riding the two horses in double harness should be noted: the high costs of industrial inputs, whether domestically produced or imported, that result from high protection are almost bound to become obstacles to competitive exporting. These processes of structural change and adjustment through foreign trade have given rise to a copious literature, to massive empirical researches, and to forceful theoretical controversy.

The present section will merely highlight a few relevant points from the record. As a start, Table 1.12 presents some main features of the changing product composition in world trade in manufactures, once more returning to the simple division of the world between three major groupings, from 1963 to 1976. There are parallels (despite differences in classification) between the relative growth rates in trade and those in manufacturing production. It must be remembered, however, that the production trends are measured in volume and the trade trends in current dollar values, since dollar export prices of manufactures approximately doubled during the period. Thus the 16 percent annual growth rate of world trade in manufactures, shown in Table 1.12, represents somewhere near an 8 percent growth rate in volume, which is consistent with the growth rates in the volume of manufacturing output (see Table 1.5) of 5 percent a year in the developed market economies and 7½ percent in developing countries (the faster growth of international trade than of production being a familiar feature of the time).

In discussing growth rates of output, it was pointed out that differences between fast- and slow-growing industries are not immense, other than a few extreme cases. Similarly, the range of export growth rates is fairly narrow—from 19 percent a year in motor vehicles and 17 percent in other engineering products and chemicals, to 13-14 percent in textiles and clothing and miscellaneous manufactures. Trade in metals shows relatively slow growth. (The range would appear even narrower if expressed in terms of volume.)

In most of the product groups, the exports of developing countries increased most, followed by those of the industrial West, while the exports of the socialist countries (partly because of more-stable prices) increased least. It should be noted, however, that:

1. The lead of the developing countries over the industrial West in export growth is really large only in engineering products and iron and steel (for which the developing countries' shares of world exports are still very small—see the second half of Table 1.12) and in textiles and clothing and miscellaneous manufactures, where developing countries account for substantial shares of world exports.

2. On the other hand, in nonferrous metals, the developing countries' share of world exports has fallen away.

3. Thus the structural change through trade, as indicated by shares of the world export market for total manufactures, has hardly been dramatic during the period 1963-76. The industrial West has maintained its dominance at about 80 percent. The developing countries have increased their share from less than 6 percent to approximately 8½ percent. And the socialist group has dropped from 13 to 9½ percent, the most striking change, if we take into account the size of the trade, being in engineering products.

4. Among the individual product groups, the only substantial weakening of the dominance of the industrial West is in textiles and clothing—a drop from nearly 75 percent to 63 percent.

Table 1.12 The Changing Structure of World Trade by Regions and Product Groups, 1963–76

		Value of exports 1976 (in $ billion) and growth rates 1963–76 (% p.a.)				Percentage of shares in world exports			
		Industrial west[a]	Eastern trading area[b]	Developing countries	World[c]		Industrial west[a]	Eastern trading area[b]	Developing countries
Total exports	V (Value) G (Growth rate)	622.8 15	94.0 13	253.1 17	991.0 15	1963 1976	64.1 62.8	12.2 9.5	20.5 25.5d
Total manufactures[e]	V G	477.7 16	56.2 13	49.2 19	588.9 16	1963 1976	80.3 81.1	13.1 9.5	5.7 8.4
Chemicals	V G	61.7 17	4.9 14	4.0 20	71.8 17	1963 1976	85.5 86.1	9.3 6.9	4.2 5.6
Engineering products[f] (excluding road motor vehicles)	V G	205.6 17	29.4 16	11.7 34	247.8 17	1963 1976	84.3 83.0	14.1 11.8	1.1 4.7
Road motor vehicles	V G	64.5 19	3.9 15	0.8 31	69.4 19	1963 1976	90.6 93.0	8.5 5.6	0.4 1.2
Iron and steel	V G	36.8 15	5.3 11	1.6 21	44.7 15	1963 1976	78.0 82.4	18.5 12.0	1.9 3.6
Nonferrous metals	V G	13.0 12.5	2.0 14	5.3 11	21.7 12	1963 1976	58.9 60.1	7.6 9.2	30.1 24.4
Textiles and clothing	V G	32.2 12.5	4.7 13	13.9 19	51.3 14	1963 1976	74.5 62.8	9.9 9.1	15.3 27.1
Other manufacturing	V G	63.9 13	6.0 6.5	11.9 19.5	82.3 13	1963 1976	75.7 77.6	16.0 7.3	6.9 14.4

a OECD Europe, North America, Japan, and Yugoslavia; excludes Australia, New Zealand, and South Africa.

b USSR, Eastern Europe, China (People's Republic), Mongolia, North Korea, and Vietnam.

c Including Australia, New Zealand, South Africa (which is why percentages do not add to 100). Excluding trade *between* China, Mongolia, North Korea, Vietnam, and these countries' trade with rest of Eastern trading area.

d Of which OPEC 13.5, others 12.0.

e Excluding food, drink, and tobacco manufactures.

f Includes metal products as well as machinery, etc.

Source: Adapted from GATT, *International Trade 1969*, Table 7, and *1977/78*, Table K.

Table 1.13 North-South Trade in Manufactures

	Exports from industrial West to developing countries					Exports from developing countries to industrial West			
	(in $ billions)			Percentage of total manufactured exports		(in $ billions)		Percentage of total manufactured exports	
	1963	1976	of which, to oil exporters	1963	1976	1963	1976	1963	1976
Total manufactures	16.95	114.30	47.30	24.5	23.9	7.84	31.70	62.7	64.4
Chemicals	2.25	13.59	3.28	28.1	22.0	0.32	2.00	51.3	49.4
Engineering products (excluding road motor vehicles)	7.11	60.79	25.99	26.8	29.6	0.64	6.80	25.0	58.1
Road motor vehicles	1.78	13.50	7.49	27.0	20.9	–	0.20	–	25.0
Iron and steel	1.38	8.71	3.86	24.0	22.7	0.14	0.80	50.0	50.0
Nonferrous metals	0.30	1.49	0.40	10.7	11.4	3.03	4.10	89.5	77.4
Textiles and clothing	1.66	5.44	2.01	24.3	16.9	1.69	9.55	52.8	68.7
Other manufactures	2.47	10.78	3.24	19.5	16.9	2.02	8.25	60.3	69.6

Source: Adapted from GATT, *International Trade 1969*, Table 7, and *1977/78*, Table K.

NORTH-SOUTH INTERDEPENDENCE

We look next at some aspects of the interdependence between the industrial West and the developing countries (Table 1.13). The trade patterns are still basically complementary, even within the manufacturing sector. Well over half the exports from North to South are engineering products; well over half the exports from South to North are textiles, clothing, and miscellaneous manufactures. Yet there is clear evidence of change in the pattern: from 1963 to 1976, the share of textiles and clothing in total North to South manufactured exports fell from 10 percent to 5 percent; and the share of engineering products in South to North exports rose from 8 percent to 21 percent.

The major dichotomy lies in the different degrees of market dependence of each region on the other. The developing countries represent less than a quarter of the markets for the exported manufactures of the industrial West.[35] The proportion varies for the different product groups, rising (in 1976) to 30 percent for engineering products, but falling to 17 percent for textiles, clothing, and miscellaneous manufactures. By contrast, of the South's limited exports of manufactures, nearly two-thirds go to the North, and the proportion is of the same order for each of the major product groups, except motor vehicles and metals.

In this sense, the overall export dependence of each group on the other did not change significantly between 1963 and 1976. But there have been changes in some product groups: the big decline in the South as a market for the North in textiles and clothing; and the big increase in the importance of the North as a market for the South's engineering exports (starting from a low base), as well as for the South's more-important exports of textiles, clothing, and miscellaneous manufactures.

Of course, one reason for this imbalance is the greater and more long-standing degree of economic integration in manufacturing among the Western industrial countries (although our figures in Table 1.13 show that the ratios of trade within to trade between the groups were much the same in 1963 and 1976) than that between North and South. Trade in manufactures between France and Germany is, in a way, a different kind of animal from that between, say, France and India. The relative market dependence can therefore be better appreciated by relating North/South trade to the total manufacturing *outputs* of the two regions. Thus, for the industrial West, exports of manufactures to the developing countries probably represent not much more than 3 percent of total manufacturing output. But for the developing countries as a group, exports of manufactures to the industrial West account for something like 7 percent of manufacturing output. The imbalance of mutual dependence remains. (It is of course partly offset by the opposite imbalance in primary products, reinforcing the still essentially complementary character of the two regions' economic structures.)

This discussion has largely ignored the immense differences between trends in the individual economies. The concentration of manufactured exports in a dozen or so developing countries — the newly industrializing countries (NICs) — is well known. A tabulation of the twelve largest exporters of manufactures among the NICs is given in Table 1.14; it shows the remarkable relative expansion of Taiwan, South Korea and, to a much smaller extent, Brazil, and the correspond-

Table 1.14   Principal Developing Countries Exports of Manufactures

	1976 Value (in $ million)	1963 (percentage)	1976 (percentage)	1976 percentage of manu- factured exports to industrial West
Hong Kong	7882[a]	20.3	18.4	83
Taiwan	6922	4.2	16.1	73
South Korea	6770	1.3	15.8	78
Singapore	3020[b]	11.6	7.0	50
India	2801	22.3	6.5	49
Brazil	2500	1.5	5.8	55
Israel	1880	6.7	4.4	68
Mexico	1010	4.8	2.4	75
Argentina	975	2.6	2.3	32
Malaysia	824	2.1	1.9	36
Pakistan	629	3.6	1.5	...
Philippines	608	1.1	1.4	84
Total of above 12	35,821	82.1	83.5	...
All developing countries[c]	42,894	100	100	64

[a] Includes reexports (about 20 percent of total).
[b] Includes reexports (about 40 percent of total).
[c] Greece, Portugal, Spain, and Yugoslavia excluded.

Source: World Bank, *World Development Report, 1979*, Annex Table 12. Manufactures consist of SITC sections 5–8, excluding Division 68 (nonferrous metals).

ing relative decline of India, as major exporters of manufactures.[36] The table also shows the high degree of dependence of the major exporters of manufactures among the NICs on sales to the industrial West; others, notably India, Argentina, and Malaysia, depend more on manufactured exports to other developing countries.

At the same time, there have been significant changes during the last 15 years in the market patterns of the Western industrial countries' exports of manufactures. From 1963 to 1973, the strongest stimulus came from the rapid expansion of trade among themselves: this intra-trade rose from two-thirds to nearly three-quarters of their total exports of manufactures, with a corresponding fall in the proportion going to developing countries. After 1973 these changes in pattern were reversed (see Table 1.15). The industrial West's exports to the OPEC markets expanded rapidly (by nearly 40 percent a year in value) after the rise in oil exporters' prices

Table 1.15   Exports of Manufactures from Industrial West by Destination

To	Percentage of exports to the world			Percentage per annum increase	
	1963	1973	1978	1963–73	1973–78
OPEC	4.4	4.6	10.4	16	39
Other developing countries	20.1	14.1	14.8	10	19
Total developing countries	24.5	18.7	25.2	12	25
Eastern trading area	3.3	4.4	5.0	19	21
Other industrial West	67.3	73.7	66.4	16	15
World	100	100	100	15	18

Source: GATT, *International Trade 1969*, Table 7, and *1978-79*, Table G. Areas defined as in Table 1.12 above.

and incomes; by 1978, the OPEC countries' share of industrial countries' manufactured exports had risen to one-tenth, while the share of other developing countries remained at 14–15 percent.[37]

Among the developed countries, the major change in the competitive picture is the rise of Japan as an exporter of manufactures, accompanying the decline of Britain and the United States. It is worth indicating some of the individual products for which the trade record demonstrates with particular force the exploitation of Japan's apparent comparative advantage. Table 1.16 shows the principal products in which Japan's share of the world market is now greater than her overall average share for manufactures, or in which Japan has increased faster than average.

By 1977, Japan's total exports of manufactures were approximately equal in dollar value to those of the United States and were exceeded only by those of the Federal Republic of Germany.

It is possible to regard Japan—formerly, but no longer, a low wage economy—as in some sense a predecessor of the manufacturing exporters in the developing countries in penetrating Western European and North American markets. Thus it is useful to compare their relative competitive positions in these markets at present.[38] In fact (in 1977 and 1978) both Japan and the developing countries accounted for 8–9 percent each of the total imports of manufactures into the Western industrial markets (other than Japan), equivalent to around 2 percent of consumption. But there are two significant differences. The first concerns the product composition of trade in manufactures. Textiles and clothing now make up only about 2 percent of the Western industrial countries' imports from Japan, against about one-third of their imports from developing countries

Table 1.16   Japan's Export Successes: Percentage of Japanese to Total OECD Exports

SITC		1965	1977	SITC		1965	1977
	Total manufactures[a]	9.4	15.6	7321	Passengers cars	3	21
7329	Motor cycles, motorized cycles	52	75	722	Electric power machinery	5	14
735	Ships and boats	16	47	725	Domestic electrical equipment	4	14
891	Musical instruments, recording equipment, etc.	23	42	715	Metal-working machinery	3	13
724	Telecommunications apparatus	20	35	714	Office machinery	2	10
864	Watches and clocks	4	28				
731	Railway vehicles	9	27				

[a] SITC Sections 5–8.

Source: OECD, *Statistics of Foreign Trade*, Series B.

(see Table 1.13). It is the Japanese who compete most strongly in the products where the other industrial countries hold their main comparative advantage. The second difference concerns the market composition. For Japan, the Western European and North American markets account for more than 40 percent of Japanese exports of manufactures; the manufactured exports from developing countries (mainly, as we have seen, from the handful of NICs) are much more concentrated, at over 60 percent, on Western Europe and North America. This difference in export orientation is relevant to the question whether the NICs are likely to follow Japan in widening their range of markets.

THE IMPACT OF NIC MANUFACTURES IN THE INDUSTRIAL WEST

A detailed account of the product composition of imports into Western Europe, from all non-OECD countries, is displayed in Table 1.17.[39] The imports from non-OECD countries are mainly from developing countries but also include imports from the socialist countries (nearly all from USSR, Eastern Europe, and Yugoslavia); the items coming mainly from the socialist countries are signaled by footnotes.

    A main purpose of this table is to bring out the difference in quality and product-mix between (a) the exports of the industrial countries to each other and (b) those of developing countries and socialist countries (most of the latter share with the NICs the characteristic of being among the NICs, although more, and sooner, industrialized).[40] For this purpose, the c.i.f. unit values, in dollars per ton, of Western European imports from non-OECD countries have been calculated as percentages of the unit values of imports of the same product class from other OECD—i.e. basically industrial—sources. To achieve as much homogeneity as

Table 1.17   Selected Imports of Manufactures into OECD Europe, 1977

		Imports from non-OECD countries		
SITC		Unit value (cif) as % of unit value from OECD countries	In $ million	As % of total imports
	Chemicals, etc.			
561	Manufactured fertilizer	80.8	305	16.7
6291	Rubber tires and tubes[a]	72.5	70	4.1
	Textiles			
6522	Cotton woven fabrics, other than gray cloth	61.6	228	12.3
6535	Synthetic woven fabrics	57.3	187	9.2
656	Made-up articles of textile materials	50.9	352	32.3
657	Floor covering, tapestries, etc.	421.0	754	35.6[c]
	Clothing			
8411	Clothing of textile fabric, not knitted	52.3	2812	39.9
8414	Clothing, knitted[a]	60.4	1188	30.4
851	Footwear	43.1	564	17.0
	Glass and pottery			
665	Glassware	74.5	87	8.3
666	Pottery	74.5	82	13.1
	Iron and steel			
673	Bars, rods, angles, shapes, sections	68.7	236	6.0[b]
	Machinery			
7151	Metal-working machine tools[b]	32.5	155	8.4[b]
7142	Calculating and accounting machinery	85.5	79	6.3
	Electrical equipment			
7222	Apparatus for electrical circuits	45.5	96	2.8
7242	Radio receivers	73.0	424	22.7
7249	Telecommunication equipment[a]	97.4	150	6.0
725	Domestic electrical equipment[a]	50.8	108	4.7
7293	Thermionic valves and tubes	73.1	291	9.6
	Vehicles			
7321	Passenger road motor vehicles[a,b]	50.4	188	1.5[b]
7328	Motor bodies and parts	78.4	138	1.6
	Other items			
821	Furniture[b]	106.9	453	22.8[b]
831	Travel goods, handbags, etc.	59.4	276	35.7
8614	Cameras and flash equipment	99.2	74	10.7
864	Watches and clocks[a]	56.2	146	14.5
8911	Phonographs, tape, and other recording equipment, etc.[a]	64.2	93	8.6

[a]EEC imports only (some importing countries do not report in tons).
[b]Main non-OECD supplies are from Eastern Europe, USSR, and Yugoslavia.
[c]Non-OECD sources: India, Iran, Morocco, and Pakistan.

Note: Unit values are expressed in $ per ton.

Source: OECD, *Statistics of Foreign Trade*, Series C, 1977.

possible of the product classes, we have used four-digit items where available in the source. The table covers all items in which the relevant imports exceeded $70 million in 1977.

It must be explained that unit values are not regarded as indications of the prices at which identical products are being traded by different exporters. Although such prices, in the strict sense, enter into unit values, as do the corresponding production costs, instead we may regard differences in unit values as signifying differences in product-mix, or quality, between goods from different sources going under one statistical description.[41]

In almost every item shown, the unit values of OECD–Europe's imports from non-OECD sources are far below those of imports from other OECD countries. No doubt there are cases where the lower unit values indicate products of equal quality sold at lower prices to gain access to new markets. For the most part, however, the lower unit values represent an element in the structural difference, almost at the microlevel, between the old and the new industrial economies; they reflect the tendency in the newly industrialized countries to specialize, whether by design or by necessity, in the lower and, presumably, simpler or down-market end of the product range, where their comparative advantage lies, within each category. This may well be a structural advantage of equal significance to the more-familiar contrast between the less- and the more-sophisticated large industrial sectors. Specialization and comparative advantage, in fact, may be conceived in terms of low grade against high grade textile fabrics or machine tools as much as in terms of the textile industry in general against mechanical engineering in general. This within-product specialization is of obvious importance to full understanding of structural change and of the pattern of international trade.[42]

Exceptions in Table 1.17 to the general rule of low unit values for Western European imports from non-OECD countries are few: floor coverings (where nearly all the imports come from a few specialist carpet industries), telecommunication equipment (covering an exceptionally large variety of items), furniture (where Yugoslavia is a major supplier) and cameras.

INTRAINDUSTRY TRADE: AN INSTRUMENT
FOR STRUCTURAL CHANGE

Another aspect of the importance of specialization *within* product-groups (parts and components as well as final products) is displayed by the concept of intraindustry trade—the exchange between countries of products (or their components) falling within the same product category. Its importance as a way of securing the benefits of specialization, long runs, and other economies of scale has been emphasized for some years by many analysts of international trade patterns.

Measures of intraindustry trade vary, but essentially they represent the extent to which a country's exports of a given product group are balanced, during a given period, by imports of the same product group. The relative importance of intraindustry trade can be assessed by seeing what proportion it bears to total turnover (imports plus exports) of the product-group concerned. Naturally the measure depends on the degree of disaggregation employed. If the product group is simply passenger motor cars, the proportion of intraindustry trade will generally be high. If the product is disaggregated down to harvest gold, four-door Austin 1300 vintage 1972, intraindustry trade is by definition zero. It is, however, found that disaggregation on a more-modest scale than this (say from the three-digit SITC code to the four-digit) reduces the proportion of intraindustry trade, but not by a great deal.

Among Western industrial countries, the proportion of intraindustry trade in manufactures is very large. One recent estimate puts intraindustry trade at an average of more than 60 percent of the total trade in manufactures of 20 OECD countries in 1973.[43] The proportion is highest among the more fully industrialized countries (although lower in Japan). It is not as large in the less-industrialized Southern European countries. Further, the proportion has been increasing in the last decade. The effect of a large and increasing proportion of intraindustry trade over a wide range of product groups is, of course, to render the export and import structures increasingly similar. Studies of trade structures have illustrated their increasing similarity, most markedly among the fully industrialized economies. To quote Hufbauer: "Export vectors mesh better with import vectors when the importing country is a richer nation."[44]

The lower level of intraindustry trade in economies of recent industrialization is also shown by estimates for Eastern Europe, although specialization within rather than between the branches of industry has long been a basic principle of integration policy in the CMEA.[45] In the chemical and machine industries, specialization among socialist countries—as reflected in high rates of both imports and exports—has gone a long way, assisted in many cases by industrial cooperation schemes with Western firms. But intraindustry trade seems to be smaller in other sectors of industry than in the West.

Estimates by Balassa for a number of Latin American countries suggest a much lower intraindustry component in the trade of these economies than that in the industrial West.[46] He shows that intraindustry trade (a) is strongest in machinery and chemicals, as in Eastern Europe, but weak in textiles and primary metals; (b) is strongest in the larger countries (Mexico, Brazil, Argentina) than in the smaller and less-industrialized ones; (c) as a rule is more important in trade with other LAFTA members than with more-remote developing countries or with developed countries. The rather low level of intraindustry trade between developed and developing countries may seem surprising in view of the importance of the transnational companies, many of whose transactions (in parts and components for final assembly at the home base, or vice versa) are certainly of the nature of intraindustry trade. Nonetheless, the quantitative importance of transnationals in North-South trade in manufactures is not large; thus U.S. imports of manufactures by transnationals from developing country affiliates in 1976 were only 10 percent of total U.S. manufactured imports from developing countries, and appear to be declining as export business comes increasingly into the hands of national firms.[47]

It might have been expected that intraindustry trade would be an ideal form for North-South economic relations. It permits developing countries to establish a base in a wide range of industries and at the same time to develop specializations in particular product lines. Yet it does not appear, in general, that development strategies have been designed to take full advantage of the opportunities: for example, tariff structures associated with import substitution in developing countries may bear more or less equally on all variants of a given product group, thus failing to discriminate in favor of those variants offering to a domestic industry the most-favorable chances of developing an export business by specialization. At the same time, of course, tariff and quota structures in developed countries tend to bear most heavily (or no less heavily) on the items within a product group in which the developing countries could most easily specialize.[48]

MARKET PENETRATION IN TEXTILES AND CLOTHING

The changing structure of international trade reveals only part of the picture of structural change through market penetration. We now examine in more depth the product groups where import penetration from developing countries has been strongest in the West — textiles and clothing. For this purpose, the most-relevant statistics are those showing the changing shares of imports, and especially of imports from developing countries, in the total consumption of the industrial West. The impact on the domestic markets of nine major OECD industrial countries is illustrated by Table 1.18 for the period 1959-60 (average of the two years) to 1975, based on valuable estimates by the UNCTAD statisticians.

In *textiles* at the end of the 1950s, the share of imports from developing countries in these industrial markets was negligible, except in the United Kingdom where such imports already took 5 percent of consumption. By 1975, the proportions increased in the other markets but did not reach the 5 percent share still held in the United Kingdom. At the same time, trade in textiles between the industrial countries also increased, although more slowly; but such imports, even among the six founding members of the EEC, did not exceed 6 percent of the market, except, again, in the United Kingdom. In the United Kingdom by 1975, imports from other *developed* countries amounted to a quarter of textile consumption.

The significance of these increases can also be seen, as in Table 1.18 (the two rows showing growth of imports as percentage of growth of consumption for both textiles and clothing), by comparing the *increment* of imports with the *increment* of total consumption during the period. Again, the figures are very small except for the United Kingdom, where increased imports accounted for half the rather moderate expansion of consumption. But it is imports from other industrial countries (mainly EEC) that account for the great bulk of the increased import share (40 percent of the increase in consumption) and explain most of the stagnation of British textile production.[49] Imports from developing countries played only a secondary role. (Of course, the impact of imports from the developing world on the markets of the industrial countries would be greater if expressed in physical quantitites, because of their lower prices.)

The story for *clothing* (which in Table 1.18 includes a few other items) indicates a somewhat stronger impact of imports from the developing world; such imports, very small in 1959-60, had by 1975 reached 9-10 percent of consumption in the USA and Japan, 13 percent in Britain, and 6 percent in the EEC Six; they accounted for about a fifth of the increase in consumption in both the USA and Britain. Again, however, their impact was rather less in Britain than that of imports from other developed countries.

It must be remembered, of course, that imports of textiles and clothing from developing countries have since 1974 been limited by the Multi-Fibre Ar-

Table 1.18   Textiles and Clothing: Growth of Consumption and Imports in Major Developed Market Economies, 1959/60 to 1975

	Six EEC countries	UK	USA	Japan	Total of nine countries
Textiles[a]					
Apparent consumption[b] (annual percentage increase)	8.4	4.6	4.7	14.0	7.4
Imports as percentage of consumption:					
From developing countries					
1959/60	0.85	5.16	1.59	0.10	1.62
1975	4.12	5.41	2.49	2.23	3.25
From developed market economies					
1959/60	4.94	8.29	3.94	0.96	4.48
1975	6.44	25.37	3.52	2.08	5.94
Growth of imports as percent of growth of consumption:					
From developing countries	5.4	5.6	3.3	2.5	4.1
From developed market economies	7.0	42.3	3.1	2.3	6.7
Clothing[c]					
Apparent consumption[b] (annual percentage of increase)	10.0	5.3	4.8	20.0	7.1
Imports as percentage of consumption:					
From developing countries					
1959/60	0.56	3.91	0.77	0.71	1.02
1975	6.41	13.28	9.98	9.13	8.63
From developed market economies					
1959/60	1.70	5.16	2.69	0.71	2.62
1975	6.08	16.56	5.17	4.66	6.41
Growth of imports as percentage of growth of consumption:					
From developing countries	8.1	21.0	19.0	9.6	12.7
From developed market economies	7.4	25.9	7.6	4.9	8.5

[a]Textiles includes SITC 65 and 267.
[b]Apparent consumption is value of gross production (free of intraindustry deliveries) at manufacturing factor cost, less exports plus imports.
[c]Clothing includes footwear, other leather products, luggage, and handbags (SITC 61, 83, 84, 85).

Note: Percentages are derived from data in current dollars.

Source: Derived from UNCTAD, *Handbook of International Trade and Development Statistics, Supplement 1977*, Table 7.1.

rangements (and earlier by the somewhat less restrictive Long Term Cotton Textile Arrangements). The direct result has been a substantial reduction of the share of developing countries in the Western industrial countries' total imports of textiles and clothing; this share, after rising by the end of the 1960s to about 15 percent, fell to 10 percent in 1977 and 1978.[50] But the Arrangements have had a number of side effects. They have relieved the pressure on the industries of the Western industrial areas, to the advantage of the more-competitive among them (including the lower cost industries in Southern Europe). They have made it particularly difficult for developing countries without an established export business to enter Western markets. Finally, the established exporters among the developing countries have tended to move up-market, toward more highly processed and higher quality goods, partly to get a larger income from quotas expressed in physical units.

Notes

1. UNCTAD, *Dimensions of the required restructuring of world manufacturing output and trade* (Supporting paper for UNCTAD IV, TD/185/Supp. 1 1976, Table 1), and UNIDO, *World Industry since 1960* (1979), p. 34.

2. See, for example, a series of bilateral comparisons between East and West European industries of labour productivity in terms of physical output per worker: UN/ECE, *Structure and Change in European Industry* (1977), p. 212.

3. UNIDO, op. cit., Annex I.F.

4. But the industrial (and GNP) growth rates in the 1960s as a whole were profoundly affected by the disruptions in the early years of the decade following the "Great Leap Forward" of 1958–60 and by the further disruptions of the Cultural Revolution in 1967 and 1968.

5. World Bank, *World Development Report 1979,* Annexe Table 2, comparing GDP growth rates in 1970–77 against 1960–70. Of 80 countries cited in the table, 35 showed some acceleration.

6. It is of purely arithmetical interest to report that if the 1970–76 rates of manufacturing growth in the developed market economies and the developing countries were to continue until 2000 AD, the relative weights of the two groups would fall from about 7.5:1 in 1975 (See Table 1.1) to about 2.7:1. One interpretation of the Lima target (by which the developing countries would by 2000 account for at least 25 percent of world industrial production, the world apparently including CMEA but not socialist Asia) arrives at somewhere near a ratio of 2:1 between manufacturing output in developed market economies and developing countries. (Based on UNCTAD, *The dimensions of the required restructuring of world manufacturing output and trade in order to reach the Lima target,* TD/185/Supp. 1 1976.)

7. Ingvar Svennilson, *Growth and Stagnation in the European Economy* (Geneva: UN Economic Commission for Europe, 1954).

8. H. B. Chenery, "Patterns of Industrial Growth," *American Economic Review,* September 1960: see also Afred Maizels, *Industrial Growth and World Trade* (Cambridge: Cambridge University Press, 1965), especially Chap. 2, for a longer historical survey. United Nations, *A Study of Industrial Growth* (New York, 1963).

9. Heavy industries represent capital goods and intermediate goods, while light industries are mainly consumer goods. But this distinction holds only up to a point: the engineering industries, which are all included as heavy, include durable consumer goods — vehicles and household appliances. Paper, pharmaceuticals, fuel oil, etc., are also defined as heavy while including consumer goods; and light industries include a proportion of intermediate inputs into capital goods.

10. The slowing down of fixed investment in the recession clearly had a special impact on the heavy industries.

11. See UN/ECE, *Structure and Change in European Industry (1977),* p. 229.

12. Some express doubt that the rapid growth of plastic products will continue, in view of possible substitutions.

13. The importance of chemicals in the developing countries might be a little exaggerated, because oil refining might be included in some countries. This appears, from the UNIDO source, to be the case in Brazil, where the reported share of chemicals in total output is particularly high.

14. Note the extreme diversity of the electrical machinery industry, which comprises everything from heavy generators to prosaic domestic refrigerators to advanced technology in computers and light electronic products.

15. Calculation based on 1970 weights and 1960–74 growth rates in Table 1.5. Assumes 1970 pattern of value added prices.

16. Half the developing countries report some output in iron and steel, but in some this may mean only processing of scrap (UNIDO, *World Industry since 1960,* p. 74).

17. I.e., the standard deviations between the 1960–74 growth rates in Table 1.5, weighted by their shares of output, as percentages of the overall growth rate, in each of the two groups of countries.

18. Some experts believe that new technology in electronics, e.g., in the production of chips, reduces the advantages of production in low labor-cost countries and can lead to a transfer of output back to the home base.

19. A trivial statistical coincidence illustrating the process of development by stages: the proportion of manufacturing output in textiles and clothing in the developing countries in 1970 (Table 1.5), at 16.5 percent, is almost exactly equal to the corresponding proportion in Australia (17 percent) in *1913* (as given by Alfred Maizels, *Industrial Growth and World Trade,* Cambridge: Cambridge University Press, 1965, Table 2.3).

20. UN/ECE, *Structure and Change in European Industry* (UN, 1977). See, especially for Western Europe, Part 1, Chapter 1.

21. The original six countries of the Community, except Luxembourg, plus Finland, Norway, Sweden, the United Kingdom, and Yugoslavia.

22. UN/ECE, op. cit., page 17, data for earlier periods being based upon V. Paretti and G. Bloch, "Industrial production in Western Europe and the United States 1901 to 1955" (Banca Nazionale del Lavoro, Quarterly Review No. 39, 1956).

23. Comparing UN/ECE, op. cit., with data in UN, *Growth of World Industry,* 1973 edition.

24. H. B. Lary, *Imports of Manufactures from Less-Developed Countries,* National Bureau of Economic Research (New York: Columbia University Press, 1968).

25. Notably the chapters by Hufbauer and by Gruber and Vernon in Raymond Vernon, ed. *The Technology Factor in International Trade,* NBER (New York: Columbia University Press, 1970).

26. UN/ECE, *Structure and Change in European Industry,* Part 1, Chap. 2 for factor intensities in Western Europe, and Part 2, Chap. 3, for Eastern Europe and the Soviet Union.

27. UN/ECE, op. cit., Part 1, Table 2.14 and Chart 2.2. The coefficients of determination (R^2 adjusted for degrees of freedom) of the independent variables are: for labor skill 0.69, for research intensity 0.63, and for physical capital 0.60.

28. Because of the extreme values for the handful of very high capital-intensive branches, the mean for all manufacturing falls far below the median. The measure of physical capital intensity used here is an average of four indicators: investment per worker, investment divided by labor costs, profits (nonwage value added) per worker, and profits divided by labor costs.

29. The low pay in textiles and clothing is not simply an indication of poor skills in the ordinary sense. It is due also to the high proportion of women in the labor force (not to mention general economic conditions).

30. UN/ECE, *Structure and Change,* op. cit., p. 15.

31. Ibid., p. 88.

32. UNCTAD, *Recent Trends and Developments in Trade in Manufactures,* 1977 Review (TD/B/C.2/190; March 21, 1978).

33. UNIDO, *World Industry in the 1960s* (1969), p. 227.

34. Summarized in H.F. Lydall, "Employment Effects of Trade Expansion," *International Labour Review,* vol. 111, 1975. Productivity is expressed in dollars since the analysis is intended to exhibit the consequences of potential trade expansion on employment. For a review of other studies of the employment effects of changes in trade flows, see OECD, *The Impact of Newly Industrialising Countries on the Pattern of World Trade and Production in Manufactures,* Annex II (1979).

35. And more than 40 percent of these markets are the oil-exporting countries, where the dependence relationship is certainly not one-sided.

36. An inconvenience of statistics from some of the UN agencies on this, as on other, matters is that almost the largest NIC, Taiwan, has been excluded since the admission of the People's Republic of China to the UN.

37. Of which, two-thirds went to six principal NICs (Brazil, Mexico, Hong Kong, South Korea, Singapore, and Taiwan).

38. Data mainly from GATT, *International Trade 1978-79.*

39. The table is restricted to OECD Europe. This is because comparable data on unit values of imports are available only for OECD Europe (United States, Canada, and Japan often report in different physical units, and United States and Canada value f.o.b.).

40. Of course, Czechoslovakia, the GDR, and the Soviet Union cannot be regarded as NICs, although their entry on a substantial scale (or for Czechoslovakia and the GDR, reentry) into Western markets for many manufactures is relatively recent.

41. The assumptions, obviously not to be taken literally, are that prices of identical goods must be equal in the world market and that different kinds of goods under a single statistical description are largely substitutable for each other.

42. The significance of differences in unit values applies not only to comparison between developed and developing countries. Comparisons of unit value of the trade in a variety of engineering products between Britain, France, and Germany, showing for most products low unit values of British exports, are taken to indicate the relative technological backwardness of much of British engineering (Christopher Saunders, *Engineering in Britain, France and Germany,* Sussex European Research Centre, University of Sussex, 1978).

43. P.W.B. Rayment, "Intra-industry Specialization and the Foreign Trade of Industrial Countries," in S. F. Frowen, ed. *Controlling Industrial Economies* (forthcoming). These estimates are based on data at the three-digit SITC level, but Rayment shows that disaggregation to four-digits, although quadrupling the number of items, reduced the proportion of intraindustry trade by less than 10 percentage points in nearly all cases. The formula used here is to take the lesser of imports or exports as a percentage of exports plus imports.

44. G. C. Hufbauer in R. Vernon, ed. *The Technology Factor in International Trade,* NBER 1970, p. 201. See also UN/ECE, *The European Economy from the 1950s to the 1970s* (Economic Survey of Europe in 1971, Part 1, 1972).

45. UN/ECE, op. cit., p. 60.

46. Bela Balassa, "Intra-industry Trade and the Integration of Developing Countries in the World Economy," *World Bank Staff Working Paper* no. 312 (January 1974). Balassa also quotes estimates of his own for EEC countries, which seem consistent with those of Rayment just cited. Balassa's figures seem to be the only estimates available of intraindustry trade in developing countries. Further investigations could be profitable.

47. See Balassa, op. cit., p. 27.

48. The U.S. tariff concessions on products processed in developing countries from U.S.-supplied inputs, and similar (but sometimes more restrictive) arrangements in Western European tariffs, are exceptions.

49. The *volume* of United Kingdom textile production (apart from man-made fiber production) hardly increased in the 1960s and early 1970s, whereas at least modest increases are reported in most other Western industrial countries.

50. Data from GATT, *International Trade 1969,* Table 7, and *1978/79,* Table 9.

2 Causes and Kinds of Industrial Policy

JOHN PINDER

Introduction

The last chapter has shown how industrial production and trade have been growing in all parts of the world. Mankind is a manufacturing and trading animal and becoming more so. He is also a political animal, forever changing the arrangements that govern his activities; and some of the characteristics of the growth in production and exchange of manufactures have caused him to change the arrangements that govern these particular activities, in ways that are called industrial policy.

MARKET IMPERFECTIONS, ADJUSTMENT COSTS, PROBLEMS OF INTERDEPENDENCE

The growth of production in the last three decades has been accompanied by a great growth in the skill, capital, and research and development employed in most manufacturing sectors. The cost of establishing or ceasing production has increased correspondingly. Large sums of capital must be raised in order to start producing, particularly in sectors subject to economies of scale or to massive research and development; the investment in education and training for the necessary skills is also big, whether or not the cost is paid by the producing firm; and part of these investments will be wasted if production is wound up—whether the cost is borne by the firm, by the employees who may not be able to use their skills again at least for a time, or by the taxpayer or others. Thus the cost of adjustment from one economic activity to another has risen, and in this respect the markets have become more imperfect. Governments have responded with policies to promote training, investment, and research and development and so help to pay the costs of starting new production.

Production has also become more specialized, which tends to reduce the number of producers of a particular product, increase the element of oligopoly and of price-making rather than price-taking, and again to make markets more imperfect. Antitrust or competition policy is one reaction on the part of governments. The scale of production has at the same time increased, widening the market geographically and bringing into it new producers from other countries, which intensifies competition and abates, to that extent, the trend toward market imperfection. Where new competition has become uncomfortable for existing producers, governments have often responded with import restrictions or subsidies, and sometimes with policies to modernize these industries or promote new activities into which their resources can be transferred.

41

In the 1950s and 1960s, manufacturing industry, which before World War II had been concentrated mainly in the United States and northwest Europe, grew rapidly in other parts of Europe and in Japan. Trade in manufactures expanded extremely fast within Western Europe, and the OECD area as a whole progressed far toward becoming a single market for manufactures. This brought both the benefits and the problems of interdependence. The benefits included the division of labor and the economic basis of a new, pacific political relationship among the industrialized countries. The problems included a loss of control by individual national governments over economic forces that were becoming increasingly international. Macroeconomic trends were rapidly transmitted from one country to another. More and more industrial sectors felt the pressure of international competition. For the most part this stimulated them toward higher efficiency and specialization, but some sectors that were harder pressed, or less adaptable, secured protection against the imports. Textiles and clothing have become the classic example; the Long Term Arrangement regarding International Trade in Cotton Textiles was concluded in 1962, to protect North American and European industries against cheap imports from less-developed countries and Japan, and was later followed by the Multi-Fibre Arrangements to be discussed in Chapter 4. Competition from less-developed countries remained concentrated, through the 1960s, on a few products such as textiles, clothing, and footwear. But Japan, with a growth rate double that of most other countries and an economic system uniquely adapted to the rapid development of selected industrial sectors, began to challenge its OECD partners across a growing range of products. Partly in reaction, many OECD countries introduced industrial policies for troubled sectors and a variety of new barriers to trade. By the time the initiative for the Tokyo Round was taken in 1971, it was clear that the focus of trade negotiations would be on nontariff distortions as much as on the tariffs that had dominated previous rounds.

In the 1970s, the problems in a growing number of industries intensified, and hence also the pressures toward more industrial policy. Stagflation made adjustment slower and costlier. Slow growth lengthened the periods in which new investments would earn their pay-back or overcapacity would be taken up. Unemployment raised the costs of adjustment for both workers and the public purse. Monetary squeezes, intended to reduce inflation, at the same time raised the cost of new investment. Lacking adequate profits, companies cut their research, development, and investment programs. The higher costs of adjustment, and industries' reduced capacity to finance it, strengthened the rationale for industrial policy to stimulate the establishment of new economic activities and help pay the price of winding up old, uneconomic ones. These costs, both economic and social, also stiffened the resistance to the winding up of old activities, through industrial policy of a protectionist type.

THE NEWLY INDUSTRIALIZING COUNTRIES

Despite the stagflation and industrial difficulties in most OECD countries, they continued through the 1970s to increase their imports faster than production and thus to intensify interdependence, with its problems as well as benefits. Among the OECD countries themselves, the range of products exported by Japan to the others widened, and Japan continued to open its own market for imported manufactures. More progress was thus made toward a single OECD market for manufactures, albeit with discomfort for a number of industrial sectors in the importing countries, leading to further measures of industrial policy and protection. But Japanese competition is not a new combination of words in the English language, whereas newly industrializing country is. This reflects a momentous new development in the 1970s, clearly brought out by Saunders in Chapter 1: the rapid growth of a wide range of exports of manufactures from countries that hitherto exported primary products and a narrow range of labor-intensive manufactures, so striking as to point unequivocally toward a world market for manufactures in which the competitors in a growing number of sectors come from a growing number of countries and will doubtless eventually come from many more countries, containing a big majority of the world's population.

Of course, the idea that an industrialized West could forever exchange its manufactures for primary products from the rest of the world, who would conveniently remain unindustrialized or keep their manufactures to themselves, was neither morally acceptable nor tenable in practice; and a constant widening of the market is the only way to combine continuing specialization with a competitive market system. But the process of widening the market to include new production can be hard on the existing producers. The new production may grow faster than the market, forcing them to contract at a time when, as in the 1970s, it is difficult to replace old activities by new. The new producers may have radically different factor costs (low wages in less-developed countries), growth rates (Japan in the 1960s, South Korea in the 1970s), or economic systems (Eastern Europe); and exports from any of these can cause the sort of disturbance that results if one suddenly opens the gates between two canal locks containing water at sharply different levels. Beyond the difficulties of particular sectors, moreover, it is not fanciful to fear that constant pressure from the industries of countries catching up from a lower level of development could eventually induce a state of general economic weakness in the older industrialized countries. This seems to have happened to Britain; it may now be happening to the United States; and the examples of regions such as Wallonia, Clydeside, Pas de Calais, and New England are not encouraging.

The newly industrializing countries which have emerged in the 1970s have given an additional impulse to the development of industrial policy in the OECD area; and since the number of such countries and their capacity to export manufactures will probably continue to increase, this pressure is likely to remain with us indefinitely. Nor is the trend toward higher costs of adjustment in the industrialized countries likely to abate, for industry will continue to become more specialized and to require more skill, capital, and research and development. Even with full employment and fast growth, public policy needs to help pay some of these costs and to facilitate the adaptation of our economies to the new patterns of industrialization in the world. With unemployment and slow growth, there are yet greater pressures toward industrial policy, both with the positive aim of adapting to new and more-viable economic structures and, negatively, in defending the old ones.

General Industrial Policies

The term industrial policy is often taken to imply policies relating to specific industrial sectors. These are indeed the principal focus of this book, because they pose the most-immediate challenge to the international system. But they are only a part of the subject, because many of the market imperfections that industrial policy should aim to correct, such as restrictive practices or high costs of adjustment to individuals and firms, are widely spread across the economy. It does not follow that a need for sectoral policies arises only if more-general policies to encourage industrial development and adaptation have failed, because particular sectors may share problems, such as costly R and D or chronic overcapacity, which fall through the net of general adaptability. But the need for sectoral policies, and hence the scope for international conflicts, will certainly be reduced if policy helps industry in general to be more adaptable than it otherwise would be; and welfare will be enhanced if policy encourages a steadier and smoother development of industry than we have seen in the 1970s. Before proceeding to consider sectoral policies, in the last part of this chapter and the following two chapters, it therefore seems appropriate to review briefly the various kinds of more-general industrial policies, which provide a background for the sectoral policies, as well as much of the instrumentarium on which sectoral policies can draw. These general policies can be divided into those that apply to factors of production, to firms, and to geographical areas.

Policies Relating to Factors of Production

The costs of adjustment that deter the winding up or slimming down of old economic activities and the start or expansion of new ones relate to the different factors of production. Policies to reduce these costs to the individual or firm therefore apply to factors of production, such as labor, capital, or (a combination of the two) research and development.

The policies relating to labor, or manpower policies, themselves comprise a vast subject that requires a separate book. But it must be noted here that manpower policies are needed because labor markets are so imperfect, not just or even mainly because of restrictive practices in them, but because the high level of skills in the modern economy and the low propensity to move house in modern society constrain the mobility of workers, both occupationally and geographically. A government role in training, placement, and the location of jobs has accordingly become normal in most countries and is not contested by most liberal economists. The subsidizing of labor in various ways, to preserve or create employment, has been widely practised in the 1970s and has given rise to more controversy.

The encouragement of capital investment has roots in the 19th century, when state-supported banks were established in a number of countries to promote investment in response to the challenge of British industrial dominance. Whether the justification was then Listian protection or the infant industries exception to free-trade doctrine, it has since become generalized in the form of fiscal and financial encouragement for industrial investment, on the implicit assumption that the relationship between cost and risk is otherwise not favorable enough to investment in a capital-intensive economy. In addition to the general fiscal and financial incentives, investment is promoted through public sector investment programs, public purchasing of goods that require capital investment to produce, and a variety of other schemes relating to particular sectors.

Research and development is an investment in innovation and in some countries attracts general fiscal incentives in the same way as investment in equipment. If there is a bias in the modern economy against innovation being sufficient to create full employment and to adapt our industries to a new division of labor in the world such a general incentive for research and development is justified. More usually, however, public support for R and D has been heavily concentrated on those sectors where the costs are particularly high and where defense capability is generally a motive, such as aircraft and nuclear power.

POLICIES RELATING TO FIRMS

Another set of industrial policies concerns the size and behavior of firms. Antitrust or competition policies control or break up monopolies and cartels, inhibit mergers, and ban restrictive practices. Merger policies, on the contrary, encourage the fusion of two or more firms into a single enterprise, usually in order to concentrate in it enough resources for costly development or large-scale production, or to create a national champion to compete in the international market. At the other end of the scale, there is a tradition, in many countries, of public support for small firms, which has social and political rather than economic origins. Economists have usually regarded this as a backward-looking policy, inimical to efficiency and progress. Recently, it has become more usual to regard small firms as a major source of new employment and innovation in a modern economy, so that support for them can help to reduce unemployment and revive the flagging dynamism of industrialized countries.[1] Small firms can be said to suffer from the effects of a number of market imperfections: in the administrative complexity of the modern economy with which they are ill equipped to deal, in the bias against them in the provision of investment funds that is inherent in the financial institutions of at least some countries, and in the difficulty of obtaining all the necessary market and technical information in a complex, swiftly changing world. Tax remissions, relaxation of administrative or employment protection requirements, special institutions to provide investment finance or information and advice have been some of the policy responses to these disadvantages. In this way, public policy can promote the growth of small and new firms to provide the employment and value added that is needed in the place of employment or production reduced elsewhere. The problem may be to ensure that the support for small firms helps the energetic and innovative more than it protects inefficiency and restrictive practices.

POLICIES RELATING TO GEOGRAPHICAL AREAS

The third kind of general industrial policies relates to geographical areas in which industry is chronically underdeveloped or depressed. The Italian Mezzogiorno is a well-known example of an under-developed region, to which many of the instruments of industrial policy have been applied. The market imperfections that hold such regions back are related to the externalities and linkages that provide the basis for growth in the more-dynamic areas: the concentration of skills, services, financial institutions, suppliers, buyers, infrastructure, and a whole industrial culture. As well as applying the policies relating to factors of production, therefore, governments have developed physical and social infrastructure and established industrial complexes with the aim of carrying the region forward under the impetus of poles of growth.

This is a generalization from individual industrial sectors to whole regions of the infant industry argument, which had already been developed in the 19th century. More recently, it has become apparent that the externalities can turn against an industrialized region too, trapping it in a vicious circle of declining industries, high unemployment, out-dated infrastructure, and unenterprising mentality. Policies are then devised to regenerate industry in the region, by renewing the infrastructure as well as promoting new enterprise and subsidizing the factors of production (labor as well as capital, for such regions lack the advantage of cheap labor that is common in the less-developed areas).

From policy to favor the development of industry in an underdeveloped or an old industrial region, only one more step in the argument leads to protection of the industry of a whole country. Protection has been, historically, the most-important instrument of industrial policy. Apart from Britain, all the major industrial powers—the United States, Japan, Germany, France, Russia—built up their industrialization behind protective walls. In their means, the main differences between national protection and regional policy are that regional policy lacks tariffs, quotas, and currency manipulation. In their ends, the differences can be deeper, reflecting the presence and probable dominance of the other regions of a state in the making of regional policy, as opposed to the absence or, at best, arms-length relationship of other states in the making of a country's policy of national protection. "Les absents ont toujours tort": regional policy is more likely to take account of the interests of a state's other regions than national policy is to allow for the interests of a state's trading partners. It was for just such reasons that the GATT (General Agreement on Tariffs and Trade) was created, with rules to control the levels of national protection and procedures for negotiating their reduction. This worked well enough among countries which did not feel the need for general protection to foster their industrial development. But now most countries feel the need for industrial policies to deal with the problems that have been described; and the industrial policy of one state can affect the interests of another state quite as much as a tariff (which is indeed just one form of industrial policy). A natural, liberal reaction is to view other industrial policies in the same way as tariffs and to argue that they should be reduced and eventually eliminated, as was happening to tariffs in the GATT. But this view fails to recognize the importance of the needs to which industrial policy responds. The aim must be not to suppress this response, but to ensure that national industrial policy takes the interests of other countries sufficiently into account and that there is a capacity to make international industrial policy when the dimensions of the problem require it. The control of national policies and, still more, the formation of common policies present formidable difficulties for the international system. Five sectors in which these difficulties are evident are considered in the following two chapters. Before we present these examples, however, it may be useful to provide a framework within which sectoral policies can be analyzed and judged.

Sectoral Policies

Textiles have been cited as the classic example of an industrial sector that has, in the industrial countries, secured protection and attention from industrial policy as a result of low-wage competition. It is however an example of only one kind of sector for which industrial policies have been devised: a labor-intensive sector in which low-wage countries have had a pronounced advantage. Note the careful use of the past tense; textiles are, as Saunders showed in Chapter 1, no longer a labor-intensive sector, if defined in the strict sense that excludes clothing; it is clothing that remains labor-intensive (even if that too may change with the development of automated production). For the genuinely labor-intensive sectors, policies can aim either to defend the status quo or to secure the sector's contraction.

Saunders also shows that only a few sectors are much more capital-intensive than the average and he lists chemicals, oil refining, basic metals, and paper-making. Such sectors face special difficulties if they suffer from overcapacity, as did a number of them in industrialized countries in the 1970s; they are trapped between heavy capital charges and weak price structures, which make it hard for them to finance the capital charges, let alone new investment. Since the great majority of sectors in the contemporary economy are more or less capital-intensive, this difficulty can strike a wide range of sectors. The policy responses may aim either at stabilization, if the overcapacity is attributed to a trade cycle, or contraction, if it is expected to be longer lasting.

Aircraft and nuclear power have been mentioned as sectors requiring costly research and development. Saunders adds electrical machinery (which includes data-processing) and chemicals. Governments promote such sectors by support for R and D as well as by other means, at least in part to raise the level of innovation in the economy and the pace of industrial development. Policies of industrial promotion may also be applied to other sectors that are thought likely to contribute to objectives such as the creation of employment or improvement of the balance of payments.

The rest of this chapter considers the three types of sector in turn (labor-intensive, capital-intensive, R and D–intensive) and the types of policy which can be associated with them (defensive/contractionary, stabilization/contractionary, promotional). The typology is put forward only in order to simplify the analysis of a complex problem. Most industrial sectors contain features of two or even three of these ideal types; different product-groups within a sector can have different features, as is the case with textiles and clothing, which are often put together in one category called textiles; and a group of products can move from one type to another, as textiles have moved since the 1950s from labor-intensity to average capital-intensity. For all these reasons, the policy-maker has to approach any sector with the expectation that a combination of aims and a range of instruments may be required, even if one of the main types of policy may, for a particular sector and period, predominate.

LABOR-INTENSIVE SECTORS; DEFENSIVE AND
CONTRACTIONARY POLICIES

It is ironic that the zenith of the classicial economics was the Manchester School, while Manchester was the capital of a textile industry that was destined to suffer a decline which has lasted for two-thirds of a century so far and looks like continuing for a while yet. For even if the classical model does not imply that adjustment to a change of comparative advantage is immediate and costless, the classical economists showed scant concern about the time and cost involved. As soon as the Indians, Japanese (then a low-wage country!) and others had learned to make cloth in large quantity with cheap labor, Lancastrian entrepreneurs should evidently have applied their talents and Lancastrian workers should have obtained employment in other industries and, if necessary, places. But markets were, alas, not so perfect. Entrepreneurs hung on to their old written-off machines, making little or no profit and hoping something would turn up; workers remained for long periods unemployed; and the whole region was run-down for many years, with decaying infrastructure and lost momentum. Adjustment was agonizingly slow, with appalling costs for the people in the industry and for the national economy as a whole.

Lancashire, which in 1913 dominated the world market for cotton textiles, had farthest to fall. But other old textile-producing regions have also experienced an erosion of employment amid a similar immobility of factors of production. An almost universal reaction has been the defensive one of protection against imports from the low-wage countries, which was enshrined in the quotas of the Long Term Arrangement for cotton textiles and the subsequent Multi-Fibre Arrangements. Unlike the protection of the 1930s, which cut imports, this has allowed an annual growth in the quantity of trade. Unlike the policies of some countries, however, these international agreements have not stressed measures to render the protection unnecessary in the future, either by reducing the sector's capacity or by making it more competitive.

Typically, the measures to ease the contraction of a sector include the training of workers in skills required in other sectors and their placement in new jobs, with enough jobs created where they are needed through various forms of regional policy, and more-specific encouragement to job-creating firms. While incentives for new capital investment are thus used to encourage job creation, incentives can also be employed to reduce capacity in the contracting sector, as was done when the Bank of England guaranteed a loan for the British cotton industry to buy out millions of spindles in Lancashire between the two World Wars, and as has been done in various countries since.

More positively, as far as the threatened sector itself is concerned, industrial policy can help to make it competitive again. Recognizing that the low-wage countries are hard to beat at the cheaper end of the trade, policy can help the industry to move up-market, by providing the appropriate training for managers and other workers, together with finance on favorable terms for the reequipment that is required. Such was the policy for the Swedish clothing industry. German textile-makers, building on their aptitude for making capital-intensive industrial products, had government help to concentrate their production on industrial textiles, and Germany is now the world's largest textile exporter. The British government promoted mergers in order to strengthen the textile industry, to the point where four firms now account for half the national production.

Such measures are likely to be taken after a long period of erosion has weakened the sector. By then the process may be like pushing water uphill — possible, but requiring disproportionate effort. The art of efficient industrial policy is to respond to early signs that a sector's position may be weakening, so that the process of reorganization within the industry or redeployment outside it can be set in motion in good time. For the stimulation of new job opportunities outside the sector is not done in a day, and modernization or reorganization within it becomes more difficult as the sector itself becomes weaker. Here, as in many other respects, there is a lesson to be learnt from Japan, as Hosomi and Okumura show in Chapter 5.

CAPITAL-INTENSIVE SECTORS; STABILIZATION OR
CONTRACTIONARY POLICIES

A sector can suffer from overcapacity if there is an unexpected change in the trend of demand or the pattern of production. In the 1970s this happened in several industries, including synthetic fibers, other basic chemicals, steel, other basic metals, shipbuilding, and a number of others. Demand for the products of each sector was much less than had been assumed by those who undertook new investments before 1974; and production from newly industrializing countries, which in several sectors would have been readily accommodated if demand had continued to grow as in the 1960s, accentuated the problem that such sectors face when severe overcapacity lasts for an extended period.

The problem is, essentially, that firms in the sector must earn enough to pay not only their running costs but also capital and other overhead charges; and they should do better than this if they are to stay in business as the industry reequips with yet more expensive investments. Even if they cannot cover all these costs, it is better for them to produce than not to produce, provided that the production covers their running costs and makes at least some contribution to the fixed costs. In proportion as the sector is capital-intensive, its capital costs are high; and in proportion as a country has laws or practices that make lay-offs difficult or expensive, labor assumes some of the attributes of a fixed cost, leaving only raw materials and energy as running costs in the full sense (and only insofar as these are not obtained under long-term contracts).

Normally, such industries have survived and thrived through oligopolistic pricing conventions, often following a price leader but in any case ensuring that fixed as well as running costs are covered, with something over for profit and future investments. Experienced oligopolists can survive a fair measure of excess capacity in this way. The competition may be imperfect, but it works. In the 1970s, however, there were several sectors in which it did not work well enough. Even experienced oligopolists differ in their trade-offs between production volume and profit margin, in the extent to which they have capital charges to bear, and in their financial ability to sustain a low level of capacity utilization. If demand remains for long far below capacity, some of them will break ranks and force prices downward in order to increase their sales. When new producers enter the field, often with lower costs (with cheaper labor, the most-modern equipment and layout, sometimes with subsidized capital) and without experience of oligopolistic behavior, they are even more likely to price below average cost in the sector in order to get orders that will occupy their full capacity, and to bring the other producers, fighting to retain their share of the weak market, down to that level. In bad times like the 1970s, the price structure can be so fragile that firms accounting for only a small share of the total production can pull down the price level to a point where the mainstream firms are unprofitable (see, for example, Chapter 3, p.76).

Once prices reach such levels, firms can enter a vicious circle where low prices lead to low profits (or losses), low profits lead to low investment, and the firms cannot improve their efficiency without a revival of demand. Yet the financial strength and credit rating of many such firms is enough to enable them to endure those conditions for quite a long time; and their contribution to employment, the balance of payments, or national security may be such as to bring governments to their rescue to prevent bankruptcy. If a number of sectors are locked in a vicious circle of this kind, and hence fail to provide their share of investment demand, the prospects for a general revival of demand are correspondingly reduced.

Such are the problems presented by imperfect markets, in this case the immobility of capital rather than of labor, to the policy-maker in the contemporary economy. He has devised ways to deal with these imperfections, most comprehensively and explicitly in Japan, where the solution goes under the name of *recession cartel* (see Chapter 5). Here, production is shared among the existing producers by formal or informal quotas, and new investment is controlled until demand recovers to the point where the recession cartel is no longer required. This method has, of course, been applied by cartels in Europe and America, and it is a purpose of antitrust or competition policy to prevent such behavior. The difference with the Japanese recession cartel is that the government approves the arrangements and can thus ensure that the firms do not abuse their position contrary to the public interest. The European Community has the power to arrange crisis cartels in the coal and steel industries, although it is hard to secure the consent of enough member governments to such schemes; but the Community and the United States have both applied minimum prices to steel imports since 1978, and the Community has also taken measures to enforce price discipline on Community producers with respect to certain steel products (Chapter 3 will examine the steel industry in detail).

The main thrust of the Community scheme for steel and the center of the American one have been to prevent imports from undermining the price structure in the domestic markets. Neither informal oligopolistic behavior nor a more-formal recession cartel can achieve this if suppliers from outside are allowed to disrupt it. In the particular case of steel, the United States and the Community fixed the floor price for imports at a level that covered the costs of efficient Japanese producers; and this has suited the Japanese too, as the consequent recovery of prices has restored the profitability of the Japanese industry. The same may be said for other exporters, although the Community has backed its minimum prices by import quotas for its various suppliers, some of whom may feel that they lacked the bargaining power to secure an adequate quota.

This raises a considerable difficulty when recession cartels are to be supported by the allocation of import quotas or by an international system of production quotas. For whereas the Americans and the Japanese were able to agree on a fair price for the American imports of steel, and the Community adopted the same level, it is extremely difficult to secure international agreement on what constitute fair shares of production or import quotas; and if import quotas are imposed without such agreement, there is the danger of a slide from the law-abiding trade regime of the postwar period into the arbitrary behavior of the 1930s.

This difficulty becomes more acute when overcapacity is judged to reflect not the temporary weakness of demand during a recession but a long-term, structural maladjustment. For capacity then has to be permanently reduced, rather than be put in mothballs for the time being. This has clearly been the case with shipbuilding in the second half of the 1970s (see chapter 4); yet it has not been possible to reach agreement on a multinational reduction of capacity, either in the European Community or among the OECD countries. Several countries have decided to reduce capacity autonomously, but the reduction amounts to less than would appear to be rational in the common interest; for it is less attractive to cut capacity when the result is that another country may take the share of the market you would have supplied, than it would be if all countries reduced their share in proportion.

Until the European Community or the wider international system becomes better able to manage an agreed reduction of capacity, the issue has to be handled by the national governments separately. Here, the problem is not so different from the contraction of labor-intensive industries. Capacity can be bought out, or incentives to reduce it can be provided in the form of loans on easy terms, as the Japanese have done in shipbuilding. Policy can, as with the labor-intensive sectors, make the reduction of capacity easier by stimulating the provision of new employment opportunities where they are needed and by ensuring that workers can get the necessary training to fill the jobs. An industry can, either of its own accord or with official encouragement, reduce employment or capacity steadily over a period of years and hence without too much strain, as the German steel industry has done, rather than cut savagely in haste when forced by a financial crisis, as did the British and the French. Industrial policy can help to make the remaining capacity more competitive by modernization, specialization, or relocation. It also happens that some suppliers of equipment, and shipbuilders in particular, have been helped by the requirements of health, safety, or pollution regulations, which have obliged the buyers of equipment to make new investments in order to comply. If the effect is to be more than marginal, however, the higher standards must be applied by the main international competitors so that the higher costs affect them all, or the industry in question must be sufficiently insulated from international competiton, as are the American shipowners who have made substantial new investments on these grounds.

RESEARCH AND DEVELOPMENT SECTORS;
PROMOTION POLICIES

Among the R and D–intensive industries are some, such as aircraft, nuclear power, and data processing, where the cost of R and D is so big that it can be financed only with public support. Purchasing is often undertaken or influenced by the public sector and may be related to strategic needs. The markets could hardly be more imperfect, and the influence of public policy is inevitably great. International implications arise where the finance of R and D is shared among two or more countries, because the cost is too high for one to bear alone, and where there is multinational purchasing or production. Examples of all these are shown in Chapter 4's discussion of aircraft manufacture. Naturally, when governments are so deeply involved in industries that are important in their own right and also have strategic significance, issues of foreign policy can arise and diplomacy must deal with them.

In the excitement about glamorous and defense-related industries, the more-ordinary sectors where innovation is important must not be forgotten. Here industrial policy mainly takes a more-general form, as was noted earlier, which does not raise much of an issue for international relations. But with widespread weaknesses in employment and industry in many countries, efforts to promote selected sectors are almost bound to be intensified; and the demand may arise for a certain international coordination of policies in these sectors too.

This brings us back to the international implications of industrial policy as a whole. For, as the sections on labor-intensive and capital-intensive sectors have shown, promotional policies are likely to relate not just to R and D but also to incentives for new investments and job creation in general whether within the threatened sectors or outside them. On the one hand, the promotional policies will reduce international conflict if they succeed in taking the pressure off the troubled sectors that are the main source of tension; on the other hand, the efforts to promote new activities or to make old ones more efficient could develop into a new source of competition between national industrial policies, which could be dangerous if the international system fails to accommodate and control it.

A POSITIVE INDUSTRIAL POLICY

We will return in the concluding chapter to the impact of national industrial policies on the international system. Meanwhile, it will be clear from the foregoing that industrial policy should not be regarded just as a threat to the international order, but as a response to the imperfections of modern industrial markets which is an essential part of effective economic management, even if, like most policies, it may be open to political abuse. Thus an appropriate selection from the array of instruments of general and sectoral policies that have been considered above should be brought to bear on those situations where imperfect markets impede the development of a healthy economy; the regular and efficient use of instruments in this way could suitably be called a positive industrial policy. Seen in this light, the international system will have to find ways to accommodate and encourage positive industrial policy rather than to minimize it. As the following chapters will show, the international system is not yet well adapted to this. Nor are most countries generally skilled in the pursuit of positive industrial policy. Yet along with the failures and abuses, the reader will find in the following chapters some examples of successful policies relating to the sectors and countries we have studied, as well as the outstanding success story of Japan, industrial policy's most-skillful exponent.

Notes

1. See, for example, David L. Birch, *The Job Generation Process* (Cambridge, Mass.: Massachusetts Institute of Technology, 1979).

3 The International Politics of Trade and Production in the Steel Industry

STEPHEN WOOLCOCK

Introduction

Change in the pattern of trade and production in any industry is a continuous process. In steel as in other industries this change takes place in a setting that is determined by a combination of developments in demand, technology, and cost factors, as well as by the interaction between market forces and public and corporate policy. What has characterised the steel industry in the 1970s is the rapid change in demand that has resulted in an intensification of activity on the part of policy-makers.

The steel industry has a long history of public intervention and private, restrictive business practices. In the 1930s the international problems of the industry led to the creation of international cartels, most notably the *Entente internationale d'acier.*[1] But although the problems of many national steel industries in the 1970s had international implications, one cannot draw close parallels with the 1930s. In the world of the 1970s there were a larger number of steel-producing countries and more-developed forms of competition policy to limit possibilities of building effective cartels. Furthermore, there are various forms of direct and indirect intervention by government, ranging from subsidies or the provision of public risk capital to the retraining of workers. In short, the formulation of public policy in steel has become more complex as national governments and, in the case of Europe, supranational institutions have struggled with the task of balancing the burden of adjustment. The measures adopted in the 1970s can in no way be compared to the crude market-sharing of a 1930s cartel.

In the 1970s the steel industry faced the problem of stagnating demand, which has meant that the frictions of adjustment could not be eased by growth. Consequently, the initial response to the problems facing the industry was to introduce anticrisis measures in an effort to maintain, temporarily, the status quo and thus reduce tension between national sectoral interests and international trading partners. Any changes from the established patterns of behavior could be expected to produce a real or perceived unfair distribution of the burden of adjustment to change. This chapter will look at how policy-makers at the national, regional, and international levels have reacted to the pressures exerted in both the domestic and international spheres by structural changes in the industry.

Problems Facing the Steel Industry

DEMAND

The steel industry is accustomed to periodic cyclical recessions, but the sharp downturn in demand that began at the end of 1974 was not only the worst the industry had faced since the 1930s, but it also exhibited characteristics different from those of the traditional forty-month steel cycle. In the initial phase of the crisis there were those who believed that the industry was merely experiencing a deep cyclical recession, but when there was a severe collapse of the market in the autumn of 1977, it was generally acknowledged that the cyclical fluctuations at the beginning of the 1970s had in fact only disguised more-fundamental structural problems.

Steel demand is determined by the growth of the main steel-consuming industries. During the 1960s the rapid growth of steel-intensive industries, such as automobiles, shipbuilding, and consumer durables, provided a large and growing market for steel. In the USA, which was first to experience this consumer boom, the growth in steel consumption was already declining in the 1960s, and from 1967 to 1977 U.S. steel consumption grew by only 6 percent, despite a real GNP growth of 30 percent.[2] In Western Europe,[3] where the growth in major steel-consuming industries occurred later, the growth of steel-consuming industries surpassed that of GNP during the 1965–70 period; but at the end of the 1960s this trend was reversed and the income elasticity of demand for steel fell to 0.69 for the period 1965–74, compared to 1.03 from 1965–70.[4] In Japan, steel demand grew at an average annual rate of 13 percent between 1964 and 1973, and it was not until 1974 that the growth in demand for steel fell below that of GNP. The prospects for improved growth in steel demand are not good, since future growth in the industrialized countries is unlikely to be steel-intensive. In the developing

Table 3.1   Crude Steel Production by Main Region of World, 1974–79

	1974	1978	1979	1979/74	1979/78
	million tonnes			percentage change	
EEC	156	133	140	– 9.8	+ 6.0
USA	132	124	123	– 7.0	– 0.9
Japan	117	102	112	– 4.7	+ 9.3
Other industrialized countries	59	62	67	+14.5	+ 8.2
Total industrialized countries	464	421	442	– 4.6	+ 5.1
Total developing countries	31	47	54	+74.8	+13.9
Total Western world	494	468	496	+ 0.3	+ 6.0
USSR and Eastern Europe	185	211	210	+13.5	– 0.4
China and North Korea	29	37	39	+34.6	+ 6.5
Total Communist countries	214	248	249	+16.3	+ 0.6
Total world	709	715	745	+ 5.1	+ 4.2

Source: International Iron and Steel Institute.

world steel consumption per caput is exceedingly low, at approximately 40 kg per annum in the more-populous countries, such as India and Brazil. [5] Whether this potential from growth in the developing world, where steel demand is expected to grow at twice the rate of the Western industrialized countries, can be exploited by steel producers in the latter will depend on the growth of steel capacity in the developing and newly industrializing countries.

SURPLUS CAPACITY

The decline in demand after 1974 resulted in large-scale surplus capacity, mainly in Europe and Japan. Although there are major problems in determining the actual effective installed capacity, estimates suggest that capacity utilization dropped to between 58 and 62 percent in the European Community (EC) in 1977, with finishing processes generally operating at lower rates of utilization than crude steel production. [6] In Japan, capacity utilization also fell to about 70 percent and remained at this level in 1978 and 1979. Although investment declined after 1974, some extra capacity was added as a result of decisions taken during the 1973–74 boom. Recent estimates put EC capacity at about 200 million metric tons, [7] Japanese capacity at about 150 million in 1980, [8] and U.S. capacity at 142 million. [9] These figures can give only the order of magnitude, since capacity utilization can vary from product to product and plant to plant. There are also marked differences in the costs of operating at less than maximum effective capacity. For example, most Japanese producers were able to improve their financial performance substantially after 1975; in the Federal Republic of Germany, most steel producers returned to profitable operation in 1979, despite lower rates of capacity utilization that the bigger loss-makers in Europe.

In general, however, most steel producers in the industrialized countries suffered heavy losses in the first years of the recession. This weakening of the financial position of the major steel producers prevented them from generating the funds necessary to improve their international competitiveness. Table 3.2 gives one estimate of the losses of the major European steel producers in 1977–78. In the USA, Bethlehem Steel made a loss of US$477 million in the third quarter of 1977, partly owing to the cost of plant closures. In 1978 and 1979 the performance of the U.S. producers improved, owing to the improved market conditions and the trigger price mechanism introduced by the government in early 1978. In the latter part of 1979, however, the situation deteriorated once again; US Steel, again partly owing to the cost of closures, incurred a record loss of US$562 million in the last quarter of 1979. In Japan more economical energy consumption and stock adjustments, combined with the rise in export prices due to price measures taken in the USA and EC, enabled producers to improve profits in 1978/79.

In an effort to reduce losses and improve productivity, all steel producers made large reductions in the labor force, often in areas already suffering from high unemployment, where the steel industry was a major employer. In the USA more than 54,000 workers were laid off between 1974 and 1976, a reduction of 14 percent of the 1974 labor force. Despite this labor shedding, the steel producers in the USA were still unable to compete with their international rivals, and up to the end of 1977 another 20,000 workers were affected by 16 plant closures or cut-

Table 3.2   Financial Results for European Steelmakers Published in 1977-78

	Loss per tonne (£)
Sacilor	42
Usinor	29
BSC) Italsider)	25
Cockerill	24
Kockner	21
Ensidesa	16
Estel	13
Arbed	11
Salzgitter	11

Source: Statement by Sir Charles Villiers, British Steel Corporation Annual Press Conference, July 4, 1978.

backs.[10] The closures announced by US Steel in the autumn of 1979 involved redundancies for another 13,000, many in the same areas — for example, around Youngstown where earlier closures had taken place.

In the EC, 90,000 jobs, or 12 percent of the labor force, were lost between 1974 and the autumn of 1978. Thereafter plans were announced to shed a further 20,000 jobs in the French steel industry over the period 1979-80, mostly in Lorraine where the steel industry accounted for some 20 percent of the total industrial employment. In the UK the British Steel Corporation (BSC) decided in 1979 to shed a third of its labor force or 50,000 jobs, once again in areas dependent on the steel industry. For example, steel accounted for 28 percent of total industrial employment in Clwyd (Shotton), where plant closure could be expected to push up unemployment to about 15 percent.

These plans led to major labor unrest in France, the UK, and some trouble in Belgium, where the majority of jobs lost are in French-speaking Wallonia. In 1979 in Germany, the industry suffered its worst strike since 1945 on the related issue of a shorter working week, which was seen by the unions as a means of promoting work-sharing and thus reducing the cost of adjustment for the labor force.

The pressures caused by excess capacity, falling prices, and the desire to minimize the dislocation of labor in politically sensitive areas spilled over into trade policy. Owing to the cyclical pricing policy of steel producers, which is designed to balance revenue over the steel cycle, steel exports have traditionally been sold at prices below domestic prices during a recession. While these practices were tolerable when the steel cycle was still working, the structural recession of the 1970s intensified feelings in the USA, which was the largest single export market for the Europeans and Japanese, that subsidized foreign steel was being dumped on the U.S. market. Although the problems of the U.S. industry cannot be explained away by foreign subsidies to steel exporters or unfair pricing practices,[11] the recession did heighten the sensitivity of the U.S. lobbies to fears that the domestic industry was bearing a disproportionate share of the costs of the recession. As a result the U.S. industry filed a series of antidumping actions against foreign steel producers. When, in October 1977, a tentative determination of dumping was reached in the Gilmore case, the large number of antidumping actions in the pipe-line threatened to provoke serious problems in trade relations with the EC and Japan. By the end of 1979, a similar situation had again arisen.

Options for the Steel Industry and Public Policy-Makers

When considering the various responses of the steel producers, governments, and other interest groups, it will be useful to bear in mind the options open to the industry and governments. The options for the steel producers can be summarized as follows: to press for protection, subsidies, or market sharing, to restructure in order to reestablish international competitiveness, to move up-market and produce higher value-added products, to relocate plant in lower cost or less pollution-sensitive locations, or to move out of the industry altogether.

For public policy-makers, who are generally committed to helping the steel industry even if they do not own it, the options are less clear cut. For political and ideological reasons, few governments in the Western industrialized countries could commit themselves to a long-term policy of protection — certainly not the USA, EC or Japan. Apart from ideological reasons, long-term protection for the steel industry would endanger the position of steel-consuming industries if their foreign competitors could draw on lower cost steel. The vital domestic market for steel could then be gradually eroded by "indirect imports" of steel-intensive-manufactures, such as cars. Short of extending protection to cover steel-consuming industries, protection is neither economic nor strategically wise in the long term. Politically, such a policy would also run up against a strong lobby of the steel-consuming industries.

Faced with mounting losses in the domestic steel industry and possible bankruptcies, governments would find it exceedingly difficult, if not impossible, to stand back and do nothing. Of course the responses of policy-makers depend on the severity of the problems in the industry. Some governments may well need to do little if the industry is healthy. But in order to avoid the collapse of some producers and unacceptable dislocation of employment, governments tend to intervene by introducing temporary anticrisis measures that give producers time to restructure and help to ease the social and political costs of labor-shedding rationalization.

As in the case of long-term protection, anticrisis measures, such as those designed to increase prices or regulate trade, involve ideological, economic, and political problems. If the appearances of a liberal policy are to be kept up, some means must be found to ensure that temporary anticrisis measures are just that and not the beginning of permanent regulation. In economic terms, temporary measures that attempt to minimize the immediate impact of excess capacity will ultimately result in increased costs, unless restructuring can reestablish competitiveness.

A restructuring policy depends on how policy-makers assess future demand and the intentions of other policy-makers. If restructuring is to involve retrenchment with capacity reduction, what is the expected domestic and export demand? A government might well aim to maintain the traditional market shares. But if this means reducing capacity, what guarantee is there that other governments will not provide sufficient "unfair" assistance to their industries and thus increase their market shares?

Rather than allowing the industry to retrench in order to consolidate its position, and thus retain its market share, a more-aggressive policy of support could be followed that aims to improve competitiveness and increase market share. In all events policy will depend largely on the diagnosis of the industry's problems. Competition in the steel industry has historically concerned capacity as well as price. Owing to the cyclical nature of demand, producers who invested in a new plant in anticipation of the next upturn in demand could be expected to increase their market share when competitors were unable to deliver during booms.[12] Thus a diagnosis of short-term cyclical problems would favor a policy of at least retaining existing capacity and possible expansion, bearing in mind the long lead times for the construction or modification of plant. On the other hand, a diagnosis of long-term structural decline would favor a reduction in capacity.

The option, for producers, of diversifying out of steel altogether has major implications for public policy, and could, if followed on a major scale, lead to increased import dependency. While steel does not retain all its earlier strategic significance, excessive dependence on foreign steel could result in the domestic steel-consuming industries paying a price premium during supply shortages.

Finally, it cannot be stressed too strongly that public policy entails a delicate balance between, for example, the costs of large-scale disruption of employment in politically sensitive areas and the interests of steel-consuming industries, whose competitive position will be weakened by higher priced domestic steel. Alternatively, the higher costs could be carried by the state. If domestic friction were reduced by protection or subsidies, this gain would have to be balanced against the costs of increased tension in international trade.

The Response of the United States

The continuous process of adjustment in the iron and steel industry is shown by the shifts in the shares of world steel production of the major producing countries. In 1950 the U.S. steel producers accounted for 47 percent of world steel production, but by 1976 this share had declined to 17 percent. The UK's share fell from 37 percent in 1870 to 3.2 percent in 1975. In contrast, Japan's share rose from 2.5 percent in 1950 to 16.5 percent in 1975. These shifts in the relative shares of world steel production have been the result of faster growth in newer steel-producing countries rather than an absolute decline in production in the established producer countries. But a correlation is to be expected between growth of performance and of productivity (see Chapter 1, page 23). Although only over a short period, this is also borne out by Table 3.3. Higher productivity and international competitiveness then combine to form the kind of virtuous circle which has resulted in the rapid growth in Japanese steel production.[13]

Table 3.3 Labor Productivity and Cost for the Major Steel Producers

	Total number of employees (000)	Production mill (tonnes)	Output per man year (tonnes)	Labor cost/ tonne produced $ at current exchange rates
Japan				
1973	321	119	372	17
1976	320	107	335	27
Federal Republic of Germany				
1973	220	50	255	27
1976	213	42	200	38
United States				
1973	603	150	250	66
1976	543	128	236	103
France				
1973	152	25	167	24
1976	155	23	150	38
Italy				
1973	90	21	234	15
1976	98	23	241	17
United Kingdom				
1973	190	27	140	33
1976	181	22	123	49

Source: European Coal and Steel Community, U.S. Department of Labor, American Iron and Steel Institute, and the Japan Iron and Steel Federation. See **Merrill Lynch**, *Japanese Steel Industry: A Comparison with Its United States Counterpart* (New York, 1977).

The problems facing the U.S. steel industry can therefore be largely explained by the slow growth in demand for its steel throughout the 1960s. Neither the claims that the problems have been caused by the dumping of subsidized foreign steel on the U.S. market, government price controls, and onerous pollution control regulations, nor the counterclaims that management has failed to invest and has encouraged imports by its pricing behavior, provide a full explanation of the problems of the industry.[14] Imports into the U.S. market have preempted its growth; they rose from 4.7 percent in 1960 to 17.8 percent in 1977, with peaks in 1968, 1971, 1977, and 1978. But there is equally little doubt that the decline in competitiveness of the U.S. industry was partly responsible. While the causality of growth in imports and low investment in the United States remains contentious, it is clear that the U.S. industry has experienced a downward spiral of slower growth and lower investment. The question that concerns us is how the U.S. industry and policy-makers have responded to these developments.

In 1968, when imports passed 15 percent of apparent consumption for the first time, unions and producers pressed the government to act. As a result, voluntary export restraint agreements were concluded with Japanese and European producers, which limited growth in imports to 5 percent per annum. In 1971 these agreements were renewed with a growth rate of 2.5 percent and extended to include the UK. The objective was to stop foreign producers preempting the growth in demand in the US and thus to enable the domestic industry to strengthen its competitive base. The results do not suggest that the U.S. industry used the period of restraint to improve productivity and competitivenss, and investment in the US declined. Indirect government intervention certainly inhibited investment, especially after 1971 when price control measures were introduced, but the fact remains that such short-term defensive measures were not, by themselves, enough to ensure that investment and productivity improved.

In the 25 years to 1977 only two new greenfield plants were built in the US. The importance of such investment is illustrated by the fact that the second of these, Burns Harbor, built in 1967, has been able to match Japanese productivity levels. While new greenfield plants are not always essential, there are indications that much of the U.S. capital stock is obsolete. Taking the form of steel conversion as a proxy for obsolescence of plant, open hearth furnances, which are much inferior to oxygen-blown steel processes in terms of output per man, accounted for some 13 percent of U.S. crude steel production in 1977, compared to 8 percent in the ECSC and 1 percent in Japan. (A further interesting comparison is that about 60 percent of Soviet production uses the open hearth process.) The US Steel Corporation, the largest producer, still relies on open hearth furnaces for nearly 30 percent of crude steel production.[15] This lack of investment in new plant has contributed to the higher labor costs and lower productivity of the U.S. industry compared to, for example, Japanese producers, with U.S. labor costs consistently accounting for half of production costs, while Japanese labor costs have been held at about 30 percent despite rapid increases in wage rates.[16] It has also added to the costs of antipollution control.[17]

The voluntary export restraint agreements expired in 1973 and were not renewed because of strong demand at the time; indeed, steel production reached all-time highs in most industrialized countries in 1973-74. This boom was followed by an unprecendented fall in demand in 1974-75, so it is understandable that many steel specialists viewed this as a purely cyclical down-turn, the traditional steel cycle that had endured over the previous decade lasting approximately 40 months. In 1976 the U.S. specialty steel producers filed a complaint under the 1974 Trade Act, claiming the imports were "a substantial cause of serious injury." The Ford administration delayed imposing a quota, after the International Trade Commission suggested a quantitative restriction of 146,000 tons net in January 1976, in the hope that agreement could be reached on voluntary export restraints. Only the Japanese agreed to this within the 90-day deadline, however, the European Community and Sweden rejecting any form of orderly marketing agreement. As a result, quotas were introduced in June 1976 for a period of three years.

During 1977 it became clear that demand was not again rising; indeed, toward the end of 1977 there was a marked deterioration in the market. Faced with the prospect of what by then had generally been accepted to be a structural trend in demand, the steel lobbies put pressure on the U.S. government to do something about the low demand, poor financial performance, and major dislocations of labor. In October 1977 a tentative determination against Japanese producers was reached in the Gilmore case. Nineteen cases of antidumping had actually been filed since 1975, so this precedent threatened to lead to large-scale disruptions of trade relations with Japan and the EC. Imports continued to rise toward the end of 1977 as expectation of trade-restraining measures mounted. In Congress the steel caucus of more than 150 not only threatened to act against imports if the government failed to do so, but also considered pressing for delay in the conduct of the Tokyo Round.

In October 1977, President Carter met steel producers and unions to discuss the situation and to report on the consultations that had taken place within the then still informal OECD steel committee. It became clear that the Europeans and Japanese were not prepared to consider a renewal of voluntary export restraint agreements, because the last agreements between the U.S. government and exporters had resulted in actions in the U.S. courts against various steel producers, in which the U.S. industry claimed triple damages under U.S. antitrust law. The U.S. government appears to have resisted unilateral quota restrictions, probably for fear of causing trade frictions at a time when it was attempting to accelerate the Tokyo Round negotiations. In addition, a report published at that time concluded that the problems of the industry could not be solved unless investment increased.[18] The imposition of quotas could not be expected to lead to more investment.

The response of the government was to announce a *Comprehensive Program for the Steel Industry,* which sought to maintain the existing market share held by the U.S. steel producers and to balance the costs of the necessary adjustment of the industry between workers and producers while reducing tensions and uncertainties in steel trade (a reference to the numerous antidumping actions pending).[19] The document also expounded the commitment of the US to an open world trading environment, which should be ensured by international consultations on the problems confronting the industry.[20]

The response of the European Community and the Japanese will be discussed later, but there were consultations between the US and its trading partners throughout the autumn of 1977. Indeed, the anticrisis measures in the form of the trigger price system could work only with the cooperation of the Japanese producers, whose prices were to form the basis of the trigger prices. The trigger price mechanism was installed early in 1978, and antidumping actions were subsequently suspended. The fast-track antidumping procedure provided for in the trigger price system had been used only on one or two occasions up to the end of 1979, certainly less than the industry would have liked.

The anticrisis measures in the form of the trigger prices were only one element of the government's program for steel. Although the improvement in prices, which was in fact partly due to stronger demand, improved the cash flow for the producers and thus made investment easier, the government's proposals went further.[21] The program recognized the need for the U.S. industry to invest and improve productivity if it were to retain its market share, but as the U.S. industry is completely privately owned, government could only prod it by indirect means toward a more-active investment program. First, the government eased tax policy by reducing the Asset Depreciation Range (ADR—the depreciation allowances) for the industry slightly to enable steel plant to be depreciated over a period of about 12 years,[22] but the industry continued to maintain that this was longer than for foreign competitors.

The 1977 policy also provided for loan guarantees to help in restructuring. The loan guarantee fund, administered by the Commerce Department's Economic Development Administration, was not used extensively compared, for example, with loans provided to the European industry. Up to December 1979 only two major loans totaling about US$200 million had received backing.[23] These loan guarantees, which benefit the steel companies as distinct from steel-producing communities, met with strong protest from the other steel producers, ostensibly because the provision of loan guarantees to their competitors undermined the U.S. steel industry's case against the unfair trading practices of other steel-producing countries which provide financial assistance.

Public aid was also provided for communities affected by the rationalization of the industry, and a recommended US$20 million was set aside under title IX of the EDA for this purpose. One further measure taken to ease the process of adjustment was to ask the Department of Justice to expedite the passing down of Department-enforcement intentions in the antitrust field (merger control). This seems to have been an attempt to speed up the processing of merger or cooperation agreements between firms who wished to rationalize production by this method, thus avoiding any question of easing antitrust law. One area where the government moved to ease restrictions on the industry was that of environmental control, although the extra flexibility in the operation of control regulations has not weakened overall limits on emissions.

The effects of these policy measures were not immediately apparent. The trigger prices eased the situation for the industry in 1978 and the first part of 1979, but when the market began to decline in mid-1979 the pressures for action that had been seen in 1977 again began to mount. In February 1980 the American Iron and Steel Institute called for "firm assurances" that imported steel would not disrupt the domestic market, either by excessive volume or unfair pricing, during the next five to eight years, the vital initial period of a 25-year revitalization program that the Institute believed to be necessary. The renewal of calls for a dual trigger price system or indeed import quotas did not suggest that tension in trade policy had been reduced by any restructuring that had taken place during the two years after 1977. It thus seemed reasonable to expect the continued use of export restraint on the part of the Japanese and of temporary anticrisis measures on the part of the Americans.

Anticrisis and Restructuring Measures in the European Community

The steel producers in the European Community assume an intermediate position between the Japanese and the Americans in terms of growth. Furthermore, although the situation throughout the EC varies from country to country and producer to producer, the industry was, in general, midway through a process of restructuring when the crisis began in 1974. While the slow-down in growth of demand began to affect the EC in general toward the end of the 1960s, the picture differed from country to country, with the UK suffering more than most, owing to the weakness of its steel-consuming industries.

Capacity utilization is generally lower in the EC than the US but once again there are differences between member states. The German industry generally operates at lower capacity utilization than most others during recessions; for example, 58 percent in crude steel production in 1977 compared to about 70 percent in the UK.[24] It is interesting to note that the German producers, like the Japanese, have been able to minimize losses, or indeed to improve profitability in the case of Japan, despite lower capacity utilization, indicating that the degree of excess capacity is less important than the ability to operate profitably at lower output.

As a net exporter of steel, the EC's ability to adjust to lower demand will influence not only import penetration, as in the US, but also the ability to maintain export markets. Over the past 15 years the scope for European exports has been reduced by various factors: the growth of Japanese export capabilities, the import restraint in the U.S. market, and finally the new steel producers in the developing countries. Dependence on extra–EC exports varies from country to country. In absolute terms the German steel industry exports most to third markets, both directly in the form of steel and indirectly in the form of steel-intensive manufactures. But the Benelux producers export a higher proportion of their output, although there has been a shift toward greater dependence on intra-EC trade in recent years (Table 3.4 shows the EC trade pattern).[25]

These structural differences, along with differences in productivity (see Table 3.3), help explain the different responses of national governments and steel producers to EC policy. To these differences one must add two further important factors. First, there is the differing importance of the steel industry as a provider of industrial employment. The closure of plants in areas which depend on steel for up to 25 percent of total industrial employment in Lorraine, Wallonia, North and South Wales, and other areas in the UK had a greater impact on employment than, for example, in the worst case in Germany, where steel accounts for 12 percent of industrial employment in the Saar. In Italy the steel industry also has a major importance in regional employment policy.

One more difference between the EC steel producers that has had a major bearing on the formulation of Community policy is the degree of state involvement. In the Federal Republic of Germany 90 percent of the industry is privately owned but, more importantly, privately controlled. In the UK 90 percent is in public ownership. In Italy there exists a dual structure in which the large, integrated

Table 3.4   Patterns of Trade of Principal Importers and Exporters (percentages)

European Community: Imports	1975	1978
Sweden	14	10
Austria	13	12
Spain	8	15
East Europe	20	27
Japan	25	9
Others	20	26
Total	100	100

European Community: Exports	1975	1978
West Europe	28	20
East Europe	18	13
USA	14	22
Central and South America	12	6
Middle East	10	20
Other Asia	4	13
of which India	1	2
China	2	7
Others	12	6
Total	100	100

USA: Imports	1975	1978
EEC	39.7	40.2
Spain	1.3	3.4
East Europe	0.7	2.4
Canada	6.6	11.0
Japan	46.5	27.2
South Korea	2.8	3.7
Others	2.4	12.1
Total	100.0	100.0

Japan: Exports	1975	1978
EEC	5	2
EFTA	2	1
East Europe	3	2
USA	17	16
South America	11	5
Asia	44	64
of which Iran	6	6
South Korea	3	9
China	10	21
Total	100	100

Source: European Communities Eurostat, *Iron and Steel Yearbook 1979.*

coastal plants are run by public enterprise, while the numerous northern (Bresciani) producers are strongly independent of both national and Community control. In France and Belgium the state has extended its influence via capital restructuring and exercises a good deal of leverage via planning agreements or other forms of planning.

ANTICRISIS MEASURES

Soon after the recession began in 1974, pressure was exerted on the Commission to use its powers to regulate prices, delivery quotas, and external trade.[26] However, in accordance with Art 57 of the Treaty Establishing the European

Coal and Steel Community, on the question of regulation of deliveries, and derived from Art 46 ECSC, the Commission gave preference to indirect forms of action. In mid-1975, indicative targets were introduced for the main products by country.[27] As the recession continued, the French pressed for the imposition of minimum prices and the declaration of a "manifest crisis," which would empower the Commission to establish production quotas and impose a levy on any excess tonnage. Such measures were opposed by the Germans, who feared that minimum prices would finally lead to regulation of imports into the Community and in turn to retaliation against EC exports.[28]

The discussions in the spring of 1976 therefore did not lead to a tightening of the anticrisis measures. In December 1976 the recommended delivery programs were elaborated down to company level, each company being notified of the recommended levels by a letter from the Commission.[29] The response to these recommendations was generally good, and a slight improvement in the market in 1976 helped producers to keep within the guidelines. In all but one of the main product groups covered, 90 percent of production was more or less in line with the guidelines. In the case of reinforcing bars, however, which were the main product of the Bresciani producers, only 50 percent of production was covered by companies that were keeping to recommended deliveries. Consequently, minimum prices were set for this product in May 1977. At the same time guidance prices were introduced for the other main products, and surveillance licensing was introduced on imports into the Community.[30]

Toward the end of 1977 the market deteriorated further; when it became clear that the US would also impose anticrisis measures, the resistance to more restrictive measures, mainly from Germany, finally receded. In January 1978 the full Davignon Plan was introduced.[31] This included minimum prices for a further two of the six main products, and increased guidance prices and import base prices as well as import quotas. The external element of the anticrisis measures involved inviting exporters to the EC market to agree to tonnages and prices. Bilateral agreements were finally concluded with a range of EFTA, Eastern European, and developing countries, as well as Japan which was already exercising export restraint. Once an agreement was reached, any speedy antidumping actions against exports that were sold below the import base prices were stopped, and no further measures could be taken without consulting the exporting country. The import tonnage was based on 1976 figures less some 8 percent, to account for the decline in demand in 1977 and 1978. Importers were, however, allowed a 4 to 6 percent import penetration margin below the producer base price at any point in the EC market. These measures remained largely unchanged in 1979. For 1980 the minimum prices for reinforcing bars were suspended, as were the bilateral agreements with developing countries.

In general the anticrisis measures were effective in increasing prices, by some 20 percent by December 1979, and maintaining traditional levels of imports. There were some problems with Spain, which exceeded the agreed tonnages, but otherwise there were few complaints from steel exporters.[32] The recommended delivery program was able to keep actual deliveries more or less in line with the quarterly Forward Programme provided by the Commission.

In general then, the anticrisis program was successful in its objective of raising prices to a level where the more-efficient producers could cover costs. Yet it was not so restrictive that it protected the less-effective producers from incurring losses. Despite differences between the various steel producers within the EC, national governments held to the common policies adopted after extensive consultations and did not resort to unilateral protective action. All sides were obliged to move to reach a common policy. For example, the Germans were forced to accept some minimum prices and import regulation; at the same time, at least until after the summer of 1980, they were able to avoid recourse to the use of Art 58 ECSC (manifest crisis) and were finally successful in getting a more-effective code on direct aid to the steel industry.

LONGER-TERM POLICIES OF RESTRUCTURING

The Community's policy on steel, like that of the U.S. government, comprised not only short-term anticrisis measures, but also a policy on how the industry should restructure in the longer term to achieve a balance between supply and demand and reestablish international competitiveness. While the Commission and the Community retained extensive reserve powers in the field of prices and deliveries, responsibility for investment rested with the companies and the national governments, with the Commission having only an indirect influence.

This indirect influence consisted of four elements. First, the anticrisis measures adopted by the Community determined the general environment within which producers and governments developed their policies on restructuring. As we have seen, this did not mean that ineffective producers were featherbedded so they could avoid the need to restructure. Second, the Commission provided indicative targets and information on medium- and long-term trends in supply and demand in the form of General Objectives, Forward Programmes for each quarter, annual Investment Surveys, and detailed information on employment.[33] Third, the Community was able to provide finance by various means for steel producers, the redeployment of workers, and the regeneration of economic activity in areas affected by plant closures or reductions in employment; Community funds for both industry and social reconversion in 1977 amounted to about 20 percent of total investment in the industry.[34] Finally, the Commission has the power, and refined its application of powers, to control the provision of state aid to the industry. As with the provision of Community finance, the approval of state aid to the industry is made conditional on the fulfilment of certain requirements in terms of restructuring or adjustment of the companies concerned. In each case reference is made to the overall objectives of Community policy in line with the guidelines set out in the General Objectives.

THE POLICIES OF THE NATIONAL GOVERNMENTS

The data in Table 3.5 give an indication of the trends in EC production and capacity.[35] Despite a gradual improvement since 1975, EC crude steel production was in 1980 still below 1973–74 levels. Additional capacity was added up to 1977–78 as a result of the long lead times of decisions taken at an earlier stage. Assuming a 3 percent growth after 1980, there was still a need to reduce capacity by some 30 million metric tons by 1982 if a capacity utilization rate of 88 percent was to be regained. The Commission has not publicly specified how much EC

Table 3.5   Trends in EC Production and Capacity

	Actual production			Production potential		Expected production potential	
	1975	1978	1979	1975	1978	1980	1982
Federal Republic of Germany	40.4	41.2	46.3	62.9	68.9	69.2 (67.7	67.1 65.6)
Belgium	11.6	12.6	13.3	19.0	20.0	19.7	19.1
France	21.5	22.8	23.4	33.7	32.4	31.8	29.1
Italy	21.8	24.3	24.1	32.7	35.7	36.7	37.1
Luxembourg	4.6	4.8	5.0	7.5	7.6	7.3 (6.6	7.5 6.8)
Netherlands	4.9	5.6	5.8	6.3	8.3	8.3	8.6
United Kingdom	20.2	20.3	21.6	27.0	27.9	29.7 (23.5	32.0 25.5)
Denmark	0.6	0.9	–	0.7	1.2	1.2	0.9
Ireland	0.1	0.1	–	0.1	0.1	0.2	0.3
Total EC	125.7	132.6	136.0	189.9	202.1	204.4 (200.0	201.7 197.0)

	Production		
	1974	1978	1980
Estimated demand	155.6	132.6	135.0*
Capacity utilization (percentage)	88	66	69*

Asterisk * signifies estimate. Figures in parentheses indicate estimated capacity after considering closures announced after the completion of the 1979 Commission investment survey. For example, in the case of the UK, the figures in parentheses include BSC's closure program.

Source: Commission of the European Communities, *General Objectives, Investment Surveys,* various years, and press for recent closures.

capacity should be reduced, but it was clear that, despite significant moves already made, more restructuring would be necessary.

In the initial phase of the recession all governments supported the anticrisis measures, although with some reluctuance in the case of the Germans. National policies were influenced by the desire to ensure that the burden of adjustment was shared, and this also applied to capacity reductions within the EC. Up to 1977 the major concern was to ensure that the anticrisis measures were introduced and operating effectively; thereafter the attention of the Commission, national governments, and producers turned to the problem of reducing excess capacity. At the end of 1977, as has been shown, the existence of structural problems was

generally accepted. All governments accepted that a certain degree of retrenchment was necessary, but the question remained as to how much and by whom.
This could not be resolved by a simple balance between the various steel producers or countries, because of the divergence between structural problems and
productivity levels. A balanced reduction in the EC would involve more complex
balancing of, for example, the interests of workers and producers, and market
forces and *dirigisme*.

Belgium. The restructuring of the Belgian industry after 1977 serves to illustrate
the wide range of representation in the decision-making process. After the
reorganization of the industry into three groups, the Belgian government increased public ownership of the industry in June 1979 by converting debt into
public dividend capital. The Charleroi grouping became 50 percent public owned,
Cockerill 30 percent, and state ownership of the smaller private producers was
also increased. After this capital restructuring, the government set up a *Comité
National de Planification et de Contrôle* (CNPC), consisting of representatives
from government, producers, and trade unions, and with an observer from the
Commission of the European Community. The task of this body was to stimulate
and coordinate investment in steel, and in early 1980 Bfr.44,000 million were set
aside for this purpose. The ojective of the Belgian steel plan was to improve the
productivity of the industry. There were no clear plans for reducing capacity; in
fact it was suggested that the industry would grow.[36] Improvements in productivity would not be possible without further reduction in manning. Employment
declined from about 60,000 in 1974 to about 45,000 in 1978. The measures announced in January 1980 implied a loss of 6,000 more jobs, bringing the total
reduction in employment since 1974 to 21,000 or 35 percent of the 1974 total.

France. In France public control over decision-making in the steel industry dates
from the modernization committees formed under the first plan at the end of the
1940s. Through planning agreements, provision of investment capital, and indirectly through price control, the state continued to exercise a fair degree of control over the industry throughout the 1960s and 1970s, and was partly responsible
for encouraging the process of concentration that resulted in an industry centered
around three main groups in the mid-1970s. The Barre plan for the industry was
delayed until after the 1978 elections, but then the process of restructuring began
in earnest. The state restructured the finances of the major steel producers and
reduced their number to two, Usinor and Sacilor. In 1979 the total cost of the
restructuring program was estimated to be Ff.20,000 million, with Ff.13,000
million for the steel producers and Ff.7,000 million for the reconversion of those
affected by closures. Capacity in crude steel was reduced by about three million
tons from 1977 to 1980, resulting in the loss of as many as 37,000 jobs between
1975 and 1980.[37]

The bulk of the redundancies were in Lorraine, where the announcement of the
plans led to some of the worst rioting since 1968. The government did, however,
make efforts to attract new industrial activities to the area and used its influence
to ensure that Peugeot and Citroën built automobile plants there. Apart from the
older plants in the east of France, most of the French steel plant is relatively
modern, and there are potentially competitive coastal plants at Dunkirk and Fos.

The steel industry hopes that the French restructuring policy, which has also liberalized price controls and has become more oriented to market conditions since 1977, will enable it to break even by 1980 or 1981.[38]

Federal Republic of Germany. Unlike the French industry, which has been rationalized along national lines with the prompting of the state, the German industry has resorted to transnational rationalization in the case of the problematical Saar industry. In 1978 the Federal government provided a DM900-million loan guarantee for the private banks' financing of Arbed, the Luxembourg-based steel giant, which took over control of the Saar plants. By supporting this private solution to the problem of rationalization of the Saar industry, the German government avoided becoming directly involved.

The process of adjustment in the German industry, which began in the 1960s, has been controlled and coordinated by the private sector by means of rationalization groupings *(Walzstahlkontore* and then *Rationalisierungsgruppen).* By sharing orders to improve productivity and phasing the installation of new capacity, these groups have served the kind of central coordinating function that the state has fulfilled in other countries. The government has generally preferred to see such private formations or even mergers rather than to take a direct hand in restructuring. The Commission of the EC, for its part, to which responsibility for controlling mergers falls under the ECSC treaty, has generally adopted a relaxed attitude to increased concentration, while imposing certain conditions on the form of mergers. When the private sector steel companies sought to extend the rationalization groups to include Benelux producers in an organization which went under the name of Denelux, however, they met strong opposition from both France and the Commission. France was particularly concerned that this would develop into a gigantic German cartel. As a result, Eurofer was born in early 1976. This included all the European steel producers in one industry association; but contrary to popular belief Eurofer remains rather weak, since the divergent interests and structures of the national industries inhibit any process of cartelization in such an institutionalized form.

One of the major concerns of the German government and industry is that they feel other member states within the EC have consistently provided financial assistance for their domestic industries and thus distorted competition within the common market. Consequently the Germans attempted to make their support of the Davignon Plan dependent on the introduction of an effective code on state aid to the steel industry.[39] After some two years delay the Community finally accepted a code on state aid when Britain withdrew her reserve (Italy was then the only state to have reservations about the, by then, less-restrictive code, and was reluctantly obliged to accept it).[40]

In summary, the German policy has been one of nonintervention. In contrast with the private steel industry in the USA, German producers developed longer-term strategic planning that has resulted in the continuous rationalization and adjustment of the industry. In the case of the Saar where the private sector had not planned its adjustment well, the Federal and Land governments intervened to ease the social costs of the more crisis-inspired restructuring by providing loans to the industry and regional aid for the areas affected. The state may also have indirectly helped the steel industry to adjust output during periods of slack demand

and thus minimize costs, by the provision of short time working compensation for steel workers. As shown in Table 3.5, the German industry has the largest capacity in the Community, but despite low rates of capacity utilization it has made only relatively minor reductions in capacity since 1977. Job displacement in Germany has been gradual but consistent; between 1974 and 1977, for example, nearly 20,000 jobs were lost, which was the highest rate in the Community over that period.[41]

Italy. The Italian steel industry has tended to be out of step with the other European producers.[42] This may be partly due to the fact that the electric steel producers in the north benefit from low-priced scrap during steel recessions and thus tend to operate in an anticyclical manner compared to the rest of the Community. In addition Italian policy has used the steel industry as an instrument in the regional economic development of southern Italy. Italian policy-makers are proud of the fact that the industry has grown consistently from 2.4 million tons output in 1950 to 24 million tons in 1978, an average annual growth rate of 9 percent, which has put it in second place behind Germany in Europe and sixth place in the world.[43] This rapid growth is reflected in productivity, in which Italy compares very favorably with other European producers (see Table 3.3). Indeed, the growth of the Italian steel production exhibited similar characteristics to that of Japan in that it was able to benefit from the rapid growth in domestic demand. Under the guidance of Finsider the industry was able to construct internationally competitive steel plants.

Since 1975, however, domestic demand has begun to stagnate, and intense competition on international markets has reduced the scope for exports. Consequently the losses of the public sector industry rose to L.395,000 million in 1977 and remained at that level through 1979. Debt charges also rose to 15 percent of Finsider's turnover in 1978–79. In order to counter the effects of declining demand and mounting losses, the Interministerial Committee for the Co-ordination of Industrial Policy (CIPI) approved a restructuring plan for the industry in March 1979.[44] The plan's estimated cost was put at L.600,000 million; its aim was modernization of the more-obsolete plants and realization of the full capacity of Taranto. In the private sector the plan envisaged certain indicative guidelines for the smaller producers.

The Italian industry did not go along with EC suggestions that it should reduce capacity, and the only concession made by Italian policy to the pressure to reduce capacity in line with producers north of the Alps was the postponement of the extension of the Gioia Tauro project. These frictions between the Italian public sector and, for example, the privately run German industry surfaced in the dispute over the code on state aid to the steel industry.

In summary then, the Italian industry has tended to follow an independent policy, has added nearly four million tons to crude steel capacity since 1974, and has resisted the attempts of the other European steel producers and the Commission to reduce Italian capacity in the future.

United Kingdom. The British industry emerged from the 1960s suffering from the effects of being used as a political football for the preceding decade. Investment was low, and delays in the implementation of a corporate strategy for the nationalized steel industry,[45] caused by further direct intervention by the government, meant that the industry finally launched its investment program just a short time before the 1974 recession. The initial plan was to concentrate production in five major integrated coastal plants, but the recession made the process of rationalizing obsolete plants exceedingly difficult, because of the social and political costs of closing plant. In 1975 the steel closure program was revised, and closures were in several cases postponed or suspended.[46]

As the recession progressed it became clear that the objective of developing an internationally competitive industry on the scale envisaged in the Ten Year Development Strategy could not be achieved.[47] The high losses incurred by BSC necessitated a "step-by-step approach which [would] retain flexibility to adapt to unexpected changes in the situation."[48] These vague statements notwithstanding, retrenchment had in fact already begun, and in 1978 the closures of older plants were negotiated with the unions and led to the announcement of the closure of six plants, affecting 17,000 jobs. Thus despite the initial resistance to reducing employment (from 1974 to 1977 only some 4,500 jobs were lost), the heavy burden of losses led to a gradual increase in redundancies. By August 1979 closures affecting some 40,000 jobs had been made or announced, affecting some 18 percent of 1974 employment. At the end of 1979 a radical retrenchment policy was announced that would reduce crude steel capacity by 6.5 million tons and the industry by 50,000 jobs by August 1980, bringing the total employment in the UK industry down to 100,000, less than half the 1974 level.

This retrenchment was brought about by the recently elected Conservative Government which was committed to a reduction in public spending and hence of losses in the publicly owned steel industry. There can be little doubt that a Labour government would not have been able to reduce the size of the industry in such a radical manner, but the policy decision to retrench, albeit at a socially acceptable pace, had already been made.

British policy in steel was, then, plagued by repeated changes in policy by consecutive governments. When a corporate strategy finally emerged it ran full tilt into the worst recession the industry had experienced since the 1930s. While the public steel sector in Italy was able to benefit from the rapid growth in domestic demand during the 1960s, by the time the UK industry was in a position to benefit from rationalization, the growth in demand for steel had already slipped below that of GNP. Furthermore, the BSC inherited a structure in which most of the obsolete plants were located in areas of relatively high unemployment, in which the steel industry was a major employer.

Public Policy on Steel in Japan

It has been shown that the Japanese industry grew faster than any other iron and steel industry during the 1950s and 1960s. From 1950 to 1969 the average rate of growth in output was 34 percent per annum, compared to 1.5 percent in the USA, 2.7 percent in the UK, 6.8 percent in Germany, and 13.3 percent in Italy.[49] This exceptional rate of growth provided the Japanese industry with an opportunity to exploit innovations in production technology in a growing and stable world economy and thus improve productivity and international competitiveness. This international competitiveness in turn increased the growth potential of the industry through increasing exports, thus facilitating the task of both private and public policy-makers for the industry.

In 1950 the Ministry for International Trade and Industry (MITI) developed the first rationalization plan for the Japanese steel industry. This consisted of tax incentives for investment and the provision of investment finance through the Japan Development Bank, the Long Term Credit Bank, and indirectly through the Bank of Japan; and the first plan coincided with a major effort to promote heavy industry. By stimulating demand for steel-intensive heavy industries, such as shipbuilding and chemicals, government policies in the early 1950s sowed the seeds of future rapid growth of the major steel-consuming industries over the next twenty years.

The second rationalization plan for the steel industry from 1955–60 followed similar lines, with the role of MITI again being mainly indirect. Once steel-consuming industries began to grow, the steel industry was ensured of a sound domestic market on which to base its expansion. As the steel industry grew in stature the need for even indirect government support declined, so that by the mid 1960s the industry itself had taken full control of investment and pricing policy.

The Japanese industry is strongly influenced by the five largest integrated steel producers, which in 1977 accounted for 95 percent of pig iron and 77 percent of crude steel production.[50] Nippon Steel Corporation plays a dominant role as a price leader in flat products as well as in other areas, such as wage negotiations and dividend payments. As in the EC, the nonintegrated producers, being more numerous and smaller, tend to compete more intensely than the larger ones. As a result, prices of long products, a typical product for the smaller plants, have been more volatile than for flat products – as is also the case in Europe, where price minima have been found more necessary for these products.

As the leader in the steel industry in more than one sense, Nippon Steel Corporation's relations with the government are of some significance to Japanese public policy in steel. Apart from the fact that the need for government assistance declined as the industry grew in strength, Nippon Steel has taken on semipublic responsibilities and often considers the well-being of the whole steel industry, and indeed Japanese industry as a whole, to be as important as the interests of Nippon Steel. There are also strong personal links between the industry and other important institutions; for example, the president of Nippon Steel is also head of the influential Keidanren employers' federation. Nippon Steel itself was formed from the previously publicly controlled Yawata Steel Company.

Public policy has continued to be relevant in various areas of the steel industry. First, import restraint in the USA and Europe has necessitated the coordination of steel exports in order to avoid trade frictions, and the government has provided guidelines for steel exporters.

Competition on the domestic market, which, as in Europe, has been partly in the form of competitive capacity expansion, led to price instability and low profitability during the latter part of the 1960s. After gathering information from the industry, the government provided recommendations on the phasing of investment in new blast furnaces. These recommendations were made by the Iron and Steel Subcommittee of MITI's Industrial Structure Council.[51]

This procedure may be compared with that provided for in Art 54 ECSC, under which the Commission can make known its opinion on any investment of which it is notified by the steel producers. MITI also provides indicative quarterly production guidelines similar to those employed in the EC since the beginning of the crisis. While these EC and Japanese instruments are not dissimilar, they operate in different environments. In the EC there are a larger number of steel producers in different countries competing in one market, and as has been shown, the national governments have a fairly direct role in all but one or two of the national industries. In Japan there is one business culture and the presence of Nippon Steel, so that MITI is better placed than the EC Commission in Brussels to influence events informally when this may be required.

The capacity of Japanese steel producers increased from 120 million tons per year of crude steel in 1973 to 147 million in 1978. With the addition of one further blast furnace in 1980, total capacity will have risen to 150 million tons, where it is likely to remain for some years to come.

After the recession began in 1974, Japanese steel producers were experiencing losses owing to excess capacity and low prices. Efforts were therefore made to improve energy consumption, adjust inventories, and add modern automation to continous processes. In December 1977 the USA and the EC decided to introduce measures to regulate prices, which had the effect of raising Japanese export prices. These actions together caused a substantial improvement in the profitability of the Japanese steel producers, who by 1978/79 were able to operate at only 70 percent effective capacity and still boost profits in that financial year by up to 100 percent more than in the preceding year.[52] There was therefore no immediate reason why the government should promote capacity reduction policies, as in the case of many European countries. Equally, there was little incentive to expand capacity, given the depressed conditions on the world steel market. The policy of the Japanese steel producers has therefore been to consolidate their position and ensure that they do not make the same mistake as the U.S. industry, which did not invest in productivity improvements.[53] While the steel industry is conscious that future growth will not be steel-intensive and that there probably will be a gradual process of disengagement of the economy from steel, this does not imply that there will be a major retrenchment in bulk steel. Inevitable diversification, for example, into steel plant and more-specialized steels, will take place, but in contrast to many steel producers in Europe and the USA, the Japanese industry will have the financial resources to accomplish it. An immediate threat of competition from new steel-producing countries is considered unlikely, despite the fact that South Korea, for example, can undercut Japanese prices in some basic steel products. The new steel producers of the 1980s will have to cope with a less-stable trading environment than in the 1950s and 1960s, and are not likely to benefit from being able to apply more advanced technology than their Japanese competitors, as the Japanese did in relation to the Americans and Europeans.

In trade policy the Japanese steel producers were prepared to accept the trigger price mechanism in the United States and the voluntary export restraint to the EC, because some form of trade restraint was inevitable given the U.S. and EC pressures. It was moreover advantageous to accept price measures, which compensated for a decline in export volume by increasing export prices, and thus to maintain export revenue. In 1978-79, export volume fell by 9 percent compared to 1977-78 but export prices rose by 19 percent. Japan has also diversified the direction of her exports, and for a short time in 1978 China became her largest export market.[54] In 1977, 50 percent of Japan's steel exports went to Asia, 10 percent to Europe (of which 4 percent to the EC), 20 percent to the USA, and 10 percent to South America.

The Developing Countries

The Third World is an important market that offers better growth prospects than the industrialized countries. Estimates by UNIDO for the growth of consumption in the industrialized and developing countries are given in Table 3.6. Based on these assumptions, the UNIDO study has estimated that the Third World share of world steel production will be approximately 11 percent in 1985 and between 22 and 25 percent in the year 2000, while the share in consumption of steel could be 16 percent and 23 to 34 percent, respectively.[55] Estimates of future trends in steel consumption and production are difficult, owing to the uncertainties in forecasting caused by changes that have tended to throw doubt on the relationship between GDP and steel demand.[56] There seems little doubt, however, that, in line with the growth potential from the very low current levels of steel consumption in the developing countries, their share of world production will continue to grow.

It is possible to distinguish various categories of developing countries according to the development of their iron and steel industries. The first group has long-established expertise in the industry and had the beginnings of a steel industry before the 1950s. Other than China, these countries (Argentina, Brazil, Egypt, Yugoslavia, India, Mexico, and Turkey) have a total population of 800 million. With total production of about thirty million tons, representing only 40 kg of steel per head, the potential market in these countries is immense. Nevertheless, the growth of the steel industry depends on industrialization in general, and thus on the progress made in manufacturing industries. China holds a rather special place. The present capacity in China is estimated at thirty million tons and plans were envisaged to build 10 new steel plants of six million tons capacity each, but these plans have since been drastically scaled down. In general neither China nor the other populous countries with long-established steel industries can be expected to cope with increased domestic demand in the future. Investment in the iron and steel industry will be made as and when the growth in manufacturing and construction require increased output. Indeed, experience has shown that steel production often lags behind domestic consumption. A number of developing or newly industrializing countries do have rather advanced capabilities in know-how and technology. India and Mexico are particularly important in this respect, and Mexico has led the development of the direct reduction process for reduction of iron ore.

The second group of developing countries consists of developing countries which established an iron and steel industry during the 1950s. Of this group of 10 countries, South Korea and Venezuela are the most important, with Taiwan, which has set itself the optimistic target of twenty million tons by 1990, aiming to follow South Korea. South Korea followed the pattern of development of Japan most closely, and it was Japan which provided the Koreans with the capital and expertise to start their industry. Subsequently, Korea developed domestic sources of know-how and, helped by its rapid growth of domestic demand, has become

Table 3.6 Estimated Rates of Growth of Steel Consumption and Production in the Industrialized and Developing Countries (percentage per annum)

	Consumption	Production
Industrialized countries		
1975–1985	3.0	2.8
1985–2000	1.5–2.5	1.5–2.6
Developing countries		
1975–1985	7.8	12.0[a]
1985–2000	5.8–9.4	7.7–9.4

[a] As Table 3.1 shows, the production of developing countries continued to grow at a rate of somewhat more than 12 percent in 1978–79.

Source: UNIDO/ICIS, *Worldwide Study of the Iron and Steel Industry 1975–2000*, 1976, p. 35.

Table 3.7 Crude Steel Production in Leading Developing Country Steel Producers (million tonnes)

	1978	1979	Percentage change
Brazil	12.2	13.8	13.7
(Spain)	11.3	12.1	7.3
India	10.1	9.4	−6.5
South Korea	4.9	7.6	53.1
Mexico	6.7	6.9	3.7
Taiwan	3.4	4.2	23.8
Yugoslavia	3.4	3.5	2.3
Argentina	2.7	3.1	14.7
Turkey	2.1	2.4	12.2
Venezuela	0.8	1.3	60.0
Total	57.6	64.3	11.6
Percentage share of world steel production excluding USSR, Eastern Europe, China, and North Korea		12.9	

Source: International Iron and Steel Institute.

one of the four leading steel producers in the Third World. Thanks to the ability to install new capital equipment to cope with a rapid increase in demand, Korean productivity at the Pohang works is about 288 tons per man year, which compares favorably with productivity rates in the OECD countries. Comparing the average cost per ton of medium plate and hot rolled coils (products widely used in, for example, shipbuilding and general manufacturing) one estimate put Korean cost per ton in 1978 at about US$230 (at full operation) and the corresponding cost in Japan at more than US$300 (assuming exchange rate of 220 yen to US$1) at 67 percent capacity utilization.[57]

Venezuela is interesting because it has based its steel expansion plans on the direct reduction process, and has recently commissioned the largest integrated steel works yet built using the direct reduction route to production of flat steel products. This method of producing steel has two major advantages for Third World countries. First it is smaller in scale than the blast furnace/oxygen steel route, and economies of scale can be achieved for smaller plants serving the smaller Third World markets. Second, the use of natural gas opens up possibilities for gas/energy–rich developing countries to use gas reduction processes. Indonesia, Iran, Iraq, Saudi Arabia, and Mexico have also used this strategy, so that with rising energy prices they are able to compensate for higher construction costs, which are in any case lower for these smaller plants. These countries make up the core of a group of 15 countries which installed steel plants at the end of the 1960s and the beginning of the 1970s.

The final group of developing countries consists of thirty countries in which steel plants are planned or under construction. While many of these will be small in scale, they will increase the degree of self-sufficiency of the Third World in the production of iron and steel. In 1977 the Third World was 61 percent self-sufficient in crude steel. In view of the potential growth in demand, the availability of smaller-scale plants that are more suitable to the needs of the LDCs and the advantages of some LDCs in terms of energy costs, it seems likely that the degree of self-sufficiency will continue to increase. One estimate puts self-sufficiency at about 79 percent in crude steel in 1985, assuming a 6 percent growth rate for LDC demand.[58] There are, of course, many problems to be solved by the LDCs before they can achieve 100 percent self-sufficiency or even become net exporters of iron and steel. Perhaps the most important for many developing steel producers is the cost of a new plant.

The development of the iron and steel industry in the Third World does not represent a threat to the OECD producers in terms of the volume of direct exports from the Third World to the OECD, at least not during the 1980s. The existence of capacity in the Third World does, however, affect the OECD producers in various ways. First, imports, even of an insignificant volume, can have a disruptive effect on markets owing to low prices or disorganized marketing practices, especially during a recession. This is possibly one reason why the EC has controlled the price of imports from some Third World countries, and may have been a contributing factor in the USA's decision to introduce a trigger price rather than voluntary export restraint agreements. (South Korea was the fourth-largest exporter to the USA in 1977.) In addition, and possibly more important, is the potential the new steel-producing countries have of undercutting the OECD exporters on third markets in the developing world, thus undermining attempts led by the Europeans to make export price increases stick. Second, the proliferation of steel-producing countries has made the organization of world trade in steel more difficult. Moreover, efforts within the OECD countries to raise prices and control capacity expansion could be expected to promote expansion of capacity in the developing countries, since they increase domestic production to avoid paying inflated prices for steel imports. Finally, the long-term structural changes indicating that steel demand in the Third World will grow much faster than in the OECD represent a challenge to the OECD producers. In an industry that is experiencing a general slowing of growth in demand, the Third World market is one of the few bright spots in an otherwise somewhat depressed market. With a high degree of state involvement in the developing steel industries (see Table 3.8), one can expect industrial strategies to aim at a high degree of self-sufficiency in this basic industry. If the LDCs can harness this growth potential, the OECD producers could be faced with a declining share of world steel exports. The possibility that a few newly industrializing countries will approximate Japan's successful growth model casts a shadow over the future of the industry in the 1990s and beyond. If, as we shall see in the next section, the OECD governments wish to be able to anticipate future structural problems in the steel industry and thus avoid recourse to short-term protectionist measures, the new steel-producing countries must be included in any appraisal of future developments.

Table 3.8 Percentage of Production Capacity of the Iron and Steel Industry Controlled by the State or by the Public Sector in Various Countries

	1975 capacity	Forecast capacity for 1985–1988
Argentina	70	80
Brazil	60	80
Chile	100	100
Mexico	50	65
Peru	100	100
Venezuela	86	90
India	65	75
Iran	100	100
Republic of Korea	100	100
Saudi Arabia	–	100
Libya, Tunisia, Algeria, and Morocco	–	100
Spain	51	65
Turkey	90	90

Source: UNIDO/ICIS, *The World Iron and Steel Industry* (second study), 1978, p. 124.

International Implications of National Steel Policies

Divergent patterns of growth in demand for steel during the 1960s and 1970s have resulted in shifts in the pattern of trade and production. These have led not only to increased intervention at a national level but also to tensions in trade relations. Such divergent patterns of growth are likely to continue to cause friction in the future, unless international norms for anticrisis and structural adjustment policies can be evolved.

The response to shifts in the pattern of trade and production of steel are important because the industry is closely associated with the major steel-consuming industries, which continue to form the basis of employment and industrial production in the industrialized countries. In this sense the steel industry retains a strategic importance, because the continued strength of the major steel-consuming industries depends on the supply of reasonably priced steel. In the long term, therefore, policy-makers could be faced with the option of defending an inefficient steel industry, with all that this implies in terms of lost competitiveness in steel-consuming industries, or of allowing the steel industry to decline and accepting greater dependence on foreign sources of lower-priced steel. In practice, of course, all public policy in steel follows the objective of ensuring a cost-effective, competitive steel industry. But in order to do this and avoid the collapse of the less-efficient steel producers during the recession, temporary anticrisis measures were introduced, thus requiring a trade-off between the short-term costs for steel consumers and the longer-term chances of reestablishing competitive steel production. Such measures have introduced frictions in the international trading environment because, for largely historical reasons, some steel producers and steel-producing nations are more efficient than others. Consequently the anticrisis measures introduced during the late 1970s had to be accompanied by commitments to national policies of restructuring, in order to reestablish the balance between supply and demand. Public policy in steel has also taken account of the distribution of the costs of this process of adjustment between workers, producers, and general economic welfare, and has promoted international conciliation in order to prevent national policies that would shift the burden of adjustment onto other countries or groups of steel producers.

In the United States, where the effects of stagnating demand began to appear during the 1960s, the government was forced to introduce defensive measures in order to prevent foreign steel producers from preempting the little growth that still remained. By 1977 it had become clear that import regulation without more investment would not facilitate the revitalization of the industry. Therefore the *Comprehensive Program for the Steel Industry* recommended that measures be taken to promote investment. At the same time the U.S. government has endeavored to avoid undue friction in trade relations while the industry restructures. The trigger price mechanism was, as has been mentioned, generally acceptable to the USA's trading partners. Within the United States, however, the industry, unions, and government were well aware that longer-term solutions had to be found for the problems of the steel industry. In June 1978 the steel caucus in the House and Senate pressed the government to find a longer-term solution to the problem of subsidized imports. The pressure for the establishment of an "international steel-monitoring agreement" suggested that the Tokyo Round package would not be given a smooth ride unless there were a separate agreement on steel.[59] The government's response was to press for the formation of a permanent steel committee within the OECD. The U.S. objective, which was supported by the French although for different reasons, was to monitor steel policy in general and not just trade policy in steel. The U.S. industrial lobby also pressed for international consultations, which included the most-important steel producers in the developing countries.[60]

The European Community was not opposed to discussions at an international level; indeed, it had considered that such discussions should have taken place before the introduction of import control measures in the EC.[61] In the autumn of 1977 there were extensive consultations between the EC, USA and Japan, after which the USA introduced the trigger price system, a lead which the EC followed. The position in the EC was that there was little agreement on what should be done to facilitate restructuring, partly because all the steel producers were hoping that either demand would pick up or others would begin retrenchment first. There was, however, more consensus on the need for anticrisis measures, it being generally easier to agree on the maintenance of the status quo than how the burden of retrenchment should be distributed. Sharing the burden of adjustment in the EC did not take the form of a crisis cartel, because a continued commitment on the part of some member states, notably Germany, to competition within the common market prevented such a policy, as indeed it did in the manmade fibers industry (see Chapter 4). In addition, as has been shown to be the case in Japan, there were still strong competitive forces due to the pressure to maintain output levels and thus cover fixed costs. The process of burden sharing in the EC took a more-sophisticated form involving indicative delivery guidelines, the regulation of state aid and the provision of adjustment assistance for workers and steel producers.[62] In the negotiations on the EC steel policy there was an element of trading off internal competition against external competition. In other words the external measures of the Davignon Plan, in the form of control of import prices and quantities, were accepted by Germany, for example, in return for not using powers to control delivery tonnages and for the ultimate introduction of more-rigorous control of state aid.

In the process of developing policies aimed at sharing the burden of adjustment within the EC, the Commission has initiated policies with scope for wider application in the future development of EC policy. For example, the use of Community loans combined with interest rebates to provide maximum leverage at minimum cost was first used in the steel sector and then introduced for the EC in general in the so-called Ortoli Facility. In the steel industry the Commission has also developed the policy of linking the provision of Community assistance or the granting of national aid to the establishment of restructuring programs, which could well be extended to other industries such as shipbuilding and synthetic fibers. Finally the Commission's proposals on work sharing in the steel industry were seen as a test for the Commission's approach to this form of adjustment to slow growth. The work-sharing proposals, which have been called for by EC trade unions for some time, were intended to reduce the costs of adjustment for labor. The Commission's proposals on work sharing involved the provision of financial assistance for lowering the retirement age, working a further shift, a shorter work week, and restrictions on overtime. The costs of these measures were to be distributed between governments, employers, workers, and the Community.[63] In general, the adjustment assistance policy in the EC was far more developed than that in the USA. As all these measures could affect the competitiveness of the European industry and thus its ability to sell steel to the United States, there was a strong, though not entirely justified, feeling in the US that such measures, especially specific aid to the steel industry, constituted unfair trade and were a major cause of the problems of the US industry.[64]

The OECD Steel Committee was therefore formally established in October 1978.[65] The objectives of the committee are to avoid practices in the operation of the anticrisis measures that have the effect of shifting the burden of adjustment onto other states, to facilitate needed structural adaptations that would diminish pressures for trade actions and, inter alia, to avoid encouraging economically unjustified investment while recognizing legitimate development needs. The initial work program for the committee was to examine the effects of government policies on trade and adjustment in the steel industry and to examine the effects of government export credits for steel plant and equipment. While the policies relating to development needs and to export credits have not been a major issue in the work of the committee, they have been mentioned because they reflect some concern about the potentially important problem of the relations between the OECD countries and the developing steel producers in the Third World.

It is hard as yet to assess the effects of the steel committee on national steel policies, but any effect it does have will be indirect. The initial discussions in the committee concerned various national policies, and the exchange of views may well have influenced policy-makers. The requirement to notify the committee of trade measures should help to inhibit unilateral trade protection, and may have been influential in the suspension of U.S. quotas on special steels announced in 1979.

In the field of relations with developing countries the initial intention to include four non-OECD countries—India, South Korea, Mexico, and Brazil— has not been fulfilled. Some of these countries suspected that the OECD countries wished, in some way, to influence their future development plans. India has little sympathy for the concern in the developed countries on the worldwide surplus capacity. While South Korea may feel it has more need for the international recognition it would get by participating in the committee, it is unlikely to be able to move officially without India, which openly rejected the invitation, and Brazil, which showed little interest. The committee's objective of avoiding the encouragement of economically unjustified investments aroused a good deal of suspicion. It was not clear how unjustified investments should be defined.

One area in which greater consultations between developing and industrialized countries could be useful is in the preparation of sectoral studies on future demand and supply along the lines of the two UNIDO studies. There has already been a consultative meeting of UNIDO on the world steel industry in New Delhi in 1979, but UNIDO proposals on industrial adjustment have not met with general approval in the industrialized countries.

Conclusions

The developments in the steel industry in the 1970s show that, in addition to trade policy measures, a wide range of national and Community policies have become a matter of international concern.

The problems in the steel industry have shown that national policy responses can be largely explained by structural factors, such as the extent to which national industries have been affected by the decline in demand, and the impact the rationalization of production can have on areas that are dependent on the steel industry for industrial employment. The extent to which national policies can maintain productive capacity and employment does, however, depend on the costs of such support, and the UK in particular has been obliged to make large reductions in the size of the industry for this reason. Other producers have been able to operate profitably despite low rates of capacity utilization, for example, Japan and Germany. In general Japan has little immediate need to restructure and reduce capacity. Europe has begun to complete the process of modernizing and rationalizing the industry, which was delayed at the onset of the crisis, while the USA has still some way to go in restructuring before trade restraint by Japan and other exporters will be redundant.

The problems in the industry have resulted in an increase in public intervention, but this has not been designed merely to maintain the status quo. The now familiar temporary defensive measures have been introduced, but they have been accompanied by longer-term policies of restructuring. While some countries have not felt they were committed to help establish a balance between supply and demand by reducing capacity, few have followed policies designed to increase capacity and thus take advantage of the reductions in capacity elsewhere.

The social and political problems involved in restructuring the industry have resulted in increased representation of interest groups in policy formulation. All industrialized countries have had some form of tripartite consultative procedure with unions and producers. In the USA and Germany this has been informal and ad hoc, while in Belgium, for example, the consultations have been institutionalized in a planning committee, on which the EC Commission sits as an observer. With pressure from organized labor in the industrialized countries,[66] steps have been taken to provide a forum for international tripartite consultations, in the form of a symposium organized by the OECD.

The steel crisis has also resulted in the provision of better information on future trends in supply and demand, both at a national and Community level; MITI in Japan and the Commission of the EC both provide quarterly indicative guidelines on delivery tonnages. Within the OECD steel committee the prospects for various markets have been analyzed, for example for steel plants, and at the global level the UNIDO has held consultative meetings.

There has been little direct control of investment in the steel industry by governments. When public capital has been used for restructuring, public control is naturally greater, as it is in the case of nationalized industries; but the indicative guidelines on investment in Japan and in the EC are not enforceable and have been used only as a normative instrument. More generally, government policy in the field of taxation or price control has also had an indirect effect on investment in the steel industry.

In the USA the government is restricted in its steel policy because of the lack of structural policy instruments. In addition, the opposition of the steel industry to the provision of federal loans to the weaker steel producers reduces the ability of the government to exercise leverage over investment decisions, and increases the importance of trade policy or trigger price mechanisms as a means of providing a suitable climate for investment. As regards the choice of policy instruments, experience in Europe suggests that when the costs of a particular instrument are visible, there is less chance that support for the industry will be continued when the costs become excessive. In the case of public finance for investment or subsidies, the costs are visible and concentrated on public policy-makers, and when assistance does not improve the performance of the industry there is strong pressure to cut losses and adopt a policy of retrenchment. In the case of more indirect assistance, such as measures designed to raise prices or protect the domestic market, the costs are more dispersed.

The initial response to the crisis was to adopt anticrisis measures in order to mitigate the economic, social, and political costs of structural change. As a result of the pressures stemming from the costs of public support for inefficient plants, and from the steel consumers and international and Community bodies, steel policy has been extended to more active restructuring of the industry. These active policies include the diagnosis of longer-term market trends, the development of structural policy instruments, and international and Community monitoring of their application.

The developments in the steel industry in the 1970s suggest that when structural problems result in a high degree of public intervention, industrial structural policy should be strengthened in order to ensure that intervention promotes adjustment to changes in the longer-term patterns of demand and trade. Without such a strong industrial structural policy, there is a danger that reactions to problems as they occur will result in the perpetuation of "temporary" anticrisis measures.

Notes

1. See, for example Kent Jones, "Forgetfulness of Things Past: Europe and the Steel Cartel," *The World Economy,* January 1979.

2. U.S. Department of Commerce, *Long Term Trends in U.S. Steel Consumption: Implications for Domestic Capacity,* May 1979.

3. While much of this chapter will center on the European Community because of its importance in policy-making, these trends in steel demand are general for most Western European producers.

4. Commission of the European Communities, *General Objectives for Steel 1980-85,* 1976, p. 28.

5. This compares with some 500-700kg per caput in the European Community: see *General Objectives,* ibid., 1976.

6. Commission of the European Communities, *Investment in the Community Coalmining and Iron and Steel Industries,* 1978 Survey, p. 15. There were also differences between member states of the EC, with capacity utilization in the UK higher than in France and Germany. In 1977 the respective average rates of utilization were 71, 66, and 58 percent.

7. See Commission of the European Communities, *Investment Survey,* 1979.

8. Nomura Research Institute, *Prospects for Japanese Industry to 1985,* vol. 1, Financial Times Management Reports, 1979, p. 120.

9. See Peter F. Marcus et al., "A Western World Steel Supply/Demand Scenario for the 1980s," in Paine Webber Mitchell Hutchins Inc., *World Steel Dynamics,* October 23, 1979, and Table 3.1, herein, for 1979 steel production.

10. *A Comprehensive Program for the Steel Industry,* Report to the President, Task Force, Anthony M. Solomon, Chairman, December 1977.

11. For a discussion of what is unfair see M. J. Marks, "Remedies to Unfair Trade: American Action Against Steel Imports," in *The World Economy* (London: January 1978).

12. K. Stegemann, *Price Competition and Output Adjustment in the European Steel Industry 1954-1975* (Tübingen: J.C.B. Mohr, 1977.)

13. For a detailed study of how faster growth in demand can enable steel producers to benefit from innovations in production technology that improve economies of scale and productivity, what has been termed the "vintage effect," see F. Wolter, *Anpassungsprobleme der westdeutschen Stahlindustrie* (Tübingen: J.C.B. Mohr, 1974).

14. For a discussion of these issues, see The Federal Trade Commission, "The U.S. Steel Industry and its International Rivals: Trends and Factors Determining International Competitiveness," mimeographed (Washington, D.C., November 1977).

15. *Financial Times,* January 7, 1980.

16. Federal Trade Commission, op. cit., p. 60.

17. For detailed discussions of U.S. and Japanese production costs, see Hans Mueller and K. Kawahito, *Steel Industry Economics* (Middle Tennessee State University, 1978); for a defense of the U.S. industry, see *The Economics of International Steel Trade: Policy Implications for the United States* (Newton, Mass.: Putnam, Hayes and Bartlett, Inc., 1977). For an example of the continuing discussion of U.S. and Japanese costs and pricing behavior, see H. Mueller and K. Kawahito, *Errors and Biases in the 1978 Putnam, Hayes and Bartlett Study on the Pricing of Imported Steel,* Monograph Series No. 17 (Middle Tennessee State University, 1979).

18. See The Council on Wage and Price Stability, *Report to the President on Prices and Costs in the U.S. Steel Industry,* October 1977; see also Federal Trade Commission, op. cit. It was also thought that the last voluntary restraint agreements had resulted in an increase in imports of fabricated steel, and while there is no evidence of a direct causal link, indirect trade in steel did move into deficit during this period. See *A Comprehensive Program for the Steel Industry,* op. cit.

19. Op. cit.

20. Ibid., pp. 7-8.

21. See *Metal Bulletin,* November 2, 1979.

22. *Metal Bulletin.* April 27, 1979.

23. See *Metal Bulletin,* various issues.

24. See Stegemann, op. cit., p. 150.

25. Also see Stegmann, op. cit., p. 195, which shows an increased dependence of German steel producers on third markets up to 1975, and a decrease in extra-EC export dependence for the Benelux producers.

26. The member states retain ultimate jurisdiction over external trade under the Treaty of Paris. See on this point, and on the powers of the Commission in general, the Treaty Establishing the European Coal and Steel Community, especially title III chapter X and title III chapter I-VII.

27. For a general presentation of Community policy at this stage see Commission of the European Communities, *Guidelines on Iron and Steel Policy,* COM(75)701, 1975.

28. See 175th Session of the Consultative Committee of the ECSC analytical records.

29. The Simonet Plan; see Commission of the European Communities, *Guidelines on Iron and Steel Policy,* COM(76)543, 1976. These indicative delivery guidelines did not include exports to third markets.

30. See Official Journal of the European Communities, L 114 of May 5, 1977.

31. See Official Journal of the European Communities, "Community Steel Policy," EC C303/3 1977, L352 and C316.

32. The negotiations with Spain were complicated by the fact that the country had applied for accession to the EC. When Spain does finally join, it will not be without implications for the EC steel industry, since Spain, which suffered from excess capacity for some time, will add about 10 percent to the Community's total steel capacity.

33. See, for example, Official Journal of the European Communities, "General Objectives 1980-85," C232, 1976; Commission of the EC, "Investment in the Community Coalmining and Iron and Steel Industries," October 1979; "Forward Programme for Steel," OJ C98/75, April 30, 1975; and "Social Aspects of the Steel Policy," SEC(78)2636. July 7, 1978.

34. See "Social Aspects of the Steel Policy," ibid.

35. For a detailed breakdown of these figures by product and region, see Commission of the European Communities, "Investment Survey," op. cit., 1979.

36. See, for example, *Metal Bulletin.* February 5, 1980, p. 36.

37. *Le Monde,* February 6, 1979.

38. See *Metal Bulletin,* January 4, 1980.

39. For a discussion of the issues from the point of view of the UK, see House of Lords Select Committee on the European Community, Session 1978–79, "State Aids for Steel," January 1979.

40. For a general discussion of the Commission's policy on state aids see Commission of the European Communities, "Communication on Sectoral Aid Schemes," COM(78)221, 1978.

41. See *Commission of the European Communities,* "Social Aspects of the Steel Policy," op. cit.

42. See, for example, Stegemann, op. cit., who discusses price and output competition.

43. See, for example, statement by Chairman Sette of IRI, the holding company controlling the Finsider steel group; *Metal Bulletin,* April 12, 1979.

44. See *24 Ore,* March 9, 1979.

45. UK Government White Paper, "Steel: a ten year development strategy," Cmnd 5226, 1973.

46. Department of Industry, "Steel Closure Review," Beswick Report, 1975.

47. "British Steel Corporation: the Road to Viability," Cmnd 7149, March 1978, p. 4.

48. Ibid.

49. A. Cockerill, *The Steel Industry: International Comparisons of Structure and Performance* (Cambridge: Cambridge University Press, 1974).

50. Nomura Research Institute, op. cit., p. 104.

51. See Ira C. Magaziner and Thomas M. Hout, *Japanese Industrial Policy,* Policy Studies Institute, Report No. 585, January 1980; also Chapter 5, this volume.

52. *Metal Bulletin,* August 7, and September 4 and 14, 1979.

53. Nomura Research Institute, op. cit., p. 127; and *Japan Metal Bulletin,* July 5, 1979, for Japanese investment envisaged in 1979–80.

54. *Metal Bulletin,* May 22, 1979.

55. UNIDO, *Worldwide Study of the Iron and Steel Industry 1975–2000,* International Center for Industrial Studies, 1976. These estimates have been revised in the 1978 study—*The World Iron and Steel Industry* (second study), ICIS/UNIDO 1978—which takes a far more cautious line owing to the uncertainties in the forecasting of future steel trends.

56. See International Iron and Steel Institute, *Steel Intensity and GNP Structure,* 1974, and UNIDO, op. cit., 1978.

57. Nomura Research Institute, op. cit., p. 109.

58. U.S. Central Intelligence Agency, *The Burgeoning LDC Steel Industry: More Problems for Major Steel Producers,* July 1979.

59. See letter from the group of steel senators to Robert Strauss, *International Herald Tribune,* June 5, 1978.

60. Ibid.

61. See, for example, Commission of the European Communities, 'Guidelines on Iron and Steel Policy', COM(75) 701, 1975.

62. Commission of the European Communities, "Draft decision of the Commission establishing Community rules for specific aids to the steel industry," C(79)70/3, February 1, 1979.

63. See Official Journal of the European Communities, "Social Aspects of the Steel Policy," op. cit., p. 13.

64. For the Commission's proposals for a general program of work sharing, see Commission of the European Communities, "Communication from the Commission to the Council on Work-Sharing," COM(79)188, final, May 7, 1979.

65. OECD, Council Decision establishing a Steel Committee, October 26, 1978.

66. See, for example, the resolution of the International Metalworkers Federation in Frankfurt, 1977, *Frankfurter Allgemeine Zeitung,* November 7, 1977.

4 Four Sectors: Textiles, Man-Made Fibers, Shipbuilding, Aircraft

GEOFFREY EDWARDS

Textiles

The textiles and clothing industries in Western Europe and North America have rarely been free from difficulties. The problems of shrinking markets due to world depression and competition from low-cost producers faced by the industry in the inter-war period appear only to have foreshadowed those of recent years. The problems have also multiplied, not least with the advent of many more low-cost producers, in the context of a continuously high rate of technological innovation. Although the situation of the industry in the developed West improved somewhat by the early 1970s, the recession since 1974 has intensified its difficulties. Domestically, the importance of the industry, both economically and socially, has led to an extensive range of state aids — some temporary, some more permanent — designed to encourage adaptation, rationalization, and efficiency while limiting social dislocation. Externally, unilateral action in the 1950s against foreign competitors was gradually absorbed within the multilateral framework provided by the GATT. A Short Term Arrangement came into effect in 1961 to be followed by the Long Term Arrangement regarding International Trade in Cotton Textiles (LTA) in 1962. Additional refinements were added with the more widely based Arrangement regarding International Trade in Textiles, or the Multi-Fibre Arrangement (MFA), in 1974 and further restrictions were allowed under the Protocol extending the MFA in 1977. The Arrangement is being renegotiated in 1981, and most of its associated bilateral agreements are due for renegotiation in 1982. The industry in Western Europe and North America has pressed its case for a further renewal. It is convinced that the protection afforded by the MFA is of vital importance for its continued survival.

One of the basic problems that has confronted the industry has been the continuous need to adapt to new technology in conditions of relatively low demand and intense competition. Developments such as man-made fibers, new, highly efficient knitting machines, or, more recently, shuttleless looms have placed a high premium on the ability of the industry to invest. Obviously, within the OECD area there have been wide variations in the speed and ability of the industry to respond, although common to all is the important role played by small and medium-sized firms. There is, for example, a sharp distinction between the highly developed or less-developed OECD members. Ireland, Greece, Spain, Portugal, and Turkey, often with considerable government support, are increasing their capacity and their exports substantially.

Japan, having been one of the major sources of concern to Europe and the United States in the inter-war period, renewed its challenge to the U.S. industry in the 1950s and early 1960s. By the later 1960s, however, it too began to face some of the problems that have afflicted the industry in Western Europe, in part because of its own increased labor costs and also because of the growing competitiveness of other Far Eastern producers. The 1971 textile agreement with the United States further compounded the industry's problems of overcapacity. In the US, although there remains considerable diversity within the industry, there tended to be a higher growth in productivity than in most of Western Europe, because firms responded earlier to higher wages with an intensive investment policy. Also, its industry has traditionally had much higher tariffs, in some cases more than 40 percent. In general, however, the import penetration of the U.S. market was higher than that of many Western European markets, the UK being the major exception because of its traditional policy toward Commonwealth producers.

In Western Europe, sluggish demand and the pressures of competition compounded already severe structural problems. The multiplicity of small and medium-sized firms and fragmentation within the industry meant that vertical and horizontal integration has been slow (particularly during the 1950s and early 1960s). It continues to be a problem in many countries, despite the number of companies that have either gone out of business or merged. One factor that has caused companies to be reluctant to forego their autonomy has been that competition has affected them at different times and to different degrees. The clothing industry remains particularly fragmented and much more labor-intensive than textiles. Increasing wage costs have therefore further reduced its profitability. But low profitability in both industries has inhibited investment in modernization and the scrapping of obsolete machinery, although levels have varied from country to country. Many companies in these circumstances have deemed it too risky to concentrate on more-sophisticated specialized goods. One response in which West German firms have taken a lead has been the development of outward or offshore processing, the practice of exporting cloth to be made up where labor costs are cheaper and then reimported, the process remaining under the direct or indirect control of the company sending it out.

Nonetheless, there has been a steady increase in productivity within the industries in Western Europe, in part at least through government support for private initiative. Between 1945 and 1960, for example, productivity in some countries trebled because of accelerated technical improvements and better organization of work.[1] The number of firms in the textiles industry has shrunk enormously whether through bankruptcies, rationalization, or mergers. In the United Kingdom, the number of companies fell by 36 percent between 1959 and 1967.[2] But greater productivity has brought with it new problems or intensified old ones. As the textiles industry became more capital-intensive, the work force was reduced. It has been estimated that in the 1960s some 40,000 workers a year were being laid off in Western Europe, particularly in the cotton and woolen industries.[3] Between 1973 and 1976 a further 438,000 were made redundant in the textile and clothing industries within the European Community, including 178,000 in West Germany, 80,000 in the UK, and 32,000 in the Netherlands.[4] Many of those laid off have been women, traditionally a high proportion of the workforce. Their relative lack of mobility has served to intensify the problem of concentration of the industry in areas already suffering from considerable economic difficulties, which have been made worse in Canada's case, for example, by its concentration in the politically sensitive province of Quebec.

The alternatives for most governments appeared to be either to become extensively (and expensively) involved in support of the industry or to allow it to contract until only the most-efficient domestic producers, many of which are multinational, compete with low-cost producers.[5] No government has been prepared, for strategic if not employment considerations, to allow the industries to disappear completely. The alternatives have proved not to be mutually exclusive. Governments have intervened sooner more often than later: the UK, for example, from 1959 in the cotton sector, the Japanese from 1967. Loans, subsidies (both directly to the industry or through regional policies), and fiscal measures have been used, together with retraining or relocation schemes for the redundant work force. The UK and Japan initially concentrated their efforts on subsidizing the scrapping of old or surplus machinery and the installation of new modern plant. Only gradually (in Japan especially since 1974) was the emphasis shifted toward encouraging greater consolidation and integration. The Swedes, on the other hand, in 1970 launched a particularly active manpower policy and offered government support for companies moving into more-sophisticated products and away from those produced by low-cost countries.[6] The importance of the industry—the second largest in Italy for example and the third largest in the UK—and its location have proved compelling for most governments.

The extent of government support has created widespread concern over distortions of trade. Within the European Community especially, a great deal of discussion has concentrated on the need for subsidy discipline. The European Commission has been insistent that subsidies should be temporary, transparent, and geared to restructuring or reestablishing viable industries in new areas of activity. Nevertheless, its 1978 guidelines for a textiles and clothing industrial policy, which suggested inter alia the coordination of national and EEC financial aids, increased research and innovation, specialization, and the use of new technologies, were not accepted by the Council of Ministers. Governments have therefore continued to pursue their own policies within the Community, although not without some tension both among themselves and between them and the Commission. Within the Commission itself there have also been differences between the Directorates General: between, for example, the Competition and Regional Policy Directorates General on aids to the textile industry, and the Competition and Industrial Policy Directorates General on the man-made fibers cartel.

Despite government intervention, the textiles industry in most developed countries has continued to decline. In 1963 developed countries accounted for nearly 75 percent of world exports; in 1976 their share was just under 63 percent, much of which was made up of trade among themselves and especially intra-Community trade. The share of world exports taken by developing countries grew, despite the recession, from just over 15 percent to 27 percent over the same period.[9] The shift in trade patterns for developed countries has almost inexorably been toward a growing deficit with developing countries, particularly Hong Kong, South Korea, and Taiwan. The deficit is especially severe in clothing; many developed countries have retained a small surplus in textiles (see Table 4.1). The continuously growing pressure of imports from low-cost developing countries has led to ever more elaborate controls by developed countries.

Table 4.1   Net Trade[a] in Textiles and Clothing in Selected Countries, 1973 and 1977
(in US $ billion)

	Textiles[b]		Clothing[b]		Total	
	1973	1977	1973	1977	1973	1977
EEC	1.97	1.70	−0.89	−2.68	1.08	−0.98
Belgium-Luxembourg	0.68	0.89	0.01	−0.40	0.69	0.49
France	0.29	−0.13	0.45	0.19	0.74	0.06
W. Germany	0.30	−0.07	−1.63	−2.99	−1.33	−3.06
Italy	0.62	0.15	1.11	2.24	1.73	3.39
Netherlands	0.19	0.12	−0.45	−1.26	−0.26	−1.14
UK	0.19	0.05	−0.38	−0.30	−0.19	−0.25
Finland	−0.19	−0.23	0.15	0.28	−0.04	0.05
Norway	−0.17	−0.28	−0.17	−0.45	−0.54	−0.73
Sweden	−0.32	−0.42	−0.26	−0.67	−0.58	−1.09
Austria	−0.03	−0.05	−0.04	−0.24	−0.07	−0.29
Switzerland	0.14	0.33	−0.38	−0.58	−0.24	−0.25
USA[c]	−0.36	0.17	−1.88	−3.45	−2.24	−3.28
Canada[c]	−0.63	−0.86	−0.21	−0.49	−0.84	−1.35
Japan	1.32	2.84	−0.20	−0.41	1.12	2.43
Australia	−0.58	−0.70	−0.90	−0.28	−0.67	−0.98
Czechoslovakia[c]	0.12	···	0.08	···	0.20	···
Hungary	0.03	···	0.17	···	0.20	···
Poland[c]	0.02	···	0.23	···	0.25	···
Rumania[c]	−	···	0.24	···	0.24	···
USSR	−0.49	−1.07	−1.03	−1.67	−1.52	−2.74
Greece	0.04	0.12	0.04	0.20	0.08	0.32
Portugal	0.22	0.18	0.17	0.21	0.39	0.39
Spain	−0.01	0.13	0.09	0.14	0.08	0.27
Turkey	0.07	···	0.05	···	0.12	···
Yugoslavia	−0.05	···	0.13	···	0.08	···
Israel	−0.02	···	0.08	···	0.06	···
Egypt	0.14	0.19	0.03	0.02	0.17	0.21
Hong Kong	−0.48	−0.83	1.27	2.72	0.79	1.89
India	0.68	···	0.10	···	0.78	···
South Korea	0.14	0.73	0.74	2.05	0.88	2.78
Pakistan	0.41	···	0.02	···	0.43	···
Singapore	−0.28	−0.27	0.09	0.12	−0.19	−0.15
Argentina	0.00	···	0.03	···	0.03	···
Brazil	0.16	···	0.08	···	0.24	···
Mexico	0.09	···	0.01	···	0.10	···

[a] Exports fob minus imports cif.
[b] SITC divisions 65 (textiles) and 84 (clothing).
[c] Imports fob.

Source: GATT, based on UN, *Commodity Trade Statistics*, Series D; national trade returns; Vincent Cable, *World Textile Trade and Production* (London, Economist Intelligence Unit, 1979), p. 48.

Tariffs have rarely been a deterrent to exporters from countries once described as being able to "export at prices defying all competition.[10] Most OECD countries have therefore attempted to control trade through quotas or voluntary restraint agreements of greater or lesser strictness, including the United States which has retained higher tariffs than most other Western countries. Nonetheless, the pressures during the 1950s were such that there were increasing calls for a multilateral regulation of trade in order to share the burden of competition. The initiative was taken especially by the United States, which was suffering from a swift influx of Japanese imports: its trade deficit with Japan in cotton goods rose from $37 million to $256 million between 1952 and 1962.[11] The U.S. moves coincided with the UK interest in regulating imports of Commonwealth textiles, which by 1959–60 had reached more than 5 percent of consumption.[12] Japan accepted a multilateral solution in preference to the threat of unilateral regulation. The result was the Short Term and later the Long Term Arrangements covering woven cotton textiles. The ostensible aim of the LTA (as with subsequent arrangements) was to establish a more-orderly expansion of trade while giving importers the right to prevent the disruption of their domestic markets. The Arrangement, the first to attempt to deal with the problem of industrial decline in one geographical area and its expansion in another, specified inter alia that any quotas imposed for more than a year should allow for a 5 percent annual rate of growth in the volume of imports. By the end of five years, which would allow a breathing space for structural adjustments in developed countries, import restraints were to be phased out.

The LTA was not an unqualified success. Tighter restrictions were introduced, especially by the United States. In 1962 the US had a formal, voluntary restraint agreement only with Japan; by 1972 it had agreements with thirty suppliers of cotton textiles. Newer producers, with a smaller initial base in Western markets, were as a consequence hampered in the expansion of their exports of cotton goods. At the same time, outside the framework of the LTA they were increasingly subject to restrictions on the amounts of other textiles, particularly synthetic textiles and clothing, that they could export to developed countries. As a result they exerted increasing pressure for quotas to be enlarged and ceilings on growth to be raised. On the other hand, developed countries, particularly those of Western Europe whose markets proved increasingly vulnerable to low-cost imports, were insistent that the Arrangement should be both tightened and extended. Still, the initiative for a new agreement again came from the US, directed especially against Japan and other Asian producers.

The Multi-Fibre Arrangement of December 1973 was signed by fifty governments and covered some 85 percent of world trade in textiles and clothing. Taiwan, because of its ill-defined status, was the most-notable absentee. The objectives of the MFA were in many ways similar to those of the LTA, namely: "to achieve the expansion of trade, the reduction of barriers to such trade and the progressive liberalization of world trade in textile products, while at the same time ensuring the orderly and equitable development of this trade and avoidance of disruptive effects in individual markets and on individual lines of production in both importing and exporting countries."[13] In place of the 5 percent annual growth ceiling of the LTA, and against some demands from developing countries for a ceiling of 15 percent, agreement was reached on an annual increase of 6 percent, with the possibility of some derogation in cases of exceptional hardship. The basis of the agreement, however, was that the restrictions were only temporary and that the bilateral quota agreements would eventually be phased out. In addition, the Textile Surveillance Board was set up with the aim of bringing a more-impartial judgment to claims of market disruption and of reconciling differences. With a membership of both industrialized and developing countries, the TSB has regrettably tended to become an additional arena for the North-South dialogue rather than the authoritative body it was intended to be.

The agreement of the developed countries to the 6 percent growth rate was based on estimates derived from the growth of demand between 1968 and 1973 that, with the 1973-74 oil crisis and subsequent world recession, have proved exceedingly optimistic. The rate of growth in demand has tended to be even less than 2.5 percent per annum. Production levels in 1978 were often only about the same as those of 1973. The ability of producers to cope in such conditions has varied widely. The United States has fared somewhat better than most Western European countries, in part because of higher tariffs but particularly because it was extremely prompt in signing bilateral agreements with most low-cost producers under the MFA. Members of the European Community faced more difficult circumstances. In attempting to reconcile the differing interests of its members, the Community's decision-making process tends at best to be slow and cumbersome. In 1974 it was not assisted by the need to absorb new members, one of which, the UK, was one of Europe's largest textile and clothing producers. As a consequence, not until 1976 was it able to enforce its bilateral agreements. In the intervening period there was a flood of imports to beat the deadline, estimated at nearly three-quarters of the world growth in imports.[14] Nor did the situation improve radically in certain sectors, especially in clothing, during 1977. France, for example, although the penetration of its markets remained relatively low, took unilateral action under Article XIX of the GATT in June 1977 before the Commission introduced its more-liberal proposals.

The French action foreshadowed the tough position it took in the preliminary negotiations leading to a renewal of the MFA. In doing so it was strongly supported by the British and backed up by COMITEXTIL, the Communitywide textiles trade association; in its submission to the European Commission, COMITEXTIL declared: "The European textile and clothing industries cannot understand why the Community can knowingly accept continual deterioration of the external trade balance for textiles. Each additional tonne of deficit corresponds roughly to one job lost — in the short term, a loss of hard currency; in the longer term, a weakening of the Community's economic power."[15] Not all member states agreed. West Germany, for example, in balancing the advice of its textiles industry against the greater buoyancy of its economy, its increasing adaptation to outward processing, and its investments overseas in several low-cost producers, tended to emphasize the need to maintain the principle of free trade as far as possible. The Dutch also opposed too rigid a position, particularly on the grounds that the aims of the MFA were the promotion of economic and social development.[16] The resulting compromise allowed for a renewal of the agreement instead of proposing a new type of agreement, but the Commission was nonetheless given little freedom to maneuver in negotiating a more-restrictive agreement. It was made clear for example that the Community would remain a party to the MFA only if it could renegotiate satisfactory bilateral agreements with lost-cost producers to include provisions for greater protection. Such an approach placed the low-cost producers in the dilemma of accepting further constraints on their exports, either unilaterally by the Community or through bilateral agreement. The fact that the system of bilateral agreements was to continue undermined their ability to maintain any common front.

The resulting Protocol renewed the MFA for a further four years. Both major aims of the Community were accepted. The GATT Textiles Committee reached a consensus, for example, on "the possibility of jointly agreed reasonable departures from particular elements (of the MFA) in particular cases." Although emphasis was placed on the need for mutual agreement, and the Textile Surveillance Board remains in existence, there are no agreed definitions as to what might constitute the basis for departing from the norm. Definitions remain largely dependent on what the importing country's government and industry deem an acceptable level of penetration, which has varied substantially. Under the Protocol, however, the formerly sometimes loose categorization of textiles and clothing was tightened up considerably. In the European Community, for example, there are now 114 generally applicable categories grouped according to their sensitivity, and another nine applicable to state-trading countries on linen or related products. In the most-sensitive group, where import penetration has been highest, modifications have been made to the 6 percent norm, which have restrained the growth of imports to only modest increases above their 1976 levels. European Commission figures indicate that from 1976 to 1979 the average annual growth rate of imports from countries which concluded bilateral agreements with the Community was 2.3 percent for all MFA products and only 0.8 percent for the eight most-sensitive items.[17]

The growth of trade has been restricted by the MFA and its agreements, but it has grown steadily nevertheless. At the same time, since the extension of the MFA in 1977, there has been a certain revival of confidence in the West, reflected in increased investment and production. There have been a number of problems, however, some of which will affect the negotiating positions taken up when the MFA expires. The problem of China as an exporter of textiles, for example, has only recently arisen. Contrary to the usual pattern, the Community reached an agreement before the United States. Despite relative stability and indeed a decline in its textiles and clothing imports, the U.S. industry has persuaded its government to renegotiate tighter restrictions in its bilateral agreements with several low-cost producers, including Hong Kong. Within the Community there also have been some strains. One issue that has taxed the British especially has been the general slowness of the Commission to act in implementing quota limits. In part this has been caused by a lack of comprehensive and up-to-date information, but there has also been a certain reluctance on the part of the Commission to approach supplying countries until quotas have been clearly exceeded, especially on less-sensitive products. A much more difficult problem faces the Community with the prospect of further enlargement. During the period of the initial MFA, Mediterranean countries which had various forms of Association agreements successfully demanded that they should be treated separately from others. In place of formal bilateral agreements voluntary arrangements were therefore accepted, many of which were exceeded. The Community as a result resorted to unilateral action in some cases, notably against Turkey. But the problems relating to the three applicant countries are especially delicate, for all three have invested heavily in textiles. The problem is severest for Portugal, both because textiles make up some 20 percent of its manufacture and 30 percent of its exports, and because of the general fragility of its economy. Freeing trade within an enlarged Community will create problems for existing Community industries on top of the continuing challenge from low-cost Asian producers, and will inevitably reinforce the pressures for continued protection in the negotiations on a successor to the MFA.

It is unlikely that any technological developments in the textiles and clothing industries in developed countries will be sufficient to offset their present disadvantage vis-à-vis low-cost producers. Several arguments suggest that, despite the efforts of developed countries, low-cost producers may even add to their existing strengths. The present quota system itself may help to strengthen some of those developing countries with a large initial base in developed markets, although the protection offered to them against late-comers may be limited. As far as European Community markets are concerned, the four principal suppliers — Hong Kong, South Korea, India, and Brazil — achieved an average annual growth rate between 1976 and 1979 of only 1.2 percent, compared to an increase of 3.4 percent on the part of other suppliers. But while quotas limit growth in certain sectors, they encourage expansion into others. While not all low-cost producers have the flexibility or capability to diversify in the immediate future, some do. And such moves are frequently supported by governments, the rapid development of synthetic fibers production perhaps being the prime example. Much has been made recently of outward processing. To some countries such as West Germany and the United States, this has proved attractive, and they have taken advantage of lower labor costs elsewhere. With high levels of unemployment, however, there have been criticisms in a number of countries against firms that "export" jobs. Moreover, although there is substantial Western investment into research and development in the textiles and clothing industries (although often less than in other industries) frequently supported by government funds (and, in the clothing sector, by European Community funds for joint research programs), similar government-sponsored or -supported efforts are being made in the low-cost producers.

The reaction of the industry in most developed countries is very clear. Few regard the MFA and its associated bilateral agreements as merely a short-term breathing space in which to adapt to external, low-cost competition. The industry, especially in the Community and North America, continues to believe that quotas are necessary. Indeed, the U.S. industry has increased its pressure on the administration to tighten its bilateral agreements with several Asian producers, and in its February 1979 Policy Statement the Carter administration indicated that it would take steps to introduce unilateral import controls if the MFA were not renegotiated. The industry in Europe has been pressing for similar government statements, while also calling for improved anti-dumping legislation patterned on the American model. The industry has also argued that in the renegotiation of the MFA, greater emphasis should be placed on measures that would offset their comparative disadvantages. Such measures might include greater reciprocity on reducing tariff and other barriers, an issue that has frequently been fought over in North-South relations and indeed North-North relations. Little, for example, was achieved in the Tokyo Round beyond reductions by the European Community and the United States, and some U.S. tariffs, especially on woolen goods, remain high. There has already been some concern over the degree of burden sharing, with the Europeans critical of U.S. and Japanese restrictions. The attention of some low-cost producers may also concentrate less on Europe than on the United States and Japan. The Koreans, for example, are Japan's leading market yet are only in eighth place in the Japanese market, and even this is largely because of exports from Japanese-owned companies.[18] Finally, there is likely to be another increasingly common bone of contention in North-South relations, the question of human rights, for example freedom of association in trade unions. Issues such as minimum wages, maximum working hours, the use of child labor, and health and safety standards have particularly concerned the International Labor Office as well as both sides of industry in the West. The latter have suggested that future agreements should commit signatories to uphold ILO rules. Their pressure has found some sympathy in official statements; Vicomte Davignon, the commissioner responsible for Industrial Affairs, has for example declared, "reciprocity is the golden rule of free trade; yet there cannot be reciprocity until the rules of the game are the same for all the players. It is impossible for the EEC to maintain its high level of salaries and employee protection while at the same time leaving its market to the mercy of competitors whose system of production is founded on totally different social and cultural bases."[19] There are thus a number of reasons why the renegotiation of the MFA in 1981 should be even more difficult and bitter than that in 1977.

Man-Made Fibers

The man-made fibers industry in the advanced industrial countries has inevitably experienced many of the problems that affect the textiles industry as a whole. The sluggish demand of its major customer, the clothing industry, in the face of intense competition from low-cost producers has been particularly important. Even in 1971 there was some concern over the growing overcapacity in the fibers industry, in view of the substantial programs for expansion that were underway. The 1973–74 oil crisis and its aftermath were therefore of increased significance for man-made fibers, since not only was demand reduced but costs were sharply increased. The result was extensive overcapacity, particularly in Western Europe and Japan, with firms producing only 60–70 percent of their capacity, and the inevitable difficulties and problems of contraction to bring supply more in line with demand. At the same time, however, low-cost producers continued to expand their production and thereby further reduced the West's export opportunities and increased Western imports of low-cost textiles and clothing. Western industries have therefore strongly supported other sectors of the textile industry in pressing for restrictions under the MFA. In addition, Western Europe especially has recently experienced considerably more competition from increased American exports, largely as a result of U.S. energy and monetary policies.

Man-made fibers – that is, cellulosics, such as rayon and acetate, and synthetics, such as polyester, acrylics, and nylon – are a relatively new industry. Although cellulosics were produced before World War II, it was only with the development of synthetics in the 1950s that the industry expanded rapidly. Demand for cellulosics has since tended to flatten out and even decline. The development of synthetic fibers within the petrochemical industry — synthetics now account for some 25 percent of all petrochemical products — has given the industry a markedly different structure from others within the textiles and clothing sector. Synthetic producers tend to be large, often multinational companies with interests diversified throughout petrochemicals — a factor vital in the industries' approach to the post-1973 recession. In the United Kingdom, for example, six companies, only two of which, Courtauld and ICI, are wholly British, account for some 99 percent of production; in Western Europe, 13 companies account for over 90 percent of production.

The cheapness of the basic raw material, oil, and high levels of profitability and investment led to a quadrupling of production of synthetic fibers between 1965 and 1973. Even despite the post-1973 recession, the production of nylon, the least dynamic of the three main synthetics, was still 125 percent higher in 1978 than in 1968. Prices were halved between 1955 and 1965 and again between 1965 and 1971, while the price of cotton nearly doubled over the same period.[20] Demand for synthetic fibers grew on average at about 15 percent per annum during the 1960s.[21] In Western Europe the share of mill consumption taken by man-made fibers in general increased substantially from 43 percent to 64 percent between 1966 and 1973, while that of cotton declined from 41 to 26 percent.[22] And even though there were fluctuations in the demand pattern — intensified because production is at the end of a long pipeline — the trough of one cycle during the 1960s was not far below the peak of the previous cycle. In Japan production of synthetic fibers grew relatively steadily after 1960 at more than 15 percent per annum. By the mid 1960s the rise in demand was such that the industry had outgrown the special policies introduced in the early 1950s to establish a synthetic fiber capacity. Prospects of continued growth encouraged a further investment, in the industrial West and not least in several developing countries, which reached a peak in 1973. Even in 1971, however, there were warnings of serious problems of overcapacity. In 1972, surplus capacity was estimated at 25 percent within the Community of the Six.[23] Not only was additional production coming on stream within Western Europe and in countries producing low-cost textiles and clothing, but there was a fairly abrupt flattening out of the rate of substitution of natural by man-made fibers.

The 1973–74 oil crisis therefore had particularly severe repercussions for the man-made, and especially synthetic, fibers industry. Western Europe and Japan bore the brunt. As the industry's chief new raw material quadrupled in price and household incomes ceased to rise, it was inevitable that demand would fall, although few in the Community were prepared for a 15 percent drop between 1973 and 1975.[24] Nor did it begin to rise over the following three years. During the worst period of 1974–75 the industry in Western Europe and Japan was utilizing little more than 60–70 percent of capacity. Losses were substantial, and in some cases continued to be throughout the 1970s (see Tables 4.2 and 4.3).

The pattern in the United States has been somewhat different. Demand recovered more quickly to 1973 levels, even if further growth has been slow. The U.S. industry, working at about 80 percent capacity, has been in a far healthier position than its European and Japanese rivals. In contrast to the industry elsewhere in the developed world, it has undertaken a further significant expansion in capacity, perhaps as much as 250,000 tons.[25] Insofar as it has been able to

Table 4.2 World Production of Cotton, Wool, and Man-Made Fibers (in million kilograms)

| | | | Man-made fibers | | | | | |
| | | | Synthetic | | Cellulosic | | | Total |
	Raw cotton	Wool	Fila-ment	Staple	Fila-ment	Staple	Total	of all fibers
1900	3,162	730	...	...	1	...	1	3,893
1940	6,907	1,134	1	4	542	585	1,132	9,173
1950	6,647	1,057	54	15	871	737	1,677	9,381
1960	10,113	1,463	417	285	1,131	1,525	3,358	14,934
1970	11,784	1,602	2,397	2,417	1,391	2,187	8,393	21,779
1973	13,714	1,432	3,820	3,912	1,361	2,499	11,592	26,738
1975	11,809	1,510	3,764	3,672	1,136	2,065	10,638	23,957
1977	14,138	1,445	4,332	4,829	1,155	2,379	12,695	28,278

Source: Organon World Cotton Statistics, cited in Vincent Cable, *World Textile Trade and Production*, EIU Special Report No. 63 (London: Economist Intelligence Unit, 1979).

take advantage of scale, the U.S. industry has also been marginally more efficient: significantly, synthetic yarns and fabrics carry a much lower tariff than other textiles imports. But the industry was also considerably assisted by low U.S. prices of oil and gas and the weakness of the dollar. In addition, the Department of Commerce has worked closely with the industry, (for example, in undertaking extremely detailed foreign market surveys) to maintain and increase its exports. As a result of such measures, the United States has been able to maintain its share of world trade at about 32 percent.

In contrast, Japan's share of the world market fell from 18 to 13 percent between 1970 and 1976.[26] Although the Japanese trade balance was assisted by a decline in imports, in the short term its exports were not assisted by the appreciation of the yen. In the longer term, too, Japanese exports are seriously affected by the expanding production of man-made fibers in its traditional Asian markets, particularly South Korea. Korea's ban on inward investment also halted further outward processing to take advantage of cheaper Korean labor. Together with the slump in domestic expenditure, the industry suffered large losses, the aggregate losses of the top seven companies being valued at $250 million a year between 1974 and 1976.[27] Business failures reached a record level. Although production of man-made fibers was closer in 1978 to its 1973 levels than other textile production, it still utilized only about 70 percent of capacity. As a result, the industry was included within the provisions of the 1978 law for the stabilization of specific structurally depressed industries, the aim being to oblige the industry to undertake some radical rethinking, on both the more-immediate problem of overcapacity and the longer-term problem of rationalization and contraction.

Table 4.3   Geographical Distribution of Production of Man-Made Fibers
(in thousands of tons)

	Western Europe	USA	Japan	Rest of the world	Total world
1970	2,628	2,268	1,511	1,987	8,394
1973	3,420	3,435	1,818	2,911	11,584
1975	2,611	2,983	1,435	3,645	10,674
1977	2,995	3,643	1,707	4,555	12,900

Source: Textile Organon, cited in Vincent Cable, op. cit.

Government measures, for example, sought the permanent elimination of a quarter of the industry's capacity. The labor force was reduced from more than 91,000 in the peak year of 1975 to little more than 55,000 in 1978.[28] Rationalization has also caused several leading companies to merge, such as Tayobo and Mitsubishi Rayon, which together produce about 40 percent of Japanese acrylic fibers, with government guaranteed funds in support.[29]

The position in Western Europe has been similar in many respects to that of Japan. Its share of world production fell from 31 to 23 percent between 1970 and 1978. There have been variations of course, not least the continued expansion of the industry in Italy and Ireland. Only in Italy among the major European producers has output actually overtaken that of 1973 (see Table 4.4). West Germany, the largest synthetics producer, suffered additionally from the appreciation of the mark. The UK too imported more, particularly after sterling began to appreciate. While costs have risen considerably, prices have tended to be depressed because of competition — both intra-Community and from third countries — and low demand. The result was that the problem of surplus capacity became acute. In order to break even, production units are estimated to need to work at 85 percent of their maximum capacity.[30] Yet it has been suggested that while the use of capacity has varied, the average overcapacity in Europe has been 30–40 percent (see Table 4.4).[31] Large losses have therefore been incurred, possibly $2 to 3 billion between 1975 and 1978.[32] Most companies, however, were able to absorb their losses because of the profitability of their other sectors. The result also was that companies were obliged to tackle the problem of overcapacity, both by halting or modifying planned expansion and by closing their older and less-efficient plants (with some transnational problems, such as that between the French government and Montedison on the closure of one of the latter's plants in Eastern France). Between 1977 and 1979 the eleven leading European producers cut back production of their six main textile fibers by some 325,000 metric tons (especially continuous polyester and polymide yarns).[33] The contraction of the workforce has been substantial: in the UK some 10,000 left the industry between 1973 and 1979 (from a total of just under 40,000); in France some 8,000; in West Germany, 14,000; and even in Italy, 8,500.[34] Temporary short-time working

Table 4.4   World Noncellulosic Fiber Production and Capacity (except Olefin) (in thousand metric tons)

	Beulux	Ireland	France	Federal Republic of Germany	Italy/Malta	Spain	United Kingdom	German Democratic Republic	Poland	Rumania	USSR	United States	Japan	Taiwan	South Korea	Brazil	Mexico	World total
1971	138	–	214	600	277	77	358	57	67	37	203	1803	1103	77	62	52	63	5609
1973	163	10	266	808	337	131	454	93	81	52	287	2641	1246	128	116	103	105	7640
1975	123	12	205	625	277	119	361	112	118	85	362	2945	1021	235	263	126	155	7353
1977	139	15	244	690	330	160	359	124	147	114	456	3037	1280	364	350	160	186	9141
1978	143	34	246	729	354	189	406	128	152	117	475	3218	1375	464	440	181	199	9946
1979	178	50	370	922	599	279	583	143	164	125	600	3930	1527	586	490	230	274	12538

Source: Textile Organon, June 1979.

has also been introduced, sometimes with government-supported compensation schemes, as in the UK.

The pressures to reduce capacity were such that discussion began within the European industry on the possibility of a coordinated approach to the problem. All eleven leading European companies took part, while Dupont and Monsanto, the two largest U.S. producers in Europe, were kept closely informed of discussions (neither wished to participate because of U.S. antitrust laws). The initial aim of the discussions was to reach agreement on investments and the reduction of excess capacity by scrapping older plants rather than merely by placing them in mothballs, much of which was already planned on an individual basis by several companies. The initial plan was based on the assumption of the continuation of the status quo as far as markets were concerned. Largely at the insistence of the Italians, however, the market share element became more marked, with an agreement on quotas that took account of new Italian production coming on stream. The plan had been drawn up with the active support of the Commissioner for Industrial Affairs but became increasingly bogged down in a debate, led by the Directorate General for Competition, over compatability of its market-sharing provisions with the interests of the consumer, the only basis on which market sharing is permissible under the Treaty of Rome. While the debate continued the companies operated in something of a legal limbo. But the plan was finally rejected by the Commission in December 1979. The companies involved have nonetheless continued to implement their own plans to reduce excess capacity, for which, under an ad hoc Regulation of 1979, they can qualify for Community aid.

The extent to which governments have intervened in the man-made fibers sector of the textiles industry has varied. The Irish, with an extensive range of subsidies, have been particularly successful in attracting producers to establish plants. New plants have also been an integral part of Italian plans for the development of Sardinia and the Mezzogiorno. But few governments have gone as far as the Italians in keeping inefficient plants in operation, much to the concern of other members of the Community.[35] Despite such differences, however, the Council of Ministers was able to agree to the Commission's proposal in 1977 to refrain for two years from extending further subsidies to the industry that would merely enlarge existing capacity. In December 1979 member governments further agreed to the Commission's proposal for a regulation extending aid to the industry. Aid, in the form of investment premiums, has been available for conversion, diversification, and restructuring: i.e., investment by other undertakings in order to create new jobs for workers made redundant in the fibers industry through total or partial closures; investment by the fibers industry to change types of activity; and investment designed to reduce production capacity.

Such internal moves have been complemented by a strong stance of the man-made fibers industry on the need to control the import of downstream products from low-cost producers. The expansion of output, especially of polyester, in South Korea and Taiwan, for example, has continued unabated, seemingly unaffected by the oil crisis and the recession. Between 1968 and 1978 more than half the increase in world consumption of man-made fibers took place outside Western Europe, Japan, and the United States. Some 80 percent of this increase was met by the rest of the world's own production and only 20 percent by net exports from developed countries.[36] While the extent to which this expansion has contributed to overcapacity in Europe and Japan is arguable, it is certainly emphasized by the industry. The industry's reaction has been to play an important role within its various pressure groups and associations in bringing about the tight quotas on the import of yarns and fabrics from low-cost countries under the Multi-Fibre Arrangement. But capacity in Eastern Europe is also increasing substantially, giving rise to concern over dumping. This has been felt particularly in Western Europe; the situation in the United States and Canada has been less difficult, in part, perhaps, owing to the practice of publishing at an early stage applications for antidumping action. Since 1977 the Commission of the EC, rather than the member governments, has had responsibility for applying antidumping procedures. As the Commission's investigations can take between six and twelve months, the industry has often called for greater speed and flexibility.[37]

In addition to the problems posed by low-cost producers, subject at least to MFA agreements, the European industry has experienced growing competition from other developed countries, particularly the United States. During 1979 and 1980 the Community imposed antidumping duties on certain U.S. acrylic fibers that had caused problems particularly for the Italian industry (and which had led the Italian government to take unilateral action) and removed them when prices ceased to be regarded as disruptive. In February 1980 the Community also allowed protective measures to be taken against imports into the UK of continuous polyester filament and textured polyamide carpet yarns, U.S. imports of which had risen particularly fast. Although a further UK demand for protection against U.S. imports of tufted carpets was rejected, the Commission introduced surveillance over U.S. fiber imports into the Community. It was recognized that the U.S. industry had an advantage over many of its European competitors because of its organization and structure, and that the depreciation of the dollar had also worked in the industry's favor. But the Commission held that the U.S. industry was able to take advantage of government regulations, which set the price of fuel and raw materials well below world levels, to penetrate Community markets. The price advantage offered to European customers was estimated to be approximately the same as the advantage the U.S. industry received through the regulation of petroleum and national gas prices. The differential pricing system is being phased out, however, and is ending in 1981 for petroleum and 1985 for gas.

Such intra-OECD problems have complicated the recovery of the man-made fibers industry in Western Europe. In addition, the price of oil has continued to rise while the demand from the clothing industry has remained sluggish. Since the consumption of man-made fibers continues to be largely within developed countries, companies have been urged to expand their markets in the less-developed areas of the world. Many NICs, however, have imposed particularly high tariffs on synthetic fiber imports: Brazil's tariff on synthetic fiber cloths woven in 1979, for example, was 205 percent, Korea's 60 percent.[38] In addition, production in the NICs and Eastern Europe continues to expand, further reducing developed countries' export opportunities. In such circumstances, U.S. plans for large-scale investment in new plants are exceptional; Western Europe and Japan are concentrating more on reducing excess capacity, up-dating machinery, and improving the qualities of man-made fibers. They havel little motive to be any more responsive than other sectors of the textile and clothing industries to the demands of the NICs in the renegotiation of the MFA in 1981.

Shipbuilding

Demand in the shipbuilding industry has traditionally been cyclical. Rarely, however, has the collapse of the market been as severe as in the mid-1970s, or its recovery as delayed and surrounded by as many complicating factors. The expansion in merchant shipbuilding during the 1960s and early 1970s was rapid. In 1960 world output was 8.4m gross registered tonnage (grt). By 1975 it had reached 34.2m grt (see Table 4.5). Expansion was particularly notable in tankers and dry cargo bulk carriers. Japan overtook Western Europe as the predominant center for shipbuilding during the mid-1960s, accounting for around 50 percent of grt in 1975. With the 1973–74 oil crisis and subsequent recession, however, demand for new shipping collapsed. While orders derived from the earlier optimistic forecasts of continued expansion cushioned the immediate impact, by 1978 the world order book was at its lowest in 13 years. The result was enormous overcapacity, possibly as much as 50 percent in 1977, huge losses, and thousands of jobs made redundant. Few countries have been able to avoid the effects of the recession, although the impact has varied depending on such factors as the level of concentration on tankers and bulk cargo carriers, the level of protection afforded to the industry, and the involvement of government in staving off or mitigating the full effects of the crisis. Whatever their general attitudes toward free trade and competition, all governments have become involved, although the emphasis they have placed on aid for rationalization or more direct support subsidies has varied. Such aids were perhaps unavoidable, given the severity of the crisis and particularly the regional significance of the industry. But the crisis has also brought out the structural problems of many traditional shipbuilders in the face of competition from several NICs, including South Korea and Brazil, and Eastern European countries, especially Poland, for whom shipbuilding and its related industries have been a vital part of their economic development plans.

The result has been a costly battle of subsidies. Various attempts have been made to introduce an element of discipline, notably within the OECD and more effectively, perhaps, within the European Community. But the problem remains of adapting both to a shrunken market, that is unlikely to recover significantly until the mid to late 1980s, and to the changing nature of international competition. Within the developed West it is to a considerable extent a European-Japanese problem, in view of the limited exports and insulation of the highly protected U.S. industry. Rationalization and contraction have had to be balanced by the need to maintain a viable industry for both strategic considerations and the social problems involved in contraction, while awaiting the hoped-for recovery in demand. Nevertheless, the major question is: Who will be in a position to take what shares in the new circumstances of the late 1980s, particularly in view of the comparative advantages enjoyed and exploited by the NICs?

The expansion of world trade during the 1950s and 1960s brought about a strong and, for the most part, steady demand for new ships. The growth in demand for tankers, of progressively larger tonnage, was especially marked (about 12 percent per annum during the 1960s), followed by bulk carriers (about 7 percent per annum). Transport of oil as a proportion of total seaborne trade grew from some 34 percent in 1965 to 44 percent in 1973. Even more marked was the growth of new centers of production. In the early 1950s the present members of

Table 4.5 World Output of Merchant Ships, 1960 to 1979 (in million gross tons and percentage shares)

	World[a]	North America		Western Europe[b]		European Community		Japan		Eastern Europe[c]		LDCs[d]	
	mn grt	mn grt	%	mn grt	%	mn grt	%	mn grt	%	mn grt	%	mn grt	%
1960	8.4	0.6	7.2	5.7	68.4	4.4	52.3	1.7	20.7	0.2	2.7	–	0.6
1965	12.2	0.5	3.7	5.9	48.1	3.6	29.3	5.4	43.9	0.3	2.8	0.1	1.1
1970	21.7	0.4	1.7	9.6	44.3	5.6	25.9	10.5	48.3	0.9	4.0	0.3	1.4
1975	34.2	0.6	1.9	13.7	40.2	7.8	22.8	17.0	49.7	1.7	4.9	0.9	2.8
1977	27.6	1.2	4.3	11.3	41.1	5.6	20.4	11.7	42.5	1.6	5.9	1.5	5.4
1978	18.2	1.2	6.4	7.0	38.3	3.7	20.3	6.3	34.7	2.0	11.1	1.6	8.9
1979	14.3	1.2	8.2	5.0	34.8	2.8	19.5	4.7	32.9	1.6	10.9	1.9	13.4

aExcluding People's Republic of China.
bIncluding Yugoslavia.
cIncluding the USSR, incomplete information.
dExcluding the European LDCs.

Note: Figures for the period 1960 and 1965 concern ships launched, thereafter ships completed.

Source: **Lloyd's Register of Shipping**, London, 1980.

the European Community produced 70 percent of world output (35 percent in the UK alone). By the mid-1970s, although production had increased from 4.4m grt in 1960 to nearly 8m grt, the Community's share had dwindled to little more than 20 percent. In contrast, Japan's production rose from 1.7m grt in 1960 to 17m grt in 1975, 50 percent of world production. The Community's decline in the face of this expansion was largely the result of higher costs, including rising labor costs, and the existence, despite some attempts at rationalization, of too many, often relatively small-scale, and not always highly productive shipyards. Japan's conquest of the world market, on the other hand, was helped by close cooperation between the government, shipbuilders, shipping and trading companies to ensure that Japan's growing volume of imports, especially of oil and raw materials, was carried in Japanese-owned ships built in Japanese yards. Particular emphasis was also placed on tankers and bulk carriers to meet the surge in world demand, so that by 1976 tankers and bulk carriers accounted for almost 90 percent of Japan's total output. But if the 1960s witnessed the huge expansion of Japanese production, the slump in demand since 1975 has taken place against the background of the continuing expansion of the industry in several less-developed countries: in Europe, in Spain and Poland (the latter even between 1977 and 1978 increasing its output from less than 500,000 grt to 700,000); in Asia, especially in South Korea (which, even within its first Five Year Plan for shipbuilding, produced more than 800,000 grt in 1976); and in Latin America, particularly Brazil.

The immediate effects of the 1973–74 oil crisis were the cancellation of perhaps a third of existing orders and the collapse of demand for new ships. Demand in 1976 barely reached one-third the level of 1974 and, despite considerable efforts by governments to stimulate demand, remained low through the rest of the decade. During 1978 the industry was completing ships at almost twice the rate that new orders were being received.[39] The fall in demand was especially dramatic in tankers and bulk carriers. With 32 percent of existing tanker tonnage not needed, many vessels were either laid up or put to other uses, such as storage;[40] and whereas in 1976 tankers had accounted for some 60 percent of total output, in 1978 the figure was only 25 percent. Yards concentrating on tanker production were inevitably hardest hit. Those industries that were heavily dependent on exports were also severely affected by the sudden check to industrial growth rates in the developed West and to the continued expansion of seaborne trade. But even those yards that had diversified into more sophisticated shipping, such as liquified natural gas or chemical carriers, did not escape the effects of the slump, nor did those already heavily supported by governments.

The collapse in demand has forced the shipbuilding industry in the West to face the controversial and sensitive issue of contraction. Since most forecasts predict no upturn in demand before the mid to late 1980s, there has been considerable domestic dispute over the capacity to be retained until then, intense competition on the means of financing it, and disagreement over the possible shares that each national or regional industry may have of the future market. Shipbuilding has never been a simple matter of profitability; there have always been strategic considerations and hence some degree of government intervention. Naval contracts have always played an important role, especially during periods of low demand for merchant shipping. But of particular importance during the current recession has been the question of employment in the industry. Its share in total manufactures is substantial only in a few countries, although its impact on other industrial sectors can be extensive. In Norway, for example, direct employment in shipbuilding is more than 10 percent of the total, whereas in Germany it is less than 1 percent. But the special importance of the industry lies in its location. In many if not most countries, shipbuilding is a major or the largest employer in otherwise depressed areas: in the UK for example, 90 percent of shipbuilding workers are located in development areas. The industry has therefore been eligible for a wide range of grants and loans provided by governments to such regions. But in most countries, governments have also provided more-direct subsidies and credits. In Europe certainly, direct support was considerably extended to prevent shipyards from collapse in the face of Japanese competition during the 1960s. Most governments also encouraged some degree of rationalization and/or programs that emphasized particular types of ships, such as the Danes with tankers or the French with more-specialized tonnage.

Shipbuilding in the United States has been described as "probably the most heavily protected industry in the world,"[41] and was therefore able to weather the crisis much better than was Japan or Western Europe. It has also acquired one of the largest order books in the world, although largely with U.S. shipowners. Various measures have been introduced or extended to maintain and expand the proportion of U.S. trade carried by U.S. merchant ships built in U.S. yards. As a result of the Merchant Marine Act of 1970, for example, employment in shipbuilding increased from 128,000 in 1968 to 184,000 in 1977. Government construction cost subsidies were granted to U.S. owners building in U.S. yards, based on the difference between high domestic and foreign building costs. Substantial support has also been given for technological developments and specialization. Moreover, although the U.S. industry has not fully escaped the effects of the recession, the U.S. administration, with strong congressional support, appears to be moving against the trend by emphasizing the construction of tankers within the context of a national cargo policy. In order, at least in part, to stimulate further work in U.S. yards, the administration has also begun to enforce strictly the safety and antipollution agreements reached within the OECD for all tankers using U.S. ports. In addition, under the Jones Act of 1920, which requires that only U.S. flag ships carry trade between U.S. ports, the demand for tankers to transport Alaskan oil will increase. As elsewhere, naval ship construction is also planned to expand substantially.

In Japan, with an estimated annual capacity of some 19m grt, orders of 50m grt had been reached in 1974. In 1977 the order book had declined to 10m grt and in 1979 to 9.3m grt. With 90 percent of its output in tankers, the crisis was particularly acute; profits slumped and dramatic losses were incurred by many Japanese yards. There have been numerous bankruptcies in shipbuilding and related industries, with smaller or less-diversified companies inevitably suffering most. The number of jobs in shipbuilding declined from 116,000 in 1975 to 70,000 in 1979. In contrast, the contraction of the Japanese industry has been carried out with the close cooperation of the government. In 1976 the Japanese Shipbuilding Association, made up of the 23 leading yards, and the 100-member Association of Smaller Shipbuilders agreed to a long-term overall reduction of capacity to 65 percent of the level of 1975, the reduction of operating ratios varying between 34 and 49 percent for the principals. This overall ceiling has been maintained with government support for scrapping, freezing, or transferring excess facilities. Those yards facing bankruptcy were also supported under Japanese rehabilitation legislation. Such measures were agreed within an overall objective of maintaining Japan's share of the market, during both the slump and the expected recovery in demand.

In Western Europe those industries that had concentrated on bulk tonnage also suffered immediately and severely. Sweden, for example, Western Europe's largest shipbuilder, produced 10.6 percent of the world's output of tankers in 1976, mostly for export. Because of Japanese competition in the 1960s and in view of Sweden's substantially higher costs (labor costs, for example, are some 50 percent higher than those in Japan), the government became progressively more involved in ownership. But while public ownership may have assisted the reorganization of the industry, it could not prevent an acute crisis. In 1978 losses were estimated at over £233m,[42] and between 1976 and 1978 some 30 percent of the workforce was cut back, from over 25,000 to less than 18,000. Denmark, with 6.2 percent of world production of tankers in 1976, more than half of which was produced for export, was also affected immediately and severely. Again between 1975 and the beginning of 1979 the workforce contracted from more than 16,500 to 11,000.[43] In West Germany, although the industry was less heavily dependent on bulk carriers, it was equally dependent on exports. With German labor costs some 50 percent higher than Japan's, the effect of the slump has also been serious. Between 1975 and early 1979 the civil shipbuilding workforce was reduced from nearly 47,000 to just under 27,000. The impact of the crisis was felt less immediately in France and the UK. The French industry with government support had undergone a gradual reorganization since the 1950s, with a greater emphasis on more-sophisticated shipping. In 1976, for example, it produced over 30 percent of the world tonnage of liquified gas and chemical carriers. Nonetheless, the impact was severe enough to cause the industry to work far below capacity and to lose nearly 6,000 workers. In the UK the effects of the slump were also somewhat delayed by government intervention. Indeed, the industry was at the same time going through a protracted process of nationalization. Like the French industry, the British had already undergone extensive rationalization and contraction, although its output remained constant at around 1.2m grt. The British share of world production shrank from 35 percent in the early 1950s to 3.5 percent in the mid-1970s, while the civil labor force, the largest in the Community, was reduced by 45 percent over the same period to 45,000.[44] Further contraction inevitably took place, despite considerable union opposition, although a considerable number of workers (16 percent) were merely transferred from merchant yards to naval work.[45]

In Europe, therefore, the 1974 crisis tended to intensify problems of long standing rather than to introduce wholly new ones. Confronted by the collapse of demand, all governments resorted to extensive subsidies of one sort or another in addition to those already granted. Some subsidies have been tied closely to adaptation and rationalization plans; others have been designed more simply to attract the few orders around. In Sweden, for example, where contraction of the industry was undertaken within a gradual process of nationalization, initial reactions were based on the hope that the slump was merely cyclical. A two-year scheme was therefore introduced in 1976 to build for stock, which has proved extremely expensive. Within the Community, the French, German, Italian, Dutch, and British governments have extended production subsidies to the industry, ranging from 15–25 percent in France, 20 percent in Germany, up to 30 percent in Italy, and 25 percent (or 30 percent in special cases) in the UK. The Dutch government undertook to meet 75 percent of the losses in certain yards within a scheme linked to a restructuring program.

All governments have also been generous in the subsidies they have allocated to domestic buyers. In contrast to the U.S., the Japanese have been able to rely on a greater loyalty from their own shipping lines, together with attractive subsidies. Subsidized loans for up to 75 percent are available from the Japan Development Bank, with a three-year moratorium. Most Community members also have Home Credit schemes: in Belgium, for example, loans of up to 80 percent over fifteen years at 1 percent interest and a further 10 percent at 6 percent over fifteen years have been available with a two-year moratorium; in Denmark, loans of up to 80 percent over fourteen years at 8 percent interest with a four-year moratorium. The Italians have also had a long-standing scrap and build scheme, although it has been little used. Such terms have not always been sufficient to attract domestic shipowners; the French government, for example, resorted to a ban on import licences for two ships to be built for a French company in Japan. Many governments have also offered more generous terms on exports to developing countries; although orders have tended to be small, they have sometimes been important in view of the dearth of other orders.

In view of the costly battle in subsidies, early efforts were made within the OECD to draw up possible guidelines. In 1974 the OECD Understanding on Export Credits was reached, setting limits to officially supported credit terms. These suggested a norm of 70 percent of the contract price to be repaid over seven years at 8 percent. Credits granted to developing countries were excluded as long as there was a genuine development aid intention. Despite the sievelike quality of the Understanding, it remained as a guide until December 1979, when the minimum down payment was reduced to 20 percent, and the maximum duration of the credit extended to 8.5 years. The interest rate remained as the accepted guideline. In 1976 additional guidelines were introduced calling for appropriate reductions in capacity, the avoidance of aids preventing long-term adaptation, and the maintenance of fair competition. These purely normative levels have been extended further by members of the European Community. The Fourth Directive of April 1978 attempted to reaffirm the link between aids and restructuring; aids to shipbuilding were permissible as long as they were intended to alleviate a crisis or acute social problems, were tied to measures making for greater competitiveness, and were intended to be temporary. The original 1974 OECD Understanding was also given legal sanction by the European Community, as was the agreement on cost escalation insurance, as long, again, as it was linked to the contraction of the industry and was designed to be progressively reduced. Although most governments have had difficulty in abiding by the guidelines or the Directive, the latter especially has had a constraining influence over government action. The Commission's conclusion, in its report on the industry in August 1979, was that "generally speaking. restructuring policies lag behind market developments."[46]

In view of the importance of the shipbuilding industry and the dearth of orders, continued competition in government aid has been inevitable. But the situation has been made even more difficult for developed countries by the advent of new, lower-cost producers, such as Spain, Poland, South Korea, and Brazil, all of which are heavily supported by their governments on terms similar to or even more attractive than those of the more-traditional producers. The Spanish industry expanded dramatically during the late 1960s and 1970s; its order book in 1978 placed it sixth in the world with 1.3m grt. Spain is, however, a member of both the Association of Western European Shipbuilders and the OECD, which has placed some constraints on its actions. Its comparative labor cost advantage is also being undermined. Poland, the most-dynamic shipbuilder in Eastern Europe, is in many respects in a separate class. Much of its expansion has been the result of the planned expansion of the Soviet and Eastern European merchant fleet which has already caused much concern in the West because their low freight rates appear unrelated to rational costs. A similar concern was felt when Poland was reported to sell two ships in 1979 at a price lower than that which had been offered in 1978.[47] Brazil's expansion has been largely a result of a determined effort not merely to industrialize but to enlarge its national fleet to carry 40 percent of its seaborne trade. South Korea also has ambitious plans to increase the amount of trade carried by its own ships, but it is much more geared to exports than Brazil. Under its Shipbuilding Plan, output was to be trebled by 1986 to exceed 6m grt, a huge figure given some estimates of an annual world output of around 20m grt by the mid to late 1980s.[48] Although the industry continues to be heavily supported by the government, with significant Japanese investment, there have been increasing problems caused by inflation and rising labor costs. Nonetheless it is usually assumed that the share of world production taken by newly industrialized countries will continue to increase significantly, largely at the expense of the industry in Western Europe.

Against this background, Western Europe and Japan face extremely difficult decisions on their relative capacities and their share of the world market. On the one hand, all governments have accepted that there is a need to reduce their shipbuilding capacity. On the other hand, all governments, strongly supported by their industries, have been opposed to significant reductions out of step with others when competition is so evidently distorted by government aids. Thus discussions have been not merely on pricing policy but on market shares. The Japanese have been determined to maintain as nearly as possible their 50 percent share of world output achieved in 1975. The Western European industry has challenged this claim arguing that if compensated grt (i.e., grt taking account of labor costs), is used as the measurement, Japan's share is reduced to about 40 percent. In addition, others such as the UK have claimed that since they took no part in the general expansion in shipbuilding in the 1960s, their industry should not be obliged to contract even further. During 1976–77 these arguments led to extensive and sometimes bitter exchanges between the Western European and Japanese industries and between governments within the framework of the OECD. After strong pressure was exerted by the Europeans, the Japanese eventually accepted a pricing agreement in January 1977, but they have been strongly critical in return over Europe's slowness to reduce its capacity.

Whereas the Japanese industry has remained confident that it can retain its share of the world market, few believe that Europe can retain its share. With the prospect of further contraction the Commission of the EC has attempted to introduce a number of proposals to aid restructuring and to stimulate demand. Its first proposals in November 1977 for coordinated action, based on a Community output of only 2.4m cgrt (compensated gross registered tonnage) against a 1975 output of 4.4m, were sharply critized, not least for their vagueness over the crucial question of how such cutbacks were to be shared out among the member states. Most governments had already introduced cutbacks, some over a long period; others had undertaken programs to reequip and modernize their yards in order to specialize in those vessels likely to be in greater demand; others believed that their industries were already more efficient or simply economically more important. Given the notoriously poor accuracy of past forecasts, few were prepared to accept new ones based on the worst years of the slump. There was, and remains, a concern that the European industry inadequately reflected the shares taken by Community member states in maritime trade, a factor influential with most other governments, including the Japanese and American. Of the Commission's initial proposals, therefore, only those that sought to stimulate the industry through the enforcement of antipollution and safety standards were generally welcomed, the Council of Ministers resolving that greater emphasis should be placed on the maintenance of a healthy, competitive industry of a size consistent with the Community's maritime trade and its social and strategic interests.

In 1979 the Commission prepared a further, more-positive, proposal of scrap and build. Its aim was to stimulate Community output to 3.4m cgrt by 1982 and save an estimated 35,000–40,000 jobs by offering incentives to shipowners to scrap a target figure of 2m cgrt per annum and subsidize new building up to 1m cgrt per annum. The costs, estimated at more than $65m in incentives to scrap (made up of the difference between the secondhand value and the probable scrap price) and $85m in subsidies to build, would be borne by the Community. The proposal, although drawn up in consultation with the industry, did not win unanimous approval among the governments. While the Italians, with their own limited 1:1 scrap and build plan already in being and whose costs might be transferred to the Community, were in favor, Denmark and West Germany were opposed. The industry, together with the Commission's Directorate General for Industrial Affairs, nonetheless continued discussions on various alternative scrap and build possibilities.

But such policies would provide solutions only for the short or medium term. It will remain extremely difficult for the Community to compete effectively with either Japan or the newer low-cost producers, many of whom are not even subject to the normative guidelines agreed within the OECD. The newer producers are likely to continue to have the advantage of developed producers (including Japan) because they can impart the technology, know-how, and machinery, while their costs remain lower, especially in the production of more-standardized tonnage. On the other hand, European builders may be able to maintain a viable industry through greater concentration on more-specialized shipping (although some yards have not always proved particularly flexible in the past), although it is significant that a similar trend is occurring in some low-cost producers. Poland, for example, has been specializing in chemical carrier producers, liquified gas carriers, and container ships. Other possibilities may occur—such as an increase in demand for dry bulk carriers for transporting coal (rather than oil) and iron ore, as steel production also moves to lower-cost producers. But while such demand may increase world output, it is significant that many low-cost producers are also increasing their own shipping lines with government support. Therefore, the main preoccupation of the European shipbuilders in particular will continue to be to maintain a viable and competitive industry with a sufficiently diversified capacity, and to protect jobs or at least to bring about a controlled reduction in the workforce.

Aircraft

The aircraft industry offers significant contrasts to the other industries considered in this chapter. The later 1970s saw the beginnings of a considerable expansion in the output of new airplanes and engines in both Western Europe and the United States. This expansion was continued, fuel crisis notwithstanding, in order to meet the continued growth in demand, new noise regulations, and the need for more fuel-efficient engines. Similarly, the military market is buoyed by the need for a new generation of fighters and higher defense expenditures. But the industry's present position needs to be viewed against the problem years of the early 1970s when there were serious overcapacity and heavy financial losses. Nor can one ignore, for the future, the problems created for the world's airlines by the rising cost of fuel and for the manufacturers by the growth of their own costs, especially in research and development.

Nonetheless, the aircraft industry is frequently picked out as an area of growth for the developed West because of its sophisticated technology, specialization, and the high levels of investment required. At present, the United States dominates the market, producing some 90 percent of the world's airplanes, and is likely to continue in that position, although possibly against a more-coherent and united challenge from Western Europe. The U.S. predominance has been achieved despite (or perhaps partly because of) the extensive involvement of European governments, directly and indirectly, in their national industries. European governments have frequently supported projects that compete with other European and American designs and have largely determined the final choice of aircraft for their national airlines. Production runs have therefore tended to be short, even when exports have been relatively high. Few European companies have been able to break into the hitherto all-important U.S. market. They have tended to fail less because of tariff barriers, which although significant in the past are due to disappear under the 1979 GATT agreement, than because of closer relations between American airlines and manufacturers, greater flexibility in design on the part of the latter, and financial terms comparable with or better than their directly supported European rivals. In Europe, the lack of commercial success (even when the industry is technologically competitive) and the ever-rising costs of developing and producing aircraft have led to not always wholly compatible outcomes. The industry has undergone extensive reorganization. In the UK, for example, the industry (at least temporarily) has been either nationalized

(British Aerospace) or taken into public ownership (Rolls Royce). Elsewhere, as in Germany, government contracts have been used as additional levers to bring about mergers; nevertheless the two larger companies, Vereinigte Flugtechnische Werke (VFW) and Messerschmitt-Bölkow Blohm (MBB), resisted pressures to amalgamate for several years. The lure of the American market, and American money and know-how, have also led many European companies to seek cooperation with U.S. companies, such as SNECMA and General Electric, while others have sought either subcontracting work, especially from Boeing, or licenses to manufacture in Europe. At the same time, extremely slowly and with considerable difficulties and many false starts, European manufacturers have begun to collaborate among themselves, most notably with the Tornado multirole combat aircraft (in which France does not participate) and the Airbus (from which Italy is absent). In reply, for defensive reasons (in order to keep a firm foothold in Europe) and more-positive ones (to share risks and costs), American companies have shown an increasing willingness to collaborate rather than merely to license manufacture, but for a number of reasons the results have been limited. For the Europeans, particularly Britain and France, there has been a certain ambivalence as to whether the long-term aim is competition or cooperation with the United States, or some sort of combination of the two.

So far the issues within the aircraft industry have largely involved only Western Europe and the United States, but recent moves by Japan to increase its involvement in aerospace may add a further dimension. Moreover, the increasing demand for airplanes in the third world could create additional complications. Some countries, such as Brazil and Korea, have already taken steps to establish their own embryonic aircraft industries, in part as a logical extension of their development plans. Foreign exchange constraints in particular may lead others to follow suit, at least to manufacture aircraft under license, an extremely effective means of receiving sophisticated technology, or to become involved in the production of equipment, especially perhaps in the electronics sector. That is not to suggest that non-OECD countries are about to throw down a challenge to existing manufacturers. But it does mean that there will be new factors for the latter to take into account when competing for third world markets in the future.

The strategic importance of the aircraft industry has caused governments to be involved more intimately as purchasers and financiers than even in the shipbuilding industry. Defense contracts have for most companies been more than a cushion for protection against fluctuations in the civil market and the tendency — itself encouraged to some extent by government involvement — toward overcapacity. The strategic balance creates a perpetual demand for ever moresophisticated weaponry. Given the time-lag between the conception of a new project and its readiness for service, the emphasis placed on technological innovation, and the inevitable escalation of costs, government support has been unavoidable. Moreover, 47 percent of the physical assets of the British aerospace industry in 1961 were financed by borrowing, compared to 4 percent in manufacturing industries in general.[49] It is unlikely that many aircraft manufacturers could exist solely by borrowing on the basis of future contracts had governments been unwilling to lend; several companies, including Rolls Royce and Lockheed, have had to be rescued even while receiving substantial government support. In the United States in recent years, some 80 percent of official funding in R & D has

Table 4.6   Turnover in the Aerospace Industry at 1970 Prices (in million European Units of Account)

	Federal Republic of Germany	Belgium	France	Italy	Netherlands	United Kingdom	Total European Economic Community	United States
1970	770	39	1310	227	113	1576	4035	21,779
1971	764	50	1310	205	110	1479	3918	18,292
1972	761	58	1359	319	139	1898	4534	18,057
1973	823	48	1580	313	115	1988	4867	18,168
1974	771	50	1690	295	88	2081	4975	17,178
1975	746	59	1779	358	125	2071	5138	16,587
1976	808	57	2164	346	134	2122	5631	16,519
1977	689	53	2130	363	126	2181	5542	16,632

Source: Commission of the European Communities SEC(79)995, July 2, 1979.

been provided by the Defense Department.[50] Such support has not only been geared to specific projects; it has also been given in order to maintain a viable, appropriate R & D capacity. Such support for R & D, while substantial, has been only one facet. A wide variety of subsidies and fiscal incentives has also been employed; and having supported the production of the aircraft or engine, governments have also become involved in encouraging their sales, especially through military aid programs and subsidized prices.[51]

Commercial aircraft and engine manufacturers depend to a greater or lesser extent on military contracts. But the civilian sector, too, receives substantial governmental support. In sales, for example, at least in Europe, considerable pressure has been exerted by governments on national airlines to buy the domestic product — with, in many cases, compensation paid for any additional costs, or losses simply written off. It has usually been a matter of national prestige, however lack-

Table 4.7 Breakdown of Overall Turnover by Subsector in EC Countries in 1977
(percentages)

	Federal Republic of Germany	Belgium	France	Italy	Netherlands	United Kingdom	Total European Economic Community	United States
Airframe	58.2	41.9	61.7	64.4	81.1	40.2	54.5	45.6
Engines	10.7	22.1	18.5	20.1	–	32.0	21.5	14.1
Equipment	18.2	14.3	17.9	12.0	7.4	26.2	20.1	18.4
Space	12.9	21.7	1.9	3.5	8.5	1.6	3.9	21.9

Source: Commission of the European Communities SEC(79)995, July 2, 1979.

ing in commercial viability because of the small size of the market, for national airlines to use nationally produced airplanes. The civil sector also receives further support: in the UK, for example, the industry by 1977 had received £1500 million from the Treasury toward the development of civil aircraft and plane engines, with less than £150 million recovered.[52] Moreover, the precise separation of the military and civil sectors can never be wholly clear in view of the many spin-offs from the military to the civil sector. The General Electric–SNECMA CFM-56 engine is but one example, the engine being a derivative of the F-101 used in the B1 bomber (a fact that caused security problems during the initial period of the companies' collaboration). The importance of the military sector for civil manufacturers tends to be most obvious during threatened or real cutbacks in government spending, a major fear of the industry being that its technological lead, and hence its export opportunities, might be adversely affected. One American observer has remarked, "When things are going well the companies stress the idea of free enterprise with no need for government regulations. But when things aren't going well, they suddenly become a close partner with government and want it to bail them out. All they have to do is to threaten collapse and the government pours in more money."[53]

National governments, whether directly or through other national concerns, remain the mainstay of the aircraft industry, both through support for R & D and as the major purchaser. The U.S. government, for example, purchased 71.5 percent of the total sales of the U.S. industry in 1978, 77 percent of McDonnell

Douglas's output and 57 percent of Lockheed's.[54] Such a role necessarily gives government a strong hand in determining the structure as well as the projects of the industry. In view of the costs involved, governments on both sides of the Atlantic have tended to concentrate on fewer projects and, with the pressure of withholding contracts, have encouraged rationalization and efficiency within the industry. But whereas the U.S. government has been able to continue its support indirectly, even to the extent of having to bail out Lockheed in 1971, European (and the Canadian) governments have tended to resort to public ownership. In Britain and France, for example, rationalization was encouraged through mergers from the 1950s onward. During the 1960s, government-sponsored mergers resulted in Hawker Siddeley and the British Aircraft Corporation becoming the national leaders; but in 1977, after considerable delays and uncertainties, both companies, together with Scottish Aviation, were nationalized to form British Aerospace (BAe). In aircraft engines, Rolls Royce became the national leader after merging with most of the aircraft engine divisions of the aircraft manufacturers, but was itself taken into public ownership in 1971 after going bankrupt. In France a similar pattern emerged when the nationalized Aerospatiale was formed in 1970. But two companies, Dassault (makers of the Mirage series) and Breguet, were left in private hands, although they merged into one company and the state recently acquired a blocking minority of shares. In Germany also, by 1970 the smaller aerospace industry was organized into three groups. Several Länder governments have interests in VFW and MBB, Bremen in VFW, and Hamburg and Bavaria in MBB; Dornier, the third manufacturer, remains in private hands. Federal efforts to bring about the merger of VFW and MBB were of long standing, and were finally successful in 1980. The merger brought an end to the only example of a cross-frontier merger; VFW had joined with the Dutch company Fokker in 1970.

Although these mergers were intended to improve the viability and international competitiveness of national industries, the United States has remained overwhelmingly predominant. Even in 1978 when U.S. turnover had declined and Europe's had expanded, Europe purchased 25 percent of the world's non-communist airplanes but produced less than 10 percent of them; the US, on the other hand, purchased 50 percent and manufactured 90 percent.[55] This predominance has frequently caused consternation among European governments. During the 1960s the aerospace industry, viewed both as a growth industry and one to which governments were heavily committed, became an element in the debate on the so-called technology gap between Europe and America. Harold Wilson, then prime minister, declared in 1967 that continued American domination of such strategic growth industries was "the road not to partnership but to an industrial helotry."[56] In 1967 also J. J. Servan-Schreiber published his best-seller, *Le Défi Américain.*[57] The debate, however faulty many of its premises, continued until the early 1970s. It included some emotive elements, such as the threat of a massive brain-drain across the Atlantic, but to a considerable extent the gap was less one of technology than of management and the inability to implement R & D. As the 1968 OECD Report, *Gaps in Technology,* put it, "The size and homogeneity of the U.S. market, including that portion made possible by government procurement, helps American firms to commercial discoveries because it facilitates the prediction of market requirements. The European market, considered as a whole, has a greater potential size . . . However, its present . . . diverse political and contrasting social structures result in fragmentation."[58] This fragmentation of the market has inevitably caused relatively high costs and short production runs and therefore heavy losses for the European industry (a situation not always assisted by the choice of projects). National governments, in committing themselves to their national industries, have thereby spread their resources thinly over a wide range of sometimes competing programs.

Collaboration among European governments and industries was a logical step in the interests of sharing costs, greater efficiency through economies of scale, and the challenging of U.S. predominance. In encouraging such collaboration, albeit from the sidelines, the Commission of the EC noted that the aeronautical industry is a major source of employment (see Table 4.8). "It is one of the chief representatives of a type of employment – highly skilled, commanding sophisticated technologies and a high level of investment – towards which the Community must necessarily move in the future as the industrialisation of the Third World proceeds and a wider international division of labor unfolds." Second, R & D in the aircraft industry has provided important scientific and technological innovations in other areas; and third, Europe's capacity to contribute to its own defense required a strong aircraft industry.[59]

Despite the commitment of heads of government at their summit meeting in 1972 to establish a single industrial base and the adoption by the Council of Ministers of the Commission's "Action Programme for the Aeronautical Sector" put forward in 1975, little has emerged of substance. In 1977 for example, the Council of Ministers agreed only to a list of general criteria on which future joint programs should be based. The reasons for such limited progress are several, although, as two of the authors of the Colonna Report on Industrial Policy presented in 1970 later commented, "a genuine common industrial policy, particularly for key industries such as aerospace, data processing and electronics, can only be developed to the extent that the construction of Europe takes on a political dimension which at present is still lacking."[60] One aspect of the problem has been that the Treaty of Rome provides only a limited basis for Community action in the industrial sector. Certainly it provides no legal basis for Community involvement in defense, the exclusion of which, as the Commission recognized, would make any common aircraft policy wholly incomplete. France especially, although not alone, has consistently objected in the Council of Ministers to any substantive linkage. The matter has nevertheless been debated in the European Parliament.[61]

Efforts to establish an institutional basis for increased collaboration in the military sector have also proved to be limited in their results. The debate on the technology gap, the impetus given to conventional forces by the 1968 Soviet invasion of Czechoslovakia, and U.S. congressional disquiet over the U.S. contribution to Western security, especially in its troop commitments, were all factors leading to the formation of the Eurogroup in 1968 by the European members of the Atlantic Alliance apart from France. Common procurement and collaboration have since been a major preoccupation of the Group, although to only limited effect. Increased tension in U.S.-European relations, however, in many ways epitomized in Dr. Kissinger's "Year of Europe" exercise during which he stated that "unbridled economic competition can sap the impulse for common

Table 4.8 Workforce in the Aerospace Industry

	1972	1974	1976	1977
Federal Republic of Germany	52,455	52,982	51,367	52,416
Belgium	4,941	4,422	5,015	4,895
France	108,525	106,769	107,454	103,295
Italy	28,500	30,000	31,991	32,080
Netherlands	6,600	6,555	7,865	7,320
United Kingdom	207,500	210,100	227,402	219,251
European Economic Community	408,521	410,828	431,094	419,257
United States	922,000	965,000	899,000[a]	890,000
Canada	28,800	28,400	25,300	27,400
Japan	26,000	25,550	26,746	23,756

By subsector	EEC	Percentage
Aircraft	206,698	49.3
Engines	99,061	23.6
Equipment	113,498	27.1

[a]For breakdown of US 1976 figures, see below.

Source: European Commission SEC(79)995. The Commission suggests that these figures be treated with caution because of the difficulties of establishing common definitions for all occupational grades.

United States Aerospace Industry Workforce Distribution (1976)

Aerospace:	aircraft	− 262 000
	engines	− 132 000
	equipment	− 91 000
	total	485,000

Missiles and space	85 000
Communication equipment	135 000
Other	194 000
Total	899 000

Source: Commission of the European Communities SEC(78)3298, 1978.

defense,"[62] and increased U.S. pressures for greater standardization in NATO military equipment to improve efficiency pointed up the political problems faced by European governments dependent on U.S. defense policies. Standardization was regarded by several governments as a cause for concern, since U.S. standards were likely to be those imposed, and in its place interoperability was emphasized; one French General for example declared, "provided a military aircraft can land on most bases, replenish its fuel tanks and ammunition and have no trouble with its telecommunications, it is effectively 100 percent operable. Who cares whether it has the same wing-span or the same number of turbine blades as its competitor?"[63] The continued predominance of the U.S. industry, as shown in the F-16 agreement of 1974 in which the Belgian, Dutch, Danish, and Norwegian governments chose the U.S. fighter against European competitors, led the Eurogroup to reemphasize "the need to maintain a highly developed technological, scientific and industrial base in Europe whilst seeking to achieve the closest possible cooperation in arms production between the countries of North America and Europe."[64] Its conclusion, to seek to establish a European Defence Procurement secretariat, echoed that put forward by others such as the Commission of the EC. But in order to include France in the plan, the resulting Independent European Programme Group (IEPG) not only emphasized the divergence between European and U.S. interests, but also continued European cooperation on a procedural basis rather than within a new institutional structure. The U.S. reaction was mixed. On the one hand the U.S. government increasingly recognized Europe's need to retain its technological base through its support for the two-way street concept. Congress, however, while accepting the two-way street, laid particular stress on the competitive basis for any procurement, an emphasis that favors the U.S. industry. Moreover, the U.S. government successfully sought to establish planning groups within NATO on all future requirements, and thus undermined the European attempt to keep greater control over the programs designed specifically for European needs. The result has been that the IEPG has so far been largely ineffectual, partly because of U.S. policies but largely because of the inherent problem facing European governments in emphasizing European interests at the possible expense of those of the Atlantic security system itself.[65]

The lack of political will on the part of the European governments to pool national resources has frequently been reinforced by a number of more-practical difficulties. In the defense sector, for example, differences in tactical doctrines have to be taken into account—a procedure that has often led to a number of variations being built, inevitably at greater cost—and different replacement timetables. Industrial capabilities are also radically different, particularly between the four largest Community members (Britain, France, Germany, and Italy) and other European countries. The latter's position in financial terms may be little improved, since European equipment is often more expensive than American, a factor which "detracts from the functioning of the . . . [IEPG] as a fully cooperative organization."[66] But even among the big four countries, differences of capability and capacity help to create problems in collaboration. For example, there are both political and economic constraints over the division of labor within any project plus the differences in national regulations, standards, and procedures. Increased experience has helped to smooth out some of these difficulties, for example, in Panavia, which produces the Tornado multirole combat aircraft, and Airbus Industrie. But collaboration, while spreading the costs of the project among the participating countries, does not often result in a more competitively priced final product. A number of estimates have been made of the extra costs resulting from added time, translation, geographical separation, transaction across the exchanges, etc., which range from 20 percent to more than 50 percent if several versions of the equipment are produced.[67] In addition, the possibilities of delay in any collaborative venture tend to be all the greater.

Despite such difficulties collaborative ventures have been undertaken in Western Europe and with some success, even if they have as yet been on an ad hoc basis that leaves each country's industry free to compete with the others on other projects. Among early examples of collaboration in the 1960s were the Anglo-French Concorde, a technological success even if an economic albatross, and the Anglo-French Jaguar fighter. Management of the latter showed some advance on that of Concorde, and further refinements were made for the Tornado project. Although the venture was confined to Britain, Germany, and Italy after the Canadians, Belgians, and Dutch dropped out in 1969 (the French with their own project pursued an independent line), most commentators have viewed its management under the German-registered company Panavia as a success. British Aerospace (BAe) and MBB each have a 42.5 percent share in the airframe, and Aeritalia 15 percent. Rolls Royce, MTU, and Fiat have similar interests in the engine company Turbo-Union. At its peak the project has been estimated to give employment to 70,000 in the three countries, with 809 aircraft being produced at a cost of £8 billion over ten years.[68]

The success of the Tornado has been complemented in the civilian sector by the success of the Airbus. The joint project was initiated by the French and German governments in 1969, and the German company Deutsche Airbus (in which both MBB and VWF have holdings) and the French Aerospatiale had 47.9 percent participation. The Spanish CASA took a 4.2 percent share, while the Dutch Fokker (without government support in terms of compensation for any losses) has had a special status. Britain, which was involved in the early discussions, officially withdrew in 1969, although Hawker Siddeley (later incorporated within BAe) remained on a contractual basis to produce the wings. The British decision was based in part on the uncertainty that Rolls Royce would provide the engine (in fact General Electric was chosen for the A300B) although it was largely preoccupied with its U.S. links (with both Lockheed on the RB211 and Boeing on the RB211-535), uncertainty that the Airbus would be competitive enough, and a reluctance to enter into another French-led costly exercise when Britain had its own possibilities. Italy also stood aside from the venture largely because of its strong links with Boeing. Under the Franco-German agreement, undertakings were entered into not only to share development costs (estimated at DM2.7 billion) but also to extend production subsidies to compensate for currency losses and differential increases in costs in the United States and Europe, sales subsidies so that prices and terms were competitive with U.S. rates, and credit guarantees to German firms—a total estimated at DM 9.7 billion.[69]

Despite some show of reluctance by the French, the reinvolvement of the UK was always considered a desirable end. This became especially so with the evolution of the concept of a family of airliners, beginning with a smaller version of the A-300, the A-310, the possibility of a small short-haul aircraft, and a stretched version of the A-300 for longer hauls. The importance of such a family lies not only in the possible continuation of the consortium, thereby providing a nucleus for a European aircraft policy, but, as Boeing has so often shown, in the sales potential of inter-related aircraft. The British, persuaded by the increasing signs of success and the possible future involvement of Rolls Royce, officially returned to the consortium on January 1, 1979. BAe became a 20 percent risk-sharing participant in the consortium and took a substantial share in the development costs of the A-310 and an entitlement to a substantial share also in future Airbus activities. BAe also agreed "that there will be no individual participation in programmes conflicting with the present and future programmes of Airbus Industries."[70]

British ambivalence was further demonstrated by the decision to allow British Airways to purchase the Airbus's main rival, the Boeing 767, and with Rolls Royce's links with Boeing on the launch engine of the 757. This seeming lack of commitment to European collaboration has not been confined to the UK. Aeritalia, for example, is a risk-sharing participant in the Boeing 767. The French national aero-engine concern, SNECMA, formed a joint company with American General Electric to produce the CFM-56. The agreement, drawn up in 1971, came about on an initiative of the French government which, with the promise of loans to assist in the venture, encourage SNECMA to seek foreign collaborators and so provide both a more-secure future and a challenge to the dominant position of Rolls Royce in Europe. General Electric was chosen largely because cooperation with an American firm would provide greater credibility in the American and world markets and, as General Electric was second in the United States only to Pratt and Whitney, the partnership was likely to be one of equals. For its part, General Electric, financially tied up with its CF-6 engine, favored the agreement, which maintained GE's position as a serious competitor to Pratt and Whitney and provided a valuable foothold within Europe that might have been lost if SNECMA had reached an agreement with Rolls Royce.[71]

The challenge to U.S. predominance, presented or at least threatened by developments such as the Airbus (especially in the light of the decision by Eastern Airlines to buy it), has caused a certain defensiveness in the American industry. American companies have traditionally been able to rely at least on licensing production in other countries, as with the F-16. But in the face of growing European criticism, U.S. companies have more frequently sought closer collaboration with European and other countries, either on a sub-contractual basis or as joint risk-sharing partners. Boeing's investment in other countries, for example, is substantial, with major subcontractors on the 757 and 767 in Canada, Australia, Japan, Italy, and Britain.[72] Greater collaboration has been seen as a necessary means of maintaining its position in Europe. But there have also been more-positive reasons for such collaboration as costs continue to mount. In the military sector, T. A. Callaghan in his report prepared for the U.S. State Department and later to Congress argued in favor of greater collaboration and of spreading the U.S. technological base to Europe because the United States itself can no longer fund its own arms development program adequately, with the result that many arms projects crawl along or become obsolete before they can be completed. In his view the United States needs Europe to undertake many such programs so that these, whenever undertaken, can be fully funded and move to completion.[73]

A number of reasons nevertheless suggest that such trans-Atlantic collaboration is likely to remain limited. Collaboration is an effective means of transferring highly sophisticated technology, design, and engineering know-how to sometimes extremely receptive collaborators and potential competitors. The American industry has often been critical of the transfer of private American technology and of a lack of reciprocity by the European industry. The European industry for its part has often been reluctant to enter into projects with a high export potential, because of U.S. restrictions on arms transfers to non-NATO countries. Moreover, neither production under license nor collaborative ventures necessarily remove the barriers established against imports. Insofar as American airplanes, civil and military, have in the past been significantly cheaper than their European competitors' planes, European tariff barriers have been largely irrelevant in controlling the flow. When, as in the F-16 case, the Community imposed duties (although, under the off-set arrangements, work to the value of 40 percent of the total of European purchases was carried out in Europe), it was seen largely as a bargaining counter to try to persuade the United States to cut its tariffs on European imports. When the US refused, the Council of Ministers simply lifted the tariff.[74] But exclusion from the American market has long been a bone of contention for European manufacturers. As the WEU Assembly Report of 1977 put it, the US has "a policy of near autarchy in weapons procurement." Not only has the Buy American Act protected the U.S. market to a level of 50 percent of domestic costs, but "when the US does purchase European equipment, such as . . . the Harrier vertical take-off aircraft, agreements for manufacture under licence are demanded."[75] Nor has (reluctant) Congressional acceptance of the two-way street significantly altered the situation. European civil aircraft have faced even greater difficulties, not least because of price; hence the excitement when Eastern Airlines ordered 25 Airbuses with an option for nine more. The Community again attempted to persuade the Americans to suspend duties of 5 percent. Again the United States refused, and Airbus Industrie undertook to pay the duties. Moreover, although such duties are being removed, doubts remain about the extent to which the new Code will radically change the situation.

Nonetheless, European manufacturers have been sharing the optimism over the future. Estimates prepared in 1979 for the ICAO and by Boeing forecast future demand for some 3,500 aircraft, 30 percent to replace existing fleets and 70 percent for traffic growth.[76] In the military sector, estimates predict a need for 5,000 new combat aircraft of all kinds. Moreover, other estimates suggest that the American market will become less important as the demand increases in the rest of the world. But while East-West tensions may maintain the current buoyancy of the military sector, severe problems face the civilian sector despite the prevailing optimism. The continuation of the economic recession is a damper. Airlines are being increasingly squeezed between cut-price competition over fares and spiraling running costs, due especially to oil price increases. Although new engines are more fuel-efficient, airlines may yet face the need to cut services, with some inevitably adverse effects on their orders for new aeroplanes. At the same time, the need for fuel conservation and the examination of alternative fuels, such as liquid hydrogen or nuclear power, creates increased pressure for additional R & D and may have profound effects on the next generation of engines and aircraft in the 1990s.

In addition to these problems, the shift in demand and the ever heavier burden on trade balances has led other countries to increase their activities in the aeronautical sector. As early as 1968 the French industry pointed to possible future difficulties if the French government failed to help maintain domestic demand "at a time when several countries – Germany, Japan, Italy and India have decided to develop their aeronautical activities."[77] Germany at least now seems indispensable to any European collaborative venture, although Italy retains its links with America (except in the Tornado). The Japanese have quietly and steadily expanded their activities, particularly by means of licensing agreements. Such an agreement was reached with Rolls Royce-Turbomeca on production of the Adour engine, designed for the Anglo-French Jaguar, for its F-1 and T-2 fighters. But increasingly there has been considerable interest, supported by government funds, in going beyond such defense equipment. In 1980 agreement was reached with Rolls Royce on the development of its RB 432 engine for short-haul aircraft by Mitsubishi, Kawasaki, and Ishikawajima-Harima. Discussions were also begun with Fokker and with Airbus Industrie on the development of a short-haul airliner. An increasing number of developing or newly industrializing countries, notably Korea, are following the Japanese example.[78] Brazil's agreement with Piper to produce light aircraft has been cited as a specific example of how the threat can be used to deny an expanding market to importers unless they negotiate a coproduction agreement. Once the agreement with Piper had been reached, Brazil increased its tariff on light aircraft from 7 to 50 percent.[79]

The increased attention paid by Japan especially does not pose an immediate challenge to established producers. Yet the need to prevent the Japanese and others from closing their markets while building up their own industries was considered sufficiently important by the United States for it to press for the inclusion of civil aviation within the Tokyo Round. European governments supported the American lead largely to open up further America's own market. The resulting Code, which has not been accepted by most developing countries, required the removal of tariffs on trade in civil aircraft, engines, components, and parts; restraint on government support policies (including export credits) so as not to affect adversely the expansion of trade; and pricing policies based on reasonable expectations of recouping all costs. While the signatories have begun to remove tariffs there are doubts whether all protective devices and influences will disappear. As most developing countries have not signed the Code, they will not be subject to its measures. But in the present cycle of reequipment, competition remains confined largely to Western Europe and the United States, with the continued predominance of the latter. The continually spiraling costs of R & D, production, and acquisition are likely to reinforce moves toward greater cross-frontier collaboration, whether intra-European, trans-Atlantic, Europe-Japanese, or U.S.-Japanese, and may extend them increasingly beyond traditional producers. The transfer of technology and know-how through collaboration encourages governments and industries to extend their activities for both strategic and balance-of-payments considerations. The process has been and is likely to remain a gradual one, but the worldwide structure of the industry during the next reequipment cycle forecast for the 1990s may show some significant changes.

Notes

1. OECD, *Modern Cotton Industry: A Capital Intensive Industry* (1965), p. 18.
2. Vincent Cable, *World Textile Trade and Production,* EIU Special Report No. 63 (London: Economist Intelligence Unit, 1979).
3. Camille Blum, "The Textile Policy of the European Community," in S. Warnecke and E. N. Suleiman, eds., *Industrial Policies in Western Europe* (New York: Praeger, 1975), p. 208.
4. *The Economist,* October 15, 1977.
5. The options posed by the Capelin Report 1970 discussed in Blum, op. cit.
6. See, for example, S. Mukherjee, *Free Trade is good but what about the workers? — Trade Liberalisation and Adjustment Assistance,* PEP Broadsheet 543 (London: Political and Economic Planning, March 1974), Chapter 8.
7. OECD, *The Case for Positive Adjustment Policies: A compendium of OECD Documents,* June 1979.
8. House of Lords Select Committee on the European Communities, *Textiles* (London, March 1979), p. xv.
9. See Table 1.12.
10. Blum, op. cit., p. 210.
11. OECD, *Modern Cotton Industry,* op. cit., p. 43, Table VIII.
12. See Table 1.18.
13. MFA, Article I(2).
14. *Eleventh General Report on the Activities of the European Communities, 1977,* Commission of the European Communities (Brussels, 1978), p. 221.
15. *The Times,* December 22, 1976.
16. For an account of intra-Community negotiations see Chris Farrands, "Textile Diplomacy: The making and implementation of European Textile Policy 1974-78," *Journal of Common Market Studies* (Oxford, September 1979).
17. European Commission Information Sheet, July 1980, p. 70. The most-sensitive group of textiles comprises cotton yarns and fabrics, spun synthetic fabrics, knitted shirts and T shirts, jerseys and pullovers, trousers and woven shirts and blouses. In Britain, for example, these account for as much as three-fifths of imports.
18. Louis Turner, *"Textiles, Clothing and Consumer Electronics: The Experiences of Hong King and the Republic of Korea"* (Paper presented to Conference on The Implications of NIC's for Trade and Adjustment Policies, Royal Institute of International Affairs, London, June 13-15, 1979.)
19. Quoted by COMITEXTIL in the evidence considered by the House of Lords Select Committee on the European Communities, op. cit., p. 35.
20. Vincent Cable, *World Textile Trade and Production,* op. cit., p. 11-12.
21. *The Economist,* February 11, 1978.
22. *Comité International de la Rayonne et des Fibres Synthétiques* (CIRFS), *Information on Manmade Fibres,* Paris, 1979.
23. Official Journal of the European Communities, Annex, Debates of the European Parliament No. 149, April 1972, cited in *Eighth Report on Competition Policy,* Commission of the European Communities (May 1979), p. 49.
24. *The Economist,* February 11, 1978.
25. Cable, op. cit., p. 14.
26. Ibid., pp. 12-13.
27. *The Economist,* February 11, 1978.
28. CIRFS, *Information on Manmade Fibres,* Paris, 1970.
29. *The Economist,* October 15, 1977.
30. Commission of the European Communities, *COM(80)432 final,* July 23, 1980, p. 2.
31. Man-made Fibres Production Sector Working Party, *Progress Report 1979,* (London, National Economic Development Council).
32. Cable, op. cit., p. 14.

33. Commission of the European Communities, op. cit., p. 4. The eleven leading European producers are Fabelta (Belgium), Rhone-Poulenc (France), Montedison, Societa Italiana Resine, and SNIA Viscosa (Italy), Adzo-Enka (Netherlands), Bayer and Hoechst (West Germany), and Courtaulds and ICI (United Kingdom).

34. CIRFS, *Information on Manmade Fibres,* Paris, 1970.

35. See, for example, Man-made Fibres Production Sector Working Party, *Progress Report 1978* (London, National Economic Development Council).

36. Man-made Fibres Production Sector Working Party, *Progress Report 1979* (London, National Economic Development Council).

37. Ibid.

38. Louis Turner et al, *Living with the Newly Industrialising Countries,* Chatham House Papers No. 7, Royal Institute of International Affairs (London, 1980), p. 35.

39. *Financial Times,* February 28, 1979.

40. House of Lords Select Committee on the European Communities, *Shipbuilding,* June 13, 1978, p. iv.

41. Ibid, p. 24.

42. *Financial Times,* August 14, 1979.

43. Employment figures for Denmark and other Community member states (with the exception of the UK) are taken from COM(79)469 Final, Commission of the European Communities, August 1979.

44. House of Lords Report, op. cit., p. v.

45. Ibid, p. 14.

46. COM(79)469, op. cit.

47. *Financial Times,* July 6, 1979.

48. *Prospects for the World Shipping Industry: A forecast of new building requirement to the late 1980s,* Survey No. 20, HPD shipping publications 1979. Cited in the *Financial Times,* September 19, 1979.

49. *Report of the Committee of Inquiry into the Aircraft Industry* (London: HMSO, Cmnd 2853, 1965), p. 21.

50. Commission of the European Communities, SEC(78)3298, *European Aerospace Industry,* October 1978.

51. For a list of many of the ways governments have supported the industry, see Mary Kaldor, *European Defence Industries—National and International Implications,* ISIO Monographs, University of Sussex (1972), pp. 15–19.

52. Lord Beswick in a speech to the Royal Aeronautical Society, London, January 26, 1977.

53. Ernest Fitzgerald, formerly the U.S. Air Force civilian cost control expert, quoted by Kaldor, op. cit., p. 20.

54. *Financial Times,* June 4, 1979.

55. Hanns H. Schumacher, "Europe's Airbus Programme and the Impact of British participation," *The World Today* (London: Royal Institute of International Affairs, August 1979), p. 332.

56. Quoted in R. Williams, *European Technology: The Politics of Collaboration* (London: Croom Helm, 1973), p. 21.

57. Paris, Denoel, 1967.

58. Quoted in W. R. Kinter and H. Sicherman, *Technology and International Politics* (Lexington, Mass.: Lexington Books, 1975), p. 78.

59. *Bulletin of the European Communities,* Supplement 11/75, "Action Programme for the Aeronautical Sector," p. 7.

60. R. Toulemon and J. Flory, *Une Politique industrielle pour l'Europe* (Paris: Presses Universitaires de France, 1974), p. 12. Quoted in H. Wallace, W. Wallace, and C. Webb, *Policy Making in the European Communities* (London: John Wiley & Sons, 1977), p. 130.

61. See, for example, the Klepsch Report to the European Parliament, published under the title *Two-Way Street, U.S.-Europe Arms Procurement* (London: Brasseys, 1979).

62. Quoted in Stephen Kirby, "The Independent European Programme Group: The Failure of Low-Profile High-Politics," *Journal of Common Market Studies* (Oxford, December 1979), p. 183.

63. General Cauchie to the WEU Symposium on European armaments policy. Quoted in Klepsch, op. cit., p. 33.

64. Kirby, op. cit., p. 183.

65. See Kirby, ibid, and Sir Bernard Burrows, *European Defence Cooperation: Report of a working party on the question of a European Defence Force and other possible means of European Defence Cooperation* (London: Federal Trust, 1979).

66. Burrows, ibid, p. 7.

67. Klepsch, op. cit., p. 43.

68. *Financial Times,* March 22, 1979.

69. Schumacher, op. cit.

70. Ibid.

71. J. Baranson, *Technology and the Multinationals: Corporate Strategies in a Changing World Economy* (Lexington, Mass.: Lexington Books, 1978), pp. 23–29.

72. For a complete list of major subcontractors, see *Aviation Week and Space Technology* (New York), November 12, 1979.

73. Klepsch, op. cit., p. 40.

74. *The Economist,* January 12, 1980.

75. As cited in Klepsch, op. cit., p. 36.

76. The study was prepared by the U.S. firm of T. M. Abrams and Assocs. for the ICAO, reported in *Financial Times,* June 4, 1979.

77. Quoted in Kaldor, op. cit., p. 30.

78. *Aviation Week and Space Technology* (London), October 22, 1979.

79. Baranson, op. cit., p. 35.

5 Japanese Industrial Policy

TAKASHI HOSOMI AND ARIYOSHI OKUMURA

What Does Industrial Policy Mean to the Japanese?

THREE ASPECTS OF INDUSTRIAL POLICY

The concept of industrial policy is regarded in Japan as constructive and is well accepted as a meaningful tool for the promotion of the national economy. Japanese industrial policy thus entails two main aspects:

First, Japanese industrial policy is not confined within the concept of industrial policy usually held in the industrialized countries, i.e., public policies relating to industrial organization in each industry. Indeed, industrial policy is sometimes understood as competition-maintaining policy. The improvement of productivity in industry and the strengthening of international competitiveness are not only included within the aims of industrial policy but, more often than not, these aims are the ones most stressed. Recently, stable procurement of energy resources and the development of high technology have been added as new goals. Thus Japanese industrial policy is a positive endeavor for the active promotion of industrial development. It rarely aims to develop or redress particular sectors, but is, rather, a general system of policies aimed at industrial development and promotion.

Second, Japanese industrial policy was formed during the rapid economic expansion and industrial development of postwar Japan, and it is difficult to evaluate this policy without referring to its historical context. Also, Japanese industrial policy cannot be measured by a static standard. It is dynamic, so to establish a general formula for it is nearly impossible.

Instead of trying to make an exact definition of Japanese industrial policy, we therefore start with the three formal aspects of industrial policy usually recognized in Japan: general measures, sectoral measures, and organizational measures.

The general industrial measures are common to all Japanese industries and aim to promote Japanese industry as a whole. In practice this means, for instance, the unification of weight and measure standards into the metric system; standardization of the quality, shape, and reliability of various industrial goods and parts; standardization of the description of goods; protection of patents, designs, and brand names; and determining installment payment standards and safety standards for durable goods.

Sectoral measures foster or promote individual industrial sectors and aim to upgrade the domestic structure of industries, promote their productivity, and expand employment opportunities. Examples include the modernization plans for the steel industry, a series of measures for the promotion of the machinery industry, import restrictions on computers to buy time for domestic technological development, and the rationalization plan for restructuring the textile industry. The principal measures are low-interest loans from governmental financial institutions based upon special legislation, acceleration of technology imports, subsidies to new technological developments, and accelerated depreciation allowances.

Organizational policy aims to maintain effective competition in particular sectors, and hence industrial vitality and higher productivity. Concrete measures include (a) eliminating any monopoly positions and unfair transactions in accordance with the Anti-Trust Law, and regulating bigger companies so that they do not sprawl into the area of small and medium-sized firms, (b) low-interest finance by governmental financial institutions specializing in loans to small and medium-sized firms, in order to strengthen the viability of those companies, and (c) several taxation measures to help smaller firms.

TOOLS TO CARRY OUT INDUSTRIAL POLICY: DIRECT AND INDIRECT

Two kinds of measures can be used in industrial policy: direct and compulsory measures to regulate industry performance by law, and indirect measures to encourage industries by financial incentives or official persuasion. Direct measures could be various controls, such as the allocation of important goods and funds (especially foreign currency and resources), the admission or prohibition of new business entries into specific sectors of industry, import or export restrictions, regulations on the borrowing of foreign funds, or instructions and orders for collective actions to regulate the levels of equipment investment.

Indirect measures have two aspects. Lower-interest and longer-term funds through governmental financial institutions, as well as special depreciation allowances and subsidies, produce strong income effects for the firms and thus can encourage industries to move in a desired direction. The other aspect is a kind of governmental persuasion, which should be in line with a national policy goal as well as the direction of public opinion. This is often described as "administrative guidance" and is well known and even notorious abroad.

Direct measures have had an element of protectionism, but they have gradually been reduced as the economy became stronger. The effectiveness of indirect measures such as government financial incentives has also been somewhat reduced, because firms have improved their financial positions by increasing cash flow.

History of Japanese Industrial Policy: Four Periods

What role was played by industrial policy in the course of Japan's economic development? As shown in Table 5.1, the period since the end of World War II may be conveniently divided into four ten-year subperiods. The first, from 1946 through 1955, is the post-World War II restoration period. The second, from 1956 through 1965, is the industrial up-grading period. The third, from 1966 through 1975, can be called the transition period to liberalization. And the period from 1976 to the present may be referred to as the internationalization period.

POST-WORLD WAR II RESTORATION: RECOVERY FROM RUINS (1946-55)

Increased production the main goal (1946-50). Much of the Japanese economy was destroyed during World War II. Japan lost all her overseas colonies, and by 1946 her population had increased by about one million people who had returned from former colonies. In addition, industrial facilities suffered severe damage.

Table 5.2 shows that Japan lost 25 percent of her total national wealth because of the war. In particular, one-fourth of the total production goods was destroyed, which included a 34 percent loss of industrial machinery and tools. Losses of consumer goods such as furniture and fittings came to 25 percent, and 81 percent of all shipping was destroyed.

In addition, other factors, such as a dispersion of engineers and skilled labor and a shortage of raw materials and capital funds, resulted in a drop in economic activity in 1946 to the lowest level for many years, as is shown in Chart 5.1. Industrial production in that year shrank to only 20 percent of the peak wartime level, which had been attained in 1944. Basic industries, such as iron and steel, nonferrous metals, coal, chemicals, electricity, and machinery, were among those that experienced a severe decrease in production. For example, electric power generation dropped by 27 billion kwh, against a peak of 35 billion kwh in 1944, and the production of coal fell from 56 million tons in 1941 to only 20 million tons.

In order to augment production capacity in these circumstances, the *Adjustment of the Supply and Demand of Goods Temporary Act*, a powerful law giving the government the authority to allocate important goods, was enacted. To restore the economy, necessary resources were directed preferentially to five industries: coal, iron and steel, marine transportation, chemical fertilizers, and electricity. Mostly to cope with this situation, the government established the Reconstruction Finance Bank, which at its peak supplied 25 percent of all industrial funds.

Toward an industrialized country (1951-55). The industries gradually installed more efficient equipment, modernized, and introduced a system of production control and advanced technology with a view to catching up with the advanced industrial nations. Manufacturing costs began to be reduced. The most-urgent issues were to improve industrial standards, on one hand, and to find measures to expedite capital formation in the private sector, on the other.

The *Industrial Rationalization Council*, an umbrella body with a number of subcommittees, was established as an advisory organ under the Ministry of International Trade and Industry (MITI) to produce a consensus among the government, private industry, and labor with regard to measures to be taken. The Council contained knowledgeable people from industry, trade unions, and academic circles. As a result, several targets were set up and authorized: (a) the adoption of more-efficient production equipment, (b) an increase in production capacity, (c) promotion of exports, (d) the development of modern industrial technologies, and (e) the strengthening of small and medium-sized firms.

One can conclude that this Council brought forth a kind of loose participation by the private sector in governmental policy formation, i.e., by transmitting the opinions of the private sector to the government before the official formulation

Table 5.1 Japanese Industrial Policy since 1946

Industrial Policy	Restoration period after World War II (1946–55)		Internal consummation period (1956–65)	
	Recovery from war damage (1946–50)	Adjustment of system (1951–55)	Promotion of priority industries (1956–60)	Enriching business power (1961–65)
Economic phenomena	IIP dropped to 20% of 1944 level	Serious shortage of foreign currency ($200–300 million US)	Annual growth rate of GNP is 7.4%	9.7% (higher economic growth). Foreign currency reserves, $180 mil. Surplus trend of trade balance. Sharp increase in CPI, 6% and over.
Problems in private sector	Shortage of production capacity, raw materials and funds / Prevention of import and foreign funds / Amelioration of the quality of products		Relative shortage of funds / Dual structure / Belated start in technology	Scale merit / Strengthen an international competitiveness
Trump cards in policy execution	Raw materials quota → (abolishment of the Adjustment of the Supply and Demand of Good Temporary Act) / Appropriation of government funds. / Foreign exchange allocation (import permission) / Prevention of import and foreign funds		(Amplification of private funds and strengthened business power)	
Basic policy	Maintenance of production / Financial complement / Prevention of imports, restriction on foreign funds, foreign currency control / Adjustment of basic resources / Acquisition of foreign currency, import substitution / Adjustment of quality and standard		Unification of quality and standard / Acquisition of foreign currency and intensification of competitiveness / Adjustment and development of technology	
Structural policy	Promotion of industrial rationalization / Preference policy for certain industries		Fostering industries for strengthening competitiveness / Quality improvement and funds / Efficient utilization of goods / Adjustment of key industries / Amelioration of structure	
Organizational policy	Weakening industries / Strengthening industries		Amelioration of dual structure	

	Transition Period to Open Market System (1966–75)		Internationalization (1976–)
	Reorganization under scale merit (1966–70)	Turning point of industrial policy (1971–75)	Groping years (1976–)
Economic phenomena	Annual growth rate of GNP, 12.4% / Annual growth rate of IIP, 15.1% (scale merit)	GNP, 5.1% / Foreign currency reserves, $16.7 billion (in 1971) / Rapid rise in CPI	GNP, 5.7% / Foreign currency reserves, $29.2 billion
Problems in private sector	Increase in prices / Problems of pollution, etc. / Inquietude in energy supply	Countermeasures to appreciation of yen's value / Increasing unemployment	Trade conflict / Depression, increasing unemployment
Trump cards in policy execution	1st liberalization of capital / Liberalization of technological introduction	Allocation of oil / Mass media / (Abolition of foreign currency concentration system)	(entire liberalization of foreign funds)
Basic policy (Industrial Policy)	Prevention of nuisance / Protection of consumption basis / Procurement of energy		Supervision of import / Revision of the Foreign Exchange Control Act / Protection of consumption basis / Development of energy
Structural policy	Shift from quantity to quality / Promotion of knowledge-intensive course / Intensive research and development / High-degree assembly / Fashion / Knowlege industry		Measures to counter depression and unemployment
Organizational policy	Promotion of reorganization / Restriction of entry by large companies into the fields in which small and medium-sized companies are already active.	Placing of public sector contracts with small and medium-sized companies and securing employment.	

Table 5.2   Damage Caused in Japan by World War II

Damage to national wealth (at prices at war's end)

	Damage (¥ billion)	Ratio of damage (percentages)	Remaining national wealth at war's end (¥ billion)
Total of national wealth to be considered as assets	65.8	25	188.9
Production goods of which	19.8	25	59.7
Industrial machinery and tools	8.0	34	15.4
Equipment for electricity and gas	1.6	11	13.3
Consumer goods of which	34.8	25	105.9
Furniture and fittings	17.5	21	63.4
Transportation goods of which	9.6	29	23.3
Ships	7.4	81	1.8
Buildings of which	22.2	25	68.2
Houses and stores	10.3		
Forests, roads, historic relics	1.0	–	–
Warships, airplanes	40.4	100	–
Grand total	105.7	36	188.9

Number of buildings destroyed (in thousands)

	All country	All cities
Entirely burned	2,188	2,119
Entirely destroyed	64	55
Half-burned	49	39
Half-destroyed	61	51
Total	2,362	2,264

Source: Tatsuro Uchino, *Postwar History of Japanese Economy* (Tokyo: Kodan-sha, 1978).

Chart 5.1   Recovery of Industrial Production

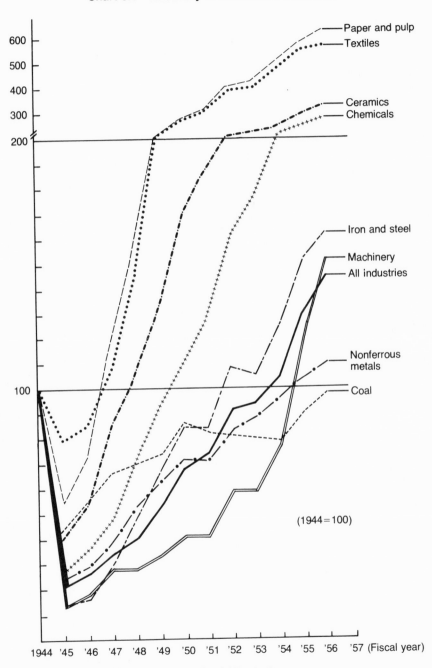

Source: General Survey on Index of Industrial Production,
Ministry of International Trade and Industry.

of any major industrial policies. This practice has smoothed the way for mutual understanding between the government and industry, industry and labor, and within the various industrial sectors. (The Industrial Rationalization Council in 1964 became the *Industrial Structure Council.*)

A most-important measure adopted during those early times was the *Industrial Standardization Act*, enacted in 1949. The *Measures Act* was next established to require compulsory use of the metric system rather than the various traditional Japanese units of measuring. This act was aimed at helping to improve the production system as well as to facilitate the introduction of advanced technology from Europe.

Because of the shortage of foreign currencies, the *Foreign Exchange Control Act* was established in 1949 to enable the government to collect foreign currency and to impose quantitative import restrictions; and the *Foreign Investment Act* was enacted to bring the inflow and outflow of capital under the control of the government. The *Export Insurance Act* was enacted in 1950 to set up a system of insurance against risks arising with exports. To avoid unstable export transactions, the *Export Transaction Act*, which allowed the government to permit the formation of export cartels, was enacted in 1952.

Tax incentives were introduced and governmental long-term credit institutions were established to encourage industrialization with adequate capital supply. The former allowed special depreciation of machinery and equipment to facilitate rationalization, and eliminated import duties on important items of machinery. Among the institutions established were the *Japan Development Bank* and the *Export-Import Bank of Japan.* This ensured a stable supply of long-term loans at reduced interest rates.

Table 5.3 shows the value of tax reductions granted to firms by the *Special Measures for Tax Exemption*, compared with the firms' internally generated funds. The tax benefits amounted to a total of 109 billion yen in the period 1951–55, made up of 47 billion yen for technological improvements and modernization of equipment and 62 billion yen for strengthening the financial standing of firms. On the other hand, the funds on hand generated by firms through retained earnings and depreciation totaled 2,929 billion yen. The contribution of tax reductions to total funds was more important during this period than subsequently.

There were clear rules for designating the firms that would benefit from tax exemption or long-term loans at low rates. The procedure was that the government made recommendations on the basis of discussions held at the Industrial Rationalization Council; the criterion for selection was the degree of contribution to the rationalization of Japanese industries. Neither arbitrary judgment by the government nor individual judgment by private firms was sufficient.

The roles played by governmental institutions such as the Japan Development Bank and the Export-Import Bank of Japan are shown in Table 5.4. The net borrowings from governmental financial institutions in the period from 1951 to 1955 amounted to 490 billion yen, while total net supply of industrial funds, both internal and external, was 7,103 billion yen. Governmental funds accounted for 7 percent, surpassing the figure realized through tax reductions. On the other hand, funds obtained from private financial institutions were much greater, at 43 percent.

Table 5.3 Tax Reduction for Private Companies by the Special Taxation Measures (average fiscal year in ¥100 million)

Purpose	FY1946-50	1951-55	1956-60	1961-65	1966-70	1971-75	1976-77
To prevent pollution	—	—	—	—	62	2,064	610
To stimulate technological development and modernize equipment	5	466	1,018	1,424	1,798	4,915	1,930
experiment and research expenses	—	—	46	183	462	864	310
overseas income earned by technological export, etc.	—	122	460	548	198	362	200
reserve for loss from reverse repurchasing of computers	—	—	—	—	94	321	80
reserve for modernization of small and medium enterprises	—	—	—	209	323	2,432	1,040
To strengthen corporate finances	—	623	752	1,301	3,285	3,792	1,340
reserve for loss from overseas market development	—	—	—	234	475	439	200
reserve for lending loss	—	—	—	—	352	226	140
Total amount (A)	5	1,089	1,770	2,725	5,145	10,771	3,880
Companies' own retained earnings and depreciation (B)	6,581	29,293	73,368	174,166	531,311	958,733	472,366
Ratio of tax reduction to own capital of companies (A ÷ B) (percentage)	0	3.7	2.4	1.6	1.0	1.1	0.8

Source: A figures derived from Ministry of Finance, *Decrease by Item in Tax Revenue Amount Caused by the Special Taxation Measures* (average fiscal year) (Tokyo: 1946–77, annually). B figures derived from Economic Planning Agency, *National Income Statistics* (Tokyo: 1952–77, annually).

Table 5.4   Net Supply of Industrial Funds (increase and decrease)

	1946-50		1951-55		1956-60	
	R(%)	A	R(%)	A	R(%)	A
External funds						
Direct						
Stocks and shares	9 (13)	2,133	8 (15)	6,058	8 (14)	15,377
Industrial bonds	2 (4)	575	2 (4)	1,581	3 (6)	6,828
Subtotal	11 (17)	2,708	10 (18)	7,639	11 (20)	21,205
Indirect						
Private finance	51 (72)	11,841	43 (73)	30,568	42 (71)	76,344
Government finance	5 (8)	1,316	7 (12)	4,900	4 (8)	8,237
Subtotal	57 (80)	13,157	49 (85)	35,468	46 (79)	84,581
Foreign funds	2 (3)	523	−1 −(3)	−1,373	1 (1)	1,308
Total	71(100)	16,383	58(100)	41,734	58(100)	107,518
Internal funds						
Retained profits	10	2,301	17	12,237	17	31,103
Depreciation	18	4,280	24	17,056	23	42,265
Total	28	6,581	41	29,293	40	73,368
Grand total	100	22,967	100	71,025	100	180,886

A = amount in ¥100 million; R = component proportion ratio, in percentage.

Source: External funds: The Bank of Japan, *Economic Statistics Annual* (Tokyo, 1946-77, annually). Internal funds: Economic Planning Agency, *National Income Statistics* (Tokyo, 1952-77, annually).

As for realignment of the industrial structure, the *Counter-Concentration of Excessive Economic Power Act* (1947) and *Anti-Trust Act* (1947) that had been established immediately after World War II were revised so that equal emphasis was placed on the strengthening of the financial standing of firms and the dispersion of their excessive power. The Acts, originally formed in the American mold, were revised because their emphasis on the division of corporate activities was deemed unsuitable to Japanese circumstances.

The Anti-Trust Act was revised three times in the six years following its enactment in 1947. Collective activities such as rationalization cartels and recession cartels gradually came to be permitted. Nevertheless, it should not be presumed that the idea of prohibiting unfair trade became less strong.

When the productive performance of Japan almost surpassed that of the wartime peak, a government White Paper published in 1955 made the symbolic statement that "Japan is no longer in the Postwar Period." The *Adjustment of the Supply and Demand of Goods Temporary Act*, which immediately after World

Table 5.4 (Continued)

1961–65		1966–70		1971–75		1976–77		
R(%)	A	R(%)	A	R(%)	A	R(%)	A	
7 (13)	32,782	3 (7)	29,822	3 (6)	54,697	2 (6)	19,905	
2 (4)	8,934	1 (3)	13,679	2 (4)	37,413	2 (4)	14,156	
9 (17)	41,716	4 (10)	43,507	5 (9)	92,110	4 (10)	34,061	
44 (74)	183,753	37 (81)	364,735	41 (80)	783,194	31 (76)	251,229	
4 (7)	17,649	4 (9)	40,126	4 (9)	85,636	5 (12)	41,490	
47 (82)	201,402	41 (89)	404,861	45 (90)	868,830	36 (89)	292,719	
1 (2)	3,874	0 (1)	4,071	0 (1)	9,643	0 (1)	3,756	
58(100)	246,992	46(100)	452,451	50(100)	970,592	41(100)	330,540	
13	57,169	25	245,447	19	364,894	19	152,079	
27	116,997	29	285,864	31	593,839	40	320,287	
41	174,166	54	531,311	50	958,733	59	472,366	
100	421,156	100	983,726	100	1,929,325	100	802,906	

War II had given the government its power to allocate key industrial goods, was abolished in 1952.

The industrial policies of the first period, directed particularly at the recovery of productive capacity, were carried out by the government's strong administrative power through which it could control a firm's operational policies directly, i.e., by allocating materials and commodities used for industrial production or by granting import licences to machinery importers. This policy was supported by public opinion and was therefore smoothly carried out.

Even during such a period, however, some differences of opinion arose between the government and private firms. For example, a plan by Kawasaki Steel Corporation to enlarge a steel mill in Chiba prefecture was assessed by the government to be on an excessively large scale in relation to the government's estimate of future steel demand. But Kawasaki Steel did not accept the official forecast and carried out the investment as they originally intended. Fortunately the judgment of Kawasaki Steel proved to be right, thanks to a rapid expansion of steel consumption. This became a famous example of Japanese entrepreneurship.

INDUSTRIAL UP-GRADING, ADVANCEMENT OF INDUSTRIAL INDEPENDENCE (1956–65)

Efforts for economic independence (1956–60). The basic nature of economic and industrial policy at this time was to achieve independence and secure steady economic growth by bringing about an expansion of the domestic and export markets. To catch up with the advanced industrial countries, policies were formulated so that Japanese industry, by improving the quality of goods and lowering production costs, could become more competitive. To this end there was an active policy for the import of machinery.

The Japanese government also favored the principle of maximizing economic growth through expanding industrial demand in the domestic market. This was achieved by fostering those strategic industries, such as iron and steel, petrochemicals, automobiles, and machinery, which have a major expansionary effort on industrial activity as a whole.

The government took other measures, such as preferential loans for equipment investment through governmental financial institutions, tax exemptions for importing particularly essential machinery, and special depreciation allowances. In some cases, collective action by firms was authorized in order to improve the unification of standards and quality. For these purposes, several pieces of industrial legislation were introduced, but the prior discussions in the Industrial Rationalization Council were always important. The *Machinery Industry Development (Temporary Provision) Act*, the *Electronics Industry Development (Temporary Provision) Act*, the *Aircraft Industry Development (Temporary Provision) Act*, and the *Japan Synthetic Rubber Company Ltd. Act* were the important bills enacted during this period to help develop strategic industrial sectors.

In addition, medium-term promotion programs for major industries were prepared, such as the streamlining program for the iron and steel industry and the promotional measures for the petrochemical industry. These programs were based on the consensus reached in the Industrial Rationalization Council on the supply-demand outlook for the medium term; on goals such as the necessary level of equipment investment, the optimum production capacity, and targets of cost reduction; and on the principles of provision for preferential loans by governmental financial institutions or other advantageous fiscal measures such as special depreciation. In order to promote standardization and unification of industrial machinery parts, a collective action suppressing outsiders was permitted. As a result, costs of machinery parts decreased substantially and production efficiency was greatly improved.

As the need grew for the introduction of technology from abroad, controversy arose about the protection of industrial proprietary rights by law. In 1959, the *Patents Act*, the *Practical Novelty Act*, the *Designs Act*, the *Trade Mark Act*, etc., were enacted, and thus the measures to protect the ownership of industrial technology were established.

As is shown in Table 5.5, there were 831 cases of the introduction of technology from 1956 through 1960. This was a sharp increase compared with the 598 cases in

Table 5.5 Introduction of Technology by Industry (in numbers of authorized cases)

	1951–55	1956–60	1961–65	1966–70	1971–75	1976
Heavy and chemical industries						
Chemical products	91	163	283	834	974	150
Petrochemical, plant-engineering	–	29	39	75	85	9
Petroleum, coal	18	22	17	103	202	14
Iron and steel, nonferrous metals	40	59	110	200	206	20
Metal products	8	33	66	153	238	44
Industrial machinery	105	170	649	1,220	1,951	352
Transportation machinery	46	44	109	247	436	77
Precision machinery	2	8	78	127	279	73
Electrical machinery	121	198	469	751	1,303	231
Subtotal	431	721	1,820	3,710	5,674	970
Light industries						
Food and tobacco	–	5	19	65	269	36
Textile and textile products	25	40	89	261	862	196
Ceramics, store and clay products	9	15	45	118	184	19
Plastic products	1	12	100	192	344	28
Other products	21	32	78	165	870	156
Subtotal	56	104	331	1,001	2,529	435
Methods of construction	11	5	27	34	147	27
Others	–	1	6	39	18	29
Total	498	831	2,184	4,784	8,368	1,461

Source: Science and Technology Agency, *Annual Report on the Introduction of Overseas Technology* (Tokyo: 1951–76)

the five previous years. The petrochemical, industrial machinery, and electrical machinery sectors were particularly active in introducing such technologies.

With the growth of exports, many inferior articles, imitation goods, or goods similar in appearance to the quality brands came on the export market, which would have undermined confidence in Japanese products overseas. In order to avoid this, the *Export Inspection Act*, which subjected export articles to quality inspection, was enacted in 1957. In addition, the *Export Designs Act* was enacted to prevent loss of confidence caused by imitation goods. The *Japan External Trade Organization (JETRO)* was also established, to collect trade information and promote and publicize Japanese goods overseas.

The Foreign Exchange Control Act of 1949 had been based upon the principle of permitting the import of industrial goods that did not disturb the promotion of key domestic industries, although its basic formula was a fundamental prohibition of imports; and the basic aim of the 1949 Foreign Investment Act was to restrict the investment of foreign capital in Japan, which would have hindered the growth of indigenous industries. Thus, strategic but infant industries – iron and steel, petrochemicals, automobiles, and computers – were given appropriate time for their development.

But industries cannot be expected to develop simply by being fostered and by being given time. During this period, each industry, with a positive, energetic equipment investment program and technological import as well as development, made voluntary efforts to catch up with advanced Western standards; and the basic drive for this active performance was a strong managerial competition among those corporations concerned. It is important to note that this peculiar combination of protection and competition was the basic feature of the Japanese style of industrial development, and that this may be possible only in a high growth economy.

The funds for these equipment investments came mainly from private sources, and the contribution of governmental financial institutions was quantitatively marginal. As shown in Table 5.4, the supply of industrial funds for the five years from 1956 through 1960 amounted to 18,089 billion yen. Forty percent of the funds were generated by firms internally, and the remaining 60 percent came from external sources. The major portion of the external funds was supplied by private financial institutions; in contrast, governmental financial institutions supplied only 4 percent of total funds. The share from governmental financial institutions was reduced by almost half in those five years from the 7 percent contribution of the 1951-55 period.

Industrial policy for internationalization: a turning point (1961-65). As is shown in Table 5.6, industrial production increased by approximately 20 percent per year in such industries as iron and steel, petroleum products, aluminium, synthetic fibers, textiles, and cement. Production of items such as automobiles and television sets increased even faster. Expansion of domestic demand resulted in the reduction of unit costs, and thus exports of television sets and steel grew steadily. Consequently, the Japanese surplus on current account became stable, and foreign currency reserves increased from $0.7 billion in 1956 to almost $2 billion in 1960.

The USA and European countries, which had already been liberalizing trade

Table 5.6 Development of Major Industries (changes in production)

Industry	Unit	1955	1960	1965	1970	1975	1979	Average annual growth rate (%)				
								1955–60	1960–65	1965–70	1970–75	1975–79
Electric power	billion kwh	65.2	97.7	161.0	283.5	374.3	474.5	8.4	10.5	12.0	5.7	6.1
Petroleum products (sales of)	million kl	10	27	79	186	215	243	22.0	23.9	18.7	2.9	3.1
Crude steel	million tons	9.4	22.1	41.2	93.3	102.3	111.8	18.7	13.2	17.8	1.9	2.3
Aluminum	thousand tons	57.5	131	292	728	1,103	1,010	17.9	17.4	20.0	6.8	-0.1
Television	thousand sets	137	3,578	4,190	13,781	12,453	14,238	92.0	3.2	26.9	-2.0	3.4
Four-wheel car	thousand cars	69	482	1,876	5,289	6,942	10,038	47.5	31.2	23.0	5.6	9.7
of which Passenger car	thousand cars	20	165	696	3,179	4,568	6,476	52.5	33.4	35.5	7.5	9.1
Textile	million cubic meters	4,477	6,173	6,607	7,750	5,955	6,757	6.6	1.4	3.2	-5.1	3.2
of which Synthetic fiber textile	thousand cubic meters	54	424	1,241	2,746	2,411	2,981	51.0	24.3	17.2	-2.6	5.5
Cement	million tons	10.5	22.4	32.2	56.5	65.2	87.1	16.3	7.5	11.9	7.9	7.5

Source: MITI, Dynamic Statistics of Production (Tokyo, each year cited).

and foreign exchange transactions, requested that Japan liberalize its market, since Japanese industries no longer needed to be protected. As a matter of fact, the Japanese began to realize the various advantages in liberalization, namely (a) that industrial competitiveness should be strengthened, and (b) that the industrial structure should be up-graded and the efficiency of the national economy increased through the functioning of the market principle. Liberalization was also a must for an advanced industrial country. Eventually, fundamental principles for the liberalization policy were decided by the cabinet in 1960.

The problem with which industry was confronted during this period was how to modernize and enlarge its production facilities to cope with the expansion of demand both at home and abroad. Fortunately, the modernization and the scaling up were successfully attained, and industrial competitiveness was greatly strengthened.

Mergers among industrial firms were also expedited. As shown in Table 5.7, the number of corporate mergers in manufacturing industries amounted to 1,700, twice as many as in the previous period. Amalgamations took place among the producers of industrial materials, such as chemicals, petroleum, coal, and metals, and in the capital goods industries, such as machinery. These mergers were made by the autonomous judgment of individual companies, based on economic rationality. This is one of the ways in which the private sector responded to the liberalization policy.

There were four aspects of industrial policy during this period.

1. *To carry out smoothly the liberalization of trade and the introduction of foreign investment*, in 1962 the concept of import policy was converted from prohibitive in principle to permissive in principle. In accordance with the policy change, the foreign currency budget system was abolished. The liberalization rate reached 93 percent in 1964, as measured by the OEEC method (imports in 1959 of items liberalized by 1964 divided by total imports in 1959).

In the same year, 1962, Japan joined OECD and adopted the full liberalization obligations under Article 8 of the Interational Monetary Fund (IMF). As a result, in addition to the liberalization of imports, Japan was obliged to fix a schedule for the regulation of foreign investments in Japan. At the same time, the government suspended its authority for foreign currency allocation, which had proved a core measure in carrying out the industrial policy effectively.

2. *To develop further the level of technology*, in 1961 the *Research Association of Mining and Manufacturing Technology Act* was passed. Its enactment resulted from the wish of enterprises to avoid the unnecessary duplication of funds and scientists that would occur if research activities were carried on by each enterprise separately. Cooperative research in frontier technologies was promoted by this law, which gave tax benefits to enterprises that organized such an association. The most-notable successful association was the one for the development of computer technology, whereby the VLSI Research Association carried out its activities from 1976 to 1980. There were, however, many occasions when research associations failed to produce results. The difficulties generally arose from conflicts of interest among enterprises, and these tended to become more divisive as the technology became more sophisticated.

The smaller contribution of the Japanese government in funding research and development than of the governments in other advanced industrial countries

Table 5.7 Corporate Amalgamation by Industry (number of cases admitted)

fiscal year	1950	1951–55	1956–60	1961–65	1966–70	1971–75	1976	1977
Agriculture, forestry, and fishery industry	11	18	22	36	62	55	4	8
Secondary industry								
Mining industry	8	30	29	57	37	60	8	9
Construction industry	10	70	82	194	270	398	79	74
Manufacturing industry	244	860	842	1,662	1,816	1,548	267	286
Textiles	56	158	113	181	227	198	30	44
Wood and wood products	5	56	54	84	132	110	23	22
Paper and pulp	–	–	4	47	43	49	13	8
Chemicals, petroleum, and coal	54	146	96	173	186	142	16	16
Ceramics, stone and clay products	20	41	32	66	111	106	13	16
Metals	23	92	81	217	250	285	36	41
Foodstuffs	34	148	158	188	266	160	39	23
Publication and printing	21	36	47	63	89	74	17	12
Rubber and leather	–	–	1	32	25	35	2	4
Machinery	31	161	206	443	420	382	60	83
Other manufacturing	0	22	50	68	67	67	18	17
Tertiary industry								
Wholesale and retail industry	94	456	565	1,073	1,584	1,759	319	407
Finance and insurance	8	45	57	60	72	71	18	12
Real estate	5	35	75	229	387	486	96	77
Transportation and communication	24	113	188	368	496	407	61	52
Warehousing business	5	15	13	}24	5	8	2	1
Electricity and gas	0	1	4	7	5	8	2	1
Services	7	66	107	295	456	535	82	85
Others	4	14	29	56	11	15	1	0
Primary industry (total)	11	18	22	36	62	55	4	8
Secondary industry (total)	262	960	953	1,913	2,123	2,006	354	369
Tertiary industry (total)	147	445	1,038	2,112	3,011	3,281	579	634
Total	420	1,723	2,013	4,061	5,196	5,342	941	1,011

Source: 1950–75: Fair Trade Commission, 30 Year History of Anti-Trust Policy (Tokyo). 1976–77: Fair Trade Commission, Annual Report, 1977 (Tokyo).

Chart 5.2 Government and Private Sector Shares of Research Expenditure

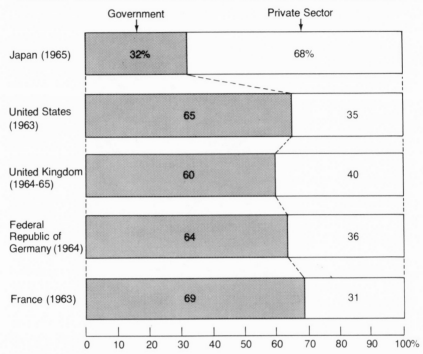

Source: Science and Technology Agency, "Science and Technology Annual Report."

caused the private sector to be particularly active in technological development. For example, government funds as a proportion of total spending on research and development amounted to 65 percent in the USA (1963), 60 percent in the UK (1964–65), 69 percent in France (1963), and 64 percent in West Germany (1964), while that of Japan was only 32 percent (1965) (see Chart 5.2).

3. *To ameliorate the dual structure of the economy* — the gap between the sector of large enterprises and that of small and medium-sized enterprises. To establish basic measures to be taken by the government in favor of the smaller enterprises, the 1962 *Small and Medium-Sized Enterprises Modernization Promotion Act* was passed to provide technology, governmental funds, and preferential tax treatment to help modernize them. The *Small Business Finance Corporation*, already established in 1953, was strengthened, and preferential tax measures for small and medium-sized enterprises were introduced.

As shown in Table 5.8, the amount of loans and discounts outstanding by government financial institutions to small and medium-sized enterprises increased from 312 billion yen in 1961 to 806 billion yen in 1965. Tax saving by means of the *Overseas Market Development Reserve for Small and Medium-Sized Enterprises* amounted to 23 billion yen during the period. The growing importance of smaller firms since 1960 is shown in Table 5.9.

4. *To foster and expedite the development of strategic but infant sectors of industry.* To cope with a ten-year forecast of industrial structure outlined in the *Doubling National Income Plan* in 1960, MITI asked the Industrial Rationalization Council to study the details of future industrial structure. The Council's advisory committee concluded that the scale of production was not yet satisfactory and that excessive competition among enterprises tended to bring about overlapping investments and to undermine the effectiveness of industrial performance. The advisory committee then recommended a closer cooperation between the government and industries so that the industries could be better prepared for liberalization by excluding any inefficiency.

Then the government proposed *Extraordinary Measures for Promotion of Specified Industries* in 1962. The proposed measures would define, under the guidance of the government, the objectives for the establishment of internationally competitive production facilities for iron and steel, automobiles, petrochemicals, and other strategic industries to be designated by the government. These included a proposal for the government virtually to control the supply of funds—private as well as public. This proposal caused a severe reaction in industrial and financial circles, which opposed stronger governmental intervention. Consequently, the Extraordinary Measures for Promotion of Specified Industries was not enacted. The government did not give up its bill and laid it before the Diet three times in the two years from 1962–63, but in vain.

This failure on the part of the government may be seen as a turning point in postwar industrial policy. As long as industrial policy is attuned to the needs of the private sector and expected to function as a useful catalyst for them, it should work effectively and acceptably. But the Japanese private sector is alert to detect whether industrial policy threatens to exceed its normative bounds. That the proposed bill was not enacted seemed to reflect this important aspect of Japanese industrial policy.

The government later established a series of Government and Industry Joint Forums on an ad hoc basis for several industrial sectors, such as synthetic fibers, petrochemicals, pulp and paper, and ferro-alloys, where they discussed new plant and equipment investments. But it is not possible to say how far these meetings influenced the adjustment of capacity, in comparison with market principles in a time of steadily growing demand.

In a few cases, government and industries had conflicts of opinion. In 1965 Sumitomo Metal Industries, Ltd., like Kawasaki in the previous decade, took a different view from MITI on the outlook for crude steel demand and proceeded with its own production plan against MITI's opposition. It took a long time for mutual understanding and trust between MITI and the company to be restored. This case demonstrates an essential aspect of consensus formation: without compromise by either the government or industries, no consensus was ever produced.

TRANSITION TO LIBERALIZATION, PURSUIT OF SCALE MERIT (1966–75)

Industrial reorganization period (1966–70). GNP in real terms grew at the high rate of 12 percent annually, and industrial production increased at the rate of 15 percent annually during this period. The domestic market continued to expand for every industry, cost-competitiveness improved, and exports grew steadily.

Table 5.8 Changes in Outstanding Loans and Discounts for Small and Medium Enterprises

		Fiscal Years										
	1955		1956–60		1961–65		1966–70		1971–75		1976–77	
	R	A	R	A	R	A	R	A	R	A	R	A
Banking accounts of all banks	(59%)	1,173	(55%)	1,994	(46%)	4,288	(45%)	10,041	(46%)	26,981	(47%)	45,596
Trust accounts of all banks	(1)	26	(1)	44	(1)	99	(1)	322	(3)	1,554	(3)	3,396
Private financial institutions	(32)	633	(35)	1,243	(44)	4,118	(44)	9,935	(42)	24,728	(40)	38,588
Government financial institutions	(8)	157	(9)	312	(9)	806	(9)	2,100	(10)	5,805	(10)	10,098
Total	(100)	1,989	(100)	3,593	(100)	9,311	(100)	22,398	(100)	59,068	(100)	97,628

A = amount in ¥ billion; R = component proportion ratio, in percentage.

Source: Small and Medium Enterprises Agency, *Small and Medium Enterprises Annual Report* (Tokyo).

This led to a regular surplus in the balance of trade, and foreign currency reserves increased from over $2 billion in 1966 to nearly $5 billion in 1970.

In this period, both demand and supply of industrial products grew and the balance between them remained favorable. It was a time when all goods produced were sure to be sold; forecasts of demand were often revised upward; all Japanese industries sought the benefits of large-scale production (scale merit); and industrial activities expanded exponentially. Following up the liberalization of imports, capital transactions were also liberalized, and the transition to an open market system began in earnest.

The pursuit of scale merit was accompanied by an active technology transfer from abroad. Table 5.5 shows the adoption of imported technology in this period, principally in the chemical, steel, general machinery, and electric machinery industries. The Industrial Rationalization Council was renamed the *Industrial Structure Council* in 1964. The *Capital Liberalization Sub-Committee*, a suborganization of the Industrial Structure Council, examined the necessity of mergers to gain the benefits of larger scale, and a consensus in favor of mergers was built up in the industrial world.

In 1967, Mitsubishi Heavy Industries was formed in the heavy machine and shipbuilding sectors. Prince Motor merged with Nissan Motor in the automobile industry. The following year, Oji Paper absorbed three Oji subsidiaries in the paper and pulp industry, and Nippon Steel Corporation was born with the amalgamation of Yawata Iron & Steel and Fuji Iron & Steel, which was the largest merger ever made. As Table 5.7 shows, the number of amalgamations in manufacturing industry from 1966 to 1970 was 1,816, the largest number ever recorded. Notable among them were mergers in the metal, chemical, oil, coal, and machine industries.

One of the problems for industrial policy in this period was to maintain effective competition despite the wave of amalgamations among companies. MITI dealt with the amalgamation issue flexibly, taking into consideration the need to strengthen industrial competitiveness and at the same time judging that such mergers were not jeopardizing a healthy competition among firms.

The simple aim of the postwar type of industrial policy, to foster industrial growth, was almost attained in this period. Subsequent industrial policy was gradually forced to become more complicated, owing to the new situation where public opinion was becoming rather critical of economic growth and big business and particularly environmental pollution.

With ever-increasing production capacity, air and water pollution became public issues. The number of complaints about environmental pollution lodged with governmental bodies was 20,000 in 1966, but increased by more than three times to 63,000 in 1970.

The *Prevention of Pollution Basic Act* was enacted in 1967. By 1970 such antipollution laws as the *Prevention of Noise Pollution Act,* the *Prevention of Air Pollution Act*, and the *Prevention of Water Pollution Act* were also enacted. The Prevention of Water Pollution Act in particular imposes strict responsibility on the polluter and is revolutionary because of its revision of the conventional idea of indemnity (no indemnity due without proven malfeasance) in the civil law. Each industrial firm had to install more-effective equipment for pollution control. The number of claims for damage from environmental pollution decreased from 88,000 in 1972 to 77,000 in 1975.

The government also strengthened the measures requiring business firms to fulfil their social responsibility. The *Basic Consumer Protection Act* was enacted in 1968 to control firms' activities, including such matters as the prevention of danger and insurance of accurate measurement, standards, and descriptions with a view to protection of consumers.

A more-diversified industrial policy (1970–75). In this period, each industry further improved in production scale and continued to catch up with the advanced nations. Durable consumer goods, such as color TV sets, refrigerators, and electric washing machines, appeared in almost all the households in Japan, and material consumer needs became considerably satisfied. At this stage, people's needs gradually diversified, and industrial policy had to change its goals as well as its nature. The pendulum of industrial policy was swinging from the fostering of industrial efficiency toward criteria of social welfare — for instance, through the prevention of pollution and the protection of consumers.

In 1971, the Industrial Structure Council concluded that the needs of people had progressed from the expansion of quantity into the promotion of quality of life. The emphasis of industrial policy accordingly changed from maximization of industrial growth to improvement of the quality of life by efficient use of the fruits of growth. Productivity and efficiency had earlier been the criteria by which to judge the performance of industrial policy. To these environmental criteria were now added. With the oil crisis in 1973, industrial policy confronted industry with a most-serious difficulty of a new kind. Probably the most-significant need for private business in this period was to convert soaring energy costs into higher final prices in a reasonable way and thus to prevent an unnecessary shrinkage of industrial activities. But industrial policy did not allow firms to pass on the rising oil costs into prices downstream.

The *Stabilization of National Living Temporary Act* was enacted in 1973 immediately after the oil crisis. This law gave the government, in a state of emergency, the authority to advise on and regulate the prices of essential goods, the quantity of their imports, stockpiles, and sales, and to ration these goods in order to meet vital needs. The government was also given authority to direct and restrain equipment investment. If some firms rejected the direction of the government, the government was to publish the names of these firms to invite social sanctions against them. Although it could be argued that the measure aimed only to counter the inflationary impact of imported energy prices, industry felt that this kind of enactment should be regarded as an excessive reaction, one too much in favor of a controlled economy.

The government's desire to freeze the prices of certain manufactured goods, such as oil products, was understandable, but it was always difficult how to determine at what level the prices should be fixed. Should the level be based on economic rationality or the pressure of public opinion? If the level is lower than that of economic rationality, production could shrink unreasonably and losses could mount in proportion to sales. On the other hand, demand for the low-priced products would continue to grow, and there would be no momentum for energy conservation on the part of the consumers. In fact, business sectors, and particularly the oil-related industries, suffered from the deficits caused by the rather directive price policy, and their financial structure was seriously eroded.

ADVANCED INTERNATIONALIZATION (1976 TO THE PRESENT)

By 1977, Japan had overcome the depression caused by the oil crisis, although at the expense of a serious profit squeeze in the oil-related industrial sectors and after a hiatus in policy-making because of political disorder resulting from the Lockheed incident.

Between 1976 and 1980, Japan achieved almost 6 percent annual growth of GNP, compared with the average of 2–3 percent for the Western countries. The Japanese GNP reached $900 billion and accounted for more than 10 percent of total GNP in the free world. Export competitiveness was well maintained, and foreign currency reserves neared $30 billion.

On the other hand, Japan experienced trade conflicts with the advanced countries as well as with the NICs. Then followed a sharp appreciation of the yen, and a new uncertainty as to the future of energy supplies. These factors led to new complications for industrial policy.

First, trade conflict has become a political issue, particularly in the fields of color TV, integrated circuits, audio sets, and automobiles, where the Japanese industries have comparative advantages over their counterparts in importing countries. Therefore, the role of industrial diplomacy has been expanding to solve these problems.

Second, several sectors of industry, such as textiles and shipbuilding, were forced to realign their capacity owing to (a) the challenge from the NICs, (b) continued wage increases, and (c) the loss of competitiveness caused by the appreciation of the yen. These sectors will in the long run be obliged to advance to more specialization in higher value added products or to a thorough rationalization by further reducing the labor element. In both cases, government intervention will be needed to expedite the realignment.

Third, industrial diplomacy is ever more necessary in the field of energy imports. Approximately 70 percent of oil supplies were procured historically through "the majors," but it is no longer rare for the government to establish direct relations with the governments of oil-producing countries to purchase the oil. Oil procurement has become politicized, and industrial policy is no longer effective unless a diplomatic effort is built into it.

The Role of Industrial Policy

INDUSTRIAL POLICY AS CATALYST

No matter how elaborate the industrial policies were, the motive force of the development of the Japanese economy was a voluntary entrepreneurship of the private sector. That spirit stemmed from the character of Japanese culture.

The Japanese nation is uniquely homogeneous, a single ethnic group speaking the same language, in which laziness is a serious shame or even a crime to the family, the basic unit of the community, or to its modern version, the corporation. Furthermore, the Meiji Restoration and the democratizing policy after World War II have brought forth a highly flexible social structure with a unique egalitarian characteristic. The harder one tries, the higher a status can be obtained, regardless of one's family background. Ambitious parents strive for their children to acquire higher education for social reasons, and the young people themselves are equally ambitious. This kind of upward-looking momentum in the community makes possible a plentiful supply of high-quality labor. At the same time, Japanese firms practice life-time employment; and their employees, who consider the firm and themselves as a family, reciprocate by faithfulness to their companies, which they regard as the source of welfare. Also, organized labor in Japan takes the form of unions organized on a company basis. This makes possible a smooth shift of the labor force within the company according to changes in the production system caused by new investment.

The highly competitive nature of the corporate society probably is a result of (a) the relatively free rein enjoyed by the Japanese corporate executives, who are allowed to be growth-oriented since they are rather free from constraints exerted by short-term–profit-oriented shareholders because of a general and secular decline of strong individual ownership; and also of (b) a perception of shame on the part of executives who are not supposed to lose the business race in any circumstances, lest they be dropped from the comfortably established club named the corporation and from the business community as well. All the business policies, such as investment, sales expansion, and even welfare or fringe benefits to the employees, are impelled by the momentum of competition.

The egalitarian characteristic of Japanese society is also reflected in the even distribution of income among the people. This structure was well established after World War II, when a revolutionary agricultural land reform was enforced by the U.S. occupation headquarters. In addition heavy subsidies have been pumped into rice farming through a special budgetary account, primarily for political reasons, which in fact have contributed to the formation of an egalitarian economy and to the creation of huge consumer markets, particularly for durable consumer goods. As can be clearly seen in Chart 5.3, Japanese real income per head increased at the rate of more than 10 percent every year, with a substantial decrease in Engel's coefficient. The disparity in wealth has shrunk yearly. (Chart 5.4 shows 1965 distribution of income in comparison to that in the United States.) At the same time, the concentration of population into the cities and a tendency for the size of a family to shrink have brought about a more-diversified pattern of consumption.

Entrepreneurship also ensured a progressive adoption of innovations. Most of Japan's plant and equipment in 1955 had been produced before or during World War II, so the need for renewal was great. Furthermore, the steadily enlarged domestic market since the postwar recovery period necessitated an increase in production capacity. There was also a large gap in productivity, since Japan had lagged behind other industrialized nations in technological progress throughout the war and for some time after it. In these circumstances, many corporations purchased new equipment from Western advanced countries, which resulted in larger capacity and higher productivity. Such machinery had a revolutionary effect, a psychological impact upon producers that new equipment was indispensable for competition, resulting in equipment-investment fever. Significant supporting mechanisms were (a) the activities of big trading companies, which supplied information on overseas capital goods markets, acted as purchasing agents, and even gave financial assistance to the final buyers; and (b) the services of professional bankers, who offered ample funds to industry. Bank loans to companies

Chart 5.3 Income Improvement and Its Standardization in Japan
Changes in Monthly Income and Engel's Coefficient

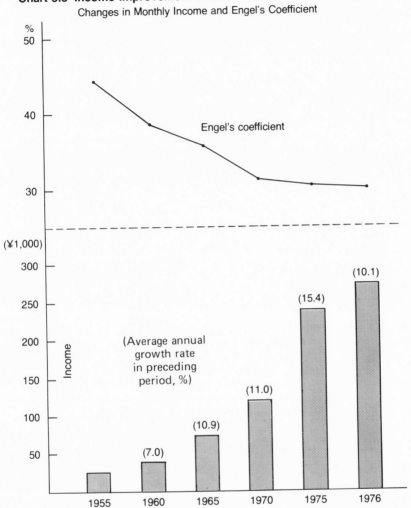

Source: Annual Reports on the Family Income and Expenditure Survey,
Office of the Prime Minister.

Chart 5.4
Comparative Income Distribution in Japan and the United States, 1965

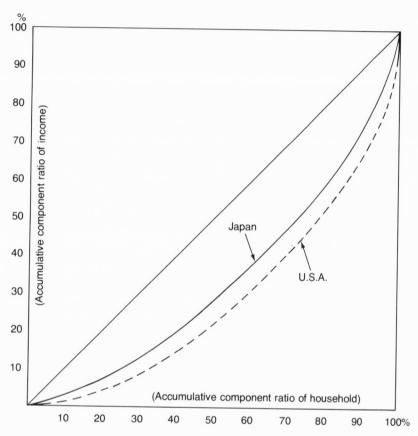

Source: Japan: Annual Reports on the Family Income and Expenditure Survey,
Office of the Prime Minister.
USA: U.S. Department of Commerce.

gave them a full leverage effect, which enabled them to enjoy an increased profit.
It is true to say that, without such strong competition among trading companies
and among banking institutions, their contribution to the expanding momentum
of industry would have been much less.

Indeed, Japan is a highly competitive society. People work for the honor of
their corporations. In such a climate, the introduction of new technological
developments induces further competition for newer technologies. This social
climate served as an important background for the voluntary development of
economic activities of individuals and firms, as well as industry as a whole.

Table 5.9   Concentration Ratio in the Major Manufacturing Industries: Share of Shipments by the Size of Establishment (in percentages)

Number of employees	1960				1970				1977			
	1-49	50-499	500-999	1,000 and more	1-49	50-499	500-999	1,000 and more	1-49	50-499	500-999	1,000 and more
Basic industries directly depending on resources												
Textiles	26	37	16	14	35	39	15	11	42	46	10	2
Wood and wood products	71	26	3	0	62	32	4	2	66	30	4	
Pulp and paper	17	43	19	21	23	45	17	15	26	45	16	14
Chemicals[a]	8	35	17	39	7	38	19	36	9	46	20	25
Petroleum, coal products[a]	5	21	42	31	5	33	63		3	34	55	9
Ceramics, stone and clay products	20	46	21	13	35	44	10	11	43	41	7	9
Iron and steel[a]	9	24	11	56	9	24	10	57	13	25	6	56
Nonferrous metals[a]	11	28	17	44	11	30	59		13	37	23	28
Assembly industries												
Foodstuffs	37	49	9	5	30	56	11	3	31	57	10	2
Rubber products	9	29	19	43	21	25	13	41	22	31	11	36
Metal products[a]	40	50	8	2	46	42	8	4	49	41	10	
Industrial machinery[a]	20	40	12	28	16	35	12	33	22	35	12	30
Electrical machinery[a]	8	23	9	60	10	26	12	52	12	31	13	44
Transportation machinery[a]	6	19	7	68	6	18	8	69	6	16	11	67
Precision machinery[a]	23	35	13	29	23	34	15	28	21	35	20	24
Other manufacturing	42	47	5	6	40	46	7	7	43	46	5	6
Total manufacturing industries	22	35	13	31	22	35	13	30	24	37	14	26

[a] Heavy and chemical industries.

Source: Ministry of International Trade and Industry, Census of Manufactures (Tokyo).

On the other hand, the role of government in the area of these industrial developments was auxiliary and complementary. Except during the period of extreme difficulty immediately after the war, industrial opinion has not been generally favorable to government intervention, and the government was able to implement strong industrial policies only when there was consensus among the government and the private sector. To reach consensus is not easy, and sometimes serious differences of opinion have arisen between government and industry, for instance on the forecasts of demand for particular goods. In such cases, consensus has been reached only by compromise. Fortunately such cases were exceptional, because the high growth rate eventually resolved the differences of opinion by justifying a higher level of industrial activity—which had in fact already been determined by a kind of disguised consensus. Without high economic growth, the consensus mechanism could not work well nor could industrial policy be successful. This kind of Japanese industrial policy may be called a catalytic one. In line with economic development, the Japanese government shifted its role gradually from a strong intervention to a weaker intervention and finally to this catalytic function.

The government still intervenes on a selective basis, in areas such as small business and the structurally depressed industries, when the appropriate economic situation for intervention arises. Slower growth as well as a contingent crisis could necessitate a *dirigiste* industrial policy. In other words, the relationship between the government and the industrial sector changes subtly according to the different stages in industrial development, to the changes in public opinion toward corporate activities, and to the phases of the business cycle. It can be said that there is no such thing as a permanent balance between the government and business and that their relationship has always developed organically in line with the changes in the international and domestic environments.

FUTURE INDUSTRIAL POLICIES

Even if the basic aims of Japanese industrial policy and the style of relationship between the government and industry are not likely to change radically in the future, the emphasis will move according to circumstances. The main features of future industrial policies will be as follows.

Long-term stable supply of energy resources. As a result of the emerging nationalism in the resource-supplying nations, energy resources have become political, not commercial, commodities. The mechanism for adjusting demand and supply has also changed and is now exposed to heavy politicization. Therefore, to procure energy resources, the government has to play a greater role—that of industrial diplomacy. This means that the government should not necessarily procure energy resources directly, but it should use diplomatic efforts to enable private energy enterprises to negotiate favorably with energy suppliers. At the same time, however, there would be a growing possibility that the government might be forced to take more directive measures in the domestic scene. To cope with any contingencies, the government's energy policy could take the form of *dirigisme* to overcome extreme shortages, and at this point the unique style of consensus formation that characterized the period of the high growth economy would be suspended, at least in relation to energy policy. *Dirigisme* is indeed a temptation not easily confined to a limited area of contingencies. For Japan in the future, it will be a serious question whether a stronger government intervention will eventually overshadow all the spheres of industrial policy.

Securing the pioneering technology. In the decades when Japan aimed to catch up with the advanced industrial countries, Japan tried to improve its living standard and promote efficiency by bringing in advanced technologies. But now the international situation is changing, and Japan can no longer rely unilaterally on the European and American countries for the development of advanced or pioneering technology.

On the other hand, as the development of pioneering technology needs enormous funds and a long lead time, so great a potential risk is involved that a single private company cannot engage in it. Although a joint development system with mutual cooperation by private companies is desirable, at times such a voluntary research and development system is hampered by conflicts of interest. For this reason, the involvement of the government in developing advanced technology has been sought for some time past. As we have already seen, the role played by the Japanese government in technological development has been minor compared with the European and American countries, mostly because Japanese defense expenditure has been small.

Consequently, if a future bottleneck in technological needs is to be avoided, the government will have to invest funds more positively in the development of pioneering technology and build a solid foundation for research and development.

Specialization and restructuring within the international cooperative system. A continued up-grading of industry is always needed to promote economic efficiency and to improve a nation's standard of living. Restructuring of Japanese industry is also needed to establish internationally a better system of inter-industry and/or intra-industry specialization so that Japan can help to mitigate economic conflicts with the advanced countries as well as with newly industrializing countries. But this is not an easy task; since restructuring of industry is a serious labor issue, any forceful measures are not permissible and sufficient time should be allowed to carry out the restructuring.

Industrial adjustment has been and will continue to be successful only when it is brought about autonomously by industrial companies, although assisted by the catalyst of official adaptive policies. The government is expected to adjust interests among domestic sectors. These adjustments usually imply assistance to a structurally inferior sector, and this should be easier when there is high growth because it is easier to shift labor from an inferior sector to a less inferior one. But slower growth could hinder the shift considerably and therefore the adjustment function of government itself.

On one hand, there will be growing pressures from overseas for Japanese industry to restructure itself to fit in with Japan's trading partners, and on the other hand, the speed of such restructuring in Japan will be constrained by her slower growth. Industrial policy-making will be more and more difficult because of a loss of steam on the part of industry, which has been the prime mover of the system.

International Implications of Japanese Industrial Policy

A Policy That Respects the Independence of the Private Sector

Needless to say, the industrial policy of one country has an influence not only on the domestic scene, but also on the international one. International implications of industrial policy may be categorized into three areas in view of Japanese realities: (a) trading policy: What are the implications of regulations on foreign trade, and of tariff or nontariff barriers? (b) policy on investment: What are the implications of controls on the international transfer of capital, in particular on direct investment? and (c) industrial adjustment: What are the implications of any protective or stimulative measures for particular sectors of industry?

The international implications of industrial policy in these categories become a matter of keen concern to foreign interests when the policy has more restrictive and protective effects on trade and investment than the level accepted among other advanced industrial nations. Yet a hasty judgment about the degree of protectiveness may not be advisable unless a comprehensive analysis is done.

Free and voluntary activities of firms. The current Japanese industrial policy is not an offensive one in the preceding three respects. The details of each policy will be described in the following sections, but the following generalities pertain:

At present, free and voluntary activities and competition between firms are the guiding principles in industry, and industrial policy plays only an auxiliary role.

Positive remedial measures are taken only for those declining sectors with employment difficulties, which need structural rescue.

Together with a free market and keen competition, adaptability to a changing market and environment is the norm. The cases of abuse of subsidies and excessive dependence on import restrictions are few in the area of industrial activities.

Fierce Competition a Seed of External Discord?

As was shown in the chronology of Japanese industrial policy, Japan's import policy is now almost completely liberalized in terms of international criteria and is among the least protection-oriented.

Japan's exports, however, have given rise to an argument that they have unfavorable implications for the industry and market of the importing country, particularly because of their "scrambling" nature. In general, when the industrial products of a country are exported, there is a demand for those products in the importing area. Such demands may be derived from quality and/or price. No one should complain because quality is good; therefore the price factor and the factor of excessive quantity are the main concern to the manufacturing counterparts in the importing countries.

The issue for industrial policy seems to be whether export prices are subsidized heavily by the government. At present we do not see any such subsidy. Therefore, any blame should be directed not at industrial policy but at the nature of competition, sometimes unnecessary competition, among the exporting firms. It is the Japanese business climate of scrambling competition among firms that can jeopardize the formation of an appropriate selling price and thus the realization of a fair rate of profit.

This business climate, in turn, produces a high barrier against direct investment by foreign firms in Japan, where the profit ratio can be lower than the standard of advanced countries. In this way, if any, the Japanese market may be said to be closed. Thus, its closed nature lies not in institutions as much as in the behavior pattern of the Japanese business community and the resulting low rate of return.

The mixture of better price, better quality, and a competitive climate produces an export scramble if there is strong demand for particular items. There may, however, be cases where Japan's exports are not welcomed, because of the slower pace of industrial production as well as adjustment on the part of the importing country, where the local industry needs to buy time to compete or to retreat.

When it is claimed that Japanese exports cause trouble or friction, the government has been ready to take realistic measures after multilateral or bilateral discussions with the countries concerned. A good example is the voluntary restriction on Japan's exports of TV sets to the U.S. market based on the Orderly Marketing Agreement between Japan and the United States, which was a remarkable success.

INDUSTRIAL ADJUSTMENT AND ITS IMPLICATIONS

Asian NICs and industrial adjustment. Japan has no clear industrial adjustment policy to cope with the challenge of Asian NICs. Instead, the general perception is that the government has a policy, if any, of benign neglect. Therefore, Japanese industry has to adapt itself to this challenge without any concrete support.

Since Japan accelerated liberalization of her market in the mid-1960s, imports from Asian NICs increased at the high rate of almost 28 percent a year. On the other hand, Japanese exports to Asian NICs expanded at the rate of 24 percent a year. The rate of expansion of trade with Asian NICs exceeded the average growth of Japan's trade as a whole, and Japanese imports of their manufactures have been growing even faster. So it appears that a mutual dependency and a kind of industrial division of labor are emerging. Increased exports of Asian NICs to Japan are in textile and textile products, plywood, leather, and miscellaneous goods such as toys, which are rather labor-intensive and require a semiadvanced technology. Recently the Japanese imports of electronic components (resistors, condensers, etc), electrical appliances (desk calculators, radios, black and white TVs), and industrial machinery (motors) have been increasing. The Asian NICs, on the other hand, are increasing their imports from Japan of capital goods, which are vital for their industrialization, and all kinds of consumer goods, which obviously reflect the growth of their incomes.

Japan has been obliged to withdraw from these product fields in both overseas and domestic markets, and its industry has had to adapt itself to the change. Policy measures have been taken in a limited number of cases, but their purpose was to reduce the loss caused by the retreat and had the nature of a positive adjustment policy.

Such fields as plywood, leather, and miscellaneous goods from which Japan had to withdraw on a large scale involved mainly smaller enterprises in provincial areas. These small enterprises did not count for much in the entire industrial structure, and the policy in their favor should be seen as a kind of social policy on a regional basis rather than an industrial policy aimed at overall structural adjustment. But, fortunately, the owners of many such small enterprises have shown flexibility and positiveness in their management and the ability to shift their activity to new fields. Until now, this has been facilitated by the expansion of new industrial opportunities in the context of high, or more recently medium, economic growth. As a result, the problem of readjustment is not yet a serious one.

Another issue is a so-called boomerang effect of active Japanese investment in the Asian NICs. There was a fear that such direct investments would eventually undermine Japanese domestic industry because of the in-flow of cheaper products manufactured by the Japanese ventures in the NICs. Reality, however, has been a little different. The export of manufactured goods with high value added by Asian NICs to the Japanese market has indeed grown to some extent. But this has stimulated the growth of incomes in those areas, which produces a new kind of expanded market for exports from Japan. Therefore, the trade relationship between Japan and Asian NICs so far has proved to be mutually advantageous.

Adjustment was also facilitated in the case of the textile industry. The textile industry, foreseeing its inability fully to maintain its competitiveness in the long run, took decisive measures: suspension or freezing of 16 percent of its equipment capacity and reduction of its labor force by 240,000 over four years, with some official help for redeployment. Long-term, low-interest loans from governmental financial institutions were offered to facilitate the suspension, or freezing, of equipment. This adjustment was arranged by the initiative of the textile industry itself, which had worked out positive measures for structural amelioration in line with their own long-term forecasting. The government took the position of advisor only.

Along with the textile industry's overall master plan of structural adjustment, each individual firm has tailored its own specific measures, which are roughly divided into three categories: those to increase the ratio of higher-grade and more-sophisticated products in the total production; those to raise the efficiency of mass production of lower-grade stuff by introducing more automatic machines with computer control; and those to diversify the product mix toward nontextile sectors. The latter course is being followed mainly by big enterprises.

These three types of response are, in fact, not limited to the textile industry. Every industry in Japan has been moving in more or less the same direction in response to such changes as ever growing international competitiveness of overseas countries and sharp increases in the prices of raw materials and fuels.

In retrospect, the challenge from Asian NICs seems to have stimulated Japan's industrial up-grading rather than to have undermined Japanese industry. The NICs have indeed been catching up with Japan but at the same time the Japanese industry has further up-graded itself, and thus the Asian NICs and Japan are described figuratively as flying like a line of geese.

Policy for the structurally depressed industries. Among the industrial policies concerned with industrial adjustment, the most-important ones are the so-called policies for structurally depressed industries. These policies specify several industries and attempt to bring about a drastic adjustment of their structure. The policies also have considerable international implications.

As a result of the oil crisis in the autumn of 1973, the Japanese economy fell into the most-serious recession in the postwar years. Unlike the usual type of recession, this developed with various structural changes, reflecting a sudden transition of the Japanese economy from high growth to a more moderate or medium-level pace. In addition, the sharp increase in energy prices after the oil crisis and the simultaneous catching-up of the NICs affected both the overseas and domestic demand-supply structures and acted as a cue for a change in the industrial structure. Those industries which could not respond smoothly to such a structural change of demand suffered from a lower production level and loss of profitability, since they were burdened with significant excess production capacity without immediate hope for an autonomous recovery. They were regarded as structurally depressed.

Various councils of representatives from private firms, the financial sector, and government conducted deliberations on how to reshape the structures of these industries. As a result, the *Law on Extraordinary Measures for Specified Depressed Industries* was enacted in May 1974. This law aimed both at the short-term adjustment of product prices through the disposal of excess capacity and at long-term industrial restructuring, with a smooth shift of excess labor to other expanding areas.

Some industries designated as structurally depressed recovered their profitability in the late 1970s. Other industries, however, such as shipbuilding and aluminum, continued to face difficulties that require a revamping of their structure.

ENERGY POLICY AS INDUSTRIAL POLICY

One facet of industrial policy that has come to be increasingly important is energy policy, because Japan is almost uniquely dependent on overseas energy sources.

Seventy five percent of Japan's energy supply depends on oil, the highest dependency of any advanced industrialized country. Its primary energy is mostly supplied from overseas sources, particularly the Middle East. So the international implications of energy policy are complicated. Even a temporary and contingent suspension of oil imports would cause great difficulty.

To deal with any serious contingencies, development of alternative energy sources must be expedited. But the length of the lead time required for the development and commercialization of those alternative devices must be taken into account. This means that the energy problem has to be tackled from the viewpoint of long-term planning and that any delay in implementation will harm the social and economic basis for sustained growth. Moreover, energy policy should be attuned to international public opinion and the tide of international realities. Therefore it will be essential to implement a policy that is based on international cooperation with advanced industrialized countries and with resource-producing countries.

To maintain a supply-demand balance under the increasing uncertainty of the energy situation, energy conservation should be promoted in every sector of industry, in the household, and in the transportation sectors. This has already been stressed, and the demand elasticity of energy to the growth rate of GNP has been declining steadily. But eventually Japan has to achieve an industrial structure with a less energy-oriented nature.

Among other conservation measures, more economical utilization of energy in industry is especially important. Economy is already being voluntarily pursued to some degree in every industry. Energy conservation policy on the part of the government will also be important, even though it be an auxiliary measure — for instance, setting up a guideline for energy consumption by industry, and financial and fiscal incentives to encourage equipment investment for energy conservation.

Second, the development of alternative energy sources to replace oil needs to be accelerated — nuclear power, coal, and LNG. Here too, greater efforts by private firms are of primary importance. But official measures are also needed, because sizeable amounts of public funds have to be allocated to finance the long lead times required for development and commercialization.

International implications. Japan, which accounted for about 9 percent of the total world consumption of oil in 1977, is the third-largest oil-consuming country, following the United States (30 percent) and the USSR (13 percent). Consequently, if Japanese energy policies can produce favorable results in energy conservation and in the development of alternative energy sources, the reduced dependence on crude oil imports by Japan will substantially ease the international oil market.

Japan can provide technical and financial cooperation in the development of other energy resources than oil in resource-rich countries by contributing to the development of infrastructure in the form of railways, ports, roads, etc. Japan could also cooperate further to expedite the local processing of primary resources so as to secure higher value added for the resource-rich countries.

WHAT JAPAN NEEDS FROM THE INTERNATIONAL SYSTEM

As has already been discussed, the security of energy and raw material supplies has become one of the most important goals of Japanese industrial policy. This security requires an international system in which the supply of such resources is managed with stability on the basis of international cooperation. Japan's energy policy, in particular, can be realized only through international cooperation. For this reason, it is especially important that Japan actively participates in cooperative schemes to speed up the conservation of oil through the development of alternative energy sources.

Another important need for Japanese industrial policy is the worldwide maintenance of free trade principles. The furtherance of industrial adjustment, which is an important task of Japanese industrial policy, can be realized only in the context of free international trade.

We are concerned about the signs of protectionism and the occurrence of trade frictions, mainly in the advanced industrial nations, over the products of high-technology and/or capital-intensive sectors. Cooperation and harmony among the industrialized nations are necessary, perhaps even more urgently than the maintenance and increase of trade relations with LDCs and NICs. In order to sustain the framework of free trade, frequent exchange of views, partial localization of production as a supplement to export, and sophisticated intraindustry specialization must be carried out among the advanced nations on a mutual basis. Furthermore, the most-significant requirement for the advanced industrial nations is a strenuous effort to increase productivity and to maintain and improve the international competitiveness of their industries.

6 Past and Future Industrial Policy in the United States

WILLIAM DIEBOLD, JR.

Unlike the other countries discussed in this volume, the United States in the postwar period has not had anything that most Americans would think of as an "industrial policy." And when suggestions have been made in recent years that the United States ought to adopt such measures, reactions have mostly been negative. But this may be changing. The 1980s have opened to a debate in which the term industrial policy is coming into use and, more important, measures are being advocated, rebutted, and sometimes put into effect that are intended to shape the structure and operation of the American economy in ways quite similar to those long made use of by the more or less well-defined industrial policies of other democratic countries. How far these new approaches will be carried, and with what results, are matters that cannot be safely predicted, but it is possible to delineate the issues, identify the pressures, and suggest some of the possible consequences of American action, or inaction, in the years to come.

That is what this chapter attempts to do, although it begins with a look backward. The historical sketch—more a collection of illustrations than a thesis—serves several purposes. It shows that flat and sweeping statements about private enterprise, the market, the place of the government in the American economy, and even planning must be taken with several grains of salt. Here and there one can discern in the American past a suggestion or two about latter-day industrial policy issues in other countries as well as in the United States. Most of all, though, the historical sketch helps explain why some contemporary American issues, attitudes, and policies take the forms they do. The chapter then goes on to examine how the issues of the current debate have arisen from structural features of the postwar American economy, some of them largely shaped by governmental measures in spite of the lack of a general industrial policy. It concludes with a section on the relation between various potential lines of American industrial policy and the changing international economic system. Long before that final section, however, it will be seen that the changing relation of the United States to the world economy has had a great deal to do with posing the structural issues the country faces in the 1980s.

An Historical Sketch

THE FIRST ONE HUNDRED AND FIFTY YEARS

The United States owes its independence in part to the reasonably clear-cut industrial policies of the British government in the 17th and 18th centuries. What one historian has called "mercantilism translated into statute law" was felt to favor Englishmen in the home islands and hurt those across the Atlantic.[1] "A colonist cannot make a button, horse-shoe, nor a hobnail, but some sooty iron-monger or respectable button-maker of Britain shall bawl and sqaul that his honors worship is most egregiously maltreated, injured, cheated and robb'd by the rascally American republicans."[2] Once independent, the colonists lived most of their first decade under the Articles of Confederation, which denied the central government both the power to tax and the ability to regulate trade. Some states introduced protective measures and not others. As the rules could not be changed without unanimous consent, a fresh start was made when the federal Constitution was adopted in 1789.

The drafters of that document took care to emphasize the role of the federal government in major economic matters. "The Congress," they said, "shall have Power to lay and collect taxes . . . to borrow [and] coin money [and] to regulate the commerce with foreign nations, and among the several states, and with the Indian Tribes." Still, the Constitution left to the states the reserve powers, all those not explicitly given to the federal government. Given the changes that 200 years have brought in the economic life, political ideas, technology, population, national size, and position of the United States in the world, it would not have been surprising if this 18th century compromise had broken down long ago. Instead, the basic structure has held, combining flexibility with the gravitation of power over economic affairs to the federal government. Except for the Civil War, which settled the issues of secession and slavery, the growth of federal power has mostly resulted from a series of factors: federal control over the West before it was divided into states; the rise of business enterprise in forms that could not be confined by state boundaries; federal control of the money supply in spite of long confusion over banking; taxation, especially after the income tax was introduced; and not least, changing concepts of the proper use of governmental powers to shape the economy, and indeed the society. The pace was not uniform, or even the direction; controversy was of the essence along with the push and pull of conflicting interests. The evolution of what we can reasonably call American industrial policy could be told in terms of the Supreme Court's interpretation of the commerce clause of the Constitution.[3]

It could also be told partly in terms of trade policy, although no such effort would be warranted in a chapter of this sort. It is worth noting, however, some respects in which American tariff history has been more than just the result of the play of political forces, with the main strength accruing to vested interests wanting protection. For a long time that was the dominant element, but the shifting structure of power makes it difficult to find a consistent theme. Interests resisting protection sometimes won, at least on some points. Another source of obscurity is the fact that throughout the 19th century, tariffs were looked at in terms of revenue as well as for their effects on trade.[4] Still, here and there one can put a finger on certain elements that reflect the kind of concern with the structure of the economy that is common to late 20th century industrial policy (or at least an awareness of structural effects).

From the very beginning, for example, the American tarriff was selective in its protection, and selectivity (differential treatment) is of the essence of industrial policy. It became more protective as time passed, especially when the duties that had been imposed to match increased excise taxes in the Civil War were not lowered when the domestic measures were removed at the end of the war. Even then, duties were imposed largely in response to the demands of existing industries, not as a fence to stimulate new investment in all forms of manufacturing (although the quest for revenue somewhat confuses the issue).[5]

Mixed duties—a combination of specific and *ad valorem* rates—were manipulated to give major protection to goods manufactured in the United States. When duties on wool were raised, so were those on woolens to assure the same effective protection (it was in fact increased). In a different sort of structural choice, when a tariff was imposed to protect Lake Superior copper it was with the clear understanding that the eastern smelters who used imported copper would be sacrificed. Free entry for various kinds of agricultural supplies and machinery was part of a continuing compromise to get farmers to support industrial tariffs on many other manufactured goods, but it had an industrial policy aspect all the same.[6]

History and common sense do not permit one to rationalize more than a century of American politics and the conflicts of interest groups into a conscious industrial policy, even a dimly drawn and erratically realized one. And yet there is a certain coherence to most of what was done, a persistence in the kind of protectionism that free traders condemned and implicit acceptance of some common values about the need to expand domestic industry, to limit dependence on imports, and to enlarge the domestic market for the supposed benefit of all, including those American farmers who needed no protection for their own output and had to pay higher prices for cloth and iron than they otherwise would have. Even free traders accepted the infant industry argument and thought in terms of prices coming down after domestic production was well established (as they often did but probably largely because of technology and scale). Producer interests dominated; compromises were with traders and other manufacturers; consumers counted for little. (Is this supply-side economics?)

In a sense and to a degree, one would not go too far wrong to see much of this history in terms of Alexander Hamilton's *Report on Manufactures* of 1792. That was much more than a protectionist tract or a politician's bid for leadership. It was a proposal for an American industrial policy, and a rather comprehensive one. In calling for tariffs, Hamilton also called for the selection of industries that were well suited to the productive circumstances of the country and to its needs. He saw what are now called backward and forward linkages in the effect of one industry in creating markets for others. The agrarian interest was to benefit both from increased home demand and from the use of the new tariffs to bargain with foreigners to open their markets to the United States. Part of the wherewithal for American development was to come from the foreign investment induced by the good rate of return from American growth, and then the prospect of protection would lure foreign capital out of "the funds" into direct investment in mills and factories. If private capital did not suffice, Hamilton would have had the government advance funds to take shares in an enterprise (but not itself become a producer, except perhaps of arms). He also saw that sometimes subsidies ("bounties") had advantages over tariffs. That all this should be clearer, more logical, and more complete in what Hamilton wrote than in what was done in practice is perhaps another characteristic of industrial policy.

Nevertheless, "that famous document had little, if any, effect on legislation," said Taussig. "Alone of his state papers, this report fell flat" observes Professor Morison.[7] The first tariff (1789, preceding Hamilton's *Report*) had imposed fairly moderate duties, largely because the shipping and trading interests of the new republic were a good deal stronger than its manufacturers or would-be industrial capitalists. It was decades later that the *Report on Manufactures* came back into the debate in an active way. Nevertheless, without trying to attribute any specific weight to its influence, one cannot help seeing the *Report* as a valid expression of some of the main themes of an epoch, a crystalization of attitudes that in later practice are fuzzier (and rarely as well put). Certainly it stands as the epitome of one view of American society, the opposite of which is generally called Jeffersonianism, or at least that part of Jeffersonianism suggested by the statement in *Notes on Virginia* that "Those who labour in the earth are the chosen people of God . . . whose breasts He has made His peculiar deposit for substantial and genuine virtue."[8]

The differences between the two views were not settled by debate, either through logic or eloquence; Jefferson left his mark on American attitudes toward farm policy as well as more clear-cut elements of American democracy. But in their time what shifted the scene markedly toward the Hamiltonian vision of the national economy were the American responses to the struggle between France and Britain: the Embargo of 1807, the Non-Intercourse Act of 1809, and then the second war with Britain in 1812–15.

With imports all but cut off, Americans began producing a wider range of manufactures. With exports cut off, farmers and others focused more sharply on the domestic market. The shipping and trading interests lost some of their power. Separated from much of their familiar old world, Americans began to think more in terms of the vulnerability that went with foreign trade and looked more to their own resources. Even Jefferson had to say, "We must now place the manufacturer by the side of the agriculturist . . . experience has taught me that manufactures are now as necessary to our independence as to our comfort."[9] Protection for the new industries was natural enough in the Tariff of 1816, especially as pent up supplies of goods from wartime Britain began entering the American market. Then the financial disturbances of 1819 in Europe and the United States and increased trade restriction abroad turned what had been thought of as a transitional arrangement into a new interest in protection that remained strong for a long time to come.

So far as shaping the structure of the American economy was concerned, more was involved than just higher tariffs and the new surge in American shipping and whaling. The events of the whole period from 1807 to 1819, it seemed to Taussig, "rudely shook the country out of the grooves in which it was running, and brought about a state of confusion from which the new industrial system could emerge more easily than from a well-settled organization of industry."[10] There is a striking similarity between this diagnosis and what the Interfutures report has to say about the "sclerosis" that blocks change in industrial societies and the implication that the postwar economic performances of Germany and Japan are related to the shakeup of their societies brought by war.[11]

There followed a period of great activity and high national self-consciousness that included a considerable emphasis on the political impact of economic measures. This was the period of the American system in which Henry Clay and John C. Calhoun joined in trying to overcome the divisive forces of interest, section, and party. "Let us bind the Republic together with a perfect system of roads and canals," said Calhoun well before he became a separatist and invented nullification. "Internal improvements, meaning roads and canals, were the complement to protection," says Morison.[12] And internal improvements involved both the federal and the state governments in a variety of activities. They made grants of land, money, concessions, and sometimes monopolies; they remitted taxes and made direct investments in private firms; they provided services, such as exploration, surveys, and removing hazards to navigation; but they also became entrepreneurs themselves, as when the federal government built the Cumberland Road, and New York State the Erie Canal. John Quincy Adams believed the government should have carried out all this construction itself and become more powerful thereby. But neither his aims nor the political purposes of Clay and Calhoun could be served except by economic results. The widening of markets and the access to supplies that roads, railroads, and canals provided made possible the expansion of the national economy, permitted many enterprises to enlarge their scale of operations, raised the value of land enormously, and altered the whole economic geography of the country. Before the Civil War the states probably did more than the federal government, except in the disposal of western lands. In any case, the aims (and results) were to bring about structural change by methods that are to be found in any lexicon of industrial policy.[13]

It was the America of internal improvements and growth in which Friederich List lived for a while in the late 1830s and of which he said, "The best work on political economy which one can read in that modern land is actual life."[14] It is not surprising that List's famous book, for all its defects, should express something of the spirit of many developing nations today. Nor was this feeling confined to outsiders. In 1840, Nathaniel Parker Willis, one of the most popular American writers of the period and who knew Europe well, was pursuing the then familiar theme of the contrast between the history-laden scenery of Europe and the American wilderness. The traveler, he said, "must feed his imagination on the *future*. The American does so. . . . Instead of looking through a valley, which has presented the same aspect for hundreds of years . . . his first thought is of the villages that will soon sparkle on the hill-sides, the axes that will ring from the woodlands, and the mills, bridges, canals, and railroads, that will span and border the stream that now runs through sedge and wildflowers. . . . He passes through . . . a town which has perhaps doubled its inhabitants and dwellings since he last saw it, and will again double them before he returns. . . . He looks upon all external objects as exponents of the future. In Europe they are exponents of the past."[15]

What came to be called in Europe "the American system of manufacturing" found its first focus in southern New England, its most famous products firearms, clocks, watches, locks, tools, and other light metal manufactures. The list grew, the area of production spread, and "there came into being the basic elements and patterns of modern mass manufacturing; that is, the principles and practice of quantity manufacture of standardized products characterized by interchangeable parts and the use of a growing array of machine tools and specialized jigs and fixtures, along with power, to substitute simplified and, as far as possible, mechanized operations for the craftsman's arts."[16] Changes in the organization of production and distribution went along with these technological shifts. A rougher finish than was expected in Europe marked some of the products, but others became some of the first American exports of technologically advanced goods. Direct foreign investment followed, notably Samuel Colt's pistol plant in England equipped with his own machinery from the United States (which failed). The American exhibition at the Crystal Palace in 1851 led to a number of visits by foreign committees to the United States, including one sent by the British Ordnance Department in 1854 to study products and processes and to buy equipment and patents. The fortunate result is a set of observations that might never have been made by Americans looking at themselves.

Structural explanations for the emergence of this American system are not hard to find: labor was scarce and costly, so there was a premium on conserving it by mechanization; craftsmen trained in traditional ways were not numerous, so there was less resistance to new methods; there seems to have been a good level of educability, aptitude, and cleverness. Much of the industrial revolution spread to the American continent in the minds of emigrants from England, sometimes in defiance of the laws that tried to keep secrets at home. (That was not the last time that immigration changed the structure of the American economy.) Even after the War of 1812, Europe was far away and travel within the country slow and difficult; the lack of a quick alternative was a spur to find ways to "make do." The Yankee tinkerer invented and adapted, but whether he made the system or the system made him is not clear.

Resources also helped shape the American system. Abundant waterpower encouraged the use of machinery; wood could be used on a scale not possible in Europe. One of the most ingenious of the American machines the Ordnance group bought was Thomas Blanchard's lathe for turning gunstocks. It was then more than 30 years old, and an earlier model had found no buyers in London because its multiple turnings cut away so much wood that stocks cost a shilling instead of seven or eight pence. But in the United States the waste of wood was negligible compared to the saving of labor: two stocks an hour instead of one to two per day per man. Blanchard's invention was also an example of dual purpose technology. Basically a device to reproduce irregular shapes by following a model, it was used to make lasts for shoes, blocks for hats, oars, and spokes.[17]

Although the American entrepreneurs mostly used their own funds or what they could raise privately from others, sometimes the government played a part with contracts, funds and facilities. Arsenals as well as private plants produced weapons and equipment. (Blanchard's machine was a feature of the Springfield Arsenal.) Eli Whitney, who said he had "the most respectable private establishment in the United States" for producing muskets, apparently found government contracts and financing important to the development of interchangeable parts, a principle that carries further than guns and the cotton gin.[18]

If one were to trace the structural effects of the American system or some of its products, the lines would fan out in many directions. The most familiar example is Eli Whitney's cotton gin and what it did, or at least seemed to many to have done, to make cotton growing truly profitable in the South and thus to give a new lease on life to slavery. When the Civil War ended slavery, the consequences for structural change in the South's economy did not show themselves quickly, probably because of the destruction and slow recovery. The war also contributed mightily to centralizing political power in the federal government and economic power in the North. For all its bloodshed and destruction, it did not stop expansion and change in the American economy. Perhaps it is only a convenience of historical hindsight (or an American provincialism) that makes one see the period after that conflict as something of a piece, very different from what went before and running roughly to World War I. At least for our purposes, such a perspective has merit. It takes us to the time when some new and important elements of the shadowy history of American industrial policy emerge.

This is the period when big business emerged on a national scale. It was national in two senses. Although corporations are the creatures of state governments, ways were found to permit them to operate across the country with great freedom. They were national also in that they were largely American owned and built, and only in exceptional cases were they extensions of foreign enterprises which wanted to get into the expanding American economy (although there was more of this in real estate and agriculture). Some of the entrepreneurs were immigrants who had made their fortunes in America; some of the capital came out of London, but mostly as portfolio rather than direct investment (and in the end there were quite a few bad debts and worthless shares, especially those of the railroads). The railroads crossed the continent and did for the whole country what internal improvements had done for the eastern part of the country before the Civil War. Again the government helped — by exploration, surveys, loans, and large grants of land to the railroads. Land was virtually given away to those who would farm it, and the discovery of minerals could establish extensive claims. At the same time that they brought new territory into the economy and connected markets, the railroads created an enormous demand for steel, rails, locomotives, rolling stock and equipment, and supplies of all sorts. The financial system was reshaped to their needs. This was the period to which what John Sawyer calls "the standard 'big' explanations of American growth" applied: "the railroads, vast continental resources . . . when population growth and rising incomes make a bigger internal market than European countries had known, and heavy industry grows apace."[19]

Although we know the names of great entrepreneurs, captains of industry, daring financiers and robber barons, this was also the period when "modern business enterprise" came to be the dominant form with its "hierarchy of middle and top salaried managers to coordinate the work of the units under its control."[20] A major result, according to Alfred Chandler's challenging analysis, was that "in many sectors of the economy the visible hand of management replaced what Adam Smith referred to as the invisible hand of market forces . . . in coordinating the activities of the economy and allocating its resources." The result was to make modern business "the most powerful institution in the American economy and its managers the most influential group of economic decision makers." A countervailing power was asserted in demands for government regulation of business and a long series of social and economic reforms. In a manner that would not have surprised Adam Smith, late 19th century American business showed how competition could lead to cartelization and monopoly and how market power rather than efficiency could shape the economic structure.

Not just the general public and elected officials moved to check the trusts, the mergers, and the railroads, but also other business groups, perhaps especially those whose traditional functions were being taken over by the vertical integration of the new giant firms. A new kind of American industrial policy took shape in the Interstate Commerce Act of 1887, the Sherman Antitrust Act of 1890, and the Clayton and Federal Trade Commission Acts of 1914.

These laws, as amended, interpreted, and supplemented by a variety of other measures intended to insure competition, limit the concentration of economic power, and make trade "fair" as well as free, continue to play an important part in shaping the economic structure of the United States and so will reappear later in this chapter. They should probably be thought of more broadly than just in terms of their specific effects. The laws and their administration and the factors that gave rise to them help provide the answer to a poignant question that Crawford Greenwalt, chairman of the board of DuPont, asked Alfred Chandler: "Why is it that my American colleagues and I are being constantly taken to court—made to stand trial—for activities that our counterparts in Britain and other parts of Europe are knighted or given peerages and comparable honors for?"[21]

Laws on the books and laws in practice can be quite different, and the period between World War I and the Depression was not a high-water mark for the reshaping of American business by the use of the antitrust laws. It could be argued that the single most-important structural development of the period for the U.S. economy was the unprecedented involvement of American financial institutions in the rest of the world. The failure of the rest of the economy to reshape itself so that the world could pay the debts built up during and after the war is well known. A specific item of industrial policy that comes to mind is the explicit replacement of the German-owned dyestuffs industry and some other chemical and pharmaceutical branches by protected American companies. Concern with dependence on imports was also reflected in the attacks that Secretary of Commerce Herbert Hoover launched on foreign raw materials cartels and combinations—German, British, and Dutch, among others—and the efforts he made to help develop alternative sources, partly by direct government help.[22]

A more ambitious history than this sketch might well find other significant features in the 1920s. It continues to stand in most people's minds as the time when the United States came closest to living by the ideology of the market (behind tariffs) and *laisser faire*. But that did not preclude the government's helping business, as Herbert Hoover tried to do in reforming the Department of Commerce and as was presumably implied by Calvin Coolidge when he said, "The business of America is business." It would carry us too far afield to consider whether that view of the government's proper place in the economy at that time was in keeping with David Potter's thesis that, while tactics have changed, "one of the key principles" of American life has been "the constant endeavor of government to make the economic abundance of the nation accessible to the public."[23] Whether or not that is the case, the New York stock market crash of 1929 marked the end of one period and was followed by the beginning of another, very different one, that leads directly to the structural and industrial policy concerns of today.

The Great Transition

The change did not come overnight. Some explanations of the stock market crash suggested a possible recuperation; business cycles were a known phenomenon, and what went down was expected to go up; and for a while the rest of the world did not show such alarming symptoms. But the path continued downward, the deterioration spread, optimism faded, and each reaction—the contraction of credit by private bankers, withdrawal of funds from banks by the public, the erection of barriers by governments—made matters worse. Traditional remedies did not work, and more venturesome ones were matters of great controversy and much criticism; Franklin D. Roosevelt's 1932 campaign included a promise to balance the budget. As important as anything done or left undone by government was the psychological effect on the people who suffered, the public at large, and on newspapers and intellectuals. The whole capitalist system came into question. The virtues of private owernship were challenged, but the main alternative was usually seen as regulation rather than socialization (although it was in these years that the always minor American socialist movement reached its peak). Faith in the market was challenged by convictions as to what could be done by planning. The reaction against banking and finance reflected an old feeling that the real economy was superior to and sounder than the illusions created by the stock market, pyramids of holding companies, inflated paper values, and the like. The glorification of business in the 1920s gave way to a wider acceptance of the pictures of America Sinclair Lewis conjured up in *Babbitt* and *Main Street* and other authors projected in a stream of stories, plays, and poems. No one could have said, in the 1930s, what a prominent clergyman had earlier said of the Woolworth Building, that it pierced "space like a battlement of the paradise of God which St. John beheld," inspired "feelings too deep even for tears," and evoked the cry "the Cathedral of Commerce."[24]

The "people of plenty" now looked on surpluses as a threat. Some felt that excess capacity was cause as well as effect of the Depression, and some advocates of planning said a major aim was to prevent new surpluses from arising, apparently on the assumption that the government could figure out what was needed while businessmen did not know where to stop. Most advocates of planning had broader aims, however, and the advocacy grew. The cliché that "planning is a dirty word in America"—or its variants—takes no account of the 1930s. Private individuals and government officials at all levels, including states and cities, advocated planning of one sort or another and made great claims for what it could do. How far practice conformed to claims is another matter. However, the word planning seems to have had such appeal that it was applied to any number of activities that might have been described differently, such as the coordination of governmental units, systematic administration, looking ahead, the collection of relevant data, and what would nowadays be called cost-benefit analysis. Only a minority were thinking of comprehensive national planning in which the government lays out fairly detailed courses for much of the economy and is given the power to steer along them. Nevertheless, the popularity of planning surely indicates a sense that past ways of doing things were no longer adequate and that some more purposive means had to be found of saving the economy. Inevitably the government would be more involved in guiding the system than it had been although what power it should have was a matter of dispute.

Certainly the New Deal greatly enlarged the federal government's part in managing the economy as a whole, as well as regulating private activities. But how much real planning was there? In 1933 a National Resources Committee was set up to survey national resources of all sorts and to advise the government on their use on a continuing basis. Charles E. Merriam, its vice chairman, said it was really a "projection" of a body recommended by the Committee on Recent Social Trends set up by President Hoover.[25]

In 1939, the Committee was turned into the National Resources Planning Board, which Franklin Roosevelt referred to as "the planning arm of my executive Office, charged with the preparation of long-range plans for the development of our national resources and the stabilization of employment."[26] The Board generated a substantial amount of research and thinking on the structure of the American economy and especially on manpower, public works, the location of industry, consumer behavior, and waterpower. It brought together representatives of many Washington agencies, but also did much work through committees that drew in businessmen and other private groups, and many leading economists contributed to its work. The Board claimed it took an over-all view, stimulated planning by other agencies, acted as a clearing house for what was being done in the field, collected data, and proposed policies.[27] Its reports might make recommendations but it often published conflicting views. Decisions were left to the executive and legislative branches of government. How much influence the Board had on those decisions or the direction of policy is hard to say.

Something similar could be said about the Temporary National Economic Committee (TNEC), made up of members of the Senate and House of Representatives and officials of the executive branch and with an expert staff. It commissioned a large number of reports, many of them very good, by people from government and private life and held hearings on the issues involved. The purpose of the TNEC was to investigate that well-established object of American concern, the concentration of economic power. Was it one of the reasons the American economy was performing so badly and that the Depression was so much more damaging than past cyclical movements? The TNEC's work reflected much concern with structure—sectoral, institutional, and the like. The stimulus to thinking and research was great, but the impact on policy—if any—is hard to discern, since just as the TNEC concluded its work, the dominant concern of the United States became the mobilization of resources for war.

From near the beginning of the New Deal, government measures concerned with structural issues were more prominent than in the past. The most ambitious attempt, and failure, was the National Industrial Recovery Act and its codes. Worked out industry by industry, their aim was to raise prices, restrain competition, spread the work and, if necessary, hold down production. By the time the Act had been declared unconstitutional—and before its effectiveness had been well tested—close observers realized that the effort to do so many complicated and unusual things in so many fields had shifted power over the drawing-up of codes for each industry from the government or the advisory groups representing labor, consumers, and business generally, to the trade associations or leading firms of the industries being regulated. Self-government of industry in a cartel-like mode seemed to be developing. The lesson — short as it was — had a bearing on the attitudes of quite a few Americans thereafter.

In the troubled bituminous coal industry, labor pressed hardest for restrictions on production. The owners feared the government intervention they thought would come from such measures; their preference for price and marketing arrangements was legitimized in the Bituminous Coal Conservation Act of 1935. In agriculture, surpluses were attacked directly by destroying them. Then followed the combination of restrictions on production and support for prices that in a teeter-totter combination marked American farm policy for a generation, influenced the structure of the economy, and gave a warning lesson about how national industrial policy measures can affect international trade.

There were other sectoral measures: a plan to rebuild the merchant marine and revive shipbuilding by subsidies, protective legislation, and preferential treatment; the separation of commercial from investment banking by the Glass-Steagall Act; the creation of the Securities and Exchange Commission with initial regulatory powers that have, over time, done much to shape the structure of the industry. These efforts have had lasting effects and are among the many elements that make the American economy of the late 20th century so different from that of the first 150 years. Some more general measures also had differential, and thus structural, effects. For example, the Wagner Act and other legislation that strengthened the bargaining power of unions was particularly helpful to the new CIO, which practiced industrial unionism instead of the craft unionism that dominated the AFL and which was especially strong in basic industries. The Tennessee Valley Authority was famous as a regional measure (of particular relevance in the United States because it cut across so many state jurisdictions), but it had no major counterparts. There were also smaller regional and river valley development schemes based on dams for flood control and waterpower. State governments came together to deal with the problems of rivers, lakes, and ports. The many-pronged attack on poverty and backwardness in the South was a kind of regional policy. Of the many ways the government tried to help businesses in difficulty, one of the most important was the provision of capital through the Reconstruction Finance Corporation. Created by Hoover but much enlarged under Roosevelt, the RFC provided loans and sometimes temporary equity investment. It can be thought of as an instrument of industrial policy, but its help was, in principle, available to all kinds of firms; so structural considerations were implicit in judgments about what enterprises could best use its aid to survive, rather than explicit in its aims.

Of different provenance and character, the Trade Agreements Act of 1934 was an early New Deal measure that was to develop into a lasting policy with continuing effects on the United States and the rest of the world. Although export expansion was a major aim, so was the reduction of American tariffs by reciprocal bargaining. There were no sectoral rules or aims, but the reduction of tariffs was selective both to preserve bargaining strength and to avoid injury to domestic interests.[28] The export effect was also assumed to be strongest in certain sectors, such as automobiles, electrical equipment, consumer durables, and agriculture. Adopted because Secretary of State Cordell Hull prized it, the Trade Agreements Act did not jibe well with other parts of the New Deal approach. It reflected a contrary spirit to that which led to the virtual scuttling of the London Economic Conference in 1933 by the American rejection of the short-run stabilization of exchange rates. Had the NRA codes lasted, there would have been many clashes with trade liberalization. Nevertheless, the Act inaugurated the longest period in American history in which tariffs were lowered, and provided the starting place for GATT, the center of a comparable multilateral achievement. In both capacities it became one of the most-important factors shaping the structure—and restructuring—of the American economy over four decades.

The dominant aim of the measures taken in the first two terms of Franklin Roosevelt was to stimulate recovery and bring about full employment, but reforms were also major objectives, partly because they were thought necessary to make the economy work well. The government's responsibilities for economic performance were enlarged and with them its powers and its involvement in formerly wholly private or unregulated activities. There was no discernible overall picture of the desirable structure of the future American economy, but there were, as already indicated, a number of measures with structural purposes and many which had structural effects, especially in the long run. There was more use of what we now call industrial policy measures than had been usual in the American economy, at least since before the Civil War. How in the end these measures would have worked out and what would have remained cannot be known because of the outbreak of war.

Little need be said about wartime policies, although a full history of structural change in the American economy would require careful study of that point. The government was engaged in expanding certain sectors of industry, contracting others, and allocating goods in short supply. A scarcity of shipping space forced choices that affected other countries as well as the United States. Only occasionally did the exigencies of the moment permit much attention to long-run factors. The expansion of aluminum production was handled so as to increase competition; novel methods of shipbuilding challenged the established yards. Anticipating the problems of the postwar transition to a civilian economy and remembering the collapse that followed World War I, a group of progressive businessmen formed the Committee for Economic Development (CED), which studied problems and catalogued opportunities for initiatives that would help insure an orderly postwar transition. Work was done along the same lines by the government. Some of this planning was done under the shadow of the fear engendered by the stagnation thesis (associated particularly with Alvin Hansen), which held that dynamism was spent in the American economy largely because investment demand was saturated. It turned out to be wrong, as several people argued at the time.

At least one problem faced at the end of the war was specifically structural. Plants to produce artificial rubber had been rapidly built. Should they, in the postwar period, be given protection or subsidies to guard against dislocation or dependence on imported rubber? Or should they be left on their own to face the competition from natural rubber continuing to be imported duty-free?

The solution was disposal of the plants to private interests by the mid 1950s (delayed by the Korean War) and then open market competition (plus surveillance to be sure the American producers competed with one another).[29] These steps were in keeping with the broad trade policy principles the United

States was advocating and, as it turned out, preserved an effectively competitive industry which developed its own specialities, made technological progress, and provided a secure home supply for a good share of American demand. The experience in other industries was often different, but our main theme for the postwar period concerns a new balance among dominant elements of American thinking about economic policy, the new measures of international economic cooperation, and the factors which generated measures of industrial policy in the United States and abroad.

Our sketchy examination of the kinds of structural problems Americans have faced and how they have coped with them has shown that there are no clear-cut lines of American industrial policy and that such continuity as can be traced is limited in time. There are also indications why some issues may be seen differently in the United States than in other countries. But nothing in even this selective approach to the American past can be regarded as evidence of why certain things can or cannot be done today or how Americans are likely to deal (or fail to deal) with some issues common to industrial democracies in the 1980s. That in itself is significantly different from the frequently heard statement that something has always been this way—or that—in the United States.

The Contemporary Debate

How the Problems Have Arisen

One cumulative effect of the Depression, the New Deal, and World War II (although any one of them alone might have been enough) was a new and more-explicit acceptance by Americans of the government's responsibility for dealing with national economic difficulties (which had always existed to some degree) and of the belief that the government could actually control the situation, at least as far as major depressions were concerned. Only slightly weaker was the realization that to achieve these desirable results would require governmental action in normal as well as critical times. Consequently, the place the government was expected to take in the economy was altered for the foreseeable future. There was, to be sure, a strong wish to get rid of wartime restraints, for shortages were irksome and "plenty" was once again something to be sought. That attitude helped speed the removal of controls and the reduction of spending for defense, but could not reverse the Depression–New Deal–wartime departures from the older presumptions about the place of government in the economy. Yet the government's role was still thought of largely in macroeconomic terms, so the implication of the changed attitude for governmental action concerning the structure of the economy was not clear.[30]

To a degree, some reversion to the older formula of limiting governmental responsibility was encouraged by the new weight given to international measures aimed at freeing trade and payments from the accumulated restrictions of war, depression, and economic nationalism. Yet it is an oversimplification to characterize American policy in that period as being concerned with the creation of a *laissez faire* world or as putting the enlargement of the markets of American business at the top of its priorities. Removing governmental restraints was a major element in policy, and so was the recovery of the world economy in which

American business was bound to play a large part. Some people believed that the results desired could be obtained only by the play of free private enterprise, and there was no doubt that competitive markets were favored over monopolies, restrictive practices, and the kinds of socialization thought to have such consequences. There was also no doubt that governments would continue to be responsible for their national economies, that they would have multiple political, social, and economic ends to pursue, and that the results would be different economic arrangements in different places.

Thus, the possibility that some countries would adopt more or less comprehensive industrial policies and others piecemeal ones was implicit in the concept of a Bretton Woods world. It soon became apparent that recovery did not mean restoration of a preexisting pattern so that each government would have to help, hinder, or initiate the inevitable changes in the structure of the world economy. Governments that failed to choose the right course of action could do much damage to their economies and place considerable burdens on their people for some time to come.

Because of its relatively comfortable position, the United States ran fewer risks than other countries. Moreover, a convergence of reasons (or interests) favored an emphasis on policies that would reduce the need for continuing governmental attention. Traditional 19th century elements in American policy were therefore strengthened, but with the explicit and major difference from that earlier time of working toward a lowering rather than a raising of trade barriers. No one could be sure how far the United States (or any other country) would be willing to go in that direction or even how firm the American commitment to freer trade (not "free trade") was. Nevertheless, events showed that the United States was willing to move vigorously, and by 1963 it could correctly be observed that whereas in the early 1930s protectionism "had the ideological initiative. . . . Today . . . the tables are turned. More often than not one hears the advocate of protection begin his statement about as follows: 'Of course I am for increasing trade and believe in lowering trade barriers, but . . .' "[31]

The United States reduced its tariffs, even though most other countries continued to restrict imports for balance-of-payments reasons until the late 1950s (with Canada and Switzerland the main exceptions). This one-sided arrangement assumed that the other major trading countries would themselves liberalize when they were able, and was politically acceptable partly because the reduction in American tariffs was fairly gradual (although cumulatively very large) and somewhat selective. The American balance-of-payments position was strong, the place of foreign trade in the American economy was still relatively modest, although growing, and there was an atmosphere favoring cooperation in what was called "the free world." The reduction of American import barriers and the expansion of American direct investment abroad brought about considerable changes in the structure of the American economy. Adaptation was left largely to private business, although the initiative for liberalization often came from the government. Resistance to lowering tariffs, in contrast, usually started with business or labor; they won government support mostly by simple political pressure but sometimes partly by what can be thought of as structural arguments (such as the industry's economic or strategic importance or the lack of alternative employment in certain regions).

Another new feature of the postwar American economy was the scale of defense industries. By its nature the military industrial complex was dependent on governmental orders, just as the ability of the government to carry out some of its security obligations depended on the economy's ability to produce a variety of arms and equipment. To trace the full effects on the structure of the American economy of defense spending — and the changes it has undergone — is impossible here, but its relevance to industrial policy must be noted. Foreign observers have often seen defense spending as a major form of government aid to industry which helped provide the edge in technology to American industry after World War II. Americans by contrast are more likely to emphasize two different points. First, the motive for and basic decisions about defense spending were concerned with security, not commercial advantage. Second, such a large outlay for military supplies and arms production is a burden to the American economy. The same resources devoted to civilian purposes could, presumably, have increased the competitive strength of American industry in a more direct manner than through the spillover of technology and government-financed research and development.

How great this spillover has in fact been is a matter of some dispute. Guesses about what would have happened if the United States had supported a smaller defense industry must take account of two conflicting arguments: (1) that no comparable amount would have been spent on science and research and development and (2) that defense spending diverted scientific skills and technically able manpower from what would otherwise have been economically productive uses. Similar arguments apply to the development of atomic energy and later to the space and moon programs. For the 1980s, the issue concerns the proper government policy toward science, technology, research and development, and how precisely those activities can be directed toward particular industrial needs.

Security considerations also introduced some specific structural concerns into American economic policy. For example, for some years the protection of the watch industry was defended on the grounds that only the watch makers had the skills necessary for the production of bomb sights; more recently, quotas on foreign oil were said to be needed to develop the domestic supply; subsidies for shipping and shipbuilding are not new. The aerospace industries present more complex issues. Civilian demand is of major importance, but government orders can be crucial to a firm's survival; products, technologies, and production facilities serve both markets. Government financing of development costs for military aircraft can reduce the price of civilian versions (even if the company does not win the military contract). Exports are large, but international competition is serious; and success in gaining orders from foreign governments frequently involves producing or procuring substantial elements of the aircraft abroad. One of the few cases of the federal government's bailing out a major firm was that of the Lockheed Company, which was saved from bankruptcy by governmental financial support. At a late stage of the Tokyo Round, a few major countries agreed to a free trade arrangement for civil aviation; in fact it goes far beyond the removal of tariffs and falls far short of eliminating all governmental measures that would influence trade and the location of industry. Dealing with standards, procurement, and related matters, this is a sectoral industrial policy agreement.[32] Its full effect has yet to be demonstrated, but there can be no doubt that in the as-yet-unarticulated consensus view of the indispensable elements of the American economic structure, aerospace has a place.

The economics of security has always influenced policy toward the supply of raw materials. The United States stockpiles "strategic" materials—the definition varies from time to time—that it lacks or that might run short in an emergency. Though buying and selling for the stockpiles was sometimes influenced by the market the use of such transactions for industrial policy purposes seems negligible.[33] The shift of the United States toward becoming a net importer of an increasing number of raw materials has raised important policy issues. Fear of shortages or import dependence led to the formation of the Paley Commission in the early 1950s, which took the reassuring view that as long as capital flowed into the development of raw material resources around the world, American buying power would suffice to command adequate supplies. After the Korean war shortages, no serious problems arose until the oil embargo and price increases of the 1970s.

Although other OPECs did not emerge, and analysis suggested they would be hard to form, dependence on foreign sources of supply once again became a matter of worry. Concern was increased by the fact that for some time governments of raw material-producing countries had been asserting increasing control over foreign investors. Sometimes this led to expropriation, sometimes only to restrictions and regulations, and sometimes to arrangements aimed mainly at increasing the government's share of the profits. Private American ownership of foreign mines was clearly no longer a guarantee of a secure source of supplies, but the best alternative was not obvious. European countries and Japan faced the same problem and relied more on governmental participation in arrangements with suppliers than did the United States. Some companies believed that new kinds of agreements with foreign governments would permit them to function effectively; others turned their attention to higher-cost sources in North America. Proposals were made for new forms of investment that relied more heavily on international financial institutions. Some consideration was given to working at trade rules assuring access to natural resources on a reciprocal basis. These possibilities remained unresolved by the early 1980s, along with such questions as the extent to which the United States should try to become more self-sufficient in various minerals.

In the decades immediately following the war, the United States continued the farm support policies begun in the 1930s, which were industrial policies in the sense that they concerned agriculture's place in the American economy. Up to the 1960s, price supports and government purchasing led to import limitations and export subsidies that required the waiver of the GATT rules, which applied to most of the rest of international trade. By the time changes in American farm policies reduced the conflict with GATT rules, European and Japanese protective policies were no longer covered by balance-of-payments rules, and required similar exceptions. This general exclusion of agriculture from the trade-liberalizing arrangements, which have done so much to shape the structure of the postwar international economy, illustrates what might happen in other fields if enough countries were to pursue industrial policies that gave priority to other results than international competitiveness.

No doubt a longer list could be compiled of American measures that had either structural purposes or effects (particularly of a localized sort), but the items mentioned are enough to show that in the first postwar decades there were some fairly important exceptions to the commonly accepted view that American policy was concerned almost exclusively with macroeconomic issues and relied entirely on private enterprise and market forces to bring about adjustment. During this period large changes occurred in the structure of the American economy, including the growth to major proportions of industries that had earlier been unknown or of negligible importance. Except through the technological spillover from defense, space, and atomic power, the government had relatively little to do with this, and to that extent the traditional view was valid. The political acceptability of this process of change is probably to be explained by commonly accepted factors, such as the expansion of the economy (although at rates less than that of the other industrial countries for the postwar period), a continuing, widespread rise in living standards, a fair amount of flexibility in shifting resources that was helped by the opening of new opportunities for people, a strong balance-of-payments position, and a general acceptance of the fact that broad foreign policy and security aims were also served by a liberal foreign economic policy.

By the early 1960s some difficulties intensified and by the end of the decade many past premises were under attack. The story is familiar. The expansion of production in Europe and Japan increased competition for American industry at home and abroad. Deficits appeared in the U.S. balance of payments. The opening of the Common Market in Europe was seen to provide some opportunities for American trade and investment but also to put the United States and other outside countries at some disadvantage. The Trade Expansion Act of 1962 envisaged a more-drastic removal of trade barriers among industrial countries than had been seriously considered before. It also created the machinery for governmental adjustment assistance for labor and business damaged by imports. The idea was not new (and, as it turned out, the machinery did not work well), but its acceptance in 1962 is significant for the subject of this chapter, since it implied a recognition that the structural changes likely to result from further trade liberalization could not be totally absorbed by unaided private markets. Or, one could say that the implication was that further major import liberalization would be unacceptable on the old basis.

The latter reason was the impetus for the American initiative for an international cotton textile agreement, which the Kennedy administration thought a political prerequisite to the passage of the Trade Expansion Act. In part the arrangements were a formalization, extension, and multilateralization of practices that had been followed by the United States and a number of other countries of requiring Japan and other producers to limit exports of some products that "disrupted" their markets. What was being set in motion—and enlarged in the 1970s—was the removal of the textile industry from the normal trade rules and the processes of liberalization in much the same way that agriculture had earlier been put into a special status. In the provisions, professed purposes, and machinery of the textile arrangements there are embryonic elements of an international policy for this industry, based on an orderly and acceptable transfer from old to new centers of production. The actual working out has been much more a matter of bilateral bargaining, unilateral measures, and disorderly development, however.[34] Although the initial American steps were accompanied by proposals for reorganization of the domestic industry, these were dropped once the protective apparatus was in place. The major changes that have taken place in the

American industry as a result of internal and external competition, technological change, and the flow of imports through and around the trade barriers have not been guided or supported in any significant way by the government, in contrast to what has been done in a number of other countries.

By the late 1960s, the strains on American economic policies had grown enormously. Many factors contributed: the deterioration of the balance of payments, the malfunctioning of the international monetary system, inadequate measures of monetary reform, the apparent loss of competitiveness of parts of American industry, stagflation, disturbances connected with the Vietnam war, the common American belief that Europe and Japan were not carrying their fair share of the burdens of defending and managing the free world, and American labor's increased resistance to import competition, combined with the belief that the large volume of direct investment abroad by American companies resulted in the export of jobs. Although the Kennedy Round was in many respects a success for American trade policy, it also added to the difficulties. The extensive reduction of tariffs emphasized the importance of nontariff barriers and trade-distorting practices, which were often deeply rooted in domestic economic policies. A common American view, especially in business, was that Japan and Europe made extensive use of these instruments while the American market was wide open to competition. All these factors and frustrations fed the outburst of economic nationalism reflected in the unilateral actions of the early Nixon administration, which severed the dollar from gold and temporarily established new barriers to international trade. Although disputes were patched up and steps taken to restore international cooperation in money and trade, no one could predict the future course of United States foreign economic policy. Equally in doubt was whether the country would continue to be as responsive to pressures for structural changes as it had been in the past and, if so, how it would respond.

The 1970s made things much worse. The energy crisis, inflation, international monetary instability, recession, and the slow and uneven recovery from the latter increased the demand for structural change in some sectors, added to the resistances to change and led governments to pursue immediate needs in ways that seem bound to cause long-run difficulties. The demands of developing countries for a new international economic order further complicated the strains among the older industrial countries and increased both the pressures for structural changes and the resistances to them. The dimensions of these difficulties and their inadequate resolution by the end of the 1970s are well known and need no restatement. What is significant for present purposes is that these troubled circumstances have played an important part in stimulating a new debate in the United States about the nation's structural problems and how to cope with them. By 1980 a question was constantly reiterated that, only a few years earlier, had hardly been thought worthy of attention: Should the United States adopt the kinds of measures other countries have long used under the general rubric of industrial policy?

More than debate was involved. As unemployment and all the other problems of recession increased, along with import competition, the threat of failure of great enterprises, and worry about the balance of trade and the state of the dollar, the American government took at least a few steps to shape (or at least prop up) the American economy. Structural as well as cyclical effects seemed probable. Past measures, some of long standing, were called into question and blamed for some of the present ills. Only some of these measures pertained directly to energy, the troubled sector in which structural change had been forced on the American economy. But implicit in governmental response when needs became pressing enough – and increasingly explicit in proposals and discussion – were basic questions of structural change and industrial policy.

NEW TALK AND SOME NEW ACTION

The difficulties of the late 1970s set in motion a number of actions and reactions that have created a completely new phase in the uneven history of American talk and possible action about industrial policy. As in other countries, many of the stimuli were cyclical, but frequently the responses have been colored by a sense that what was involved was more than the most-serious recession of the postwar period. Few people seriously argued that another Great Depression was in the making. But thoughts of that time were in the air, and not just because 1979 brought the fiftieth anniversary of the Wall Street crash. Felix Rohatyn, a New York financier, proposed a latter-day version of the Temporary National Economic Committee of the 1930s to set new goals for the national economy and advise the president and Congress how to reach them. He also called for a new model Reconstruction Finance Corporation to provide an orderly means of giving government financial help to companies in difficulty (after careful determination of the public interest and accompanied by experienced scrutiny of the firms to which money would be provided as loans or equity).[35]

Recent experience was more important than memories of the Depression in creating the view that more than cyclical factors were at work. For some years macroeconomic policies had not been working very well, for whatever reasons, but the recession called for actions that must, at least tacitly, tilt attention toward structural issues. If "pumping up demand" could not be relied on to generate adequate employment – even if the government were willing to run the risks of adding fuel to inflation – and if non-Keynesian measures of monetary policy were also unpromising in the short run, then attention had to be given to specific threats to jobs and the possibilities of creating work in certain places and certain lines of activity. Inevitably, the rationale of policy was confused. For a surprisingly long time the argument about helping out the Chrysler company was carried on primarily in terms of the merits of saving jobs versus the demerits of bailing out a company that had largely been responsible for its own difficulties. Only when Ford and General Motors began to suffer increasingly and the United Automobile Workers called for import barriers and foreign investment did larger structural issues come to dominate the debate. Even then it remained unclear whether the emphasis should be on temporary dislocation – perhaps a two-year period before enough domestically made small cars would be available – or whether government and industry alike should be thinking in terms of a much longer period.[36] In the steel industry, in contrast, the surge of unemployment emphasized long-run structural difficulties that dated back to the 1960s at least. Trouble in both steel and automobiles encouraged speculation about sectoral policies and where difficulty might next arise. Would it be in computers, if Japan's efforts in that field bore fruit? The possible settlement of the government's antitrust case against IBM was increasingly discussed in terms of what it would do to the competitive power of the American producer and the related industries.

Another push toward more structural thinking by Americans had begun several years earlier in the energy crisis. Even the great difficulty of getting agreement on steps to adapt the American economy to more costly energy played a part in this process. And when a program of action emerged to lower consumption, reduce dependence on imports of oil, and stimulate the development of alternative fuels, it comprised many elements of the kinds of industrial policies better known in other countries: targets, government investment, price and tax stimuli, direct regulation of use, and new public corporations with assigned tasks that could be accomplished only over a period of years. All this was possible only because enough people believed that energy was uniquely crucial to the whole economy. There were no close analogies with any other industries, and yet this exploration of new ways of doing things must have an influence on how future difficulties are approached. Moreover, it was plain that how the supply of energy was handled would have a considerable influence on energy-using industries, as had the original price increase. Although most of the adjustment was left to market forces, the fact that the impact differed from industry to industry meant that structural factors again came into play.

Much the same was true of government regulations setting environmental standards, which had become a central issue in American economic policy. Existing and potential rules constrain the burning of coal and open pit mining techniques, and therefore the substitution of plentiful American coal for scarce oil. The growth of nuclear power production has been slowed by concern for safety and, to some degree, by government decisions intended to reduce the risk of international proliferation of nuclear weapons. Part of the trouble in both steel and automobiles flowed from intensified concern for the environment. To ease their plight should standards be reduced or deadlines postponed? Could pollution be equally well controlled by methods that would cost less? Ought the government provide more financial help to carry the burdens it had imposed? Such questions were not really new; businessmen and some labor union spokesmen had been arguing for some years that the economy was suffering from too little regard to the impact of antipollution measures. They won over a certain body of opinion among economists, government officials, journalists, and the general public—at least when they had hard evidence of costs, avoided seeming to be callous or obtuse about the importance of environmental issues, and demonstrated that good results could be had by other means.

Other regulations raised some of the same questions. A considerable increase in rules about health, safety, noise, and food and drug standards, for example, had taken place in the 1960s and the 1970s. Sometimes rules of longer standing were being applied more intensively or broadly than before. Although the dollar figures varied greatly, there was no doubt that compliance was costly for many businesses, and that time and talent were diverted from other activities. The fact that a number of different agencies were involved that could operate separately from one another, and that consumer and other groups could not only lobby for new laws but often proceed independently in the courts to sue business or overturn government decisions, added new elements of uncertainty to corporate planning and to the costs of introducing new products. While many intemperate things were said on all sides, the seriousness of the issue was underlined when the executive branch established a committee to attempt to rationalize regulatory measures and business groups put forward proposals for reform that were not altogether one-sided.[37] The recession added fuel to this debate, especially when regulations were blamed for contributing to unemployment.

Probably, the fall in American productivity did most to spread alarm about the impact of regulation. It, too, was a longer-run phenomenon, but it became the topic of widespread and general concern by 1979 and 1980. The search for causes led many people to emphasize the relatively low levels of investment and savings in the United States compared to many other industrial countries (which was nothing new) and the decline in spending for research and development, in government and in private industry. There is room for debate about the merits of these arguments; they are mentioned here because the heightened attention to them helped stimulate the discussion of industrial policy in the United States in the late 1970s and early 1980s.

That is generally true of the new interest in supply-side economics. This is a much abused term that has been applied loosely to many different things: to some, simply the move away from Keynesianism (demand management), but to others, massive tax cuts that will expand the capacity of the economy (i.e., increase demand) by stimulating investment. For present purposes the emphasis is on a collection of views that have in common their focus on the need for public policy to pay more attention than in the past to the American productive plant. Expansion for future growth, modernization for competitiveness, and innovation to keep ahead are needs, according to this view, that can be met only by making them the explicit objectives of policy, thus overcoming years of neglect. Foreseeable bottlenecks, potential material shortages, the scarcity of skilled labor, run-down equipment, deteriorating railroads, and declining cities are among the targets emphasized by people who take these views. Among businessmen these views are often closely linked with proposals for directing more funds into investment; at another level is convergence with a broad range of policy suggestions, linked with the belief that the problems of the industrial world stem in part from the phases of the long cycles explored by Kondratieff.[38]

Drawing all these factors together some people spoke of "the reindustrialization of America."[39] Others used the term industrial policy or industrial strategy which, not many months earlier, had seldom been in general circulation. More than one group of people said to themselves, "It seems we have been talking about industrial policy all along and didn't know it." And this is true, of course, for that part of industrial policy concerning the performance of industry as a whole, or that can be said in some way or other to favor "industry" — usually thought of as manufacturing industry — over agriculture or services. But there was still much doubt about those aspects of industrial policy which especially concern structure or about measures that differentiate (discriminate) among industries or firms. Many Americans consider such measures to be regrettable departures from a general government stance of nonintervention forced by political necessity and which are in danger of becoming lasting protection or subsidy. Since few believe that the government can be relied on to "pick the winners," industrial policy is in danger of becoming a collection of measures to support the losers.

Agreeing that this last danger was real, another group of people argued that it would take some kind of industrial policy to stave off the pressures for increased protection if American industry continued to compete unsuccessfully with foreign producers, at home or abroad. It would help, for instance, if ways could be found to restore the apparently declining technological lead of the United States over other industrial countries. Measures to encourage the shift of workers and resources away from declining industries would make it socially and politically acceptable to remove some existing protection and avoid the imposition of new controls. As the competitiveness of some foreign producers seemed to be attributable, at least in part, to the industrial policies of their governments, some people wondered if the same medicine would be good for the United States. Traditional (and often tacit) assumptions of American superiority—at least in matters industrial and technical—increasingly gave way to questions as to whether the United States had something to learn from the rest of the world. The concept of *Japan as Number One* stimulated much talk and thought.[40] American labor union officials, long ideological foes of any form of worker participation in management, showed a new interest in what was done abroad, and some expressed a mixture of envy and admiration for the influence of their German colleagues and the seriousness with which they were taken in policy-making. This was quite a change from the time when American unionists considered the Germans insufficiently militant and suspected that *Mitbestimmung* would corrupt the union leaders who came to sit on the other side of the table. But as part of the Chrysler settlement, the head of the United Automobile Workers took a seat on the board of the company. And in another unprecedented move, his union invited Japanese manufacturers to invest in the United States as a way of saving jobs.

Another manifestation of the new interest in industrial policy in the United States in the first half of 1980 was shown by the activities of the executive branch of government. Earlier, in preparing to deal with the new GATT codes resulting from the Tokyo Round, the office of the U.S. Trade Representative had added some industry specialists to its staff. When important responsibilities for dealing with antidumping and foreign subsidy cases were transferred from the Treasury to the Department of Commerce, a new emphasis was put on industrial issues, which were already recognized in the way that department was organized. More was involved than trade. As she left the Treasury to take charge of the enlarged Bureau of Industrial Economics in the Commerce Department, one experienced official said: "We've milked about as much as we can from macro. To understand problems of capital formation and slow productivity, we have to probe more at the micro level."[41] With increased use of adjustment assistance, Labor Department officials found themselves facing problems of industrial structure that were difficult to deal with. The tripartite commission for the steel industry (set up pursuant to the Solomon Report) was chaired by the Secretaries of Commerce and Labor, but its activities received little attention until the spring and summer of 1980, when its discussions gained momentum and spread over a wider range of issues.

The Treasury Department played a central part in the Chrysler case. The spread of difficulties to the rest of the automobile industry triggered a number of studies, some with a long-range emphasis, and made immediate demands for current policy ideas on the Department of Transportation, the Environmental Protection Agency, and other parts of the government. When a limited number of measures to aid the automobile industry were announced in July 1980, White House officials were quoted as speaking of these as a "model" for an industrial "revitalization" policy.[42] That seemed hyperbole unless the alternatives were viewed as either doing nothing or taking major protectionist measures and nothing else. Nevertheless, even the terminology was unprecedented and a sign of the times in the new prominence Americans were giving to industrial policy. The emphasis, it appeared, was on enlisting the help of many parts of the government and on setting up a government-business-labor committee for the industry. Stuart Eizenstat, a key advisor of the president, made clear that he did not "mean every industry has to get the same treatment." Soon President Carter said that the help to the automobile industry was a step toward a more-comprehensive set of measures to revitalize U.S. industry that he would pursue if reelected. He spoke of steel and shipbuilding as possible early targets for the new approach.[43] The independent presidential candidate, John Anderson, made a speech to the American Stock Exchange, setting out what he considered to be the main elements of a sound industrial policy and what should be avoided.[44] The Republican candidate, Ronald Reagan, was not as explicit but had long favored less regulation and lower taxes.

All over the government, individuals who had concerned themselves with one or another aspect of industrial policy found new opportunities to pursue their interests, while others who had never heard of the subject were instructed to find out what industrial policy was and how it affected their agency. When a committee of the Economic Policy Group, an interdepartmental coordinating body, began preparing papers for a systematic review of the subject, it found its normal membership augmented by representatives of over two dozen parts of the executive branch.

It had taken legislation to provide funds for the Chrysler corporation, and Congress would be drawn into many other measures. The steel caucus of senators and representatives had played an important part in getting the Carter administration to act on the industry's concerns; caucuses for other industries that felt the need of help seemed likely to follow. The Senate Subcommittee on International Trade was joint sponsor with the New York Stock Exchange and Harvard University of a conference on competition, which produced a consensus statement calling for a whole series of measures of the sort mentioned earlier.[45] The Joint Economic Committee, which had conducted major studies of long-term structural change in the American economy, announced that it would hold hearings on industrial policy in the autumn of 1980, and there was little doubt that other committees would follow suit. Business groups that had long been chary of both the term industrial policy and most of the measures connected with it began preparing themselves to testify when called on and to formulate their own programs. Spokesmen for organized labor would also be heard, and it remained to be seen to what extent the considerable interest in certain aspects of industrial policy that had been manifested by individual labor leaders would crystalize into formal positions taken by individual unions or the AFL-CIO as a whole. There seemed little doubt that impetus would be given to labor's longstanding interest in strengthening the work called for by the Humphrey-Hawkins Act to improve the national economy. The President's Commission for a National Agenda for the Eighties, a group of distinguished citizens, sponsored a labor-management conference on industrial strategy in June 1980 and planned to devote significant space in its report to issues of future structural change in the economy.

The list of activities bearing on industrial policy is much longer. But perhaps, enough has been said to demonstrate that by the middle of 1980, interest in industrial policy in the United States had entered a new phase. Partly this is a matter of appearances; measures that were called by other names and that would have occupied public attention in any case have come to be called industrial policy. No doubt the term will be stretched even more; it will be used as a favorable or pejorative label for many proposals for public policy. Nevertheless, even when all necessary allowances are made for confusion, exaggeration, error, loose language, and faddishness, there is enough substance to the new American interest in industrial policy to justify speaking of a new phase. This is hardly surprising. It would be peculiar if the United States were totally immune to the responses that other industrial societies have felt. Moreover, it is hard to see how Americans can assess the problems they face without concluding, sooner or later, that they have to "think structurally" to a much greater degree than in the past.

All this does not mean that the United States is about to formulate a comprehensive industrial policy or embark on a series of measures aimed at altering the structure of its economy. For one thing the debate sketched above had only begun in earnest by the summer of 1980 as the bulk of this chapter was completed. The election that followed did not clarify matters. Although the state of the economy was much discussed, few industrial policy issues as such were debated. After his election, Ronald Reagan put primary emphasis on macroeconomic measures, such as tax cutting and the reduction of government expenditure. Though the expansion of production and productivity were the aims, they were not thought of as "industrial policy," a term abjured by many in the new administration.

There are no good grounds for predicting what will come next. Highly negative reactions to the very idea of industrial policy are not as general as they used to be, but there is no reason to expect that the balance has definitely tilted. Support for deregulation, inside the government as well as outside, has grown in recent years, and while this is not altogether incompatible with many measures of industrial policy—it can, indeed, be seen as a certain kind of industrial policy for the industries in question—it does stand as a contrast in the minds of many people. There is, too, a strong surge of concern about government intervention in the economy and a disposition to limit it, sometimes by quite arbitrary measures. But the problems which stimulated the discussions of industrial policy in 1979 and 1980 had not disappeared.

To the unpredictable can be added some features of American life that hamper the development of anything like a comprehensive industrial policy and many specific measures as well. The list starts with the separation of powers and goes through many familiar items that need only be mentioned, not elaborated on. Not only do the president and Congress have to agree on legislation, but there has to be consistency over a long period of time in how measures are carried out. The complexion of Congress changes, and different issues are determined by different combinations. The executive branch itself contains people whose views are bound to differ and officials whose duties cause them to stress quite different things. There is no mechanism for establishing a working consensus of government, business, and labor—much less other segments of the public—on objectives and methods of policy which would provide insurance against reversals when shifts in power take place. The relations of management and labor are carried on by methods that do not make it easy for them to work in close cooperation in complicated matters. Relations between government and business are also frequently adversarial, and the same is often true of labor. The financial structure of the United States does not lend itself easily to many of the methods by which industrial policy is carried out in other countries. The government does not dispose of funds or have sufficient influence over the funds of others to consistently direct the flow of capital to industries or firms that need support. Private banks, which play such an important part in shaping the industrial structure in Germany and some other countries, stand much farther from industry in the United States and do not always seem well placed to take a long view. Other countries are not immune to these difficulties, but a good case can be made for believing that the United States has less aptitude for industrial policy and more obstacles to overcome than most other democratic countries.[46]

When contemplating this array of obstacles, one might well conclude that it is beyond the powers of the United States to conduct a sustained and effective industrial policy. One could even decide that it would be better to stress, instead, whatever kinds of measures would make people more willing to adjust to changes in the world economy, allow market forces to work, and bring about these changes without counting on much government intervention. Perhaps that is how Americans will come to think — and perhaps not. After all, the United States has acted on some industrial policy matters; protectionism has structural effects and is certainly not beyond the country's capabilities; other countries have not let their own disabilities keep them from taking measures of industrial policy, however bad. If the need is great enough, the United States may overcome some of the obstacles to carrying out industrial policy measures. Or, and this seems even more likely, aims and methods will be shaped by what is possible, and the American structural measures that emerge will have their own unique cast. The chances are good, for the reasons laid out earlier, that efforts will be made in the United States in the coming years not only to think structurally but also to shape at least some measures of industrial policy. It is therefore pertinent to examine the list of problems that will have to be faced and the range of possible outcomes.

The Future

THE AGENDA OF PRESSING ISSUES

An agenda may be orderly, if someone has imposed a shape on it, or disorderly, if it reflects the demands that events impose as they arise, or something in between, if whatever the starting place, there is at least some logical connection between the parts as they ensue. Enough has been said above to give a reasonably clear idea of the way certain events have posed some industrial policy problems for the United States; a truly systematic ordering of questions would be based on an analysis of the structure of the American economy that cannot be undertaken here. We will next start with an important issue — energy — and follow where it leads. The list of subjects is not complete but comprises pressing problems facing the United States that cannot be adequately dealt with unless their structural aspects are given some attention. No attempt is made to explore these problems in any detail or to suggest solutions to them. The aim is to show what American industrial policy has to deal with, not what it will be. By the time the chapter is in print some of the situations dealt with here will have changed, but the underlying issues will remain.[47]

Energy is the field in which the United States has gone furthest toward developing an industrial policy. The slowness and difficulty of the process are important warnings about the problems the United States will encounter in other fields, although the pervasiveness of energy in the economy and its direct impact on so many voters make adjustments particularly difficult. Objectives have been set for conservation, the reduction of import dependency, the development of domestic production of fuel, and increasing supplies of alternative forms of energy. Disputes continue about prices, taxes, subsidies, and the parts to be played by private business and government. Actions taken on one matter raise questions about another. If oil companies can reduce their taxes by investment, what effect has their diversification into activities outside energy production? If a government corporation is given powers to expedite production and speed the switch to other fuels, how far should it be allowed to go in setting aside environmental standards?

Shaping an industrial policy for energy will be a continuing process. If domestic energy turns out to be higher priced than imported energy would be (as oil was in the past) and import dependence is to be limited, how will the costs be divided? What will they do to the international competitive position of the United States? To the extent that access to overseas energy supplies relies on understandings between the United States and supplying countries, further measures may have to be taken to be sure exports are supplied or imports dealt with if purchases of other goods are tied to purchases of oil.

Higher fuel costs and what is done or left undone in energy policy pose questions about the future of *energy-using industries*. Thus far most adjustment has been left to market forces, but the process is not complete as long as various government measures hold the prices of some fuels below real costs. If higher energy costs force the contraction of some industries, questions of public policy will arise that will involve not only immediate unemployment and dislocation, but also long-run regional and structural patterns, and sometimes even whether something must be done to retain the capacity to produce certain goods at home, the same consideration that motivates energy independence.

After energy, increased public concern with the *environment* is probably doing most to force American attention to structural issues. Higher environmental standards and the internalization of costs that were formerly borne by the community affect some industries more than others; smelters, for instance, are particularly hard hit, and so is the manufacture of some chemicals and other products that produce dangerous wastes. Location comes into question and the difference in the cost of prevention and treatment in new plants compared to bringing old ones up to the same standards. Whether the costs of meeting standards should always be met by the producer and consumer of the products in question (the polluter pays principle), or whether taxes and subsidies should be adjusted for some industries and areas to reflect social benefits or exceptional difficulties, ought to be judged in structural terms. If changes in environmental standards lead to a closing down of domestic activities in some lines, then questions of import dependence arise. International differences in environmental standards (or even the costs of meeting similar standards) may affect the competitiveness of some American industries in world markets. Raising standards of environmental control creates a demand for new products and stimulates R&D and innovation. Whole new supplying industries may appear, and those with a head start may have an advantage in foreign markets as other countries raise their own standards. How far government should concern itself with these responses is a question that has not yet received much attention, although there are obvious possibilities of linking the growth of the new activities with the contraction of others that results from raised environmental standards.

Export expansion is a generally accepted necessity in the United States at the beginning of the 1980s. Major governmental and private efforts are repeatedly called for, but there has been little emphasis on the potential ramifications of a serious and sustained effort to restore — or create — international competitiveness for most American industry. As on various occasions in the past, the initial stress has been on trade promotion, increased government support for business, taxes, and export credit. No doubt these are important elements, but for American industry to benefit from them on a sustained basis it must produce goods that are wanted abroad at attractive prices. The U.S. government has a limited ability to help industry from this standpoint, but it is quite possible that some policies are being pursued that impair the competitiveness of export industries. One immediately thinks of tariffs or import restrictions that raise costs, and this leads to thinking about the structure of American industry. Should production shrink in one sector in order to expand in another? Is there a public interest other than "what the market demands?" If an industry's costs are raised by tariffs on its supplies, should it be entitled to an equivalent tariff, or a compensatory subsidy, when it exports?

If exports are to be promoted, what should the government do, if anything, about *investment* abroad by American firms? The standard business view is that one invests abroad to hold a market that can no longer be held by exporting from the United States, and that this kind of investment usually generates demand for the export of still other products. If so, a policy that does not interfere with investment, or possibly even one that encourages it, is compatible with export promotion. But almost certainly there are cases in which overseas production displaces, at least temporarily, goods that had originally been purchased from the United States. Is there any way to influence this process without getting into the unacceptable position of substituting the government's judgment for that of businessmen? Other objectives also come into question. If the promotion of domestic investment is necessary for improved productivity and growth, is a tax policy that is neutral between investment at home and abroad appropriate? Even if an American firm's investment abroad pays off in the long run, its immediate effect may be to create unemployment at home. Should there be adjustment measures comparable to those that would be taken if import competition were to put some American producers out of business? Ought the cost be borne partly by the importing company?

An important American export is *technology*, in a variety of forms, and most people regard it as increasingly important to the balance of payments. But the export of technology can also be seen as the export of jobs; some people are tempted to try to find ways to ensure that technology sales or direct investment embodying the technology be delayed until the process (a) is about to be replaced by something better at home or (b) can no longer provide the advantage it had when it was new because some one else can approximate it. Many businessmen say they follow this pattern but would resist any efforts to substitute the government's judgment for their own, unless national security were involved (and their position would probably have a good deal of support in public and political opinion).

The promotion and improvement of technology, not the restrictions, began preoccupying Americans at the end of the 1970s (as had occasionally happened earlier). The loss of international competitiveness was one stimulus, but the not-well-understood fall in the rate of *productivity* growth spread even more alarm. Indeed, as was indicated above, this concern was one of the major factors to spur official and private interest in the possibilities of industrial policy, broadly conceived. Businessmen and journalists emphasized the connection between the fall in productivity and the decline in government and private spending for research and development and the low level of investment in the United States, compared to such countries as Germany and Japan. Economists were not so sure. That there were connections was clear, but how decisive they were was questioned. A leading authority on the subject, Edward F. Denison, found it "implausible" that "a slowdown in the introduction of new knowledge into the productive process" should have been the principal cause of the drop in the rate of productivity growth after 1973. He suspected the coming together of a number of elements propelled by inflation, but said that "what happened is, to be blunt, a mystery."[48]

Earlier studies by Denison and others had stressed the contribution to growth from knowledge in many forms – the education of the labor force, management skills, technological and organizational improvement. These contributions were found to be far more important than additions to capital in explaining the past growth of the American economy. Of course capital was important, but it was only one factor. "It is quite wrong," said Denison, "to blame investment for the recent sharp reduction in the growth of American output and productivity, or to suppose that merely raising investment would go far toward restoring the old growth rate of productivity."[49]

Other economists stressed the fact that spending on R&D was a form of investment and that it undoubtedly contributed to innovation; it was, moreover, often very profitable, but it was also risky and might be expected to yield slower returns than capital spent on new machinery. The effect of "government-financed industrial R&D . . . on private productivity growth, and hence presumably on technological change in industry" was not nearly as clearly demonstrated as that of private R&D.[50] There also have been questions whether the deleterious impact of government regulation on business spending for R&D is as well established as businessmen assumed.[51] In this and related matters the emphasis of the experts is on how little is fully understood; a reader of their work must also be struck with the extent to which different methods produce different results, large residual items become significant explanatory factors, and the data themselves leave much to be desired.[52]

The element of uncertainty is important, since this disagreement between the savants and the practitioners undoubtedly concerns basic issues of an American industrial policy. The gist of what the economists are saying is not that nothing should be done along the lines the businessmen want, but that it remains to be seen whether general measures, such as tax reductions to stimulate investment and an increase in government spending on R&D, will have a strong enough impact. There is no point in trying to resolve the debate before acting, but if the economists are right problems will continue and one measure will have to be followed by another. Measures that, while moving in the same general direction, can be aimed at specific targets include accelerated write-offs for tax purposes of new equipment, accounting measures that take better account of inflation and permit covering replacement costs, and concrete measures affecting R&D, in part through the patent system.[53] There will continue to be questions, however, about how far tax concessions can produce results if the major drag on investment comes from uncertainty or the expectation of slow growth. Proposals for government spending on R&D will have to make a case for choosing between basic or applied research, whether specific targets should be set or scientists permitted to forge ahead on their own, whether a massive new government project is in order or if a number of objectives should be pursued through contracts to private industry, more money for universities, or whatever.

Increasingly, Americans accept the sweeping proposition put forward by Professor Lawrence R. Klein: "We must go from being a high-consumption economy to being a high-saving economy if we are to reindustrialize and improve our standard of living."[54] That is a succinct statement of what quite a few people have been saying and could be an objective of macroeconomic policies. A number of the general measures that have been proposed concerning taxes, environmental standards, and regulation would move in that direction (as would other, more-radical, proposals that have not been mentioned here, such as the introduction of a Value Added Tax to substitute for a significant share of the personal and corporate income tax). But as this agenda shows, it is doubtful if general policies will suffice; they will certainly not meet all the existing demands. A major part of the agenda with which we are concerned must focus on the difficulties surrounding the choice and execution of governmental measures.

Plainly, though, more than governmental measures are required. Some observers have been bothered by the suspicion that some American businessmen are less entrepreneurial than they ought to be. The quarterly dividend and the price of the company's shares on the stock market are two indicators that American managers consider important to their own reputations (and jobs). But heavy investments in new capital equipment absorb profits that could otherwise be distributed to shareholders, and a fall in dividends will reflect itself in the stock market. Some American businessmen, and a number of foreigners, especially Japanese and German, believe that preoccupation with relatively short-run financial results has led some American managers to neglect the long-run strength of their companies. Support for this view comes from reports by American businessmen who have sought to take over small domestic firms that were technologically interesting and found themselves heavily outbid by foreign companies who were willing to accept lower profits for a period of years, profits that could not be justified according to American ideas of necessary cash flow. Additional but indirect support for this view can be found in the statement of Lyman Hamilton, an experienced business executive, that one reason he was arranging a major new venture as a private partnership was that "we won't be tempted to make foolish short-term decisions just to make our earnings look good every quarter."[55]

A related, and generally recognized, tendency of business is to reduce R&D in periods of low profitability because of the unpredictable connection between expenditures and return. How serious these factors are in affecting American productivity and the long-run competitiveness of American firms is impossible to say. A potential vicious circle is only too apparent since, as American businessmen are quick to point out, without a good financial record it is impossible to raise outside capital, and self-financing is reserved to those with a high profit ratio. It requires no great imagination to see a potential role for the common instrument of industrial policy, government capital or guarantees in some form, but resistance to such ideas in the United States is great and the modalities are difficult. It would in any case involve some tortuous reasoning to justify government aid to firms that by definition were not managed in their own best long-run interest. Indeed, whether any measures of public policy can usefully be taken to set right managerial deficiencies is not clear. But can we be sure that correction will come within business itself?[56]

Criticism of the quality of management in the steel and automobile industries has been common, not least among other businessmen. In the Chrysler case, in particular, it was frequently advanced as a reason for not providing a bail-out. Other counsels prevailed, but the terms of the assisting legislation required significant contributions from management, labor, banks, and other creditors, and imposed an unusual degree of public supervision on Chrysler through the Chrysler Corporation Loan Guarantee Board, a committee of high-ranking federal officials with a considerable staff.

Even when it was believed that the necessary public aid was limited to Chrysler, the consequences for the structure of the industry were of concern to the other companies, although the government or general public were not yet ready to think in those terms. Ford and General Motors had to reckon with the fact that if Chrysler collapsed, its share of the market might be taken by more-competitive foreign producers. General Motors was thought to be inhibited from expanding domestic sales for fear of antitrust action, since it already held a large share of the market.[57] By the time the federal government moved to take more general measures in July 1980, the need for thinking about the future shape of the industry was apparent. As usual, though, immediate pressures created the demand for action, and it was difficult to determine what weight to give to long-run factors or even to distinguish one set of factors from another.

The collapse of demand and the increase of imported cars was the trigger. But when the economy again improved and the retooling of the firms to produce smaller cars was complete, could the American producers be expected to hold their own without special help? If so, was investment by Japanese producers, as urged by American officials and specifically asked for by the United Automobile Workers, a proper response? Some Japanese said they would just be starting to produce in significant numbers as the American firms came back on stream. But if, as some observers thought, the Japanese companies would sooner or later want to produce cars in the United States to hold their share of that market — along the lines of what has happened in the industry in the past — would it be very disadvantageous to move sooner? Alternatively, if the price of not investing in the United States turned out to be either American import restrictions or Japanese export restraints, would that be too high a price for Japanese producers and American consumers to pay if the restraints were removed at the end of the (hypothesized) two-year period? How could one be sure?

However one answers these questions, it could be argued that policy ought to take account of the long-run forces that would shape the world industry. For example, the growth of demand for automobiles is bound to be faster in the developing parts of the world than in the more nearly saturated markets of the older industrial countries. Unless there are radical changes in the means of producing automobiles, the technology of the assembly line seems to invite increased location in middle-level developed countries. The industry has become increasingly internationalized. Ford and General Motors combine domestic and overseas output to serve the American and foreign markets in ways that reshape the American industry.[58] Should the United States government take steps that stop or slow that process? What say should the labor unions have in the matter? If long-run factors would limit the size and alter the structure of the automobile industry, what account should be taken of the impact on the industries that supply it with steel, textiles, paint, glass, and rubber?[59]

Steel, the other basic industry that has led the U.S. government into the rudiments of an industrial policy, presents quite a contrast to automobiles. A less international industry, its troubles go back at least to the late 1960s, when Japanese and European producers were asked to hold down exports to the United States temporarily. That may have been simple but limited protectionism, but it was clear that to restore competitiveness would require more investment than was taking place, and there were already thoughts in the industry about some kind of international agreement ensuring fair trade. The escape clause action that put restraints on imports of special steels in 1976 was again a more or less conventional action. Then both industry and the government moved toward unprecedented and more-comprehensive measures, first set forth in the Solomon Report of late 1977. Imports were subjected to a novel arrangement, the trigger price mechanism, and other kinds of measures were proposed to help make the domestic industry competitive. Direct governmental action was only part of the arrangement; investment by industry and, less clearly, cooperation on the part of labor were understood to be necessary elements.[60] The trigger price mechanism takes Japanese costs as a starting point and thus implicitly accepts some degree of international competitiveness as a proper standard for the American industry. In practice, the application of this standard is less clear-cut, and the trigger price mechanism seems to have been judged more in terms of the level of imports it permitted than by its price effects. When, in March 1980, the largest producer, the US Steel Corporation, brought a series of antidumping cases against Western European producers, the government suspended the trigger price mechanism. Did this mean a return to old-fashioned (and on the whole unsatisfactory) methods that emphasized fair trade and an abandonment of efforts to reshape the industry? There were indications that the steel company was as interested in pressing for action by the U.S. government as it was in checking imports. One could forsee what in fact came to be the partial compromise — restoration of the TPM at a higher level, to be followed by governmental action on tax matters. It remained unclear, however, whether further understandings would be sought with foreign producers and governments, perhaps via the Steel Committee of the OECD, which although set up some time earlier, had been little used.

In contrast to what was being done in Europe to reshape the steel industry, American efforts were guided by no publicly known program as to what was to be contracted and where new facilities would be built if the capital could be raised for investment. The reaction of communities and workers against the shutting-down of inefficient mills was inevitable, and efforts to ease transitions came after the event. There was a notable absence of public discussion of long-run objectives, including the desirable size of the industry, although more-specialized discussions suggest 15 to 20 percent of consumption as a tolerable level of imports, if their prices are not too low. How efficiency is to be assured in the 80 to 85 percent of the domestic supply produced at home is not clear. Investment by the industry, with government encouragement, is a recognized need, but the means of assuring it are not yet in sight. The diversification out of steel-making proper in which some American steel firms are engaged is itself ambiguous. Increasing profits improves the ability to invest; specialization within the steel industry increases efficiency; but if capital and management are diverted from steel-making and basic capacity shrinks, is the result to be welcomed? The answer can only be given by addressing questions about the structure of American industry that have not been dealt with as matters of public policy in the past. Similarly, the implications of any of these approaches for wages in the industry and thus for labor relations have not been explored.

In the past, one reason many Americans resisted a *sectoral approach* to problems of trade and industry was the rational fear that what is done for one will have to be done for others. While there can be no doubt that the automobile and steel industries are of exceptional importance, the old resistance to an industry-by-industry approach may now have broken down. If so, are there more candidates? Textiles and clothing were long ago accepted as special cases—but for protection, not adaptation. It is an open question whether the 1980s will see new proposals to combine private and public measures to produce an industry that can survive with less protection. Much of the rest of the industrial world shares the same problems, and it seems clear that truly free trade in textiles is not widely acceptable. But the costs of making (or resisting) major shifts, and the incidence of these costs on people and regions, present difficult issues that the United States has not been willing to consider. As the twentieth anniversary of the original cotton textile arrangements approaches, people may well ask whether it really was sensible to allow one of the largest industries to wrestle with a whole series of difficulties, many of which were widely anticipated, with no other public action than a refined protectionism (capable of being more neatly targeted than simple old-fashioned tariffs, both as to product and source of supply).

There is renewed agitation for aid to shipbuilding, partly on security grounds. Some measures to help the shoe industry met with a certain success, but little has been said about applying the same approach elsewhere. Perhaps a better way to put such questions on the agenda of American industrial policy discussions for the 1980s is in terms of an older, never satisfactorily resolved issue: *adjustment* assistance for industries suffering from import competitors. More has been done in this field in the last few years than ever before, but experience is still limited and the range of possibilities is hard to judge. New legislation may affect the link between imports and assistance. Experts have long favored the view that adjustment activities should respond to all factors of change in the economy, not just imports.[61] Nevertheless, heavy expenditures resulting from high unemployment in the automobile and steel industries have stimulated a counter-current of opinion insisting on a clear link between adjustment assistance and shifts in employment to other industries. Even if the government takes more initiative in this field, as is to be expected, and business and labor overcome some of their inhibitions about the approach, which is less probable, the contribution of adjustment assistance to hastening change is hard to predict. Politically, the existence of effective methods of adjustment that ease the transfer of resources out of declining industries and cushion the impact, especially on workers, should make the removal of import barriers (or other measures that may create disturbances) more acceptable, if not to those who are hurt, at least to politicians and voters whose interests are broader. Economically, an improved mechanism of adjustment assistance can reduce some of the costs of change and add to the flexibility of the economy. Any attempt to use adjustment assistance on a large scale as a tool of industrial policy and structural change runs into the difficulty, not peculiar to the United States, of determining how displaced labor and other resources can be better used. Any action implies some judgment about structure and some commitment to support the new status quo, at least for a time.

Somewhat related is a renewed American concern with problems of depressed areas, another possible source of pressure for structural thinking. Regionalism has a mixed record in the United States, including the use of freight rates to help disadvantaged areas and federal measures that redistribute funds from richer to poorer regions. At various times there has been an emphasis on the virtues of the Federal Reserve System in making it easy for capital to move from one region to another without triggering the kind of adjustment mechanism that caused trouble internationally (and therefore, in some formulations, avoiding the need for government programs). While a few large depressed regions have received special attention, in recent decades cities and parts of cities have been the main focus of concern. There have also been programs dealing with the impact of the closing of major defense facilities and with areas of persistently higher-than-average unemployment. As is perhaps natural, these programs have been characterized by a conservative bias (i.e., a tendency to keep existing activities going), whereas the introducing of new activities would have been more constructive. Sometimes local measures to protect health, the environment, and the unspoilt character of an area can also be impediments to industrial activity; the increase in restrictions on the transportation of radioactive wastes is a recent example.

When efforts are made to attract investment that will create new activities, another set of problems emerges. States and cities bid against one another to give away their tax funds (and sometimes federal money, too) to large corporations in ways that can only accidentally produce the most-rational distribution of industry or deal effectively with problems of structural change. Whether the recipients are domestic or foreign corporations, the federal government might be held responsible internationally for the elements of subsidization in these practices.[62] Foreign direct investment in the United States has increased greatly in recent years, stimulated by a variety of factors. Although some initial apprehension has given way to a general appreciation of the advantages of this practice at least when it is new investment, questions about the size and character of foreign investment will undoubtedly figure on the agenda of industrial policy in the future.

Whether the starting point is the avid solicitation of foreign investment that is now undertaken by American states and cities even more than the federal government, or the international competitiveness that is potentially the best criterion for American industrial policy, internal competition must be considered. High on the agenda for thinking about the structure of the American economy will be the established American industrial policy, the antitrust laws. The perspective is quite different from that in which they were conceived or, for the most part, have been used. The laws are mostly general, with a few specific exceptions based largely on concepts of natural monopoly, social policy (as in the case of labor unions), and industries subject to direct government regulation. There is, however, unavoidable selectivity in enforcement, and selectivity (or differential treatment) is a hallmark of structural policy. Government officials have to decide when to take antitrust action, against which companies, under what parts of the law, and to produce what results. Even when no action is taken there can be a selective effect, since some industries or companies are obviously more likely to attract the attention of the Department of Justice than others; prudent managers (or at least those with cautious lawyers) will avoid certain actions to reduce the risk of drawing federal fire. Once a process is engaged, a series of choices must be made that affect industrial structure: the remedies to be sought, the arrangements accepted in consent decrees, the conclusions reached by judges (and sometimes juries) as to whether competition has been interfered with; the detailed conditions a judge may then lay down for future behavior by a company, sometimes including the sale of specified assets, withdrawal from certain activities, and a ban on expansion; extended supervision of a company to see that it conforms.

Laws govern what can be done, but their application depends on explicit or tacit findings of fact. Will a merger strengthen or weaken competition? Is a company too big because it has twice anyone else's share of the market? What market is in question: a section of the United States, the whole country, the world? Does product A really compete with product B, or would the economy gain if the same firm produced both? These questions are now answered by many different people, often acting separately from one another. As far as I know, only experience and precedents provide criteria, although experts may be called on. The law provides some standards but is inevitably written in general terms; relevant concepts of competition are different for grocery stores and steelmills, and what makes sense in an industry that is thriving could be fatal to one that was contracting or shaken by the effort to adapt to changed circumstances.

Up to a point, the decentralized and ad hoc elements of the antitrust process are well able to take account of these differences. Prosecutors, judges, and juries look at the facts of the case, including the economic conditions of the industry, and not at some idealized model (or are supposed to). One may wonder, however, how such a process can produce as much continuity and coherence in the treatment of industries as sound and sustained structural policies require. Certainly, much could be done by the Department of Justice and the Federal Trade Commission through their decisions on what actions to bring and what remedies to request, and by indicating what account they would take of considerations of industrial policy. That is, this could be achieved if there were a set of industrial policies from which the Anti Trust Division and the FTC could derive guidance (within the limits of the laws they were administering).

Some recognition of these possibilities can be read into a few discrete events. The Solomon Report, noting the interest in mergers and joint ventures in the steel industry, recommended that the Department of Justice speed up its reaction to requests from steel companies about its enforcement intentions in such cases. When, in 1978, the merger of two conglomerates each of which owned a major steel company (Jones and Laughlin and Youngstown Sheet and Tube, the seventh- and eighth-largest producers) was judged not to warrant prosecution as a diminution of competition, it seemed as if the general condition of the steel industry was being taken into account. Perhaps that was also true when in February 1980 the Federal Trade Commission announced that the investigation of the automobile industry it had begun in August 1976 would be narrowed to the question whether "economic efficiency or illegal exclusionary conduct accounts for the continuing dominant positions of the market leaders, especially General Motors."[63] Judgments about proposed new antimerger laws depend heavily on what people believe would be their impact on the oil industry.

Reform of the antitrust laws, or at least some changes in their administration, are usually on the list of proposals from business groups when they discuss ways to improve international competitiveness. Generally their aim is to free firms from the worry that they will be prosecuted for overseas activities or explicitly to permit companies to join forces to deal more effectively with foreign competitors. No doubt there are often good arguments for that sort of change, but any proper examination of the subject would also have to emphasize the importance of the effective use of the antitrust laws to stimulate domestic and international competitiveness. It may well be that the international dimensions will take on greater importance in the future, not only for the United States but also for other countries. The old subject of international concern with restrictive business practices (and their structural base) will reemerge.[64]

For the future the question remains a two-sided one: (a) if the United States adopts general measures of industrial policy or at least concerns itself with certain industries, whether it should let those policies guide its use of antitrust measures (as broadly defined here); and (b) whether the "normal" pursuit of antitrust issues (i.e., the existing state of affairs) will not itself intensify the growing concern with structural problems. Those lines of inquiry cannot be pursued in this chapter, but when they are, two points ought to be kept in mind. One is that the very existence of the antitrust laws (and the attitudes behind them) plays a part in shaping the structure of business. For example, companies with a substantial share of the domestic market sometimes seek growth by investing abroad instead of expanding at home, or they may prefer diversification at home to pursuit of the specialties that have made them strong. Bankers attribute some of their overseas expansion to the limitations on domestic expansion created by the complex system of regulations. The second point is that the need to take account of foreign competition in the United States and the place of American companies in world markets does not necessarily mean that the laws should not be used to limit the size of American firms. The common business view is that the animus against bigness is anachronistic. But size does not necessarily spell efficiency, and competitiveness can usually be improved by competition. One of the weaknesses of industrial policy in many countries is that it often limits competition, shelters monopolies, and permits businessmen (or the managers of government corporations) to engage in restrictive practices. Sometimes this is necessary, but departures from competition require more justification than efforts to promote it.

The list of problems that tend to push the United States toward more structural thinking could be lengthened. Support for *small business*—a principle that has often been of more ideological and oratorical importance than economic value in the United States—is now being advocated, as it is in other countries, on grounds of job creation and flexibility in changing circumstances.[65] But whether programs can be devised in which economic rationality will outweigh traditional political reflexes remains to be seen.

All manner of questions arise about *labor* law and policy, the strengths and weaknesses of unions, the imperfections of the labor market, regional differences, and the coexistence of high unemployment among young and blacks at the same time that there are shortages of skilled workers in a number of fields. In broader terms, there is a great need to find better ways to combine job (or income) security with the flexibility in the use of the labor force that is required if the American economy is to move to a new level of effectiveness. Questions arise about the quality of work and the quality of what the workers produce and a whole range of issues of growing importance about immigrant labor, all of which bring structural issues to the fore—or would if they were calmly and systematically looked at.

Still, the greatest incentive for more American thinking about structural issues is the persistence of pervasive economic difficulties and the failure of either tried and true methods or innovations to restore the stability and growth that Americans have come to expect from their economy. Less support than in the past favors the conventional wisdom that the only way to deal with these problems is to get the macroeconomic policies right and then to cope with all other difficulties through the play of market forces with minimal government intervention. One would not question this view if such success in policy could be achieved, nor would one question the need to try to move constantly in that direction. The new realism emphasizes not only the need to supplement macroeconomic policy with other measures, also but the suspicion that one of the reasons for the lack of success of the more-general economic policies is that there is some accumulation of structural difficulties, either from neglect or a strong tendency to lean toward conservative and protectionist solutions over time.[66]

A change in thinking—whatever that means in a democracy of over 200 million with a pluralistic society and a mixed economy—is not enough to produce effective industrial policy. The obstacles to any kind of comprehensive action are formidable; the pressures to take piecemeal measures that resist change. Sustained efforts would require a change in attitudes and methods; but for some time to come, progress, if any, is likely to take the form of limited action within the old framework.

The new interest in industrial policy should not be allowed to reduce the emphasis on getting the best possible macroeconomic policies, and especially should not become the excuse for avoiding hard decisions to cope with stagflation. Realistic account should be taken of the strong preference of many Americans for dealing with problems by general measures that do not discriminate among people and enterprises. Regulations that could bring about desired results by harnessing private self-interest and market forces ought to be used as much as possible. One need not have the highest confidence that private entrepreneurs and the market will produce the best results to recognize that the lack of bureaucratic talent and of criteria that are translatable into practice and the presence of inescapable political forces will interfere with the shaping of sensible governmental decisions. Studies of the multiplication of regulatory activities, the costs of meeting some standards, the counterproductive results of some efforts, and the unrealistic and ineffective results of trying to specify precisely how good should be done and bad prevented have to be taken seriously.[67]

To a degree, the problems themselves and the disappointing experience of dealing with them in old ways will help to bring some change. In both Congress and the executive branch there is a degree of understanding that new ways must be found to handle complex issues. Champions of congressional power realize that it cannot be brought to bear constructively until the legislators overcome the disorganization of recent years. The executive branch, too, is clearly not yet ready to cope competently with the needs of an industrial policy, and any steps it may take to expand its capabilities will require some time to prove themselves.

Business groups are showing an increased awareness that to elicit from government a better understanding of their needs, they not only must be ready for new ways of doing things, but will also have to understand the perspectives and needs of politicians and bureaucrats. Some businessmen thought the most important part of President Carter's program for the automobile industry was his statement in Detroit that he sought "a very close-knit permanent partnership" of the government, the automobile companies, and the workers "within the sources of propriety in the free-enterprise system." Later he broadened the proposition, saying that if reelected he would work for the revitalization of American industry through "a much closer partnership between the Government . . . and industry . . . to make sure we have full employment and also give industry the chance to be competitive on a worldwide basis."[68] When, instead, Ronald Reagan was elected, most businessmen felt that their access to the government would improve.

The views of labor leaders on long-range adjustment to changes in the structure of the world and the American economy are, not surprisingly, unclear in a period when short-run problems of unemployment and inflation are acute. After a long period in which the dominant note was allegiance to an orthodoxy of economic views that seemed mainly intended to preserve the status quo achieved by labor in a time of upward development, new ideas and their expression are needed but have not yet appeared in any clear form. There are some hints of potentially significant advances in views about labor's relation to business and government, the interest of workers in productivity and the competitiveness of their industries, and what government should do about planning or otherwise finding ways to adapt the economy to changing circumstances. Not yet in evidence are any efforts to produce labor's own prescriptions for the treatment of industries in difficulties (other than protection) or to work out arrangements for the introduction of new technology, comparable to those used constructively in the past in the bituminous coal industry and West Coast longshore work and, less impressively, in railroading and printing. Formulas for combining job (or income) security for workers with the flexibility the economy needs remain scarce. The make-up of the organized labor movement itself, with expanding membership in the services sector but a lag behind the growth of labor force as a whole, may stimulate new approaches.

A number of labor leaders see in the Humphrey-Hawkins Act of 1978 a focus for some of the work that needs to be done in thinking through the structural problem of the American economy. That law is weaker and vaguer than many of its proponents hoped, but some people believe that a broader interpretation of its provisions would serve some of the purposes of industrial policy. It might even, they argue, be used as a vehicle for a limited degree of indicative planning, at least for a few areas of the economy. Should it not be possible, they ask, to do for other important sectors as much planning as has been done for energy—or as is normal in defense industries? Fear of the political and economic consequences of government planning still stirs negative reactions in many Americans, and in itself sometimes confuses issues. Anything comprehensive or rigorous is unfeasible, but some businessmen and others realize that to take a long-run view, or to have some assurance that the rules will not be changed, may require planned elements in public life. This is equally true if there are to be realistic targets in industrial policy. However, it is not by focusing on disputes over planning that the United States will make progress with its industrial policy issue in the years just ahead.

These are the optimistic elements. Others are not at all promising. Advocates of positive governmental action and those who would resist all government intervention in the economy are increasingly at loggerheads. Even thoughtful and constructive approaches by businessmen can make little headway when business is unpopular and regarded with suspicion by much of the public. The result is often to concentrate business pressure on getting tax adjustments and other favors and taking ideological stands. These and other factors set the stage for ineffective measures, partial policies that conflict in aims and methods according to who prevailed on which issue, and inaction, until problems are so pressing that only defensive and protective measures are acceptable.

How the contradictory forces will work out, what balance will be struck between new approaches and adherence to old ones that become less satisfactory as time passes and difficulties grow, are questions open to speculation. One set of considerations is built into the issues discussed earlier in this chapter, what happens in the rest of the world is another consideration that will have an important influence. Many difficulties the United States faces and many of the obstacles to dealing effectively with them involve primarily domestic matters. Few of them, however, can be handled successfully without regard to U.S.-foreign economic relations. In the case of many issues, external pressures and the lack of some degree of international accommodation for what is undertaken in the United States are bound either to prevent constructive action or to become active forces for negative and restrictive measures.

AMERICAN INDUSTRIAL POLICY AND THE INTERNATIONAL ECONOMY

The agenda of future industrial policy issues for the United States sounds very inward looking. The structure of production, investment and technology, job security and labor flexibility, regulation and deregulation, the impact of environmental controls on productivity and coal mining, and all the rest seem to be quintessentially domestic problems that require domestic solutions. And so they are, but such a statement is misleading. Few subjects demonstrate better than industrial policy the truth that in economic relations, at least among industrialized, democratic countries, the domestic has become international and what is international has great effects on domestic affairs, political and economic. An appreciation of this fact has major implications for the conduct of industrial policy and for the place of international understandings about national action, but before turning to those subjects, it should be made clear in what concrete ways the issues of American industrial policy are involved in the relation of the American economy to the rest of the world.

The connections are obvious and familiar. For steel, automobiles, textiles, shoes, television sets, and a long list of other industries and products, import competition has been the major force that produced action, whether protective or adaptive. The concerns with productivity, low investment, inadequate R&D, etc., are directly linked with the decline of American competitiveness. So too is much of the criticism of governmental regulation, environmental standards, and antitrust. The energy issue on which there is the most clearcut consensus is the need to reduce dependence on imports. When an industrial policy measure, whatever its form, protects higher-cost American production by restraining imports, it may be justified on grounds of national security, the balance of the domestic economy, the need to provide jobs or income for certain groups of people, or the social or political unacceptability of the dislocation that would come from increased imports. But whatever the reason, in addition to the direct cost of protection there is a risk of a further cost to the U.S. economy from foreign retaliation by action against American exports. Since an improvement in the American balance of payments is one of the objectives of American policy and since an increase in competitiveness is recognized as essential to that, the criterion of international competitiveness leaves its imprint on most issues of American industrial policy. It follows that, in addition to whatever is done to make American production more efficient, there will also have to be a sustained effort to secure the reduction of foreign trade barriers and the creation of conditions under which foreign competition in the U.S. market will be accepted as fair by some agreed set of standards.

This summary provides a good part of the answer to a question put by the authors of the national and European Community sections of this volume: What does the United States (in this case) require of the international economic system for an effective industrial policy? To be sure, the answer implicit in what has already been said assumes something about the kind of industrial policy the United States may be following in the years to come. The analysis of earlier pages has shown why that assumption cannot be made with great assurance. But to review a range of contradictory policies and spell out the international requirements of each would be tedious and largely unedifying. What does a country ask of the international system to complement a policy of resistance to change, support for inefficiency, and protectionist measures? Indulgence, or pressure to mend one's ways?

If it is risky to make firm assumptions about the future of American industrial policy, it would be downright foolish to assume that all industrial policy measures will rigorously and consistently pursue the aim of international competitiveness and to draw the conclusion that to achieve it and to maximize the economic benefits to the American people would require a high degree of adaptation of the U.S. economy to changes in the world. Nevertheless, it does not seem foolish to assume, at least for working purposes, that those aspirations will guide a good bit of what the United States does. The inherent logic of the connection between recognized domestic needs and a foreign economic policy moving in that direction has been recognized. Several of the authors of this volume have elsewhere made clear their preferences for adaptive structural policies that keep national economies open to the world.[69] The prescriptions have not been too far away from the professed aims of their governments — when they have been stated — although often far from what has been done in practice.

This earlier work showed that it is hardly credible that any major country can carry out adaptive policies in isolation; a degree of international cooperation is required, and probably a rather high degree. If leading industrial countries do not move in approximately the same direction — *mutatis mutandis*, without ignoring significant differences in national positions, the structures of national economies, and methods of policy and styles of approach — then the chances that any one of them can hold to such a course are poor and will become poorer as time passes. There must, in short, be some agreement on aims and methods that not only permit structural change but encourage it, fostering economic efficiency (broadly conceived), providing international equity, and recognizing the need to allow for diversity arising from political autonomy and difference in social aspirations.

To make anything of that sort acceptable and indeed workable in the long run each country must be free to cope with certain difficulties that are greater for it than for other countries, and at the same time each country must limit its actions by taking account of the needs of others. Effective national action must be linked to positive international cooperation, probably novel in scale and methods. The adoption of new policies cannot be postponed until some better time when difficulties may be less pressing and cooperation easier. The test of the policies lies precisely in their ability to cope with a period of stress and strain, coupled with and partly occasioned by slower growth than is desirable and by continued strong pressures for change at a pace not always politically and socially tolerable. The awkward need is to be able to deal with large problems of the change of structures — whether the emphasis is on excess capacity in important industries, the adaptation of the world to new energy costs, the emergence of the NICs, or the heavy pressure on the poorest parts of the world. Unless the structural policies of the industrial democracies are capable of dealing with these hard and immediate problems, it is unlikely that easier times (when nothing but constructive cooperation is called for) will be reached.

This general formula applies to all democracies with mixed economies, Thus, vague as it is, it becomes a major part of the prescription of what the United States would require of the international system. At least that is true as long as the United States follows what can properly be called a positive industrial policy, to borrow the OECD term but to go beyond its particulars.[70] Perhaps the characteristics of such a policy need repeating. There will have to be a general acceptance in the United States of the idea that some of the structural problems of the economy have to be addressed directly: they will neither disappear through the functioning of the market and successful macroeconomic policy nor be sufficiently small in the costs imposed on the rest of the economy to be tolerable. This means that obstacles to change will have to be minimized, whether the pressures for change come from imports or something else, and ways will have to be found of facilitating transitions that, in the past, have been either resisted or left to the play of market forces. When, for any one of a wide range of reasons, some standard other than international competitiveness is to govern in some areas — agriculture, defense, to achieve diversification of the economy, because of lack of alternative jobs — both the reason for such protection and its costs are to be made as explicit as possible and the burden borne by the nation itself rather than the rest of the world (as far as this is possible). More than adaptation to change is called for. The American economy must be made to function better than it has in recent years, both to provide alternative and rewarding uses for resources displaced by adaptation and to give the positive results in international competitiveness that seem essential to meeting the reasonable expectations of the American populace. (To what extent the expectations may have to be adjusted to become reasonable is another matter.) How much consensus this kind of policy requires on goals, how much concerted action to carry out measures, and how much could be accomplished by freeing the forces of inventiveness, investment, and consumer choice must be left to individual cases. So too one must leave aside the question of how such aims are to be pursued, by what mixture of private and public action, and by what combination of old or new methods.

Such a recipe is annoyingly general. It would never serve in the kitchen of policy where ingredients have to be more precisely labeled, measured out in the right combinations, blended in one way rather than other, mixed according to rules, and left to rise, cook, cool, or age for stipulated periods of time ("to taste" if not "until ready"). Still, the resulting list of requirements from the international economy is reasonably clear.

Many of these, as has already been indicated, can be summed up by saying that unless somewhat similar approaches are followed by at least other major industrial countries, there will be little possibility of making these measures work in the United States. In part this translates into standard and old-fashioned needs, such as the willingness of all concerned to remove barriers to trade as much as possible, to agree to common approaches to the handling of nontariff barriers that are part of the industrial policies of each, to accept the fact that clashes in investment policy — positive governmental action, inducements to private investment, or restriction and regulation of it — have to be dealt with in much the same way as trade issues have been. And so on.

This sounds like a prescription for the improvement and refurbishing of the established arrangements for cooperation in the removal of trade barriers and the like. So it is, up to a point, because those arrangements were essential to past achievements and their continued effectiveness is not to be taken for granted. But to prevent the decline of cooperation and the rise of protectionism and mercantilistic economic nationalism (often associated with industrial policy) requires something more than improved liberalization of trade and payments. National industrial policy measures often have international impacts and can be handled only by finding new means of agreeing on acceptable and unacceptable practices and results, using more complex criteria than simple liberalization. This may be thought of as establishing rules for fair trade, applying the GATT codes that resulted from the Tokyo Round, and the OECD *Orientations*,[71] or simply avoiding or settling disputes or minimizing damage. In addition, something else is likely to be needed — the fitting together as best one can of some of the industrial policy activities of major countries to reduce friction and conceivably even to do the job better than each could alone. Good and bad examples of cooperation abound in this book: steel, shipbuilding, energy, and measures to deal with temporary excess capacity, adjusting the speed of change to what is acceptable, and moderating the impact of new investment on world markets. How often this kind of positive cooperation can be formalized and how much of it will be a matter of ad hoc adjustment to what others do with no explicit commitments are matters for speculation.

If the United States were to follow this prescription, considerable demands on the US would be created. It too would have to accept the validity of other countries' needs for the opening of American markets, reasonable policies toward investment, and "positive cooperation." This is nothing new. Without outside pressures, none of the OECD countries would have come as far as they have. The difficulties the US will encounter in pursuing constructive industrial policies have been made clear enough. To some degree — different in different cases — the ability of the U.S. government to overcome some of these difficulties is enhanced by the requirement that it is accountable to other countries for the effect on them of U.S. policies. Had there been no concern for the international repercussions, it would have been much more difficult for Washington to resist the demands for restrictive action in steel and automobiles.

For this external pressure to be effective, there must be benefits to the American economy from the way the international economic system works. Otherwise there is nothing to lose — and maybe something to be gained by putting pressure on others — or simply no resistance to the instinct to hit out. For example, if the United States takes seriously the effort to be internationally competitive and finds that the GATT codes on subsidies and government procurement do not in fact prevent other countries from barring American competition in their markets (perhaps in the name of industrial policy), there might well be a repetition of the frustration that contributed to the surge of economic nationalism in the United States at the beginning of the 1970s. This would have an immediate effect on the kinds of trade and investment measures the United States would take, and in the long run would almost certainly push American industrial policy toward a troublesome blend of protectionism and mercantilism likely to damage the real interests of the United States and of other countries.

Although our supposition puts the United States in the role of *demandeur*, we should not forget that the relation is reciprocal. The United States will have to respond to the needs of others and live up to agreed standards. It is not unknown for the United States to depart from its own principles, and efforts to revitalize the economy and become more competitive internationally are almost certain to produce more such cases. Some of the U.S. measures of forthcoming industrial policy, like some of its existing trade measures, will have to be altered or eliminated to accommodate the interests of others, or the system will not work.

In addition to the ability to strike balanced bargains, the international system must be flexible. The United States should find in the international economic system — or the capitals of other major countries, which is much the same thing—responsiveness to U.S. initiatives, and naturally the US must be sensitive to the needs of others as well. An effective system of international cooperation must provide some indulgence to a country for not living up to its ideals or even, at times, its commitments. There must be limits to this margin, but they cannot be described accurately in advance, and it is perhaps particularly difficult to do so in matters of industrial policy. One is driven to use terms suggesting certain minimum vital interests or the exigencies of domestic politics to which every democratic government owes its ability to survive, or the trade-offs that make positive policies possible, or, sometimes, just the time that is needed to move from an established situation (especially one that has deteriorated) to a more-satisfactory new arrangement.

The other side of indulgence is challenge and pressure. The aim is not only to make it clear that without suitable action on the part of the United States, other countries will not reciprocate; it is also a means of strengthening those within the United States (or any other country) who understand the need to move ahead to avoid slipping backward. If the international system does not do that, there is little of use that it can do.

Notes

1. John G. Miller, *Origins of the American Revolution* (Boston: Little, Brown, 1943), p. 4.

2. *Boston Gazette*, April 29, 1765, cited ibid., p. 23.

3. Article I, Section 8 of the Constitution, cited in the above paragraph, was, as late as the New Deal, a key element in determining the constitutionality of much welfare and regulatory legislation. At that time, in a learned exposition of the history of the issue, a leading authority made an eloquent plea for a reversal of recent trends in the Supreme Court's interpretation that would "deny Congress powers over interstate commerce which were recognized as belonging to it 112 years ago." Edward S. Corwin, *The Commerce Power versus States Rights* (Princeton: Princeton University Press, 1936), p. 268.

4. It was anent this issue that Frank Taussig, the leading historian of the American tariff, spoke of its industrial policy aspects in what is the earliest use of the term I have run across in American literature. Perhaps, however, the idea was commonplace, as he does not define or characterize his expression and makes only this one use of it on p. 325 of *The Tariff History of the United States*, 7th ed. (New York and London: Putnam's, 1923). The reference is to the Tariff of 1897 and was probably written in 1898. Around the end of World War I, Taussig wrote a memorandum to President Wilson refering to the disposal of stocks of commodities as an "industrial policy." I have drawn heavily on Taussig's book in the following paragraphs, but the glossing of these measures as industrial policy is mine, not his.

5. The one exception to this I have found in Taussig concerns tinplate: it was not produced in the United States, but in 1890 a specific duty with about a 30 percent *ad valorem* equivalent (well below the run of iron and steel duties) was raised to an *ad valorem* equivalent of about 70 percent, but it was to drop to zero in 1897 unless domestic production in one intervening year equalled one-third the amount imported "during any one of the years between 1890 and 1896." It did, so the duty stayed. (Taussig, *The Tariff History of the United States*, pp. 273, 274.)

6. One result was that in the 1950s European producers almost displaced domestic firms in the American market for barbed wire, which was on the free list and had originally been an exclusively American product. More important than its tariff treatment is the way the invention and large-scale commercial production of barbed wire increased property values on the prairies and brought about extraordinary structural changes in the agriculture of the American West. The story is well told in Walter Prescott Webb, *The Great Plains* (New York: Grosset & Dunlap, n.d.) (original edition 1931), pp. 295–318.

7. Samuel Eliot Morison, *The Oxford History of the American People* (New York: Oxford University Press, 1965), p. 325. The Taussig quotation is from p. 16 of the book already cited.

8. Quoted by A. Whitney Griswold, *Farming and Democracy* (New York: Harcourt Brace, 1948), p. 30, a book well worth perusing on this theme.

9. Letter to Benjamin Austin, quoted in Morton and Lucia White, *The Intellectual versus the City* (New York: Mentor Books, 1964), p. 29. He was thus led to accept the need for cities but not to love them.

10. Taussig, *The Tariff History of the United States*, p. 62. Henry Adams stressed the positive. "Every serious difficulty which seemed alarming to the people of the Union in 1800 had been removed or had sunk from notice in 1816. . . . Not only had the people during these sixteen years escaped from dangers, they had also found the means of supplying their chief needs. . . . The continent lay before them, like an uncovered ore-bed. They could see, and they could even calculate with reasonable accuracy, the wealth it could be made to yield." *History of the United States of America during the Second Administration of James Madison*, vol. 3 (New York: Scribners, 1891), pp. 173, 174. (This is the final volume of the nine-volume work covering the Jefferson and Madison Administrations.)

11. OECD Interfutures, *Facing the Future* (Paris, 1979), pp. 6, 7, 68, 97ff, 127ff, 161ff, and passim.

12. Morison, *The Oxford History of the American People*, p. 402. The quotation from Calhoun comes from the same place.

13. The government role was called to the attention of Americans who in the 1940s and 1950s were decrying the socialism and state intervention in development in India and other developing countries. (Carter Goodrich "American Development Policy," *Journal of Economic History*, 16, 1956: 449-60.) A useful summary of much literature is in "The Role of the State in American Economic Development, 1820-1890" by Henry W. Broude in H.G.J. Aitken, ed., *The State and Economic Growth* (New York: Social Science Research Council, 1959). Adams's views, which dated from 1807 and before, are underlined as "constructive centralization" in "The Heritage of Henry Adams" by Brooks Adams in the posthumous volume of Henry Adams's papers, *The Degradation of the Democratic Dogma* (New York: Macmillan, 1920), especially pp. 13-28. He links these views, not altogether persuasively, with George Washington's plan, dating back to 1770, to build a canal linking the Potomac to the Mississippi Valley. Henry Adams, in the Chapter of his *History* cited earlier, says that the federal government's refusal to grant funds to New York to help build what became the Erie Canal proved to be only a temporary setback for New York "but was fatal to Southern hopes" for building canals which required federal aid that could not have been withheld if New York had been helped. Thus non-intervention can become a regional policy.

14. Friedrich List, *The National System of Political Economy*, trans. Sampson S. Lloyd (London: Longmans, Green, 1904), p. xlii. The first part of the book appeared in 1841.

15. N.P. Willis, *American Scenery*, 2 vols. (London and New York: J.S. Virtue, n.d.) [1840] p. 2. The text was a vehicle for the presentation to a largely European audience of engraved views based on drawings by W.H. Bartlett, one of the most popular British illustrators of the time.

16. John E. Sawyer, "The Social Basis of the American System of Manufacturing," *The Journal of Economic History* 14, no. 4 (1954): 361-79. These paragraphs draw heavily on this interesting and suggestive piece, but the twisting of the material to industrial policy purposes and structural interpretations is mine, not the author's.

17. The story of the lathe, here simplified, comes from Nathan Rosenberg, "America's Rise to Woodworking Leadership" in Brooke Hindle, ed., *America's Wooden Age: Aspects of its Early Technology* (Tarrytown, N.Y.: Sleepy Hollow Restorations, 1975), pp. 51-53 and 199-201. Other parts of Rosenberg's essay and the whole book are relevant to points made in the text, as well as being most interesting.

18. The Whitney quotation comes from Sawyer, "The Social Basis of the American System of Manufacturing," p. 370, and the earlier quote from p. 372.

19. Ibid. p. 369.

20. Alfred D. Chandler, Jr., *The Visible Hand: The Managerial Revolution in American*

Business (Cambridge: Harvard University Press, 1977), p. 3; the next quotations are from p. 1.

21. Alfred Chandler Jr., "The Adversaries," *Harvard Business Review* (November–December 1979), p. 88. Adapted from a paper for a symposium on "Business and Public Policy" (to be published in a fuller version), this statement makes a number of interesting suggestions of structural and historical reasons for the differences, and quotes an ICI executive as saying in 1937 that "the most striking difference between DuPont's business and ours arises from the existence of free competition in America" (p. 92).

22. Herbert Clark Hoover, *Memoirs, Volume 2. The Cabinet and the Presidency, 1920–1933* (New York: Macmillan, 1952), pp. 81–84.

23. David M. Potter, *People of Plenty* (Chicago: The University of Chicago Press, 1954), p. 123.

24. S. Parkes Cadman, *The Cathedral of Commerce: Woolworth Building*, foreword to 1925 reprint of a 1917 pamphlet, New York.

25. Charles E. Merriam of the National Resources Planning Board in George B. Galloway and Associates, *Planning for America* (New York: Holt, 1947). This volume provides an interesting collection of examples of the thinking and attitudes of the time as well as some description of the practical activities.

26. NRPB, *National Resources Development,* Report for 1942, letter of transmittal to Congress. The status was similar to that of the Bureau of the Budget.

27. Or at least Mr. Merriam did in the paper cited; he was a leading academic specialist in public administration and an important shaper of the reorganization of the federal government during this period.

28. The idea that tariffs could be reduced without damage to domestic producers was not quite as naive as it sounds when one remembers some of the high rates in the Hawley-Smoot Tariff and how indiscriminately some of them had been set. Not until the early 1940s was the escape clause introduced to check unexpectedly large (or cheap) imports when they resulted in "injury" to domestic producers.

29. This almost forgotten story of American industrial adaptation is well told in Percy W. Bidwell, *Raw Materials: A Study of American Policy* (New York: Harper for the Council on Foreign Relations, 1958), Chapter 9.

30. The acceptance of this change was not universal and immediate. There were those who opposed the idea of so much government responsibility and those who questioned the ability of the government to provide the expected results. A battle raged over terminology, with "full employment" becoming as objectionable to some people as "industrial policy" was later. It is no accident that the basic legislation is called simply The Employment Act of 1946. The origins, shaping, and passage of this legislation are most interestingly analyzed in Stephen Kemp Bailey, *Congress Makes a Law* (New York: Vintage Books, 1964 reprint). That book also throws much light on the elements of "planning" in wartime thinking and the fear of supporters of private enterprise that too much power was being given to the government.

31. Raymond A. Bauer, Ithiel de Sola Pool, and Lewis Anthony Dexter, *American Business and Public Policy* (New York: Atherton Press, 1965), p. 147.

32. See also Chapter 4's discussion of the Tokyo Round on page 119. The principal American negotiators' view of what was accomplished can be found in W. Stephen Piper, "Unique Sectoral Agreement Establishes Free Trade Framework," *Law and Politics in International Business* vol. 12, no. 1 (1980), pp. 221–42. A more-detailed account is Bernard J. Vaughan, "Technical Analysis of the Civil Aircraft Agreement," in the same volume, pp. 243–53.

33. An exception is the diversification of sources of supply by contracting for Canadian nickel from Falconbridge on terms that permitted that company to establish itself as a competitor to International Nickel.

34. A more detailed discussion of these arrangements is to be found in Chapter 4.

35. Mr. Rohatyn is a partner in Lazard Freres, who played an important part in the financial rescue of New York City and is frequently mentioned for future public office. The suggestions cited have been made in various talks, articles and statements to the press, for

example, "A Better Way to Bail out Chrysler," *The New York Times*, Jan. 13, 1980. Mr. Rohatyn, who was born in 1928 and came to the United States in 1942, speaks as a student of the American Depression, not an eyewitness. But his proposals are well worth considering on their merits, rather than as analogies with the older arrangements. The TNEC was concerned almost entirely with the concentration of economic power, and its influence on public policy is doubtful, as was pointed out earlier. The RFC had no guiding philosophy about the structure of the U.S. economy and operated ad hoc — first to help keep companies from collapsing and then to help shape war production. Politics are generally thought to have played a larger part in its operations than Mr. Rohatyn would like to see repeated.

36. This is a rough sketch of the general character of the discussion. Naturally, there were some people who had been thinking for some time in longer and broader terms. The issues, in this and other cases, are set forth in the last section of this chapter.

37. One of the best examples is *Redefining Government's Role in the Market System;* A Statement by the Research and Policy Committee of the Committee for Economic Development, July 1979.

38. A good example is Walt W. Rostow, *Getting from Here to There: America's Future in the World Economy* (New York: McGraw-Hill, 1980).

39. This was the title of a special number of *Business Week* that appeared in June 1980. Calling himself "the proud father of the thesis of 'reindustrialization,' " Amitai Etzioni, a sociologist temporarily serving as a senior advisor to President Carter, said it was only "a remote relation" of industrial policy. The need for "reindustrialization" was created by "decades of overconsumption and of underinvestment in the nationwide economic machine." To set matters right would take "a decade or so of shoring up its production capacity" (*The New York Times*, June 29, 1980).

40. A book by Ezra F. Vogel, a Harvard sociologist, published by the Harvard University Press in 1979. Most commentators, including the Japanese, thought the author a bit too uncritical of Japanese ways and he made only a sketchy attempt to say to what extent it was reasonable to suggest that the United States could take over Japanese ways of doing things.

41. Beatrice Vaccara, quoted in *The New York Times*, January 14th, 1980.

42. *New York Times*, July 11, 1980.

43. Interview with Adam Clymer, *New York Times Magazine,* July 27, 1980, p. 15.

44. Multigraphed, June 23, 1980.

45. A full-page advertisement in *The New York Times*, July 22, 1980, listed the statement's recommendations for job creation, tax cuts, stimulation of R&D, export expansion, improved regulatory practices, permitting firms "to work together" in foreign competition, and the development of a national consensus.

46. This whole subject is dealt with more systematically and at greater length in Chapter 6 of my book *Industrial Policy as an International Issue* (New York: McGraw-Hill for the Council on Foreign Relations, 1980).

47. The reader is reminded that this section was for the most part finished in the fall of 1980.

48. "Probing the Productivity Puzzle," *The Brookings Bulletin* 16, no. 2, pp. 7–9, a summary of Edward F. Denison, *Accounting for Slower Economic Growth: The United States in the 1970s* (Washington D.C.: Brookings Institution, 1979).

49. Edward F. Denison, "The Contribution of Capital to Economic Growth," *The American Economic Review*, May 1980, p. 220.

50. Nestor E. Terleckyj, "What Do R&D Numbers Tell Us about Technological Change?" *The American Economic Review*, May 1980, p. 57.

51. George C. Eads, "Regulation and Technical Change: Some Largely Unexplored Influences." *The American Economic Review*, May 1980, p. 50.

52. All the articles cited say something on these points. In addition, see other papers and comments in *The American Economic Review*, same issue, which reports the proceedings of the meeting of the American Economic Association in December 1979, and the papers and discussion in *Brookings Papers on Economic Activity* 1979, no. 2, pp. 264–71 and 382–462.

53. See, for example, *Stimulating Technological Progress*, A Statement by the Research

and Policy Committee of the CED, January 1980. The emphasis on rapid writeoffs of capital is particularly strong in the work of Dale Jorgenson of Harvard, who ascribes much of the fall in productivity to increases in the price of capital, labor, and especially energy. A good summary of this work, which is not taken into account in what the text says about economists' views, is provided in an interview with Jorgenson in *Challenge*, November–December 1980, pp. 16–25.

54. Quoted in *Business Week*, June 30, 1980, p. 61.

55. *New York Times*, July 6, 1980.

56. There is a discussion of management deficiencies and their possible causes and remedies, with examples, in *Business Week*, June 30, 1980, under the heading, "Managers who are no longer entrepreneurs," pp. 74–82.

57. When Ford was in difficulties after the death of Edsel Ford, Alfred Sloan of General Motors went out of his way to help his competitor hire some of GM's managers and may have talked with bankers about forming a syndicate to prevent Ford's failure, for fear that the alternative "was a government takeover that could only harm GM." Peter F. Drucker, *Adventures of a Bystander* (New York: Harper and Row, 1979), p. 292.

58. The automotive agreement between United States and Canada, which could be looked on as one of the relatively few cases of international industrial policy, is discussed in Chapter 7, since both its origin and some of its main features are more closely tied to Canadian aims and conditions than to those of the United States.

59. For a fuller indication of these factors, see the sketch of the automobile industry in my *Industrial Policy as an International Issue* (New York: McGraw-Hill for the Council on Foreign Relations, 1980), pp. 160–74. C. Kenneth Orski, Alan Altshuler, and Daniel Roos, "The Future of the Automobile," in *Transatlantic Perspectives*, a Publication of the German Marshall Fund of the United States, March 1980, pp. 1–8, raise still other issues and outline a major study being undertaken at MIT.

60. These measures and their effects are discussed in some detail, on pages 60–63. My own version of the events and their significance is set forth in *Industrial Policy as an International Issue*, pp. 107–25.

61. For example, Charles R. Frank, Jr., *Foreign Trade and Domestic Aid* (Washington, D.C.: Brookings Institution, 1977).

62. This is only one of many points at which there are potentially significant connections between the agenda of domestic industrial policy and the relation of the United States to the rest of the world. These issues are discussed in the final section of this chapter.

63. *The New York Times*, February 7, 1980. American Motors, the smallest domestic producer, had already been dropped from the investigation which was to include three Japanese manufacturers, Volkswagen, Ford, and Chrysler. The announcement was interpreted to mean that only General Motors was a serious target.

64. When negotiations between Ford and Toyota about a joint venture were reported, Professor Louis Wells of the Harvard Business School wrote to *The New York Times*, July 21, 1980, stressing the importance of import competition to discipline oligopolistic industries. "That Ford even dares mention publicly" that it had such talks shows "how far U.S. antitrust policy is from recognizing the realities of today's international marketplace."

65. One special version of the small business argument is an exception to these strictures. It has long been recognized that small firms focusing on high technology and manned by skilled scientists and engineers have been responsible for many important discoveries and innovations. In the past they have needed no government aid to attract venture capital, but with premiums for risk rising along with interest rates, there are arguments in favor of tax measures to make the rewards greater without impairing the independence.

66. Note the statement by "an American economist with important government experience" reported in John Pinder, Takashi Hosomi, and William Diebold, *Industrial Policy and the International Economy* (New York: The Trilateral Commission, 1979), p. 77. This economist stressed the underdeveloped state of the discussion of the subject in the United States and the imperative need "that heads of state comprehend that the encouraging progress on macro policy coordination and . . . lowering tariffs and at least getting a start on lowering non tariff barriers can really be subverted by industrial and structural

policies that foster . . . insidious protectionism." He is a man who, when in office, was one of the most skilled practitioners of macroeconomic policy, so his comment is worth double that of those who start from the other end of the scale.

67. An excellent summary account of some of these points and the argument for stipulating ends rather than means is to be found in Charles L. Schultze, *The Public Use of Private Interest* (Washington, D.C.: Brookings Institution, 1977).

68. The first quotation is from *New York Times*, July 9, 1980. The second is in the interview with Adam Clymer already cited, *The New York Times Magazine*, July 27, 1980, p. 16.

69. Pinder, Hosomi, and Diebold, op. cit.

70. See, for example, *The Case for Positive Adjustment Policies*: A Compendium of OECD Documents, Paris, 1979.

71. "Policies for Adjustment: Some General Orientations," in *The Case for Positive Adjustment Policies*.

7 Past and Future Industrial Policy in Canada

WILLIAM DIEBOLD, JR.

With a bit more land than the United States, Canada has about one-tenth of the people and over the years has shown about fifty times the interest in industrial policy (which Canadians are apt to call industrial strategy). Large structural problems are inherent in the nature of the Canadian economy, and differences of opinion as to what to do about them are inevitable. Potential solutions have to take account of the country's high economic exposure to the world and particularly to its next-door neighbor. For these and other reasons, the history of industrial policy in Canada is very different from that in the United States. It has long been widely accepted that the government should play a leading part in shaping the economic structure of the country, and that economic policies must frequently serve broad national purposes that go beyond simply maximizing growth or providing a setting in which private enterprise can flourish.

Naturally, Canadians have never been altogether of one mind as to means (or sometimes even ends), and as time has passed divisions have increased and the process of either building a national consensus or mobilizing support for a compromise has become more difficult. It is no surprise that nationalist appeals sometimes cover more-limited interests. In 1903, the president of the Canadian Manufacturers' Association said, "We are not manufacturers merely of articles of wood and stone, and iron and cotton and wool and so on; we manufacture enthusiasm; we manufacture Canadian sentiment; we manufacture a feeling of pride."[1] Such claims by special interest groups are not confined to Canada, but many decades later, an historian thought it worth remarking that, "No new government in Canada is without some novel scheme for using the taxpayers' money to ensure that the national consciousness is safe.[2]

The Historical Setting

For all its divisions, through much of Canadian history there has been enough of a national consensus — or governments that were in office long enough — to permit the carrying out of major economic policies that did indeed shape the structure of the economy. Successful results, in the terms in which the policies were conceived, sometimes became a new set of problems that stimulated still another debate about the proper next step in industrial policy. Some of the policies created enough opposition over time — or were seen from the first as really serving the interest of only one section or group — to be reversed when political power shifted; for example, to farmers, or Quebec, or the West.[3] Even so, the new basis often served to support policies that were maintained long enough, sometimes with growing support, to have a lasting influence on the country.

Like the Americans, the Canadians were faced with the problems and opportunities of settling nearly empty land and spanning a continent, so that similarities between the two countries leap to the eye. It is more important to emphasize the differences, however. The similarity in area is an illusion since climate limits Canada's usable terrain. Although there are now significant arctic developments, the economic history of the country is concentrated in a strip a few hundred miles wide and over 3000 miles long. The spread of the economy from the original eastern settlements came, for the most part, later than in the United States. So did independence. And always, whether under colonial rule, as a self-governing dominion, or as a fully independent country in the Commonwealth, Canada remained economically more heavily dependent on the rest of the world than the United States was except in its early years. Development for Canada meant increasing economic independence while at the same time obtaining the maximum possible advantage from external economic relations. Much more than in the United States, the position of the economy in the world both dictated national economic objectives and set limits to what could be done to achieve them.

No doubt, economic policies and practices of the colonial period shaped later Canadian attitudes toward industrial policy. Colbert is sometimes mentioned in Quebec. Harold Innis in one of his influential studies argued that "Canada emerged as a political entity with boundaries largely determined by the fur trade. . . . The present Dominion emerged not in spite of geography but because of it."[4] But the inability of the people of the thirteen American colonies to persuade their northern neighbors to join their revolution, and their failure to take Quebec and Montreal during the Revolution or to conquer Canada in the War of 1812 (when they burned Toronto, then called York) also played a decisive role in giving an impetus to the kind of structural policies Canada followed. These emerged most clearly in what can properly be called the beginning of Canadian independence, the passage of the British North America Act of 1867 that consolidated several colonies and established a Dominion with a "constitution," which to this day can be altered only by the Parliament at Westminister (although the independence of Canada has not been in question for a long time).

There was no question in 1867 of Canada in any sense choosing between the United States and Britain. Quebec's ties with France were remote and not a major factor in influencing what was done—in contrast to the "French fact" in Canada. But there was a problem of tying the parts of the country together, creating one Canada, and getting ahead with its economic development. How those national aims were to be realized depended in part on the interplay of the two sets of external relations—with Europe, and with the United States. Moreover, the choices the Canadians faced in shaping the structure of their economy would themselves also shape the external relations of the future.[5] At the beginning the economic structure, as Innis and others have pointed out, was oriented toward Europe. One road to prosperity clearly lay in cultivating those financial and mercantile ties while broadening the domestic base and using wisely the improved bargaining power that would result. At the same time, the building up of an independent national economy would have to mean curtailing dependence on Britain and especially British manufacturing. The United States provided the obvious alternative, but could it be cultivated without the creation of a new dependence? The advantages of what came to be called "continentalism" could also conflict with the aims of building Canada.

Seen in terms of this set of choices, it was a fairly easy decision to build a transcontinental railroad when the time came in 1879 and to route it entirely through Canadian territory, although that was more difficult and costly than to pass through parts of the United States. Trade policy was something else again. Here the debate was older, as there had been tariff autonomy in the Canadian colonies as early as the 1840s. Farmers, traders, manufacturers, and those mostly concerned with the processing of resources all had different views. In the old country, free trade ideas were in good order and policy was moving in the same direction. But to the south, protectionism was both preached and practiced. Henry Carey, Matthew Carey, Friedrich List, Horace Greeley, and others were all read north of the border. Similarities in circumstances no doubt increased their influence, and Mill's case for infant industry protection was also noted. Probably, though, it was not so much a choice among doctrines as the effort to build a national economy that decided matters. A careful historian says, "The weight of old-country authority behind free trade probably weakened its case in Canada. . . . [Some believed protectionist theory while] for others it was convenient to jump on a popular bandwagon. Most Canadians, however, came to regard protection as an ambitious gamble for success and free trade as stoical acceptance of continued dependence on Great Britain and the whims of world markets."[6]

That decision was not reached overnight, however. Moderate protection and a good deal of receptivity to the idea of relatively free trade with the United States marked Canadian policy during much of the middle of the 19th century. It was the Americans who ended the reciprocal free trade in some articles that existed before 1854, and the Canadians, for the most part, who attempted to reestablish that state of affairs. It was not until 1878 that Sir John A. Macdonald enunciated the full-blown National Policy that was to shape much Canadian thought and action for a long time to come. The policy proclaimed by the first Canadian prime minister "is usually taken to encompass a domestic policy of economic nationalism based on railway building, immigration and settlement, and protective tariffs. . . . But the spirit of the National Policy went much deeper. . . . Beneath [its] external manifestations was the will to build and maintain a separate Canadian nation on the North American continent.[7] Although part of Macdonald's argument was that eventual reciprocity with the United States would be promoted by a Canadian tariff high enough to be burdensome to the other country, the primary emphasis had shifted to protection for agriculture, mining, and above all, manufacturing, which was supposed to expand greatly under the new policy. In his budget speech of 1879, Sir Leonard Tilley used language that has echoed through Canadian debates of trade and industrial policy to this day: "The time has arrived when we are to decide whether we will be simply hewers of wood and drawers of water."

Although the spirit of the National Policy—and most of its specific features—came to be generally accepted, Canadians continued to differ about tariffs and about what degree of economic closeness to the United States was compatible with independence and continuation of the British connection (also a cause of differences). Some Canadians shared the views of some Americans that a merger of the two countries was inevitable and desirable, but proposals for some form of free trade often collapsed at a late stage on political grounds. For example, in 1911 there was a debate in both countries over a draft reciprocity treaty.

Although President Taft repudiated the annexationist sentiments of Champ Clark, the speaker-designate of the House of Representatives, his own reference to Canadians "coming to the parting of the ways" in choosing more trade with the United States instead of closer ties to Britain was seized on by the opposition in Canada, and the government fell.[8] In 1948, although secret negotiations for a free trade arrangement had advanced very far they were in the end repudiated by Prime Minister Mackenzie King who said that "regardless of what the economic facts might be, the issue would turn on union with the States and separation from Britain."[9] In spite of this clear and sustained sequence of political decisions, the development of economic ties with the United States continued to be both a major factor in the growth of the Canadian economy and a focus of Canadian concern that does much to explain the basic issues facing Canadians when they think about industrial policy in the 1980s.

Indeed, it was the American problem—if one can call it that—which insured that, in a Canada building itself into a nation, policies toward trade and investment had to take on the characteristics of industrial policy much sooner than they did in older countries. To develop industry by imposing tariffs meant that foreigners were encouraged to invest in Canada. Sometimes Canadian producers did not want protection carried to the point of shutting out American imports; as long as a certain flow of trade continued, some big American producers were satisfied to sell what they could instead of establishing themselves in Canada, where they would be more-formidable competitors. Access to Empire markets played a part in stimulating American investment even before the Ottawa agreements of 1932, but there is little doubt that the extension of preferential tariff arrangements at that time persuaded additional American firms to establish themselves in Canada.[10] Precision in these matters is impossible but the most careful study made during the 1930s concluded that "probably a majority of the branch plants established since the war . . . are solely creatures of the tariffs. [Few, even of the older ones] have been uninfluenced, as to their establishment, by tariffs. . . . although the majority . . . were established primarily to cater to Canada, the prospect of a wider Empire market has been attractive to an important minority."[11]

Thus a policy reminiscent of Hamilton's *Report on Manufactures*, enhanced by the Empire connection, largely succeeded. In doing so, it contributed to the next set of issues in Canadian industrial policy, but this did not become apparent at once. The war led to further American investment in Canada and at the same time postponed the clear-cut emergence of several structural problems of the Canadian economy until about the middle or late 1950s. By then, as the general shape of the postwar world economy could be seen, several aspects of Canada's problems became clear.

The success of past measures meant that there was a great deal of American investment in Canada, to the extent that many Canadians felt they were losing control of their own economy. The dominance of British investment was a thing of the past. While some the of the American-owned plants might have grown large enough to serve the whole Empire, the war more or less put an end to that possibility and in the postwar period the priorities shifted. The Canadian market was the protected area, and although it was growing it remained relatively small. Consequently, Canada had a wide variety of manufacturing enterprises but only a few that served major export markets. As trade barriers around the world began coming down—through a process in which Canada cooperated closely with the United States—Canadian industry found itself expected to accept greater competition at home through the lowering of tariffs and to improve its competitiveness abroad, even though other countries had the advantages of larger domestic markets. The creation of the Common Market in Europe and the expectation that Britain would join it added to the sense of being isolated (except for the United States, which was uncomfortably close) and the need for working out new prescriptions for Canadian policy. Canadian raw materials production (and American investment in it) had been stimulated by the war, but Canadians complained that too little processing was done in Canada (partly because of the traditional tariff structures of the United States and many other countries, including Canada, which weighed more heavily on manufactured goods than on raw materials and semiprocessed products). Thus the Canadian aspiration to stimulate the modern manufacturing sectors of its economy instead of the traditional raw materials was made more difficult.

The three interrelated problems provide keys to the difficulties of formulating contemporary Canadian industrial policy: foreign ownership, international competitiveness, and the balance between raw materials production, processing, and the growth of manufacturing and services.

Foreign Investment

The most clear-cut government measures concern foreign investment, but their effect is not at all clear-cut. There have been many years of debate, study, and the work of public commissions of various sorts, which made it reasonably clear that extreme measures were unlikely to get general support or be durable. A wide-open *laissez faire* policy would certainly not seem adequate. Any emphasis on restricting foreign investment had to cope with the view that Canada needed the capital to grow and that to borrow it all would strain the capacity of Canadian enterprises; the provinces were already borrowing heavily in New York (and sometimes the federal government as well). Canadians were investing abroad—especially in the United States—but that probably meant only that they thought it better to invest in an existing enterprise of proven value than to take fresh risks. Thus, to "buy Canada back" would require the rerouting of capital flows on a massive scale, which is unlikely without extensive compulsion; even then, it would leave open the question whether that was the best use of Canadian money that could otherwise help stimulate new kinds of economic activity. American capital could also mean managment, sometimes technology, and usually links to a continental—and sometimes global—organization that could considerably enhance the value of the Canadian assets.

For a long time after World War II the belief that Canada's gains from foreign investment outweighed all possible losses dominated many influential circles. But in a way that anyone can understand, the more investment grew, the more people wanted to do something about it. An experienced American student of the Canadian scene noted in 1975, "Although the restriction of foreign investment came to Canada more slowly than to any comparable country, public opinion surveys have shown for some time that close to a majority of Canadians would accept the economic cost of restricting foreign investment. During the past decade, this public attitude became widespread and outspoken. . . . The search for restrictive policies on foreign ownership became a pressing issue in Canada's public life during the late 1960s, and by 1972 this concern had reached a point of public preoccupation from which there was no exit except through governmental action."[12]

Governmental measures would have to be based on more than a general public feeling. If the alternative to foreign investment was not Canadian investment but no investment at all, then some Canadians, whether their immediate interest was jobs, taxes, exports, a new line of manufacturing, or the development of some natural resource, were going to be in favor of that investment. Toronto might be the center of the kind of economic nationalism that can be expected of companies glad to see their foreign competitors handicapped or of banks and investment houses happy to be given a *chasse gardée*. But in the poor areas of the Maritimes, or in Quebec where unemployment and underdevelopment were sometimes coupled with the view that, among outsiders, Americans were to be preferred to anglophone Canadians, things would look different. That would also be true in the west, where voters and provincial governments traditionally resented eastern domination and had extensive connections with the United States. Moreover, approaches to foreign investment that simply asked what to allow and what to forbid would ignore the need to improve the chances that foreign investment plus Canadian workers and managers would increase the whole economy's efficiency and ability to export.

In the circumstances, a selective policy was inevitable. In a few sectors foreign investment was limited by specific legislation in the 1950s and early 1960s: radio and television stations, some natural resources, aviation, and insurance. In 1967, when oral warnings did not stop the First National City Bank of New York from taking over a small Dutch-owned bank as a step toward expanding operations in Canada, legislation was passed that aimed at restricting foreign ownership of any Canadian bank to 25 percent. In 1971 the long-discussed Canadian Development Corporation was founded to invest government money and private Canadian funds in enterprises that might otherwise not be created or in which foreign control should be either diluted or eliminated.

Increased public scrutiny of corporate accounts and some guidelines for the conduct of foreign corporations issued during the 1960s were followed, at the end of 1973, by the most-comprehensive measure of all, the establishment of the Foreign Investment Review Agency (FIRA). Its task was to screen all proposals for new foreign investment in Canada and any transactions in which existing foreign ownership changed hands. On these occasions, the Agency was to satisfy itself that the proposed action took full account of Canadian interests. These interests were defined only in rather general terms and it seemed clear that what FIRA came to mean would depend to an important degree on the results of its negotiations with would-be investors. Different standards could easily be applied to different kinds of activity, to investors already established in Canada, and to newcomers. Conditions could be set for their behavior that might force them to choose between doing business FIRA's way or not at all. How far such steps might lead was partly a question of the bargaining power of each side and partly of the attitude of any given Canadian government (since the cabinet made the decisions, FIRA being only advisory).

Although FIRA was undoubtedly the offspring of an economic nationalism that had grown stronger as time passed, it presented itself to the world in terms of moderation and reason. The old fear that a more-aggressive attitude would scare off investment needed by Canada was undoubtedly still at work. There was also pressure from provinces against measures that would deter investments that would create jobs and build up their part of the country. Some of the provinces had objected to the creation of FIRA in the first place, but "its performance seems to have disarmed its critics." That was partly because the Act takes account of the provinces' interests in a manner "unique in federal regulatory legislation."[13]

American investors approached the new agency warily, but a few years' experience produced a general view that FIRA was a reasonable body which did not turn down any very large number of proposals.[14] Occasional difficulties arose when FIRA asserted jurisdiction over transfers of ownership resulting from mergers and other transactions between firms in the United States which had subsidiaries or branches in Canada. Not surprisingly, publishing proved to be a sensitive area, arousing concern over the autonomy of Canada's culture and the orientation of school books. It is, however, difficult to estimate how FIRA's actions as a whole affected the structure of the Canadian economy without a more-detailed study than has publicly appeared and without some idea of what foreign investors might have done if they had not had to pass under FIRA's scrutiny.

There is no clear indication whether FIRA used any consistent structural criteria. Whether government should provide guidance to business in such matters was one of the points at issue in the continuing debate about industrial strategy in Canada. Neither the Trudeau government, which was in power during most of the period, nor the short-lived Clark government was clear or decisive in these matters. By the end of the 1970s, critics of the agency were saying it had no criteria at all and was bogging down in bureaucratic difficulties.[15] But 1980 brought events that may lead to something close to a fresh start for FIRA. Its progenitor, Herb Gray, whose 1972 report had led to the FIRA legislation (and who had been for some time out of federal office) became Minister of Industry, Trade and Commerce in the newly elected Trudeau government. He soon made plain that he planned to carry out the intentions he had indicated in the electoral campaign of making FIRA more effective and broadening its scope. A major possible change would be to give FIRA some power over existing foreign investments and not just new ones. No doubt there would be some emphasis on the kinds of activities foreign companies engaged in in Canada and on such traditional targets as increasing Canadian equity and management. But structural issues would have to be dealt with at least implicitly and, if the government were able to resolve the doubts and disputes that had made for inaction in the past, there might well be a mandate making FIRA a major instrument in pursuing structural priorities. Even if government felt unable to impose an over-all pattern, FIRA could still be used to help with more-limited (although still very important) efforts that had a good bit of general support, such as making Canadian industry more competitive in world markets. How this might be done is a matter to which we shall return, but first the setting in which that issue has become central must be described.

Trade and Technology

As has been pointed out, it was trade policy—Canada's and that of other main trading countries—that led to the Canadian debates of the 1960s and 1970s that focused attention on the structural deficiencies of Canadian industry. As trade barriers went down all over the world, Canadians found themselves troubled by a diversity of manufacturing spread over products for which the Canadian market did not permit the economies of scale that existed in the United States, the European Community, and Japan. Sometimes that meant plants too small to obtain the greatest economies of scale, and sometimes the higher costs that go with having to produce relatively short runs of a variety of products with the same equipment. The difficulty of competing in the rest of the world was paralleled by the increased pressure of imports in the domestic market. There was not much that Canada could do by unilateral measures to mitigate this problem as long as it adhered to the kind of trade policy it had followed since the end of the war. To reduce the cost of production in some industries, import duties were waived on machinery that could not be produced in Canada; a flexible definition of "dumping" was used to resist foreign price-cutting on some products. The method of customs valuation protected the domestic price structure. To refuse to reduce trade barriers at all would have put Canada out of step with the rest of the democratic industrial world. As it was, it seemed to many foreign observers that Canada had dragged its feet in the Kennedy Round but could not expect a free ride from other countries for long. A unilateral removal of tariffs was no more attractive to Canada than it has usually been to other countries.

In the 1960s, however, a number of Canadians set about analyzing what could be done to make their industry internationally competitive. While the answers naturally differed a good deal from one kind of manufacturing to another, a general pattern was fairly clear. If, instead of trying to produce a range of products wide enough to meet most of the needs of the domestic market, Canadian firms concentrated on a smaller number of selected products and imported the rest, it was likely they could increase substantially the productivity of the Canadian economy and compete effectively on world markets. A key factor in these calculations was the assumption that other countries would reciprocally permit the free, or almost free, entry of Canadian products. Only under the further assumption that such conditions would last for the indefinite future would it be possible to justify the degree of restructuring of much of the Canadian economy that would be called for. Although the long-standing Canadian preference for multilateral action made it desirable to think in terms of trade with the world as a whole (or at least the industrialized world), calculations showed that free trade with the United States alone would provide substantial advantages and call for about the same degree of restructuring of Canadian industry.[16]

How this state of affairs might be achieved was, of course, a separate question. The ideas were put forward less as a program than as an indication of how, by drastic reshaping, Canada could escape from difficulties into which the gradualism of past policy seemed to be pushing it. Meanwhile, a striking step was taken toward free trade with the United States in one major industry, automobiles. The Automotive Agreement of 1965 eliminated tariffs on trade between the two countries in new cars, buses, trucks, and original parts (but not replacement parts or accessories), provided certain conditions were met.[17] This important measure did not result from the kind of thinking about the structure of the Canadian industry just described. It was the outcome of a trade dispute that threatened to do considerable damage to relations between the two countries. To expand exports the Canadians had introduced a system of grants, which the Americans judged to be export subsidies of the sort that under their law had to be met with countervailing duties.

As they sought a way out of the difficulties, negotiators from both sides arrived at a trade-freeing solution that was, from the first, intended to lead to exactly the kind of restructuring of automobile production that others were prescribing for much of the rest of Canadian industry. That is to say, in the future the Canadian automobile plants were to cut down the number of models they produced but were to manufacture the remaining cars for the whole North American market. Other models would be imported from the United States where costs were generally lower. This change in structure was greatly facilitated—some would say made possible—by the fact that Canadian automobile production was entirely in the hands of American companies, which also stood to gain by the shift. But more than free trade and company decisions were involved in the agreement. The conditions about continued production in Canada made specific the assurance Canada wanted of a "fair share" of the North American market; so did the commitments the Canadian government extracted from the companies concerning future investment in Canada. Not formally part of the agreement, these commitments were originally considered by many people to cover a transitional period only, but they have been continued at Ottawa's insistence. This has been one source of disagreement between the two governments; others have come from swings in the trade balance which affected judgments on either side of the border as to who benefited more; a third major element is the impact on the parts industries of both countries.

For present purposes it is not necessary to trace these disputes in detail or to consider the numerous changes that have been suggested—but not, to date, acted on. It is, however, important to note something that has not happened. In contrast to many people's expectations, the automobile pact was not followed by other sectoral arrangements, and the conventional wisdom has become that it is not a model that can be widely used. This conclusion rests partly on strictly structural factors, mainly the small number of producers and products. Other factors concern Canadian nationalism—the feeling that decision-making is even more concentrated in Detroit than before—plus uncertainty whether the U.S. Congress would readily accept in every field safeguards assuring the Canadians a fair share of production in spite of the fact that trade was nominally free. There seems little doubt that whenever Canadians raised questions in Washington about possible revisions in the agreement—and the issue looms much larger in Canada than in the United States—they were warned that to propose major changes would reopen the whole agreement, and it was not be taken for granted that a Congress in the 1980s would agree to all the conditions favorable to Canada that had been accepted in the 1960s. Nevertheless, possible changes, including broadening the agreement to include replacement parts and maybe tires, will continue to be considered.

Moreover, if the governments of the United States and Canada continue to concern themselves with the automobile industry, the accommodation of the two national industrial policies will affect the impact of the agreement, whether or not it is formally altered. For example, the financial help the federal government and the government of Ontario gave Chrysler of Canada, while independently negotiated, took account of the arrangements worked out in Washington. In return for loan guarantees the company made commitments about investments in its Canadian plants, a level of employment related to the size of Chrysler's workforce in the United States, and the establishment of a research facility in Ontario costing $20 million, half of which was provided by the provincial government which was to become the owner if the company went bankrupt.[18] Subsequent changes in Chrysler's U.S. activities also had repercussions in Canada. The Ford company also had to work out with the Canadian government changes in its production-sales commitments under the automotive pact. As the same union has organized the automobile industry in both countries, understandings about plant closures, spreading the work and, naturally, wages are not likely to be taken in isolation. European and Japanese investment in the production of automobiles in Canada and the United States and the terms on which this takes place may also raise new issues. The existing agreement is asymmetrical. Any cars coming into the United States from Canada would be duty free as long as they were considered to have been made in Canada (defined as 50 percent value added there). But cars made in the United States enter Canada duty free only if they are imported by a firm eligible to do so (i.e., meeting the various conditions about the ratio of production to sales in the base period), and these are only the established producers. A further potential complication is that as part of its program to stimulate manufacturing in Canada, the government in Ottawa remits import duties in proportion to the amount of Canadian content achieved by individual automobile manufacturers. Should such cars be exported to the United States, the duty remission might well be regarded under American law as a subsidy, bringing the situation back full circle to the kind of issue that led to the creation of the automobile pact in the first place.

Although the automotive pact has not led to other sectoral agreements between Canada and the United States (or any other country), the possiblity continues to be suggested (most recently for petrochemicals).[19] More important, Canadian thinking about trade issues has continued to underline the need to deal with questions of the structure of industry. In 1975 the Economic Council of Canada published a major study that, in effect, reaffirmed the findings of the 1960s work described above, i.e., that for growth Canada needed more-specialized industrial production and could best link it with widespread tariff liberalization at home and abroad. Its numerous recommendations regarding trade policy, adaptation measures, and international negotiations centered on the conclusion that while participating in the Tokyo Round, the Canadian government should "actively explore the conditions under which Canada might join an open-ended free trade area with other interested countries . . . under which barriers to trade in industrial products might be eliminated over a ten-year period."[20] In 1978, the Foreign Affairs Committtee of the Canadian Senate, after extensive hearings, issued a report concluding that "in order to resist the gradual shift of Canadian manufacturing capacity to the United States and to strengthen potentially competitive firms and industries in Canada, Canadians should seriously examine the benefits to be derived from free trade with the United States."[21] Multilateral free trade did not seem to the committee a practical possibility; unilateral moves in that direction were unwise. Proper preparation would, of course, be needed and measures taken to reduce the inescapable risks. Neither of these bodies is a potent political force, and the appearance of the reports did not mean that the tide had turned in Canada on this old issue. There are several reasons, however, to suppose these restatements should not be disregarded.

For example, the Senate Committee's report and hearings showed that there was a good deal of moderate opinion, some of it in business, that was prepared to entertain fairly drastic ideas. A second series of hearings was soon undertaken to examine more closely possible procedures and particular sectors. The Economic Council of Canada, although it has a structure that could work for understanding among public, private, business, and labor groups, is less important for consensus building than for the quality of the analyses made by its staff. Not only the report already cited, but also others about the problems of Canadian trade and industry and in particular a series of works concerning the potential effect on Canada of increased competition from Third World industrial products stressed the problems of industrial adjustment.[22] As might be expected, these studies showed that unless Canada refused to lower barriers to imports from developing countries,or imposed new restrictions, there was no way to escape a further decline in some of its industries that were quite large employers; it was essential to find alternative uses of resources that would contribute substantially to Canadian production.

A separate stream of reasoning that developed at about the same time also has a bearing on the possibilities. As they assessed the results of the Tokyo Round, Canadians saw that much of its meaning for them would depend on how effectively the codes, and the procedures under them, reduced foreign nontariff barriers to Canadian exports. The negotiations had not encouraged them to believe that Europe and Japan were especially responsive to Canadian needs. The United States had done somewhat better and was by far the largest export market. The question naturally arose whether a major target of Canadian trade policy in the years to come should not be American nontariff barriers. Whatever was accomplished in Geneva on a multilateral basis would help, but Canadian officials suspected that might be a slow process. They began to think about what might be accomplished by direct negotiations with the Americans. Government procurement was an interesting field. The market in the United States was large; in Canada federal and provincial procurement was an important instrument of industrial policy; there was already a reciprocal arrangement covering defense; the way the GATT code on public procurement was written seemed to make possible selective arrangements in civilian industries that did not raise questions of the most-favored-nation obligation of both countries.

There was also the question of what the codes might mean for Canada's own practices. Subsidies for regional development were a well-established policy, widely regarded as important to national unity. A number of additional purposes existed for which federal and provincial subsidies in one form or another would continue to be used. Assuming a "continuing need" for such assistance, Rodney de C. Grey, the chief Canadian negotiator in the Tokyo Round and then adviser to the Government of Ontario, posed at least part of the issue in very concrete terms. "Obviously, much of the resulting production must be exported, and much to the United States. Thus a vigorous United States countervailing duty system can have a serious impact on the effectiveness of Canada's industrial development programs."[23] How the United States would in fact respond depended partly on domestic law and partly on how the MTN subsidies code was to be interpreted. Canada's ability to retaliate would suffer from asymmetry. "Canadian countervail is not going to be a discipline for Americans, but merely an irritant," said Mr. Grey. Moreover, Mr. Grey pointed out there was a risk that American measures directed at third countries but applied across the board on a nondiscriminatory basis would damage Canada, even if it had no responsibility in the matter. Clearly the need was for some understanding with the Americans about what could safely be done within the code, whether or not all other countries were ready to agree. Or so it seemed to a number of Canadians.

Still another set of Canadian concerns converged on the link between trade policy and the restructuring of industry. For some time it had been a source of worry in different quarters that Canada was lagging in high technology, except in a few fields — nuclear power plants, for example. Some of the weakness was obviously connected with the more-general problem of the size of plants and markets. Some people saw these causes as an inevitable result of the high proportion of Canadian industry controlled from abroad; the big American companies, it was argued, carried on R & D at home so Canada was starved of stimulus and had fewer jobs for scientists and technicians. Whether the amount of R & D done in Canada and the level of technology in Canadian industry are that closely related is open to debate, as is the full force of the foreign ownership argument (although there is undoubtedly a connection).[24] In any case, there is little disagreement among Canadians about the desirability of improving the technological performance of their industry, but a great deal of disagreement as to how this is to be achieved.

There are success stories, such as Northern Telecom which has become a multinational with sales and production around the world, but it is not clear that the same results can be induced in other fields by government action. The sheltered market for telephone equipment helped give Northern Telecom its start but does not seem to tell the whole story. Nevertheless, that experience plus the government's involvement in the nuclear power industry, where Canada is also a major exporter, are taken by some to indicate the need for quite specific governmental intervention. Initiatives by PetroCanada, the government oil company, are given credit for significant parts of the work oil companies are doing on arctic technology. But the government can hardly set up a bellwether company in every field. As in other countries, businessmen and quite a few other people advocate general policies encouraging private spending on R & D but have little hard evidence to show that this is the best course.

Many specific ideas are being suggested. For example, one of Herb Grey's ideas about strengthening FIRA is that it should either lay down standards about the amount of R & D to be done in Canada by new or existing foreign firms, or work out case-by-case arrangements with foreign investors. The Science Council study already cited recommends regulation of the terms on which technology is imported to ensure that possible domestic sources are not overlooked. When purchasing foreign aircraft, the government of Canada has made an important issue of the amount of procurement, production, and R & D that would be carried on in the country. Rodney Grey has suggested that since governments are large buyers of high technology equipment, it would be advantageous for Canada to work out with the United States ways of extending the coverage of the MTN procurement code.[25] The Minister of Industry and Tourism of Ontario said the government was considering ways of ensuring that Canadian firms, and especially foreign-owned firms, would organize production so that Canadian factories would produce for a world market and thus at one blow overcome some of the cost disadvantages of small size, increase exports, and raise the country's technological level. This world product mandate, as it came to be called, was naturally of interest to businessmen as well and, not least, to the Canadian managers of foreign-owned companies. Some companies had long found this a useful arrangement; others seemed not to have given the matter much thought. Some businessmen pointed out that to take the initiative in this matter was better than waiting to be pushed by the government.

International competitiveness is not just a matter of technology or firm size or having a large enough domestic market to achieve economies of scale. Costs are important; there was a period in the 1970s when much of the loss of Canadian competitiveness seemed traceable to a rise in unit labor costs above those of the United States, coupled with the maintenance of an exchange rate around dollar-for-dollar parity. When the strain on the current-account balance became serious, the Bank of Canada, starting about the middle of 1976, let the rate slide until, by the end of 1978, it reached about US 85¢, which seems to be regarded as a new equilibrium. Because of the close link with the U.S. capital market and the heavy dependence on capital imports, there is a constant tension in Canada between using the exchange rate to promote stability and check inflation and managing it with the emphasis on export competitiveness.[26] The latter priority has strong supporters, some of whom would agree with one consulting economist from Toronto who said, "I cannot think of any greater national industrial tragedy, and I emphasize the word tragedy, than an early resurgence of a 'strong' Canadian dollar."[27] That the exchange rate itself is no guarantee of competitiveness is plain enough, but this explicit link with macroeconomic policy only adds to the difficulties and disagreements that beset the formulation of industrial policy in Canada.

Primary Production and High Technology

Another basic and long-lasting disagreement concerns policy toward raw materials. The concern with high technology is a natural extension of the emphasis on the development of manufacturing that has always characterized Canadian trade and industrial policy. At the same time, the production and processing of resources — agriculture, forestry, fisheries, mining, oil, and gas — remain major sources of Canadian wealth and income. Exports of raw and semifabricated materials usually make up more than 60 percent of Canadian exports. About one-fifth of this is accounted for by agricultural products, with the rest divided roughly equally (over a period of years) among forest products, fuels, and non-fuel minerals. About half the exports in the latter three categories are at least partly fabricated, with the proportion being highest in forest products.[28] In 1964 the share of these same categories in Canadian exports was over 80 percent, but almost the entire shift is ascribable to the increase in trade with the United States under the automotive pact. In Canada's exports to Europe in 1978, resource-based products (as defined here) accounted for more than 80 percent of the total, and in sales to Japan over 95 percent. Ores and other unprocessed products made up a higher proportion of these sales than for Canadian exports as a whole.[29]

Raw materials and how they are handled are clearly central to Canada's industrial policy. But as in all countries, the shifts in energy, their consequences, and the methods and prospects of guiding them are central questions. Limiting the access of others (mostly the United States) by export controls on oil was only the first step. Although Canada has become a net importer of oil, the country produces more energy than it consumes and has major exploitable reserves. Sharing the benefits and burdens of the increase in oil prices between the producing and consuming parts of the country, while keeping domestic prices below the world level, remain continuing sources of trouble that are enmeshed with the new geographical dimensions of Canadian policy-making (to be discussed below). A public presence in the industry through PetroCanada seems reasonably well established, as does the aim of expanding natural gas production. After that, major disagreements arise. Late in 1980 the new Trudeau government announced a series of measures aimed at greatly increased Canadianization of the oil industry and a higher share of revenue for the federal government. A sharp reaction by both domestic and foreign producers and several provincial governments, especially Alberta, left the future highly uncertain.

No matter who owns the Canadian oil and gas companies a series of issues have to be dealt with: the pace of production, the terms on which gas and electricity should be exported to the United States (and a few other countries) while imports of oil continue, arrangements on finance and transportation with the United States, and the long-run approach to additional domestic sources of fuel (synthetics, tar sands, etc.). While the conservation of energy is the order of the day in many industries, Canadians consume more energy per caput than the people of any other industrial country. Oil prices are kept low, at least partly to provide a competitive advantage for exports. There are strong advocates of the expansion of petrochemical production, and the energy-intensive production of aluminum from imported bauxite is also being expanded because water power is available.

Energy is a special case, and agriculture (and fisheries) have been left out of this volume by agreement. But for Canada more than for the other countries being discussed, forestry and hard minerals remain central issues of structure. A tension has existed between the high yields of these activities and the feeling that they were somehow "backward" in comparison to manufacturing and services. It may well be that Canadian tax policy at one time was biased in favor of raw material production, but in the 1970s an accumulation of provincial and federal measures undoubtedly discouraged the expansion of mining. By the 1980s there was a new debate; some economists and civil servants argued that it was the height of folly to stress the expansion of manufacturing industries in view of the high return on investment in areas of considerable existing comparative advantage, which might be expected to grow if world needs for raw materials over the next few decades enhanced their value and put a premium on secure sources. The counterview was that Canada's comparative advantage in minerals was waning as its richer veins became exhausted, environmental standards rose, and production expanded in developing countries with lower labor costs and, sometimes, cheaper capital.[30]

There was even a question whether traditional views of raw material production were not misleading. Mining is very capital-intensive and, in a country where labor is increasingly hard to come by and has a considerable turnover in the remote places where the minerals are to be found, may become more so. Mining (including the production of oil and gas but not processing) has employed only 1.5 percent of the Canadian labor force in recent years, but in 1972, before the oil price rise, its value added amounted to more than 4 percent of the GNP. In that year, the capital stock per man hour in mining was over six times what it was for manufacturing.[31] Between 1946 and 1976 the capital stock used in mining increased faster than in any other goods-producing industry. Seven times as much capital was used per worker in 1976 as in 1946 (in constant dollars). Productivity, not surprisingly, increased at twice the national average.[32] Production per worker is about twice that of the United States and perhaps eight times that in Western Europe.[33]

Such figures do not make mining a leading candidate for the provision of jobs (although wages are higher than in most industries), but they suggest a considerable contribution to the national economy. The long-standing Canadian emphasis on doing more processing of raw materials at home continues, but perhaps a little more cautiously than before. The well-known perverse tariff structure of industrial countries — duties rising with the degree of fabrication — has proved difficult to alter; expanding exports to Europe and Japan has increased the proportion of raw products; where duties have been lowered they have not always been decisive, at least partly because it is not always more economical to process near the source of production rather than the market; export controls to foster domestic processing have only occasionally been satisfactory. Nevertheless, efforts to increase processing by one means or another will continue, as in the case of Quebec's taking over an asbestos firm. This was, however, also connected with the wish to establish a public presence in an industry of symbolic importance to Quebec's "quiet revolution." The earlier Saskatchewan measures taking over potash plants had to do with improving export prices. The question of foreign ownership in raw materials will continue to raise questions especially because of the high capital needs, the question of who captures the rents, and the locus of decision-making with regard to processing, exploration, the rate of production, and a number of other basic matters.

Forestry is not nearly as capital-intensive as mining; nevertheless, the technology of both industries is considerably more advanced than would be suggested by stereotypes of miners with pickaxes and lumbermen riding logs down rivers. Canadians have begun asking themselves whether a good way to develop their economy would be to build a bridge between raw material production and processing and the creation of areas in which Canadian manufacturing and R & D could break new ground. One could at the same time find better ways to increase productivity in the raw materials industries, stimulate research, and then introduce new products in machinery and equipment, which could also be exported.

Not the least of the problems Canada faces in carrying out industrial policy is the division of powers over raw materials between the federal government and the provinces. According to the British North America Act, "lands, mines, minerals and royalties" belong to the provinces. Thus they have "the right to determine who may develop and extract the mineral resources within their boundaries and under what terms and conditions development shall take place."[34] And they may tax. But the federal government too may levy taxes on the revenue from mining. Moreover, it, not the provinces, is responsible for the regulation of trade and commerce, domestic and foreign. There is also a somewhat arcane power to assume jursidiction over "works" that are declared to be "for the general advantage of Canada," on the basis of which uranium mining has been put under federal control.

It seems to be generally understood that this last nominally sweeping power cannot in practice be used except in very special circumstances. And there is no doubt that the federal government can impose export controls as well as restrict imports. But when is a provincial limitation on production a restraint of trade, internal or foreign? Does a federal export tax interfere with a province's right to determine how its resources should be used or at least undermine its potential revenue? If federal and provincial tax measures are taken independently of one another, a private producer can be put out of business by penalty rates. Yet the division of a given amount of revenue between Ottawa and a provincial capital is plainly a zero-sum game, in which someone loses something. Naturally, Canadians have found ways of living with these problems. Customs have sprung up about how the laws should be interpreted and powers used; a certain amount of machinery has been established to coordinate action and settle disputes. In contemporary Canada, however, established ways of doing things do not always work smoothly, and when the stakes escalate (as they have in energy) it is inevitable that difficulties should increase. Federal-provincial difficulties are not, as we shall see, confined to raw materials, but the difficulties built into the raw materials situation have contributed substantially to the others.

The Difficulties of Shaping Canadian Industrial Policy

The broad problems of Canadian industrial policy sketched in the three foregoing sections are not new. None is clearly on the road to resolution. Perhaps no altogether consistent and sustained policy can be pursued because of intellectual disagreement, conflicts among interest groups, and the democratic, social, and geographical pluralism of the country. But there will have to be serious efforts to deal with these issues if any significant measures of industrial policy are to be developed. For Canada, like the other industrial democracies, faces a set of long-run problems that have been sharply exacerbated by the events of the 1970s and then given added urgency by the unsatisfactory performance of the economy in recovering from them. But the making of an effort is no guarantee of success, as recent Canadian history shows.

In the early 1970s the Liberal government of Pierre Elliott Trudeau made a considerable effort to formulate an industrial strategy that would help substantially to deal with all of the problems mentioned here. It did not succeed. There were divisions within the Cabinet on such basic issues as whether to take an overall or a sectoral approach and on how deeply and directly the government should intervene in the economy. Energy, inflation, unemployment, and the balance of payments demanded more urgent attention than could be given to devising long-run industrial strategy. Elections and the changing patterns of Canadian politics (including but not confined to the Quebec issue) played their part. Businessmen, as was to be expected, resisted the idea of too much governmental intervention, and many were opposed to or skeptical of the whole idea of an industrial strategy; often, however, they wanted the government to do specific things to deal with the problems of their own industries. The Liberal Party tried to work out a declaration on industrial strategy but could not reach a meaningful agreement. By and large, it seems fair to say that the divisions within the government that stood in the way of formulation of an industrial strategy reflected the divisions of thought and interests within the country.

Even so, certain things were done. Energy, foreign investment, regional development, and a number of other matters were acted on. The negotiations in the Tokyo Round were linked to an Interdepartmental Committee on Trade and Industrial Policy. Extensive consultations in 1977 led to the creation early in the following year of 23 sectoral task forces made up of business, labor, academic specialists, and others to work over industry profiles prepared by the staff of the Ministry of Industry, Trade and Commerce. Their reports were gone over by a second tier task force that was to seek common elements and recommend policies to the government. Late in 1978 an interdepartmental Board of Economic Development Ministers was created to integrate federal work on economic growth. Its president sat in the Cabinet and was supported by a small but select secretariat. The new board gave a generally favorable response to the recommendations of the Tier 2 committee and helped deal with the problems of several industries and regions. According to one observer, "by far the most important of the BEDM's accomplishments was its realization of federal-provincial agreements on a major program in pulp and paper modernization."[35] Whether this culmination of several years' work by other agencies was intended to open a series of major sectoral measures is unknown, since the Trudeau government fell. The Progressive Conservative government of Joseph Clark was not in office long enough to establish a new course in Canadian industrial policy. When Trudeau returned to power in February 1980 there seemed little doubt that in one way or another a fresh start would be made on the problems of industrial strategy, but by what means and how comprehensively was not made manifest by the time this chapter was completed.

Many of the difficulties of carrying out industrial policy are common to all democracies, but Canada's problems have a special dimension in the relation of the federal government to the provinces in matters bearing on industrial policy. This is not just a matter of raw materials or Quebec or the outcome of the discussions of constitutional reform, which have been under way for some time but were reopened with a new vigor in 1980. What happens in any of these fields may make an important difference, but the difficulties are pervasive. They are also not confined to federal-provincial relations, strictly speaking. Major issues arise from the relation of one province to another and from a kind of regionalism that appears when several provinces share interests and attitudes. Here we can do no more than illustrate this special facet of Canadian industrial policy.

In 1867 the drafters of the British North America Act had before their eyes the bloody near-dissolution of the United States. They prudently said that when powers were not specifically given to the provinces, they should remain with the federal government, the opposite of the American principle that left the states with residual rights. But history read its instructions the other way: the powers the provinces were given and have acquired give them a major voice in dealing with natural resources, foreign investment, and a host of other matters essential to industrial policy. The constitution lists 31 powers exclusive to the federal government, 16 to the provinces alone, and a number that are concurrent, with one or the other level of government given the right to over-ride when there is a conflict. Residual powers are assigned explicitly to the federal government. But this "impression of a centralized federal system with a clear-cut allocation of responsibilities" is misleading. Life and law have "profoundly altered the division of powers, to the point where the activities of the two orders of government are so intertangled that one cannot take action without stirring up reactions by the other."[36] The result is not only inefficiency and waste but a constant conflict between "the two orders of government . . . because neither one has a clear sphere for autonomous action." The conflict is not confined to legal issues; it affects the performance of the Canadian economy, the ability of the federal government to undertake international commitments, and the play of political forces within the country.

It would be foolish to ascribe the difficulties between Quebec and Ottawa primarily to conflicts of economic policy or to any other single cause, but there is no doubt that dissatisfaction with their economic lot and the sense that they lacked control of their own economic affairs have long contributed to rallying support among Québecois for the wish to be *maîtres chez nous*. This aspiration is shared in varying degrees by those who want to separate from Canada, by those who would use "independence" to establish a new relation with the rest of the country, and by those who believe that more can be accomplished by staying within the federation and reforming it. Although clear-cut victory for any one of these views would have immense consequences for Canada, our concern is not with these but with the way in which the existence of the Quebec issue, in any of its forms, exerts a major impact on Canadian industrial policy.

If Quebec were negotiating some kind of "sovereignty-association" with the rest of Canada, or if it had simply separated, it would be necessary to question Quebec's ability to stand alone or what would be involved in its making one rather than another kind of arrangement with the rest of Canada, or, for that mattter, with the United States.[37] Comparable questions would have to be asked about the rest of Canada and would bear heavily on issues of industrial policy. Perhaps such questions will have to be thought about at some future time. But even if it could be assumed that the negative vote on sovereignty-association in the referendum of May 1980 is definitive (a proposition the Parti Québecois would not accept), there are major questions of industrial policy to be considered that arise from the continued presence of Quebec in the Canadian federation, not from its departure. Some have to do with the way concern for Quebec's interests affects federal industrial policies. Others arise from the powers of the government of Quebec—and their use—as they affect what the federal government can do.

It is a delicate question whether any powers exercised by Quebec would have to be given to all other provinces or whether it could have its special brand of autonomy (in more than language) because it is *pas comme les autres*.[38] We need not answer it here but cannot forget that while the Quebec issue is in many respects unique, it also has aspects that are part of the broad set of issues about federal-provincial division of powers. Examples of the way concern for Quebec does much to shape federal policies on trade and industry are not hard to find.

The protection of the clothing and textile industries is of particular interest in Canada because of the high proportion of the plants located in Quebec and the widely accepted view that, for reasons of language and culture as well as habit and conservatism, the workers cannot be expected to move to anything else. Much the same is true of the shoe and furniture industries, where protection is not quite so stringent.[39] Not only measures to deal with the problems of these declining industries are involved, but also the possibilities of introducing expanding and more productive ones. In bidding for an aircraft contract, an American company went out of its way to stress the amount of work that would be done in Quebec (but lost out to a rival whose bid offered more work in Canada as a whole). Quebec has been more resistant than some other provinces to measures likely to hold down foreign investment, whether taken by FIRA or otherwise. The federal government will have to consider whether it can give special weight to the needs of Quebec in the distribution of funds to encourage the location of industry there. No doubt foreign investment in Quebec will be influenced by uncertainty — or conviction — about the future of the area.[40]

Tariffs, import controls, and regional policy can also been seen as part of the process by which some sections of Canada transfer resources to other areas. The main beneficiary of import protection other than Quebec is Ontario, a much richer province, but the one that has the other large share of declining industries.[41] As a number of studies sparked by the Quebec issue have pointed out, however, it is not enough to deal only with the location of protected industries, since a high proportion of the markets of the rest of Canada also lie in these two provinces. Each is furthermore the other's best customer. Thus there are leakages of any form of federal aid to Quebec that make for some uncertainty about the impact of such measures, whether they are taken for economic or political reasons. Nevertheless, one of the basic factors influencing future Canadian industrial policy is bound to be the fact that Ontario and Quebec, the two old centers of industry, are losing a certain amount of ground to the west, economically and politically.

In the west there is an old, established belief that the tariff is largely a tax imposed on the rest of the country for the benefit of Quebec and Ontario. That view dates from a time when the west was almost entirely devoted to agriculture, forestry, and mining. The new growth of industry in British Columbia, Alberta, Saskatchewan, and Manitoba introduces new considerations that may affect the traditional free trade sentiment, but certainly has a bearing on both the federal-provincial distribution of powers over economic activities and the sharpening of regionalism as well. This is part of a larger view characterized by a professor at the University of Alberta: "There is a tendency to view the relationship with the federal government and the 'East' generally as one of continuous strife and adversity. Confederation is seen by many as a kind of 'zero-sum game' where the distribution of a fixed stock of wealth is a function of regional political power, with the federal government's being at best indifferent to the West and at worst actively working against it."[42] Given these views, it is inevitable that the increase in economic importance of the west should have had a strong impact on the geopolitics of industrial policy with which Canada has to live.

The whole west has gained but Alberta most of all. Its gross domestic product per caput in 1977 was 34 percent higher than the national average, compared to an 8 percent advantage in 1970. Having trailed Ontario, it had moved to first place and British Columbia to second. Personal income per caput was still lower in Alberta than in Ontario and British Columbia in 1977, although only Alberta had made a marked gain since 1970, compared to a slight gain in British Columbia and a substantial fall (in comparison to the national average) in Ontario.[43] Oil and gas have propelled the shift in wealth and power. The struggle over the returns from them has been an important part of its manifestation. The division of revenue between Ottawa and Edmonton and the relation of Canadian to world oil prices involve wide areas of Canadian economics and politics, but they are central to issues of industrial policy. For example, the Alberta Heritage Savings Trust Fund, fed by 30 percent of the province's oil and gas revenues and amounting to over $5 billion by 1980 (and growing fast), requires thought about the future of the province; that in turn leads directly to decisions about what kinds of industries should be developed to provide employment and new sources of income—when, as, and if earning from oil and gas decline.

A natural candidate has been the petrochemical industry. In spite of worldwide overcapacity, the push is strong (as in other oil-producing countries) to establish new plants which, to be economical, must be big enough to export on a large scale. This would require access to foreign markets, and it is hardly surprising that Alberta should have pressured the federal government to make a reduction in American petrochemical tariffs a major target in the Tokyo Round. Subsequently there have been suggestions that the Alberta government's assent to levels of gas production permitting exports to the United States might be conditioned on American tariff action. Some Canadian producers favor a North American free trade area in petrochemicals.[44] At the same time there are established petrochemical producers in Ontario and Quebec whose future will also be heavily influenced by the investments made in Alberta.

They and other parts of Canadian industry will also be greatly affected by the struggle between Ottawa and Edmonton about the oil prices. So far, it has been federal policy to keep the Canadian domestic price below the world level but to move slowly toward it without catching up with the American price. Accepting this approach, Alberta has wished to raise the price faster than the federal government wanted to. Who is to decide the pace is, itself, one of the issues, as are such related matters as how the subsidization of imports of oil at world prices is financed and whether there should be an export tax on natural gas going to the United States. Even with the reduced price and the substantial sluicing off of income to the Heritage Fund, Alberta has been able to help finance substantial new investment in the province. Low taxes, high wages, and improved public services further stimulate industrial development. The shift in income to Alberta from the rest of the confederation is only partly offset by the various fiscal equalization mechanisms made use of in Canada. By lending from the Heritage Fund to other provinces or investing in private ventures, Edmonton gains a further influence on the pattern of Canadian economic development. It is no distortion to say that the oil price not only transfers purchasing power from Ontario to Alberta but shifts the locus of some investment decisions as well.

While not quite as hostile to Ontario and Quebec as the west, residents of the Maritime provinces and Newfoundland have also resented the tariff. Poor and rather sparsely populated, these provinces have not the political impact of the west. Although they have gained from the extension of Canadian fishing grounds and may benefit from offshore oil, they remain heavily dependent on federal aid. In 1977 they received about half the total grants made by the Department of Regional Economic Expansion and about half the total provincial revenue came from federal transfers.[45] While other provinces also benefit from a variety of payments, they are better able to take matters into their own hands. For example, in British Columbia the provincial government stepped in to prevent the control of a major forest products company from passing to a company with headquarters in Montreal. Dividends from companies located in the provinces are taxed less heavily when collected by residents than those from companies in the rest of Canada or abroad. Quebec has a similar arrangement. Sixty percent of all public procurement in Canada is by provinces and municipalities which frequently discriminate in favor of their "own" producers. Suppliers of telecommunications equipment and other products for which governments are primary customers often find themselves required to establish plants in a given province instead of delivering from larger facilities elsewhere. Where legal powers are lacking or formal arrangements eschewed for one reason or another, political pressures and appeals to local patriotism are used in the same way. The result, as increasing numbers of Canadian scholars and commentators point out, is that "province-building has come into direct conflict with country-building for Canada as a whole."[46]

It is not surprising that among the proposals for constitutional reform put forward by the Trudeau government in 1980 should be the grant of power to the federal government to intervene if provincial measures obstruct the flow of goods, labor, or capital. In part this would simply restate what the British North America Act now says, and some people might prefer a strong assertion of nominal federal powers. Constitutional reform is immensely difficult in Canada; as this chapter is written no one can say with any assurance that the new efforts to deal with the whole range of federal-provincial relations, as well as with the "French fact" of Quebec, will have significant results. Some proposals would increase the powers of the provinces by such measures as replacing the Senate (now appointive) with a house where provincial and regional interests are directly represented, or by permitting provincial governments to name members of regulatory commissions or otherwise influence the choice of them.[47] One needs to remember, too, that the original drafters of the Canadian constitution took care to create the condition they wanted, but their descendants got quite a different condition. Whether the constitutional framework is changed or not, Canada will not be able to produce effective national economic policies without effective federal-provincial cooperation.

The consequences of failure would not be just internal. The ability of the government of Canada to make international commitments on trade, industrial policy, investment, and some financial matters is limited by what is in the power of the provinces. This inability in turn limits the ability of Canada to obtain from other governments commitments about their policies that may be essential for carrying out those of Canada's industrial policies that require reliable access to foreign markets or supplies. No doubt an awareness of this problem may help Canadians to overcome it. John Holmes recognizes the "special challenges" presented by the importance of "multilateral diplomacy" to Canada. It "has done well," he believes, partly because these challenges have been met. "The need to act effectively in intergovernmental negotiations has forced us into drastic changes in federal-provincial policy-making processes, a major evolution of our constitutional practice too little noticed."[48] Whether such good results will be achieved in the future remains to be seen.

Clearly the shaping of industrial policy is made considerably more difficult in Canada than in other countries by the division of power between provinces and the central government, and the differences among provinces and regions that result both from the exercise of these powers and shifts in political and economic strength.[49] More is involved than just adding complexities and differences of interest to what is almost always a highly controversial subject in democracies with mixed economies. There is a self-feeding element in the process, arising from the fact that insofar as province-building reduces the economic benefits of the *national* division of labor, the economic advantage of national unity for one part or another (and perhaps all) is reduced. And it is the existence of the "surplus from the integration of the ten provinces" plus its distribution "in a way that is acceptable to all the participants" that offset "the sacrifices required in terms of the increased vulnerability to decisions taken outside each jurisdiction" and hold the country together.[50]

Canadian Industrial Policy and the International Economic System

Although Sir John A. Macdonald in 1878 enunciated a *National* Policy, that policy was largely concerned with Canada's foreign economic relations – and their political implications. In the years since, Canada's position in the international economic system has been a key element in determining the objectives of its trade and industrial policies and at the same time a major limitation on what could be achieved by those measures. This basic condition has not changed. Among the industrial nations, Canada remains one of those most dependent on the rest of the world. Its choices in industrial policy depend heavily on what the international economic system permits and what it demands of Canada. Even the basic political aim of the National Policy – nation building – remains part of the rationale of industrial policy today.

As in the case of other countries, a bill of particulars covering what Canada wants from the rest of the world cannot be drawn up without making hypotheses about future Canadian industrial policy. The foregoing pages have shown why no clear, coherent set of hypotheses is sufficiently credible to warrant elaboration. At a certain level of generality it is nevertheless possible to indicate some of the kinds of requirements that Canada is likely to make of the international economic system and some of the difficulties that are almost bound to arise.

Suppose, for example, that that body of Canadian opinion were to win out which favors a sustained effort to improve Canada's international competitiveness by a considerable restructuing of its manufacturing. There might still be disagreements as to the proper instruments of industrial policy but agreement that it is necessary to specialize in some lines of exports while relying more heavily than before on imports of other products. For such efforts to be successful there has to be a system of international trade cooperation in which the removal of

Canadian import barriers is matched by other countries' reduction of barriers to Canadian exports (tariff and nontariff alike) on a sufficiently broad and lasting basis to permit Canada to rely on the results for some time to come. The restructuring and the enhancement of competitiveness will entail governmental aid in one form or another, perhaps particularly with regard to R & D or a certain volume of government procurement. This means Canada will need international arrangements that permit it to carry on these activities without incurring retaliation from other countries that would nullify the advantages it hoped to gain. Perhaps this could be done simply by legitimizing the practices in question, but further steps might be needed to prevent other countries offsetting Canadian gains by their own industrial policy measures.

More is involved than just trade policies. Canadian industrial policy will be concerned with the pattern of investment, foreign and domestic, and will lay down conditions, when possible, for the behavior of foreign firms, provide tax exemptions and other forms of inducements (sometimes including assured Canadian markets) for companies that invest, and in a variety of ways will try to influence their behavior as to jobs, investments, exports, R & D, and the kinds of technology they apply. The acceptability of these practices, or at least their immunity from retaliation, will (as in the case of trade measures) be one of the things Canada asks of the rest of the world. As a raw material producer and exporter, Canada will also be interested in the possibilities of joining with other producers to enhance its terms of trade by holding up prices or—as in the case of oil—of benefiting from the actions of others even if it does not formally take part in the trade and pricing arrangements. But as Canada also imports raw materials, it is unlikely to favor all commodity agreements or arrangements intended to improve the terms of trade of all raw material exporters or transfer resources to them. As a major exporter of wheat, it has one set of interests; as an importer of many other kinds of food and feed, another. It is also of considerable importance to Canadian competitiveness that the country have sufficient control over its exchange rate to be able to keep it low enough.[51]

For the present, the international monetary system offers no threat on this last point. The extent of international agreement on investment, food, raw materials, and the behavior of multinational corporations is too modest to seem, in itself, a barrier to Canada's shaping of an independent policy on these matters. The counterpart of this last condition, however, is that there is little restraint in the international system on other countries whose actions, whether intentionally or not, might counteract the effects of Canadian policy. As to the new GATT codes, which are so clearly related to industrial policy, it has been made clear elsewhere that their full purpose remains to be worked out. Thus the question arises whether Canada should be thought of as gaining a certain freedom of action from the present state of the system of international economic cooperation or whether its greater need is more insurance against the untoward behavior (from a strictly Canadian point of view) of other countries.

If the first alternative seems persuasive, Canadians may feel that it is best to deal with difficulties pragmatically as they arise, counting on their own bargaining power (which is far from negligible and seems to be growing) and trusting to some degree to the likelihood that any given Canadian action will not be so damaging to others as to incur the wrath of powerful countries.

But if the latter possibility is taken seriously, the question arises whether, to carry out an effective industrial policy, Canada needs to try to improve the international machinery. Although it is common to think of bigger countries taking the lead in these matters—and certainly without their cooperation little could be achieved—it is not illogical to think of a major trading country (such as Canada) taking the initiative (especially within a roughly agreed framework of principles such as clearly exists in the GATT codes and is adumbrated in other matters) to make more precise the international obligations of countries. Relative weakness is, after all, a good reason to seek stronger, clearer rules that will limit the damage that might be inflicted by free-swinging, uninhibited measures by the United States, the European Community, or Japan. It would also not be a new role for Canada. As a perceptive historian of Canada's part in the making of the postwar world (who was also a participant in the process) has pointed out: "The part played by Canadians in the conferences at Hot Springs, Bretton Woods, Chicago, where the great agencies to deal with food and money and aviation were set up, was closer to the international centers of power than was their activity at San Francisco" (in the drafting of the United Nations Charter). The same was true of trade, where "Canadians required both protection and opportunity and were in the strategic position to play that middle role which international economics required of them."[52] The words seem quite apposite to the present day.

Whether or not Canada takes steps to alter the international economic system, its requirements from that system go one step beyond the kinds of reasonable assurances of restraints on unfair practices of others—or simply practices damaging Canada—that these paragraphs have suggested. The reciprocal question concerns the extent to which the system (or other countries acting independently) will accommodate Canada's views or needs when Canadian practices affect the interests of others or offend standards that are accepted as the general rule. Some degree of indulgence, some degree of license to commit transgressions, is a necessary part of cooperative systems. The strongest countries are not likely to be denied that, but for smaller and more dependent countries the need may be especially great. (Moreover, the indulgences granted them cost other countries less than would the same measures for the benefit of much larger economies and are less likely to undermine the system by upsetting the balance between freedom and restraint on which it all depends.) In the past, Canada has been the beneficiary of some asymmetry. When fixed exchange rates were the rule, it had a floating rate for a long period without suffering sanctions from other countries or the International Monetary Fund. Its tariff cuts in the Kennedy Round were less than those of the other main trading countries. Even after the Tokyo Round cuts are fully applied, it will have higher average duties than the European community, Japan, or the United States (although the customs valuation code will reduce the real effect of some duties). Canada has safeguards in the automobile agreement that the United States lacks.

No special status for Canada is provided in the GATT codes, tariff rules, or other international arrangements. There is little doubt, however, that an active Canadian industrial policy of the sort sketched earlier would involve a whole series of practices that might be challenged by other countries. For example, to build up internationally competitive units will require a period of protection of the home market while at the same time freer access to foreign markets is claimed.

To require foreign investors to undertake local processing or to increase their R & D in Canada as the price of admission will be regarded as taking those activities away from someone else, very likely the home country of the investor. Even simple regional aids are likely, as Rodney Grey pointed out in the statement quoted earlier (see note 23), to affect exports (or, for that matter, imports). That will be one of the purposes of government technology policy.

Canada's success in these matters may well depend on how far other governments will go in accepting the view that it is reasonable to take account of Canada's special problems and interests. Is this likely to be done on the grounds that a restructured Canadian economy will contribute more to the welfare of Canadians and also to the international division of labor than one in which adaptation had been blocked or distorted by foreign actions? Suppose Canadians made a case based on more than economic need and asymmetry. Given the nation-building aspect of past Canadian economic policy, and the nation-breaking tendencies now at work in the country, it would not be stretching a point to claim that some measures of industrial policy were politically essential for any Canadian government or even required for national unity. A Canadian economist has made a suggestion along these lines: "Might a refusal by the Canadian government to sustain import-vulnerable industries in Quebec contribute to a collapse of employment in that province so serious that confederation would be fatally undermined, causing upheavals in the economy of this part of the world that would be felt by all our trading partners for a considerable time to come?"[53] Thus other countries would be asked, in effect, to accept arrangements they might otherwise object to, either because they are thought to have a direct stake in the political unity and welfare of Canada or, less directly, because the economic loss to them of disturbance and perhaps the breakup of Canada would be greater than that of accepting a degree of protection for weak industries or subsidies for vulnerable areas of the country. It is not to be taken for granted that all countries will react in the same way.

Partly for that reason, and because it is in any case inescapable, Canada will have to face the question: If it does not prove possible to negotiate on a global or wide multilateral basis the kinds of arrangements that are needed, how far should Canada go in trying to work out such arrangements with the United States alone? As was noted above, the place of the United States in Canada's trade, investment, capital supply, and technology is such that satisfactory bilateral relations can take care of most of Canada's main worries. But there is much history, and quite a bit of contemporary evidence, that suggests that the idea of deliberately fostering closer economic integration with the United States is too hard for many Canadians to accept. Even the once established practice of asking for exemptions from American policies toward the rest of the world, which could do disproportionate damage to Canada, has been castigated as an undesirable kind of special relation. Some steps of both kinds have proved acceptable, however, and the debate goes on in Canada as it probably always will, as to which measures would best serve national interests.[54] Therefore, it seems likely that if Canadians are able to agree on goals of industrial policy and measures to achieve them they may also be able to agree on steps to take toward the United States, perhaps very selectively. Then two more questions will arise which are much less discussed than Canada's choices. First, how should the United States respond? And second, how far should the other principal partners in the international economic system go in accepting special arrangements between Canada and the United States as justifiable exceptions to multilateral arrangements that they were not themselves prepared to undertake on the same terms?

Notes

1. Quoted by Ramsay Cook, *The Maple Leaf Forever* (Toronto: Macmillan of Canada, 1971), p. 211. This collection of essays deals only obliquely with economic policy but does much to show the various kinds of nationalism that have done so much to shape Canadian nationalism—whether Anglo, French, or Canadian, aimed against Britain or the United States, or expressed in historiography as well as politics.

2. Ibid., p. 210

3. Reacting to the manufacturers' statement quoted above, the *Grain Growers' Guide* said, "Always bear in mind that the good old patriotic slogan of the C.M.A., 'Canada for the Canadians,' means Canada for 2,500 Canadians." (Ibid., p. 211.)

4. Harold A. Innis, *The Fur Trade in Canada* (New Haven: Yale University Press, 1962), p. 393. The original edition was 1930.

5. The theme of the two orientations is most interestingly developed by Cook, especially in his comparison of Anglophone Canadian historians in *The Maple Leaf Forever*, pp. 141–65.

6. Craufurd D. W. Goodwin, *Canadian Economic Thought: The Political Economy of a Developing Nation 1814–1914* (Durham, N.C.: Duke University Press, 1961), pp. 69, 70. This book is a most-valuable tracing of intellectual, political, and economic influences on a range of important economic problems and throws light on the whole structural approach (although it does not explicitly use these terms or concepts).

7. Robert Craig Brown, *Canada's National Policy, 1883–1900* (Princeton, N.J.: Princeton University Press, 1964), pp. 11, 12. The quotation from Tilley that follows appears on p. 12. This book is full of valuable contemporary material and balanced analysis of the interplay of trade, fishing, and boundary issues as they were worked out between the United States and Canada.

8. Quoted by L. Ethan Ellis, *Reciprocity 1911* (New Haven: Yale University Press, 1939), p. 114. This is the classic study of an intricate process which, like the Brown book just cited, brings out issues of lasting relevance to both Canadian thinking and Canadian-American relations. The repudiated statement by Clark (page 96) said he supported reciprocity "because I hope to see the day when the American flag will float over every square foot of the British-North American possessions clear to the North Pole."

9. Quoted in R. D. Cuff and J. L. Granatstein, *American Dollars—Canadian Prosperity* (Toronto: Samuel-Stevens, 1978), p. 81. Chapter 3 of this book, drawn from American and Canadian archives and private papers, is the fullest account available of this little-known episode.

10. Though it is widely assumed that this was part of the Canadian government's reason for favoring the Ottawa agreements, the point is not even mentioned in Ian M. Drummond, *Imperial Economic Policy, 1917–1937* (Toronto: University of Toronto Press, 1974).

11. Herbert Marshall, Frank A. Southard Jr., and Kenneth W. Taylor, *Canadian-American Industry: A Study in International Investment* (New Haven: Yale University Press, 1936), pp. 202, 203. The relation of tariffs and investment is discussed on pp. 199–203, 209, 210, 216–18, 241–43, 272–77, and passim. Once established, American subsidiaries often became advocates of Canadian tariff protection and "more than one of the lobbying firms at the Ottawa Conference in 1932 were American subsidiaries anxious that 'Empire content' rules be stiffened and that other protection be maintained or increased to retain their Empire markets" (p. 275). The same page of this book is the source of the point made earlier about holding some duties low enough to keep out large American producers, such as US Steel.

12. John Sloan Dickey, *Canada and the American Presence* (New York: New York University Press for the Council on Foreign Relations, 1975), pp. 105, 106.

13. This is done by stipulating that provincial policy objectives have to be taken into account by FIRA, that the provinces be kept informed, and that the federal government be told what any provinces think about each FIRA recommendation. The administration of the Act seems to have been fully in the spirit of these provisions; provincial officials who complained about other federal regulatory bodies were quite happy with FIRA, according to Richard J. Shultz, *Federalism and the Regulatory Process* (Montreal: Institute for Research on Public Policy, 1979). The quotations are from pp. 59 and 60.

14. Between April 9, 1974, and the end of 1977, FIRA approved 78 percent of the cases before it concerning takeovers (and a slightly higher share of those from American firms). The equivalent figure for new investments between October 15, 1975, and the end of 1977 was 85 percent, with a slightly lower figure for American applications. See Steven Globerman, *U.S. Ownership of Firms in Canada,* Canada–U.S. Prospects, a series sponsored by C. D. Howe Research Institute (Canada) and the National Planning Association (USA) (Montreal, 1979), p. 58.

15. Thomas G. Bakelin, "What it can be like to face FIRA," *The Financial Post* (Toronto), April 12, 1980.

16. The fullest exploration is that undertaken by the Private Planning Association of Canada, resulting in the publication of 13 volumes between 1968 and 1972 under the series title *Canada in the Atlantic Economy.* The concluding volume, which takes account of an extensive literature over and above the studies of the series, is H. E. English, B. W. Wilkinson, and H. C. Eastman, *Canada in a Wider Economic Community* (Toronto: University of Toronto Press for the Private Planning Association, 1972). A forerunner was H. Edward English, *Industrial Structure in Canada's International Competitive Position* (Montreal: The Canadian Trade Committee and the Private Planning Association of Canada, 1964). A benchmark was provided by two economists, Ronald J. Wonnacott and Paul Wonnacott, *Free Trade between the United States and Canada: The Potential Economic Effects* (Cambridge, Mass.: Harvard University Press, 1967).

17. These were principally on the Canadian side, where imports were tariff-free only for companies producing cars, buses, and trucks. Moreover, these companies had to produce vehicles in Canada in the same proportion to their sales in Canada as before the agreement and maintain at least the same absolute amount of "Canadian content" (value added by material, labor, and parts) as before. The most authoritative early study of the agreement is Carl Beigie, *The Canada–U.S. Automotive Agreement: An Evaluation* (Montreal: Canadian-American Committee, 1970). The evolution of the agreement is covered by a substantial number of official reports by both governments. An effort to put the agreement in a larger setting and to see how it might relate to other fields can be found in William Diebold, Jr., *The United States and the Industrial World* (New York: Praeger for the Council on Foreign Relations, 1972), pp. 81–95.

18. *The Financial Post* (Toronto), May 24, 1980.

19. An older agreement eliminates tariffs and some discriminatory practices in defence procurement by the two federal governments. Free trade in farm machinery between the two countries was arrived at by separate unilateral acts, not by an agreement. In fact, a fairly high proportion of Canadian-American trade moves at zero or low tariffs, but this has not been brought about through sectoral balancing. In the Tokyo Round, the Canadian government championed sectoral negotiations (especially in raw material–based industries) but with little success.

20. Economic Council of Canada, *Looking Outward, A New Trade Strategy for Canada* (Ottawa, 1975), p. 188.

21. The Standing Senate Committee on Foreign Affairs, *Canada–United States Relations, vol. 2. Canada's Trade Relations with the United States* (Ottawa: The Queen's Printer, June 1978), p. 121.

22. Economic Council of Canada, *For A Common Future; A Study of Canada's Relations with the Developing Countries* (Ottawa, 1978) is the most-comprehensive report. A substantial number of supporting papers were also issued of which the two most relevant to

this chapter are Roy Matthews, *Canadian Industry and the Challenge of Low Cost Imports* and G. K. Helleiner and D. Welwood, *Raw Material Processing in Developing Countries and Reductions in the Canadian Tariff.* Shortly afterwards, the Wonnacott brothers courageously (and effectively) reviewed the conclusions of their earlier book in the light of the criticisms made of it, new facts, and new analysis: Paul and Ron Wonnacott, *Free Trade between the United States and Canada: Fifteen Years Later,* Working Paper 1980-20, mimeographed (College Park, MD.: University of Maryland, Department of Economics and Bureau of Business and Economic Research).

23. Senate of Canada, *Proceedings of the Standing Committee on Foreign Affairs,* June 5, 1980, issue no. 4, p. 7. The next quotation comes from p. 8.

24. The responsibility of foreign ownership for low Canadian technological performance is most fully argued in John N. H. Britton and James M. Gilmour, *The Weakest Link: A Technological Perspective on Canadian Industrial Underdevelopment* (Ottawa: Science Council of Canada, Background Study 43, 1978). A thorough-going critique of this report has been made by Paul and Ronald J. Wonnacott, *The Tariff-Foreign Ownership-Technology Nexus: Towards a Less Truncated Theory of Canadian Industrial Truncation* (University of Western Ontario Centre for the Study of International Economic Relations, 1980), Working Paper no. 8013.

25. Senate of Canada, *Proceedings,* op. cit., pp. 9, 10, 17,

26. The whole story is laid out in Wendy Dobson, *The Exchange Rate as a Policy Instrument,* HRI Observations, no. 21 (Montreal: C. D. Howe Research Institute, May 1980).

27. J. J. Singer, "Practical Approaches to Exchange Rate Policies," in Canadian Institute for Economic Policy, *Our Current Account Deficit: A Need for Action,* Occasional Paper no. 1 (October 1979), p. 16.

28. As always there are some problems in definition; e.g., these figures include whiskey, and one might quarrel about the dividing line between semifabricated and more highly finished goods. The figures in the text are approximations based on data for several years. A good survey with a variety of measures, mostly for 1975, is Richard Shaffner, "The Resource Sector of the United States and Canada: An Overview," in Carl Beigie and Alfred O. Hero, Jr., eds. *Natural Resources in U.S.-Canadian Relations,* vol. I (Boulder, Colorado: Westview Press, 1980).

29. B. W. Wilkinson, *Canada in the Changing World Economy.* Canada-U.S. Prospects, a series sponsored by C. D. Howe Research Institute (Canada) and the National Planning Association (USA) (Montreal, 1980), pp. 106, 148. Exports of "road motor vehicles" were 2.2 percent of total Canadian exports in 1964 and 21.3 percent in 1970.

30. The emphasis of Canada's comparative advantage in mining is well worked out in D. J. Daly, "Mineral Resources in the Canadian Economy: Macro-economic Implications," in Beigie and Hero, op. cit. Warnings that the situation may be changing and concern about the loss of rents to the Canadian economy through foreign ownership are stressed by Wilkinson, op. cit., pp. 85-96.

31. Shaffner, op. cit., pp. 26, 29.

32. Wilkinson, op. cit., p. 81. A sharp drop in productivity in mining, quarries, and oil wells from 1973 to 1978, when the national average was going up, has been ascribed to the oil and gas industry, not to the rest of "mining." See C. D. Howe Research Institute, *Investing in Our Own Future* (Montreal: Policy Research and Outlook, 1980), pp. 52, 53.

33. Daly, op. cit., pp. 127-29. The comparisons differ according to years and the lists of products used, but the orders of magnitude make closer measurement unimportant.

34. Garth Stevenson, "The Process of Making Mineral Resource Policy in Canada," in Beigie and Hero, eds., op. cit., p. 169. Only the original provinces' ownership of minerals was confirmed by the British North America Act, but the others have gained the same status by different arrangements. The federal government still has full proprietary rights over the resources of the Yukon and the Northwest Territories. Throughout this section there are oversimplified statements that are more fully explained in Stevenson's work and in a variety of other sources.

35. Richard D. French, *How Ottawa Decides: Planning and Industrial Policy-Making 1968-1980* (Ottawa: Canadian Institute for Economic Policy, 1980), p. 129. This book is

primarily concerned with the clash of different approaches to economic policy within the Canadian government but discusses some of the issues of industrial policy more generally. I have drawn on it for some points in the last few pages but my account — along with much of the rest of this chapter — rests primarily on a continuing study of the subject over a number of years.

36. Judith Maxwell and Caroline Pestieau, *Economic Realities of Contemporary Confederation* (Montreal; C. D. Howe Research Institute, Accent Quebec Series, 1980), p. 29. The next quotation come from p. 31.

37. In 1906 Errol Bouchette, a lawyer who was librarian of Parliament, published *L'indépendance économique du Canada français* based on articles which had appeared in the *Revue canadienne*. It was reissued in 1913, and in 1977 a new edition was published (Les Editions La Presse, Montreal) with an introductory study by Rodrique Tremblay, a professor of economics at the University of Montreal, who became the first Ministry of Industry and Commerce in the Parti Québecois government. Earlier, Tremblay had published *Indépendance et Marché Commun Québec-Etats Unis* (Montreal: Editions du Jour, 1970), arguing that Quebec would be better off in a customs union with the United States than with the rest of Canada. The case for small economies existing perfectly well in the world — with European analogues — is made in Jane Jacobs, *Canadian Cities and Sovereignty Association* (Toronto: Canadian Broadcasting Corporation, 1980). The Scandinavian model has interested a number of Quebeckers, partly because of its reputation for benign social relations and economic welfare and partly for geography. See, for example, Luc-Normand Tellier, *Le Québec, Etat Nordique* (Montreal: Les Editions Quinze, 1977).

38. In an odd twist, the Parti Québecois has turned this equal treatment issue into an argument for independence. Its basic statement arguing for a yes in the referendum said, "To respond to Quebec's needs and ensure its development, it would indeed be necessary to transfer to all the provinces so many powers that now belong to Ottawa that it would add up, in the eyes of English Canadians, to the almost total disappearance of the central government." Gouvernement du Québec, Conseil exécutif, *Quebec-Canada: A New Deal* (Quebec, 1979), p. 41.

39. Measured by employment in 1973, Quebec had 52.1 percent of the country's textile industry, 61.9 percent of the knitting, 65.4 percent of the clothing, 49.9 percent of the shoe factories, and 57.2 percent of the leather glove factories. See Roy Matthews, *Canadian Industry and the Developing Countries,* Economic Council of Canada, Conference on Industrial Adaptation, June 1977, pp. 12, 13. The figures for furniture for 1979 are 39 percent for employment in all kinds of furniture and higher for the value of shipments in certain categories, such as wooden household furniture (53 percent). Senate of Canada, *Proceedings of the Standing Committee on Foreign Affairs* June 26, 1980, issue no. 8, pp. 21–24. On the whole subject, see Caroline Pestieau, *The Quebec Textile Industry in Canada* (Montreal: C. D. Howe Research Institute, Accent Quebec Series, 1978).

40. Protectionism, regional politics, and foreign investment are not the only aspects of Canadian industrial policy relevant to Quebec. It is a major producer and exporter of raw materials and of energy, in this case electricity to New York. None of these can be divorced from the peculiar mix of considerations bearing on the rest of Canada's policies and attitudes toward Quebec (and the views Québecois have of their status), and these paragraphs can only sketch the issues.

41. Compared to the figures just given for Quebec, Ontario had 42.5 percent of the textile employment, 28.6 percent of the knitting, 22 percent of the clothing, 46.1 percent of the shoes, and 25.2 percent of leather gloves. It had substantially larger shares than Quebec of electrical products, especially radio, TV, communications, industrial equipment, batteries, and small appliances. For manufacturing industries as a whole, Ontario's employment is 49.2 percent of the country's and Quebec's is 30.5 percent (Matthews, op. cit., pp. 12–14).

42. Kenneth H. Norrie, "Natural Resources, Economic Development, and U.S.-Canadian Relations: A Western Canadian Perspective," in Beigie and Hero, op. cit., p. 281.

43. Maxwell and Pestieau, op. cit., p. 70.

44. On all these points, see the testimony of representatives from the petrochemical industry before the Senate Standing Committee on Foreign Affairs. *Proceedings,* July 8, 1980, issue no. 9.

45. This last figure ranges from 47.6 percent for New Brunswick to 59.2 percent for Prince Edward Island. The importance of the transfers for personal income can be seen from the fact that while the per caput gross domestic product of the area ranged from half the national average in Prince Edward Island to two-thirds in Nova Scotia, personal income per caput was between two-thirds and four-fifths of the national average for the same two provinces (Maxwell and Pestieau, op. cit., pp. 64, 68, 70).

46. Maxwell and Pestieau, op. cit., p. 91. Chapter 6 of this volume draws together a great deal of material on this theme.

47. Some proposals are made and the merits of others discussed in Richard J. Schultz, *Federalism and the Regulatory Process* op. cit., pp. 87 ff. A committee of the Liberal Party of Quebec would abolish the Senate and create a Federal Council made up of representatives of the provincial governments who would have power over the federal government's activities in a number of fields and broad advisory powers. See the Constitutional Committee of the Quebec Liberal Party, *A New Canadian Federation* (Montreal, 1980) pp. 51-55.

48. John W. Holmes, Canadian Unity: The International Dimension, *Transactions of the Royal Society of Canada,* series 4, vol. 17 (Ottawa: Royal Society of Canada, 1979), p. 104.

49. Space makes it impossible to pursue the very important question of the large differences in regional and provincial support among the three major political parties and the differences within the parties that reflect provincial and regional differences.

50. Maxwell and Pestieau, op. cit., pp. 6, 7.

51. What "low enough" is depends not only on the exchange rates of other major currencies but on what compromise has been made within Canada betwen the conflicting tendencies regarding export competitiveness and financial stability referred to above.

52. John W. Holmes, *The Shaping of Peace: Canada and the Search for World Order 1943-1957,* vol. 1 (Toronto: University of Toronto Press, 1979), pp. 269, 270.

53. Roy A. Matthews, "Reconciling National Interests to the International System," *International Perspectives,* September-December 1979. Mr. Matthews has for some years been on the staff of the Economic Council of Canada and formerly headed the Private Planning Association. He also asks whether "some sort of categorization of nations" might be taken into account based on "the fragility of their economic or even their political and social structures" and the disproportion between the potential damage to them and to the international system.

54. Naturally, Canada will not have a completely free hand in these matters. The United States has already raised the question of federal and provincial subsidies for factory location that draw plants across the border. Considering how general the practice is, the two governments may find a bilateral understanding preferable to extended multilateral negotiations under the GATT subsidies code.

8 Industrial Policy, Trade Policy, and European Social Democracy

WOLFGANG HAGER

The new European debate on industrial policy started as an anachronism: it has not been—the question of "recession cartels" excepted—a debate among Europeans about the economic future of an integrating economy, but a debate held in the Atlantic context and initiated by the United States. The origin of the debate lies in the Tokyo Round and the policy-thinking in the US that accompanied it. Its results have been codified in the OECD framework. But if the U.S. point was valid—microeconomic interventions by governments may distort competition and have tariff-like effects—its validity applied much more to intra-European trade. For this trade is not only many times larger, but is dominated by standardized products (rather than commodities and high-technology items) and thus is sensitive to small cost changes. It can be argued that such a debate is not necessary within the European Community since here, unlike the GATT context, the rules are clear: subsidies that distort competition are ruled out by the Treaty of Rome. This formal approach would be naive; until the postrecession changes in European thinking about industrial policy, the Community was quite permissive in applying the rules of the Treaty.

In fact, what could have turned into a major Atlantic quarrel, i.e., a wholesale attack on the European mixed economy practices, became the basis for a new consensus on the virtues of market adjustments, breached rarely and only by common consent in special cases like the steel and shipbuilding industries. The sympathetic response in much of Europe to the American ideas, codified in the OECD's Positive Adjustment,[1] can largely be explained by a crisis of industrial policy, experienced simultaneously by many European countries following the recession of the mid-seventies. In many countries, the short-term response to the crisis had been a steep increase in status quo subsidies in order to keep recession-hit industries afloat. When the recovery occurred later and weaker than expected, governments risked running out of money. Since the printing of money had simultaneously gone out of fashion—the return to monetarist fundamentalism fitting in neatly with the rediscovery of market forces—the set of ideas incorporated in the Positive Adjustment approach offered a coherent and promising way out.

The Positive Adjustment approach (to be discussed more fully below) is essentially a commitment by governments not to shape their industrial structures in a certain pattern, but to improve the conditions, notably factor mobility, that will allow the *market* to determine that pattern. Such an agreement has enormous attractions from the point of view of economic conflict management, and is therefore the natural first choice for organizations, like the European Commu-

nity and the OECD, with a strong tradition of fostering international cooperation. The only other international arrangement with an equally low propensity for
conflict generation is total autarky. The one thing the international economic
system is badly equipped to handle is a collection of mixed and/or planned
economies that are each "market makers" as well as "market takers," i.e., which
try to exploit the world market where it suits them while trying to pursue volun-
taristic domestic policies.

Strangely enough, this is precisely the world we have been living in since the end
of the last war; and nowhere was the paradox more pronounced than within the
European Community itself. Something has clearly changed that has reduced the
tolerance on which the previous system rested. A first explanation could cite the
following factors:

the scale of mutual influence has grown with the rise in trade-to-GNP ratios;
the number of successful "market makers" has increased;
the amount of intervention has grown;
the costs of accommodating changing market patterns have grown, especially
in the former dominant "market maker" countries.

An essentially self-denying ordinance like the OECD's Positive Adjustment approach seeks to reverse one of these changes – the amount of intervention – while
leaving some of the others, which can also be understood as causes of the increased intervention, out of consideration. Like the trade liberalization effort of
the first postwar decades, of which Positive Adjustment is a direct successor, the
politically most-elegant solution to an otherwise divisive international problem is
underpinned by economic analysis that promises high rewards, in terms of
welfare, for system-conforming behavior. In the case of Positive Adjustment,
these are not only the usual rewards of free trade, but also a greater efficiency of
factor allocation even in purely domestic terms. This in turn provides a precious
contribution to the fight against inflation and creates the preconditions for a
resumption of growth.

The tendency of economists to develop principles of action independent of the
time and place to which they are applied is reinforced, in the international policy
context, by the need for a diverse group of countries to agree to common standards of economic rationality. Fixed exchange rates are an extreme example of
the damage that can be wrought by this process. Free trade, which was and is offered in the same spirit as a universal prescription, was formally rejected by the
Third World, was not practiced for many years by Japan, and of course is irrelevant as a guiding concept of East-West trade. Yet industrial policy – a related but
much farther reaching element of national *and* international economic policy – is
supposed to be susceptible to universally valid analysis and prescription.

A first quick check of the postwar experience shows that the worst-performing
countries, in terms of growth and international trade shares (i.e., Britain and the
US) are those which were most hesitant to practice industrial policy (British in-
terventionism being relatively recent), while the best performers as regards the improvement of their position were the interventionists: Japan, Italy, and France.
The United States has maintained its lead only in areas where it *did* have an industrial policy, i.e., the nuclear, aerospace, and related electronic fields for which
the military provided R&D finance and markets on a cost-plus basis. The suc-

cessful, industrializing developing countries all have vigorous industrial policies. Even the Eastern European countries, who were beginning to exploit the opportunities offered by the world market in the seventies—both as regards buying technology and selling products—might now be counted among the success stories, if the oil crisis had not caused them to suffer an international cash-flow crisis at a particularly awkward moment. Even without success, Eastern Europe remains a potential and actual "market maker," i.e., it pursues industrial policies with implications for trade as one of the many actors and groupings that shape the environment in which "hands-off" Western European industrial policies are supposed to operate.

The Postwar Experience in Western Europe

Since Western Europe is the "classic" region of industrial policy, all but three chapters in this book discuss its experience both on the sectoral level and more generally. A fair summary of the various national approaches on the lines of the chapters on Japan and America would require a book in itself, especially since practices in each of the European countries are at least as complex as those of their major OECD partners. Thus, the following sketch can do little more than hint at the diversity of purpose and method of industrial policy used in Europe at different times and in different countries.

Even a cursory examination of Western European experiences suggests that the decision not to engage in a voluntarist industrial policy, i.e., one that pursues specific structural aims, would constitute not the restitution of the status quo, as much as a radical break with past practice. It is difficult to sketch the history of industrial policy in Western Europe, not least because, until the seventies, structures and policies diverged widely. The story begins in the late forties, with the perceived need to manage scarcity and rebuild key industries. In the French case, this was from the beginning coupled with a long-range development plan, whose concrete result was, inter alia, the modernization and electrification of the railways. The Marshall Plan, initially intended to provide a Euro-American framework for integrating planned economies, rapidly became a force for trade liberalization. This reflected a shift in thinking in northern and northwestern Europe in matters of economic and industrial policy toward a greater reliance on market forces. In the fifties, however, Germany among others continued systematic and concentrated aid toward industrial reconstruction, coupled with a certain resistance toward trade liberalization. In Britain, industrial policy followed a basically liberal path, in line with the early adoption of Keynesian thinking in that country. There were two major exceptions to the British neglect of industry as a subject for public policy. One concerned the Labour Party's policy of ownership of the "commanding heights," notably steel; the other was the massive support, by the then prevailing standards, of high technology as part of the big power posture of the country.

This highly voluntarist concentration of British resources in the nuclear and aircraft industries can be cited as one of the outstanding failures of industrial policy, since it could not hope to match the American efforts and drained the rest of the economy of scarce engineering talent. Its failure, then, was *not* to exploit world market opportunities but to act as if that market did not exist. Most failures of industrial policy, also in the Third World, result from this parochial bias. Yet Britain found a ready, and largely successful, imitator in France, which in the fifties laid the basis for its present vigorous nuclear and aerospace industry. That essentially military motivation contributed to the failure of the second attempt, after the foundation of the European Coal and Steel Community in 1952, at a European industrial poicy, i.e., Euratom.

But the really interesting part of the French experience does not lie in the often costly attempts to create the advanced technological base for a big power role. Rather, it is the way in which that country, together with Italy, overcame structural deficiencies of long standing by the exercise of venture capitalism supported and run by the state.

The desire to remove perceived structural inadequacies that prevent accelerated economic development provides one of the oldest and still relevant motivations for states engaging in industrial policy. After the war, Italy and France perceived themselves as relatively backward and overly agricultural economies. One structural deficiency was the absence of risk-oriented capital markets, with instead a preference for secure low-return investment in, say, real estate, over productive investment. (The backwardness of contemporary Portugal is in no small part due to an extreme manifestation of this attitude.)

These economies, particularly that of France, were characterized by small family firms that failed to perform as Schumpeterian entrepreneurs. And like some contemporary defenders of the comfortable status quo (i.e. workers), they failed to seize the opportunities offered by new technologies. A number of accidents — in Italy the need for the state to take over some major banks (and their industrial holdings) when they collapsed in the inter-war period, and a similar, if ideologically motivated, take-over of credit institutions in France before the war — gave the governments of both countries new tools with which to practise venture capitalism.

In France, but hardly at all in Italy, the entrepreneurial role of the state was accompanied by planning. Where IRI (Istituto per la Ricostruzione Industriale) helped, e.g., to establish a modern heavy and light engineering industry in Italy, the French approach initially relied on modernizing a few sectors that could either be classed as infrastructure (railways, electricity) or as intermediate inputs for the rest of industry (coal and steel). As trade liberalization progressed, first in the OEEC and then in the EEC, France took the fundamental decision to create industries capable of withstanding international competition. But knowing the slow pace at which structural change took place, the government took a highly activist role in inducing small firms to merge, supplying capital to sectors that needed to replace old physical capital stock, providing technological know-how from governmental research establishments, etc.

There is a continuing and inconclusive debate on the impact of French planning, underpinned by a 70 percent state ownership (but often loose control) of sources of credit. Was the impressive postwar growth experience due to the state effort (as many European governments came to believe by the late fifties), or did France succeed in breaking out of the inter-war stagnation because of improved external circumstances and better macroeconomic policies? The evidence seems easier to judge in the Italian case. After striking success in the fifties when whole new sectors were created to give the country a broad and sophisticated industrial base, the state-owned and -financed sector increasingly escaped the hands of entrepreneurial technocrats and fell under the domination of party appointees. The creation or maintenance of industrial jobs was frequently decided on electoral grounds. By the end of the sixties the state sector, far from being in the vanguard of modernization, preempted scarce capital from a now vigorous private sector to cover its operating losses.

In Britain, state capitalism of the Italian and French kind, attempted cautiously in the sixties through the National Economic Development Council and the Industrial Reorganisation Corporation and subsequently other bodies, also had "catching up" and accelerating development as its stated purpose (the British growth rate remained stubbornly at half the continental rate). Rescue rather than innovation became its primary purpose, however.

Nevertheless, state venture capitalism remains a powerful tool of industrial development. Especially since the sixties, one particular variant of such policies has been widely used in Europe: the more or less enforced merger of firms whose size was deemed insufficient to allow them to operate profitably and keep abreast of the latest technology. Steel, shipyards, metal smelting, heavy engineering, automobiles, electrical engineering, aircraft production, and computers have been some of the industries rationalized by direct state intervention. For such purposes, the state has essentially three instruments at its disposal: the provision of credits for modernization (this applies especially to countries with a strong public banking sector, like France and Italy); the threat of withholding credits to near-bankrupt industries (Britain, Sweden, etc.); and use of the near monopoly of governments over certain procurement markets (e.g., the German aircraft industry). In Japan, the conscious fostering of strong firms and the timely weeding out (*mugi-fumi*) of weak ones has a similar purpose and the effect of accelerating adjustment to advanced technological and production requirements. In Germany, the large banks are sometimes said to perform this intrasectoral weeding-out function.

The ability of the big German banks to have detailed knowledge of all major firms in the key sectors of the economy (through their representatives on the boards of directors) and their willingness to go for long-term capital gains rather than short-term high dividends are examples of the many fortunate historically derived arrangements that lessen the need for active industrial policies in that country. Another such circumstance is the comparatively even distribution of industrial activity, reinforced by the federal structure of the country, which allows the concentration of regional policies on a few areas. (One such area is West Berlin, where the almost universal recourse to subsidies is producing a syndrome of management and labor behavior oddly reminiscent of the "British sickness.")

Concentration of (financial) resources has also been typical of both positive and defensive policies in Germany. Of the latter, coal and shipbuilding have been the major beneficiaries as well as, periodically since the fifties, steel. Among the positive policies, that devoted to nuclear power has been the major effort since the early sixties and was reasonably successful, because government remained in a supporting role (in contrast to the heavy-handed administrative interference in France and Britain). More recently, the aircraft, computer, and ocean-related industries have benefited from government help.

As in the United States, a good deal of German industrial policy is carried out not on the federal but at the state level. The Länder, more than the Federal government, have the ability to give free land, tax holidays, hosuing grants for workers, etc., and to provide credit guarantees to attract new industries or to preserve old ones. This decentralized support of industry (complemented by a similar array of instruments at the municipal level) is likely to be more flexible and effective than similar schemes run by central governments in France, Italy, or Britain. Since no aggregate statistics are available, one can only guess at the scale of these efforts, but it is at least equal to all expenditure for industrial purposes by the Federal government. As in the United States, the relative weakness of central policies fosters a myth that exaggerates the extent to which industry operates independently of public authorities.

If one looks for a general trend in European industrial policies over the first three postwar decades, it will not necessarily be found in the amount of intervention as such. Rather, a cyclical movement is apparent, with intervention being highest in the early fifties and the mid-seventies. If there is a trend, it is the steadily growing role of the international environment in providing the incentives for engaging in industrial policy. For the early developmental industrial policies pursued on the continent in the fifties, the international environment provided only the standards to be emulated — the main model being the United States — but the decision to approach "best international practice" was largely an independent domestic one. Thus, for instance, imitation stopped short of copying certain consumption patterns. The deliberate French policy of developing small parochial automobiles was an early example of disregard for world markets, as was the long delay by all European countries in introducing color television.

This changed in the sixties. Trade performance and hence competitiveness became the dominant motive for some industrial policies; another motive, almost exclusively related to the United States, was technological independence. This was thought to be important for long-term competitiveness, but also involved fears that technical creativity and the ability to shape the socio-industrial environment of European nations were being compromised by U.S. dominance, via direct investment, of advanced European industry. The combination of trade and independence objectives led to the creation of "national champions": large firms, favored by national procurement policies, capital sources, etc., and able to negotiate with American companies on the terms under which U.S. technology was utilized. As long as the primary trade competitors of such firms were other European champions, and as long as U.S. technology was crucial to success, the natural partners of such champions were American companies. In the seventies, with the technological gap narrowed, and world-market rather than intra-European competition the primary concern, the logic that led to the creation of national champions was beginning to operate in favor of creating European champions, Airbus Industrie being the prime example.

More generally, the sixties were a period of rapid structural changes within European economies. It will always remain a matter of contention whether this change was due to rapid growth as such, or to the effects of the Common Market and general trade liberalization. Nevertheless, the speed-up of change revealed more strongly than ever the unequal mobility of factors in different regions. This, then, was the period when all European countries began active regional policies that went beyond the mere provision of infrastructure: subsidies to capital became universal instruments of policy, supplemented, in the Italian and British cases, by regulations that forced industry to move to the regions. In the Italian case, the state-run sector had to invest heavily in the South. Under legislation introduced in 1971, 80 percent of new, and 60 percent of total investment had to be located in the Mezzogiorno. When one adds the fact that in certain (slump) years, the state-run sector accounted for half of all industrial investment in Italy, the significance of this becomes obvious. On the other hand, the simultaneous policy of underwriting losses incurred by the state sector in the North counteracted the regional policy and led to very high general levels of capital subsidy in the state sector. The South also benefited from a reduction of social security payments and other tax concessions worth about 70 billion lire per annum. In Britain, the "command" element of regional policy was largely limited to (the refusal of) investment licences in the rich regions.

More in line with the thinking now codified under the Positive Adjustment label were methods that did not compensate for insufficient factor mobility but were designed to increase such mobility directly. In France, mobility of capital was enhanced by a general improvement of provincial credit facilities—which in the case of Germany already existed by virtue of the Federal structure of savings and credit through the Landesbanken. More interventionist and requiring budgetary outlays were measures to increase the mobility of labor, notably through training schemes. Here Germany and Sweden became the leaders in what came to be called active manpower policies. By the end of the sixties, however, organized labor even in those countries started to question the assumption that mobility should be the principal aim of manpower policy, as the cycles of obsolescence in skills quickened and some of the most-sophisticated skill-groups, such as printing and metalworking, were threatened. The foundation in Sweden of AB Statsföretag in 1969—a state financial holding designed to save lame ducks—was the symbolic end of an unconditional commitment to adjustment that had characterized that country after the war.

During the seventies, the distinction between regional aid and aid to declining industries became increasingly blurred, especially since the areas covered by special grant schemes and the like were extended (although at the end of the decade there was a tightening of development criteria in Britain under the Conservative government). Regional subsidies can now be treated, in large part, as a subset of the more-general problem of industrial subsidies, which lies at the core of our present subject.

The Politics of Compensation

The usual mental model most people have of these subsidies is derived from spectacular rescues: shipyards on Clydeside or on the Elbe; steel mills in Wales, Lorraine, or the Saar; and automobile industries in the Midlands, perhaps in Turin, and, for that matter, in Detroit. The political explanation normally given is a straightforward one: large groups of workers and powerful capitalists can induce the state to act against the general interest. The one qualification admitted is that the general interest may be served by avoiding the multiplier effects of closure in local economies dominated by single firms or industries, which would lead to the costly underutilization of write-off of resources. But by and large, the political model is one of short-term pressures, cravenly conceded.

The reality may be more complicated. The ability of an industry to compete successfully is a function of a host of factors. Some of these relate to management: timely design changes, product and market diversification, etc. But a number of fundamental elements are determined by broad and long-lasting developments in the society at large. When these work against industry and competitiveness declines, the state, acting for society, has three choices: (1) it can remove (some of) the antiindustrial or antiefficiency biases introduced over the years: the prescriptions in the Positive Adjustment approach go in this direction (which includes allowing firms to fail), as do incomes policies designed to reduce real wages; (2) it can compensate industry for the impediments introduced by the socio-political processes, i.e., subsidize the social status-quo; or (3) it can remove the competitive standard against which viability or nonviability is measured, e.g., through trade protectionism.

What are the antiindustrial biases introduced by society? The simplest one is too-high wages, which has an influence in terms of current competitivity. But the more-interesting effect is the dynamic one: when profits (and expected profitability) are low over a longer period, the replacement of capital stock, hence increases in productivity, are no longer possible and/or economically warranted. Weak profits, which are a signal for adjustment, may in fact remove the capacity to adjust. High wages, a cause of weak profits and inadequate investment, is one of a host of other socio-political bargains struck in society: job security provisions, welfare arrangements which encourage absenteeism, agreements which prevent intrafirm job mobility, and longer holidays are some cost-increasing measures; taxes and social security payments levied on firms further reduce profits. Limits on the optimal choice of producing sites, imposed for environmental reasons, as well as costly controls on emissions or to ensure the health and safety of employees, also raise costs.

On a more-general level, society decides on the proportion of total savings to be spent on industrial investment as opposed to social-infrastructure investment. The crowding-out hypothesis advanced by Bacon and Eltis in Britain as an explanation of industrial decline encompasses this phenomenon, although it goes well beyond it.[2] But a substantial part of government expenditure in Britain, perhaps 10 percent, in the mid-seventies involved not so much a crowding-out of private investment in favor of social investment and consumption, but a substitution of government for private agents as a source of finance for industry. Here we have perhaps the strongest evidence for the logic of industrial policy which may be described as the politics of compensation. That is, the state and society remove with one hand the resources (and conditions) that allow industry to prosper, and give them back with the other. *Both* operations are carried out in the name of social objectives. It is logical for a government which imposes a stop on redundancies on industry in general, or state-run industries in particular, to make up the inevitable losses incurred. The same may be said for price controls imposed to reduce inflation, for example, which leave profits severely squeezed.

This process of compensation, of the state giving with one hand and taking with the other, is clearly a sleight-of-hand that satisfies, partly in symbolic rather than real terms, society's demand for justice, security, etc. If it were structurally neutral, one might even make a case for this process on the grounds that the partially overpriced service sector, notably public administration, makes a restitution to the productive sector on which it largely lives. As the manufacturing sector drops below 30 percent of GNP (i.e., as did agriculture on the Continent a few decades ago), such a transfer may be reasonable and even necessary, especially if wages in the service sector rise in step with manufacturing wages, irrespective of the poorer productivity performance in most of the (public) services.

The process of compensation is not structurally neutral, however. There is a systematic bias, explained in part by politics and in part by administrative bias and convenience, toward large firms, and especially toward the worst performers among them. There is thus also a transfer (and crowding-out in terms of resources) from successful firms, which pay taxes, to unsuccessful ones, which receive subsidies. Moreover, experience shows that firms ostensibly helped by the government become the object of further injunctions, which are intended to help the government's economic policies: e.g., against lay-offs and price-increases and with orders to expand in the regions. The need to coordinate with government bankers may also introduce additional handicaps for successful management.

These sorts of industrial policies are therefore a second-best way to run an industrial economy. Before turning to the alternatives, it is important to underline the strength of the forces that have contributed to this pattern. The political history of the last hundred years—and this is unique to Europe—has been dominated by the process of incorporating the industrial worker into the mainstream of society. The sharing of wealth and power (and, more subtly, the reductions of the uniquely unfavorable conditions in work itself, risk, and status) is one of the great achievements of contemporary Europe. But it is not a secure one. For the underlying distributional problem cannot be ultimately resolved; there are always those whose jobs are less secure, more unpleasant, and worse paid than those of others. But by the sort of bargains which were alluded to above, conflict can be reduced below the level of violence—most of the time. Countries without these working-class traditions, such as the US and Japan, rarely face the problem of basic political stability when deciding on industrial policies. Even within Europe, the level of mutual suspicion among classes differs widely. Single-standard recipes for industrial policy, however rationally appealing, may therefore be irrelevant or dangerous when measured against goals more fundamental to society than an increase in wealth.

Positive Adjustment

In June of 1978 the OECD Council of Ministers adopted a document entitled "Policies for Adjustment: Some General Orientations," whereby the member states committed themselves to shift from defensive policies, which impede adjustment, to policies that improve their economies' capacity to adjust.[3] Since Japan was already practicing what the document preached and the United States still thought it could limit itself to protectionism as the chief defensive instrument, the document can be read as a blueprint for Western European industrial policies. As such, it advocates a reduction to the minimum of measures that compensate for socio-economic failures. In addition, it advocates a shift of some of the social security burdens now borne by industry to the taxpayer, and greater wage differentials to aid adjustments in the labor market. In other words, the

Positive Adjustment approach not only seeks to reduce compensatory policies, but also to correct some of the distributional bargains that necessitate compensation.

The approach is best summarized in a sentence contained in the "Orientations": "Cases where specific action to protect or support individual sectors or companies in financial difficulty can be justified, and are likely to be successful, should be relatively rare."[4] Stress is laid on indirect measures: better (general) access by industry to capital, a general improvement of profitability of enterprises, improved functioning of labor markets, etc. Where aid must be given because of "unacceptably high" short-run social costs, these should be degressive, encourage the best firms (which usually means aid to sectors rather than firms), and not reward inefficiency of labor and management. Where public funds are used, participation of private risk capital should be sought. On the more activist side, the "Orientations" make three suggestions: support for long-term R&D, thus excluding the more immediately relevant D&D policies (the development and deployment of advanced product lines); support for research and investment in areas which constrain growth, i.e. energy, pollution, and health-improving measures; and improved access to venture capital for small and medium enterprises.

Except for the reference to easing the tax burden from industry to taxpayers (more precisely, the social security contributions which act as a tax on employment) and to encourage greater wage differentials, the document does not directly attack the underlying social bargains that led to the politics of compensation in the first place. The main instrument for reattaining high employment levels (and thus to solve the main problem which triggers government intervention) is a resumption of growth. Positive adjustment, by reducing rigidities and distortions introduced by government policies themselves, will create the possibility of a resumption of growth, for "otherwise with labour and capital locked into declining activities, bottlenecks will emerge and renewed inflation will constrain expansionary policies and undermine the recovery."[5] And while it is recognized that expansion itself would remove the incentives for propping-up operations, a start has to be made somewhere. The chicken-and-egg problem is solved by the advice to free factors first, so that they become available to a market in search of new opportunities.

Freeing factors now locked, by government subsidies, in activities condemned by the market translates into a temporary rise in unemployment. With successful general demand management policies, this should be a short interval. Unfortunately, general demand management in many countries is based on a strategy that also requires a temporary rise in unemployment. With the fight against inflation pursued by monetary policies that combat the bargaining power of unions by letting unemployment rise, general conjunctural policies reinforce rather than alleviate the problems posed by Positive Adjustment. Moreover, to the extent that tight money policies and falling demand simultaneously raise costs and reduce markets for industry, more lame ducks are created rather than less. This has become a familiar criticism applied to the British policies of 1979–80, but the logic is a more general one.

According to their social or political preference, people may legitimately differ as to whether the high unemployment engendered by these heroic efforts to reverse past trends in the European political economy is tolerable. The unanswered question, however, relates to the ultimate success, i.e., whether the hoped-for pay-off in terms of a dynamically growing, fully employed economy will in fact materialize, or whether the experiment will produce one more of the traumata, like the Great Depression, that have historically fostered the common man's mistrust of capital and contempt for government.

One view currently in favor with civil servants and politicians considers the adjustment of bargains on job remuneration and security as a marginal and at any rate unavoidable correction — a necessary and sufficient condition for a return to industrial dynamism in a highly competitive international environment. The other view — most recently expressed in the analytical portions of the OECD's Interfutures Report[6] (although not in its policy conclusions) — sees a strengthening, not a weakening, of the societal values that have brought about the "dysfunctionally" comfortable industrial society in the first place: equality, the trend toward nonmaterial forms of satisfaction, the growth of partly antiindustrial values, paradoxically coupled with a romantic view of industrial employment reminiscent of similar attitudes toward agriculture.

If this latter view is correct, and if the political imperatives still operate that have translated these values into rules and bargains circumscribing industrial performance, then the first view, which holds Positive Adjustment to be a marginal correction of past practices, may turn out to be justified: not in the way it is now optimistically supposed, i.e., by reestablishing European industrial dynamism through the removal of useless or even harmful state intervention, but rather by being limited to a series of minor and useful improvements on an essentially unchanged reality of mixed economy practices.

The persistence of certain values and political balances is only half the equation helping us to assess the contemporary and future context for industrial policy in Europe. The other is the gap separating the actual ability to perform industrially — to adjust and compete — from the level required to survive with a greatly reduced amount of state intervention. If wages are too high, jobs too secure, and profits too slim, by how much do they have to be corrected? What, in other words, is the standard of socio-industrial organization toward which, implicitly, Europe must move?

This is indeed a fundamental question going well beyond the discussion of a few technical fixes. As will be argued below, for most of its postwar history Western Europe can be considered, as a region, to have been a closed economy. It is now emerging as an open economy to a world composed of countries most of which are heavily engaged in the pursuit of industrial policy; and of societies who have worked out *their* particular bargains which shape their industrial performance. Yet the naive view that adjustment takes place with respect to some state of nature outside Europe, resistance to which is both foolish and immoral, is implicit in much of the contemporary discussion.

Clearly the notion that Western Europe, in the past, was a closed economy requires some explanation. After all, it is composed of countries which rightly can consider themselves to be the most-open economies in the world. But if we contrast the situation of the sixties with that of the late seventies, a number of differences stand out. Then, for most industrial products, there was no effective international competition outside Western Europe itself. Eastern Europe had not yet started on its modernization drive and could not meet elementary quality standards. Japan was still specialized in a few labor-intensive sectors, was easily kept out by restrictive trade practices, and at any rate was wholly absorbed by the U.S. market. The United States was increasingly handicapped by an overvalued currency, thus protecting European home markets and "traditional" third markets for European exports. The Third World virtually did not exist as an industrial competitor.

There was, of course, increasingly vigorous competition among European countries. But in this game most participants played by the same rules: their (productivity) wages were similar, as were the share of national income devoted, respectively, to industrial investment, social infrastructure investment, and public and private consumption. To simplify greatly (and leaving out the crucial role played by national industrial policies to make intra-European trade competition acceptable), European competition took place among firms, not societies (although it suffices to think of Britain and Germany to realize the continued significance of societal factors in intra-European competition.)

To make the same point in more-technical terms, intra-European exchanges were overwhelmingly intraindustry trade with little sector specialization. Indeed, as a UN/ECE study showed, by 1970 all the Western European industrialized countries had approximately the same distribution of sectors in their productive structure.[7] In the (extremely open) context of intra-European competition, no country could devote a disproportional share of investment capital to the development of a few industries (as Japan did in this period), since this would have weakened other parts of manufacturing industry, most of which were facing competition. At any rate, the Treaty of Rome and the EFTA Treaty contained rules that were evoked if a country in Western Europe engaged in what could be called predatory industrial policies.

But because the Western European economies, collectively, were by and large safe from international competition, there was a great deal of autonomy left to society in deciding on the two crucial components of industrial competitiveness: the cost of production, to the extent that it is determined by wages, social security, job security legislation, etc.; and the shares of GDP to be devoted, respectively, to consumption and investment.

The setting of wages can be compared to price setting in an oligopoly. In an oligopoly the most-efficient producer sets prices at levels that maximize profits on a cost-plus basis, and that maximize market security rather than market share. Applied to (productivity) wages, the central fact was that these were set by bargaining rather than by the market, even in the most-efficient producers within Western Europe. Other socially relevant components of production costs were set by even more explicitly political processes, e.g., company taxation, laws on employment practices, etc. Again, these political processes were broadly similar in all of Western Europe. Together these distributional bargains produced the mixed-economy, social-democratic pattern that makes Western Europe unique. The fact that the United States, the only other potential competitor in the sixties, was "handicapped" by some (but not all) of these processes (i.e., it had vigorous and often conservatively minded unions and an increasingly perfectionist central government circumscribing the externalities inherent in industrial production) was a further element in the de facto protection and social autonomy enjoyed by Europe in this period.

The existence of a cartel or oligopoly is never demonstrated more clearly than when a newcomer challenges it. For Europe, the period of protection came to an end in the early seventies. The undervalued dollar disappeared. The Eastern Europeans launched a program of modernization and cooperation with Western multinationals that rendered more of their manufactured products saleable. Even more important, Japan diversified both geographically — growth of the American export market being limited by U.S. protectionism — and as regards products. The newly industrializing countries began their meteoric rise, which was to give them 10 percent of world manufactured exports by the end of the decade.

The setting for industrial policy is radically transformed by these changes; yet their impact, already felt at present, is still perceived as a series of exceptional situations. The new competitive situation facing Europe can be described in several ways. One is to see the world divided into two labor markets — free and "administered." Free labor markets are characteristic of unfree societies, those that jail trade unionists. Administered labor markets are characteristic of democratic societies with diffused political and economic power. In economic terms, free labor markets reflect the tremendous surplus of labor worldwide. By the late seventies, some 74 million industrial workers in the OECD countries produced just under nine-tenths of the value added in manufactures in the noncommunist world. Some 90 million in the less-developed countries produced a further one-tenth. To these must now be added 70 million Chinese workers. By the year 2000, another 250 million jobs will have to be created in the Third World, a large part of them in manufacturing industry. Thus, in spite of the scarcity of skilled labor in some of the more-successful NICs (which simply speeds up the diffusion of some industrial activities to second-generation NICs, like the Philippines), the total outlook for the free (world) labor market is one of surplus, hence for wages that are a fraction of the European ones. A number of the NICs have shown that they can increase labor productivity faster than wages, and so strengthen their ability to compete with the Europeans, whose wages annually grow faster than productivity. The magnitude of this competitive threat depends, of course, on the number and size of the countries where "productivity wages" become and remain, across a range of industrial sectors, so favorable in comparison with the Europeans. It would be unwise to assume that they will be few and small.

The reliance on adjustment as the only feasible industrial policy in the North-South process is based on an assumption that, in the long run, seems highly implausible: that exchanges between a free market (the industrializing Third World) and an administered market will automatically find an equilibrium that allows both growth and full employment in the region with artificially high costs. Moreover, that high-cost region in this developmental model is asked to make up for deficiencies in effective demand in the developing countries, especially as regards consumption goods, while at the same time making up for deficiencies in capital accumulation through direct investment, export credits, and aid. One wonders whether such a circuit is viable, even if world development as a whole is the only objective.

The question hinges critically on the ability of European economies to find employment opportunities in activities that are either sheltered from competition, for example many services, or where comparative advantage and/or technological monopoly (near-universal for manufactures in the sixties) still apply. If such opportunities are not found, productive resources — workers, capital and infrastructure — are not shifted to better uses, but simply left idle; hence the gains from trade cannot be realized.

Pessimism on this score is indicated for a variety of reasons. First, the "basket" of products consumed in the advanced countries (which continue to represent the bulk of effective demand) does not change radically. There is, in other words, a limit to the computers, aircraft, and nuclear power stations that will be consumed in the world. Final demand will still consist largely of cars, can openers, and TV sets. While product differentiation, such as in fashion, can occasionally reconstitute the sheltered market conditions of former times, none of the standard consumption items and few of the intermediary inputs are *inherently* safe from competition. The same applies increasingly to investment goods. Adjustment (on the North-South dimension) is thus not the once-and-for-all reorganization of industrial activity involving the shedding of a few labor-intensive industries like textiles, but an accelerating race which cannot be won if labor costs remain out of line by several multiples as measured by the free-market standard.

Of course wages in the NICs increase to take up part of the growth of productivity; and exchange rates can be adjusted in response to a structural disequilibrium between NICs and Europeans, thus restoring enough price-competitiveness to secure a trading balance. This points toward the hope that, as the NICs advance into new industrial sectors, a new equilibrium will be found on the basis of intrasectoral trade between the NICs and Europe, as has already been developed among the European countries themselves. But such a view may be too complacent by far. If, in a sufficient number of NICs, productivity wages grow several percentage points slower each year than in Europe, it may be beyond the scope of exchange rates to compensate, even if European workers accept the implications for their real wages and the NICs cooperate in such an exchange rate policy. Even, moreover, if a trade balance were thus maintained by successive devaluations of European in relation to NIC currencies, the constant erosion of European competitive strength would be likely to sap Europe's industrial dynamism.

Current labor costs are only the static element of competition. The dynamic one is the speed at which capital equipment is modernized and hence the latest technological opportunities are utilized. This capacity is, if anything, even more socially determined than wages. The setting of wages takes some account of market conditions. The allocation of national wealth to different purposes, of which industrial investment is one, depends on a host of other objectives, politically fixed over decades. After-tax profitability — the bottom line in industrial terms — is one of the main determinants of the time needed to amortize capital equipment, and hence of the rate of replacement. Expectations of future profits may lead an enterprise to write off capital prematurely, as may the fear of future loss. But the capacity to do so is circumscribed by present arrangements in society.

The more a society pursues industrial development as its chief objective (i.e., the more social infrastructure investment, distributional objectives, and current consumption in general are second-order priorities), the faster — all other things being equal — its ability to replace capital stock. Another key element is the willingness of labor to allow the resultant productivity gains to be realized at all, and the resistance of labor and public authorities to job loss implications of more-efficient plants.

Moreover, the decision to introduce new technology rested until fairly recently with only two economies, those of the United States and of Western Europe, who alone had the requisite know-how and skilled workforce (as the example of steel shows, Japan was acquiring the same ability by the late fifties, but it was then still limited to a few products). In the Atlantic area, with its comfortable oligopolies, technology was often introduced gradually, as part of expansion programs. In many cases, when it would have rendered too much of the existing capital stock obsolete too quickly, the introduction of new technology was delayed.

This Euro-American duopoly control over the speed of technological change has now passed to East Asia. Henceforth, the competitiveness of green-field technology, introduced by countries starting either from scratch (Korean shipbuilding) or with rapid capital turnover, like Japan (automobiles), sets the international standard. Again, conventional wisdom underlying present thinking on European industrial policy implies that it is possible to match this standard. But doing so, if the preceding analysis is correct, involves not a quasi-technical change in investment practices, but something much more profound: an adaptation of European society to the "best international standard." This is certainly possible in some areas, although not without a strong industrial policy. But to regain a comparable rate of technological progress, and thus to maintain a general competitiveness with the faster-growing countries, a different society would be required.

Inevitably, Japan has entered the argument at this point. Europe's difficulties in relation to Japan are of course not caused by cheap labor, and unlike most of the NICs, Japan has free and effective trade unions. The problem is caused rather by society's willingness to channel resources into industrial investment rather than leisure, social infrastructure investment and consumption. No doubt, there is also a much greater willingness to work harder, but the essential element in the creation of wealth, here as elsewhere, is the rapid introduction of capital goods incorporating the highest technology-generated productivity increases; and Japan retains a striking advantage in this respect, despite the greater importance given to social goods in recent years. For Western Europe to match the Japanese challenge on its own terms would require, in the last analysis, a similar ordering of priorities for society, including a change of its political system and administrative structures.

The normative case for adapting to cost-patterns achieved by other societies is weakened by the voluntarist origin of some of these competitive advantages. All NICs, including those of South America, are heavily protectionist. Japan's formal liberalization program is, on the contrary, now second to none, although informal barriers exist and much of Japanese industry has strong de facto defense against foreign competition in the domestic market (not least as a consequence of virtuous cycles of growth, profits, and investment initiated in its long period of formal protectionism). While Europe used its period of de facto protectionism, and hence of autonomy in economic policy-making, to create what I have called the "comfortable industrial society," the autonomy enjoyed by other societies through natural or deliberate protection can be used to concentrate economic resources on a few favored sectors.

In a full-employment situation, the best strategy for Europe is to accept the cheap products resulting from these concentrated efforts of industrial development. But as a general proposition, the prescription that Europe *must* get out of any sector, like shipbuilding, that happens to be chosen by commercial partners, is tantamount to leaving the initiative to others, i.e., to have one's industrial pattern determined, not by market forces, but by the industrial strategy of others.

This problematique is not, of course, limited to the North-South context. From a European perspective, the problems posed by OECD-area competitors divide quite sharply into Japanese and U.S. problems. The Japanese problem has just been considered. As regards the United States, conflicts tend increasingly to be confined to the rather narrow range of sectors where governments engage in broadly similar kinds of (incompatible) industrial policies and/or where their common predicament as comfortable, slow-moving, and pluralist societies faced by an environment of rather different societies pushes the two sides of the Atlantic to shift part of the burden of adjustment on each other: textiles, steel, fibers, and automobiles tend to fall into this category. In some fields, Europe may seem to be the industrial aggressor, notably in civil aircraft and a few other sectors of high technology, although the military element in U.S. market dominance tends to even the score. In principle, however, the trade and industrial policy problems dividing the United States and Europe can be settled either by ad hoc "organized free trade" arrangements, as in agriculture and steel, or by something akin to a multilateral and balanced subsidy reduction. In the other cases, sectoral tinkering with the free market is insufficient.

A refusal to accept the international division of labor dictated by the interaction of market forces and industrial policies of our trading partners can aim, as a minimal goal, to maintain shares in output. This can be achieved by a heavy injection of capital, which improves productivity to the level where subsidized machines can compete with cheap labor (in the North-South context) or with other subsidized machines (in the West-West context). This injection of capital can be managed by industry-minded banks with a long-term outlook, as in Germany and Japan; by the state; or by providing a rent to enterprises via protectionism. This latter device has allowed the German textile industry to be revitalized to the point where it dominates intra-European trade. The last two strategies involve a lowering of real wages: not of the workers directly concerned, but by those who pay the higher prices for imports or the taxes for subsidies. Also, as far as employment is concerned, the result may not be very different from the consequence of declining market share under conditions of free trade and no intervention: the defense of the share in output and markets is bought by a sharp increase in productivity and hence a loss of employment opportunities in those sectors. This has been the experience of European agriculture, and, incidentally, the U.S. (protected) textile industry.

Nevertheless, the strategy employing financial or trade protectionism may result in strong sectors with the potential of adaptation in production technology and product design, rather than a series of slowly dying industries with a cumulatively declining ability to adjust. The upstream and downstream linkages are maintained. In the case of textiles, the fiber industry, the textile machinery industry, and the dye-stuff manufacturers all maintain their customers, rather than being pulled down by the decline of the textile industry. All this is desirable only if, in the economy as a whole, factors of production are not fully utilized. But this is clearly the prospect of the eighties.

The assertion that protected markets may create strong sectors flies in the face of conventional wisdom, which predicts a cumulative loss of competitiveness as industries become complacent behind high trade barriers. The evidence is derived from either developing countries with import-substituting policies behind, say, a 100 percent tariff; or from de facto autarky such as applied to France and its colonies. The evidence of postwar Japan and of prewar Germany and the United States shows on the contrary that very high levels of protection were compatible with technological innovation and growth. This was due to the importance of either competitive third markets or competitive domestic markets. Taking the European automobile industry as an example, both these factors apply, and complacency is the least likely outcome of even a permanent margin of protection. The free-trade logic becomes stronger, the further we move away from items of final consumption: costly intermediate products may create problems for downstream production, which is otherwise fully competitive. In a perverse way, this was demonstrated by the case of chemical fibers, where (artificially) cheap supplies from the United States eased the problems of the European textile industry.

In any case, trade protectionism is only one of the three options for coping with the contradictions of exchange between societies with different industrial cultures—the others being adjustment and financial protectionism. It should be recognized, however, that the conventional adjustment strategies proposed by some free-trade advocates aim at creating products that benefit, so to speak, from natural protection. These are either goods in the early stages of the product cycle based on what amounts to technological monopoly, or highly differentiated conventional goods (high-fashion clothing) that require production close to the market. In fact, neither niche in the international market appears particularly safe. The high technology sector, far from providing monopoly rents, is increasingly competitive, with America, Japan, and Europe crowding each other in a limited market. The loss-making nuclear industry of the last decades may provide a better model for the future than, say, the experience of IBM. As regards product differentiation, the same processes that increased trade in standard items—cheaper transport, transnational trading companies, rapid information transmission—can remove the putative advantages of home production in differentiated goods.

If one moves from an axiomatic rejection of protectionism to accepting it as a device that is at least sometimes necessary, the problems for political decision-makers multiply. First, even if one subscribes to the view that many of the achievements of our society, in terms of real wages, job security, work conditions, and public expenditure, are negotiable only at the price of giving up consensus-based democracy, there is clearly a vast area where changes in social policies (at national or firm level) could be made with little damage to those affected, and with considerable welfare benefits all around. Protectionism or financial subsidies that underwrite ill-thought out schemes where minor short-term benefits are bought at great medium-term cost, or schemes that buy temporary security and wage improvements for a minority at the cost of greater insecurity and lower income for the majority, are "a bad thing," whatever the politics of the observer.

One of the great virtues of the OECD's Positive Adjustment initiative is its call to governments to monitor the cost-effectiveness of their policies, taking overall social objectives as given. The OECD also attempts, in its patient way, to improve the methodology of measuring such effects, e.g., of regional policy on employment. The same process of reexamining the methods for achieving social objectives is going on at the firm level, with unions (often under pressure from their membership) discussing solutions with management, which no longer confuse the short term with the long term.[8]

The example of the automobile industry illustrates how a greater stated willingness to use the protectionist weapon may actually reduce the need to implement it. Present Japanese investment plans, together with the decision of major developing countries to step up domestic car production with mandatory export commitments imposed on the multinationals, translate into a sharp drop in the European share of the world market by the mid-eighties. By that date, the U.S. market will no longer supply growth opportunities for newcomers: improved domestic models using European and Japanese technology will see to that, if necessary with the help of protectionism. The European share of the world market, including its domestic market, will become the residual — that which has to adjust. Given the strategic importance of the industry in the economy, protectionism seems inevitable. But as usual it will come too late to prevent substantial unemployment and the expenditure of the taxpayers' money in propping up unprofitable industries. Worldwide, this translates into overcapacity, not least in Japan, at a time when capital is urgently needed for more important things — e.g., the conversion of the economy to cope with the energy predicament.

The sensible course would be to admit the inevitability of this scenario under status quo policy assumptions, and to come to an agreement with Japan, not on import levels, but on the long-term investment plans themselves. This could involve some very tough bargaining. On the Community's side, the ultimate sanction would be the possibility, not just of keeping Japanese imports at 10 or 15 percent of the market at some future date, but of reducing or even closing the market off entirely if such expansionary investment plans are implemented, so as to compensate for the inevitable loss of third markets with a larger share of the domestic market. If this kind of industrial diplomacy is handled skillfully and in good time, there is less danger of political conflict than if it is rushed through after the investments have been made and the crisis is on us. There are times when the unthinkable has to be thought, if only to stop it from happening.

So far the case for facing the inevitability of protectionism as a normal policy instrument has been made on negative grounds: there is no combination of a fall in real wages, capital deepening, and changes in work practices that can match the Japanese and NIC performance at politically tolerable cost in a growing number of the standard traded manufactures, and there is no sign that the number will cease to grow. Another reason for not pushing trade competition too far has been mentioned in passing and needs elaboration: energy. At present, the main energy policy pursued by all oil-importing nations, and in particular by Japan, is to increase exports to pay for the dearer oil. This is a zero-sum policy at best; more likely it is a negative-sum policy where everybody loses. The world's deficit with OPEC of more than $100 billion cannot be instantly compressed; and when it is reduced, past experience leads us to expect that prices will again be increased so as to widen the gap. But the attempt by individual nations to minimize their share of the deficit translates, among other things, into a serious misallocation of capital spending: efforts to improve competitive positions almost universally mean capital deepening that saves current labor cost. Since in our societies labor has to be paid a full wage (for practical purposes) whether or not it is employed, capital deepening (or rationalization) provides no saving for the national economy as a whole as opposed to the individual firm, if the economy suffers from general unemployment already. To the extent that capital deepening is achieved by subsidies or by a cut in corporate taxation, the net effect is again a lowering of real incomes. If the same money were spent on a massive program of energy adjustment instead of on trade adjustment, both domestic and international imbalances would be minimized.

Domestically, spending on changes in capital stock and infrastructure with the aim of reducing energy consumption would bring lasting benefits rather than accelerating the overcapacity crises and unemployment implicit in the race to improve trade balances. Internationally, not only would trade conflicts be minimized, but each nation using its investible savings for energy purposes would be making a contribution to every other nation's economic security: moderating oil price rises, reducing the supply risk inherent in a tight oil market, and stretching available supplies generally. Compared with this overriding concern, trying to achieve another 1 percent increase in GNP through trade-induced improvements in factor allocation would be an irrelevant luxury even in a full employment context. In a situation where the gains from trade cannot be realized anyway, the diversion from the important tasks of the eighties becomes foolhardy. To repeat: the choice on protectionism is not whether it will occur, but whether it will occur in the context of domestic and international crises, or be used as a timely device to get nations to agree on a more-sensible use of scarce resources. The developing countries — to meet a major objection in a short sentence — would be the greatest victims of a continuation of a course that is as inherently unstable as the arms race before World War I.

The Role of the Community

For some of the same reasons that have brought industrial policy to the center of the international trade debate, the European Community needed to take a view on member-state practices which might have interfered with free and equitable trade. Unlike the European Coal and Steel Community, which had potentially discretionary powers, the Rome Treaty governing the European Economic Community essentially limited the role of the Commission to policing a set of rules, i.e., a set of qualified prohibitions.

Essentially, European industrial policy has been practising for decades what the Positive Adjustment approach now preaches. The Treaty of Rome is heavily biased against subsidies and in favor of competition. Industrial policy proper, i.e., of the activist or voluntarist variety, whose first practical expression in the EEC, after five years of gestation, was the Colonna Memorandum,[9] was almost wholly concerned with accelerating positive adjustment toward high technology industries. Only much more recently, and with respect to a very few capital-intensive industries hit by, among other things, cyclical problems, has the adjustment commitment been tempered by an element of status quo preservation. Yet as regards the bulk of industrial activity, the European Commission continues to act according to the (renewed) orthodoxy of Positive Adjustment, toughening its stand on state aids. In doing so, it acts logically in defending the Common Market which, as we saw earlier, is as much affected by the recent surge of financial protectionism as is the international trading system in general.

The danger for the Community as an institution, of a confrontation with adjustment pressures with which on both technical and political grounds it cannot cope, is the gradual erosion of the Common Market. Of course, this process has already begun. The internal market order is threatened by an increase in nontariff barriers. The rise of financial protectionism has been temporarily checked, but is bound to resume when conditions deteriorate further. Most immediately threatening is the demise of the common commercial policy, as the majority of the member states refuses to accept Brussels's lowest common denominator standard, which is that of Germany.

As has been argued implicitly and explicitly, the role of Brussels in industrial policy depends crucially on a prior decision on trade policy. Its tasks will grow, irrespective of the maintenance or rejection of the free-trade norm. Under free trade, the Commission's role becomes defensive and reactive. Under the alternative scenario it can become creative. The defensive task is to police the increase in financial protectionism, aids and subsidies, and the like, which are bound to grow under free trade conditions. In extreme cases, and with the expenditure of great political energy, the Commission may succeed in putting together a damage-limiting regime in sectors where government involvement has gone too far to be reversed. It has failed to do so in shipbuilding (see Chapter 4) and only just managed to succeed in steel (see Chapter 3). The main point to grasp for those arguing from free market principles is that free trade, under given external and internal conditions, accelerates the demise of the genuinely private sector. Free trade with all comers also undermines the chances for the one genuine, free trade experiment — that existing in Western Europe — of surviving the next half-decade.

While the timely use of the protectionist weapon (as a bargaining tool more than a sanction actually applied) would lighten the Commission's task in policing national subsidy races, it would nevertheless create new tasks of great complexity. First, the fight for free competition within the Common Market would shift from concern with treaty infringements by the governments to concern over collusion by private firms. This problem should not be overstated, since the reintroduction of a modicum of oligopolistic stability must be considered desirable, given the relationship between risk and investment in an age where technologically complex production requires long-term gambles with huge amounts of capital. Moreover, competition with other suppliers in third markets would be as fierce as ever. At any rate, the efficiency gains that can be realized by Communitywide oligopolies must be compared, not to an ideal free market standard, but to the inefficiency of weak national industries clinging to national purse strings. Again, the choice is not between good or bad, but between the lesser of two evils.

Community industrial policy in a protectionist setting must shoulder an additional task: it must be the manager of the internal counterpart of the external agreements that accompany modern protectionism. For it is inconceivable that outside trading partners would tolerate a situation where protection leads to a substantial increase in the self-sufficiency ratio of the Community, coupled with an aggressive export strategy made possible by cross-subsidies derived from domestic (protectionist) rents. This means that protectionism of the modern variety will be accompanied by implicit or explicit market guarantees for outside suppliers plus, importantly, undertakings on capacity limitations and specialization. Thus, to take an early example from agriculture, the Community offered to the United States a dynamic market in feed grains, in particular soy beans, as a substitute for lost wheat and citrus markets.

This implies an activist, MITI-like role of the Commission's Directorate General for Industrial Affairs. Its power to enforce the internal counterpart of external bargains would derive from the threat to reduce protectionism (a device used in France, Japan, and the United States to influence the behavior of sectors). To some, this outlook may raise the specter of a vast, dirigiste bureaucracy, creating a plethora of CAPs in the Community. In fact, given the limited number of firms involved, their often effective organization in national and Community federations, and the rather broad nature of the guidance required, an occasional exercise of economic diplomacy between the Commission and the section of private industry involved is all that is needed. It must be remembered that the whole exercise is largely a development of processes formerly carried out by private industry, i.e., oligopolistic competition, which implies something much more modest than dirigiste administration.

What are the traditions and instruments of the Community relative to this very broadly sketched agenda? As already mentioned, the ability to conduct industrial policy proper (the conscious shaping of specific structural outcomes) continues to be hampered by the fact that it is an afterthought alien to the main thrust of the original design. If competition policy is considered part of industrial policy, however, its formal basis is firmly anchored in not only the letter but the spirit of the Treaty. The view that the industrial policy directorate is on the side of intervention, representing the mixed economy, and the competition directorate is on the side of laissez-faire market principles, is a caricature containing, as often, a substantial grain of truth. It is true that one initial impulse for setting up an industry directorate, in 1965, was to promote bigness, while one of the tasks of the competition directorate was to control it. The promotion of size in individual firms was, in a sense, the continuation of a strand of thought that was instrumental in setting up the Community itself. Both were designed to match the economic conditions of the United States.

The large continental market itself allowed efficiency gains of specialization, including economies of scale. But the United States seemed to have an additional advantage that could not be explained by large production runs as such: in crucial fields the American market seemed dominated by a few very large firms. Rather than associating this structure of the American economy with its relative failure—much slower growth than in Europe—it was seen as instrumental to its relative success: in establishing a seemingly unbeatable leadership in high technology industries: nuclear, aerospace, computers, etc. The (still) partially correct part of the diagnosis recognized that for certain kinds of long-term and complex developments of technology, success of R & D strategies depends on absolute rather than relative amounts of money. The huge sums spent on R & D by IBM on successive (and successful) generations of computers were generalized into a principle: the capacity of Europe to innovate and to stay in the forefront of developments seemed to require large firms.

Even this initial pro-merger attitude contained an element of competition thinking. It was realized, at the outset, that the alternative to large European firms were small national champions, protected from competition by national procurement markets and subsidies. True competition—and the ability to compete on world markets—could therefore be increased by *reducing* the number of what were, essentially, noncompeting firms. It is precisely this thinking that prompted Commissioner Davignon in 1980 to seek to "rationalize" the European telecommunications industry by reducing the number of competing systems to two.

On the other hand, competition policy, resting essentially on articles 85 and 86 of the Rome Treaty, was at the outset qualified by something akin to an infant-industry clause. For agreements between firms which restrict competition could be allowed where they "contribute to the improvement of the production or distribution of goods or to the promotion of technical or economic progress," albeit under certain conditions (art. 85, 3). Thus a substantial discretionary element allows the Commission considerable latitude.

Discretion, based on an even more explicit infant-industry argument, is also laid down in the second major area where the Commission acts as a watchdog of market principles: that of state aids. No fewer than seven articles (49, 75/3, 80/2, 82, 92/2/3, 93, and 226), as well as the Protocol concerning Italy, allow exceptions to the general norm of Communitywide competition.

The main point is made in article 92 of the Rome Treaty. Its first paragraph prohibits "any aid granted by a Member Country or through State resources in any form whatsoever which distorts or threatens to distort competition . . . in so far as it affects trade between Member States." Its second paragraph excepts, i.a., regions bordering East Germany; and its third provides exceptions for "aid to promote the economic development of areas where the standard of living is abnormally low or where there is serious unemployment, . . . aid . . . to remedy a serious disturbance in the economy of a Member State, . . . aid to facilitate the development of certain economic activities or of economic areas, where such aid does not adversely affect trading conditions to an extent contrary to the common interest."

If one examines the list of Commission Decisions that fall under article 92, one finds a strong predominance of Italian and French cases.[10] The comparative rarity of such decisions, about four a year, bears no relation to the importance of state aid in the Community. And although a far larger number of cases have been settled on an informal basis, the Community cannot be said to have conducted a wholesale attack on state subsidies.

This latter circumstance serves to underline a central point about article 92: the enormous amount of discretion left to the Commission, and the comparative informality of the procedures. In a negative way, the Commission's directorate on competition policy shapes important parts of Community industrial policy. Its terms of reference are pitifully vague: what is an "abnormally low" standard of living, or "serious unemployment"? There are no quantitative or qualitative standards, such as "injury," to determine when trade is affected more than the common interest allows.

In fact, the Commission, in the field of competition policy, is using exactly the method it should employ more widely across the whole area of active industrial policy: it engages in economic diplomacy toward firms and countries. For the most part, it works by persuasion and consensus, without such a consensus being necessarily spelled out and formalized. A student of Japanese industrial policy will recognize the style: it resembles that of MITI. Formal powers are used as a last resort. Pragmatism and a sense of political reality play a large role.

To rely wholly on taking a tough stand on state aids would be tantamount to making the same mistake as the OECD's approach, i.e. to consider the mixed economy character of European countries as an aberration that prevents the sensible operation of international markets. In cases where national involvement in the economy is very considerable and based on long-standing social and political objectives, the mere reaffirmation of liberal principles of undistorted competition would be utopian and ineffective. Indeed, an attempt to liberalize Community public procurement markets by means of directives (1971 and 1976) has brought about little change.[11] The Community's attempts to cope with the problem of inconsistent but well-entrenched national policies provide some guidance on problem solving even in a worldwide context, although ultimately the Community's ability to act within its boundary is, for reasons explained in Chapter 9, far greater. One can distinguish three stages of development in what is called a common policy. The first is close to the OECD means of operation: a statement of intent, prepared by the Secretariat (here: the Commission) and endorsed by governments who promise to do, each in their own way, useful things considered in the general interest. Early documents in the fields of science policy, energy policy, transport policy, and social policy are largely of this type, even though they already contain elements of the next two stages. The next higher level of achieving "communality" of policy is coordination: governments sit down together to discuss their plans for transport, energy, science policy, etc., with the aim of achieving consistency, or, as in the case of transport and technology, to prepare the ground for multinational cooperation in common projects. The third and highest stage of cooperation in mixed economy sectors involves what the Commission sometimes calls direct action, i.e., central policy execution at Community level, involving common finance where appropriate.

It is an interesting commentary on the lack of a political and legal basis for positive structural policies in the Community that in almost all cases the legitimacy of Community involvement in mixed economy sectors derives initially from the "liberal" powers granted by the Treaty, i.e., the need to improve the free circulation of goods and services. This was the fulcrum on which a common energy policy was hinged and which justified early involvement in transport questions.

Increasingly, however, Community documents develop the thesis that the magnitude of the various crises that became apparent in the seventies, and hence of the efforts needed to correct them, requires a joint, Communitywide approach. In these formulations, the need for action by public authorities is simply taken for granted. The Community is expected to provide greater efficiency and effectiveness than fragmented national policies. The great market is one of the tools for this, but the means of exploiting it are what amount to specialization agreements or joint production by governments or publicly supported firms (in the fields of high technology), or the elaboration of common investment, production and capacity targets in especially troubled sectors like fibers, shipbuilding, and steel. Of course, as long as the myth prevails that the Community introduces a novel element in an existing free market situation, rather than organizing a more-effective coordination between national and international practices, such attempts are bound to fail.

The second oil recession, which will be fully developed by the time this book is published, will serve to accelerate the learning process, notably in Germany, as to the true character of the international economic system. The adoption of mixed economy practices by the United States, including both "rescue" of lame ducks, the provision of more overtly commercial R & D funds, and the improvement of the present, excessively short-term–oriented financing instruments for industry, would, so to speak "make it unanimous." It would then become clear that all nations in the world are operating with a mixture of protectionism and financial aid in the pursuit of industrial policies, and that some organization of this uneasy coexistence is preferable to leaving the Community in the role of the residual market, which adjusts to the structural policies of others.

Europe and the World Economy

The ways in which the Community could organize itself to coexist with its partners, in a world economy in which industrial policy and selective protection are the norm, are further considered in the following chapter. But it may be useful, first, to recapitulate the argument of this chapter, sketching the background against which the Community's policies will have to be formed.

The advanced industrial countries of Western Europe are facing a competitive challenge from the NICs that is likely to intensify because it is based on cheap and pliant labor which, for demographic reasons, will remain cheap and pliant for a long time to come. The advantage this gives to a growing number of countries in a growing number of sectors is compounded by their ability to invest a high proportion of GNP and thus make much faster technological progress than the Europeans. Without the cheap labor, moreover, Japan, with its unique social system, has managed to maintain its high rate of technological progress and thus competitive superiority.

In these circumstances, protection will have to be regarded as a normal tool of policy if the strength of European industry is not to be eroded in one sector after another and jobs destroyed faster than they can be created. This does not mean that the Community will have to raise its tariffs or tighten restrictions all around. The rise of NIC competition is incremental, so protection can be imposed selectively. An active industrial policy can, moreover, accelerate the creation of viable activities to replace uncompetitive ones, thus enabling some of the existing protection to be relaxed or removed. But the Community and its member states are not as yet sufficiently skilled in conducting such an industrial policy to avoid the use of a substantial degree of protection. Whether European industry will, with the help of a growing capacity to conduct active industrial policy, eventually recover a dynamism that enables it to develop as fast as the competition from the NICs and thus to allow a decreasing amount of protection, depends on developments in both Europe and the NICs that cannot be foreseen — although on present showing this does not seem very likely. Meanwhile, it is to be hoped that both Europeans and their trading partners will develop the necessary skills of industrial diplomacy and an understanding of each other's problems, so that trade can be as large and as stable as circumstances allow and political conflict can be kept to a minimum.

Conclusion

Many, perhaps most, assertions in this chapter contradict the view of the world on which much normative writing on international economic arrangements is based. Most realists would agree that some of the policy implications of the above will in fact be implemented, although not with a good conscience and in the context of clear priorities, but with much wringing of hands, piecemeal, and ineffectively. The danger of upholding principles of behavior that are increasingly utopian in political terms and may even be bad economics is that timely methods of economic conflict management are not considered and prepared.

In order to avoid misunderstandings, the political point made in the preceding analysis is not (mainly) the familiar one: that governments have to "buy off" groups in society affected by structural change. The point is rather, that the last hundred years of political and social development in Europe have created constraints that are as real as the land constraint which figures in the normal refutation of the Ricardian adjustment model (the point being that Portuguese wine production could not be expanded sufficiently to offset the loss of textile jobs). The political constraint imposes first a real resource cost of producing in Europe that goes well beyond the wage level, but derives most broadly from successful attempts to internalize the (social) externalities of industrial production. More important are the dynamic effects of social bargains. Capital stock must be amortized over longer periods, and productivity-enhancing investment is resisted by workers or governments or both, even when profitability is still high.

The OECD's Positive Adjustment approach, and similar efforts by the EC Commission, are useful to correct excesses. They cannot—and in my opinion should not—get Europe to match "best international practice," i.e., fall back to a state of affairs where the increase of industrial production is the only criterion, where money incomes are confused with welfare, where social infrastructure investment is neglected in favor of investment in tradeables, where job security provisions are dismissed as a sentimental concession mistakenly made in a period of plenty and, in a word, where Europe goes back on the social-democratic achievements, supported by all political parties over the past decades. Wealth is, of course, not irrelevant to social welfare. German workers are not only richer than British ones, they work shorter hours and enjoy better physical conditions. They have sensibly allowed industry to make profits (albeit for most of the period behind the protection of an undervalued exchange rate), although they too are pricing themselves out of the market. Unemployment, first exported on a large scale, now hits the natives and is climbing well over the million mark.

As argued many times in these pages, the trade context is radically different from that of the sixties. The neat model, whereby a highly trained workforce sheds the labor-intensive parts of industrial production to find high value added niches up-market, suffers from at least three fallacies. The high value added sector is not a high-profit one: it is getting as crowded (and subsidized) as the lower end of the adjustment ladder. Second, the label "labor-intensive" (and by implication low-skilled) does not adequately describe the competitive position of an increasing number of newcomers in the standardized consumption goods, including motor cars, which form the bulk of industrial production and consumption. There is something unconsciously racist in the calm assurance that "They'll never get the Suez Canal to work" or, translated into modern terms, make automobiles. Thirdly, competitive advantages is the better term, since a combination of protectionism and selective export and production promotion determines the patterns of growth in the middle-range sectors.

In sector after sector we can observe a negative-sum game whereby nations strive to increase their exports by subsidizing capital, lowering real wages, or both. A powerful incentive to do just that derives from the desire of each to minimize its share of the incompressible current-account deficit that all countries run collectively with the oil producers. So we are increasingly faced with the paradox that there is overcapacity of capital stock added to (and worsening) the overcapacity of labor in a world which is still far from satisfying basic human needs or taking elementary precautions against living on the brink of oil disaster. Of course, some of these problems, for the rest of the world, would be temporarily eased if Europe adjusted fully to the demands for market access — for Japanese cars, U.S. fibers, Third World clothing. The result would surely be a near mortal structural recession in Europe, which would not only quickly dry up the market of would-be exporters, but put at risk the achievements in political civility, in the defense of which in another context people would willingly risk war.

Even if such a structural recession could be coped with politically, the economic effects would hardly serve the interests of the supposed beneficiaries. The negative growth rates — a consequence of the contraction of sectors facing competition with superior capital stock (i.e. green-field plants) and/or lower-cost labor — imply in the not-so-short term a destruction of existing capital and skill resources in Europe. Given the overall cost situation, it is not immediately obvious that the overall depressed state of capital markets, corporate balance sheets, and domestic demand that would accompany such unbridled adjustment would be propitious to new investment, which would offset the loss of wealth-creating (and employment-creating) stock. More likely, the disruption of existing input-output relationships — which involve substantial parts of the service sector (including, via taxes, public services) — would leave European economies permanently underemployed. It is quite possible, in static terms, that external accounts would be in balance with an appropriate exchange rate. But the underemployment of domestic resources, whether of a medium-term "frictional" kind or, as suggested here, more permanently in the familiar manner of depressed regions, would leave growth and income below the levels assured by a fuly employed economy. After all, the nonemployment of resources, notably of labor, is the normal condition in the world (including the United States), and it is hard to see why global adjustment mechanisms should behave in the textbook manner for Europe when they have failed to do so for most of the world. And if the vision of a "mortal adjustment recession" seems too far-fetched, it is quite enough to imagine the total liberalization (without subsidies) of just a few sectors — cars, textiles, and steel — to make this point.

It is the conviction of this writer that industrial policy — in the sense of sectoral or firm-level intervention — should be limited to a few cases if it is to be successful. A large-scale bail-out of weak firms and regions, such as took place in many European countries during the recession of the mid-seventies, distorts the economy, undermines managerial efficiency characteristic of free enterprise, and would lead to an economic (and political) Balkanization of the Western European free trade area. Without some restraints on international trade competition at the Community level (and leaving free trade agreements with EFTA untouched), this restriction on the use of industrial policy will not be practicable. Trade restrictions should concentrate, if at all feasible, on standard downstream products, i.e., not on inputs (which would make life harder for user industries) but on final consumer items. Assured markets for these would also benefit intermediate industries, for instance, steel for cars and ships.

A second set of measures that relieve the burden put on industrial policy of the interventionist kind are those suggested by Pinder in the concluding chapter, i.e., macroeconomic and capital-market policies which create incentives and opportunities for investment, including "implicit investment contracts" between workers and managers. The dear-money policies pursued by some major OECD countries, and their imitation by others concerned with their exchange rate and terms of trade, are antiindustrial policies which must, in time, provoke the need for state-supported recapitalization of the kind justly criticized by the OECD (which favors badly managed firms over those which, equally weakened, just scrape by). Still, in the same spirit of minimizing the recourse to industrial policies, the sensible suggestions of the OECD's Positive Adjustment approach should be tried, provided they are not relied upon to solve the problem by themselves, and are not pushed to the point where they significantly reduce the social security *acquis.*

As regards industrial policy proper, it is perhaps easier to say something general on methods and procedures than on substance. As to the latter, state aid designed to accelerate the introduction of energy-saving technology in production methods and end products can be justified on purely economic terms, if the discounted cash savings on energy expenditure come close to the value of fossil fuel production, which could have been achieved with a similar investment. Indeed, most people would put a large premium on the saving of fossil reserves and the environmental advantage of not burning fuels. As argued above, the greatest failure of an adjustment debate (and practice) conducted in terms of international competitiveness is that it distracts private and public resources away from the really vital adjustment needed to escape the energy constraint. Even for those who argue that high energy prices should be the chief instrument of transformation, a measure of protection may be a necessary complement (c.f. the price competition from U.S. synthetic fibers, considered in Chapter 4).

As regards standard manufactured products, adjustment processes should largely operate — provided the overall context for industry is right and provided market shares in the very large industries, like motor cars, are maintained. In these make-or-break industries, timely discussion with outside suppliers making investment plans on the assumption of major gains in European market shares would reduce the need for abrupt and politically divisive protectionist measures. Sectors that have become internationally uncompetitive should be allowed to contract, provided there is concrete evidence of alternative jobs being available in services and new industries. If not, Europeans should accept the lower real incomes that follow from consumers being prevented from buying cheap on the world markets. Again, a timely warning on the rate of market penetration to be tolerated may prevent poor countries, egged on by the World Bank's advice to practise export-led growth with export subsidies, to make costly investment mistakes. Within the EC, a policy of external protection should replace costly and mutually destructive subsidies to industry, with parallel or later discussions to follow at the OECD level.

As far as future industries are concerned, major opportunities exist at the EC level to get a better return on the considerable government expenditure that now takes place at the national level. One of the most-promising models is not the replacement of national with a single, centrally funded, Community policy, but the formation of multinational consortia able to compete on world markets. Such attempts have had only partial success in the field of computers and largely failed in standard nuclear reactor production. They look more promising in aerospace, uranium enrichment, and the fast breeder, and may extend to the key industry of the future, telecommunications. As to the latter, the Commission has taken important initiatives, notably an attempt to reduce the number of switching systems in Europe to two. Needless to say, the role of the Commission in such ventures is hampered by its lack of Community policy instruments. Like any successful broker, it needs a modicum of carrots and sticks of its own. As the examples of MITI and the most-recent French methods of arms-length guidance of private enterprise by public authorities show, such a role is facilitated if the guiding authority can reward compliance with privileged access to credit. The so-called New Community Instrument (Ortoli faclity) instituted in 1978, and in theory able to finance future industries, has so far been used for infrastructure and energy loans. The European Investment Bank devotes one-sixth of its (much larger) resources to industry, and—given the policy link between Commission and Bank—it can give the Commission some of the financial leverage it needs.

The main and prior task for the Commission and the member states is to agree on the broad lines of industrial strategy. Within the Commission, the activities of the industry, competition, and trade directorates ought to be guided by a single view of the future, with the Directorate General for Industrial Affairs being in the role of prime policy coordinator. MITI is not charged with Trade together with Industry for nothing. Leaving trade policy in the role of ad hoc conflict management deprives the Community of an essential tool of policy.

Much the same applies to competition, uneasily caught between the implementation of a legal mandate and ad hoc political expediency. Even if, for reasons of personal and national rivalry, these industrial policy tools cannot be brought under a single Commissioner—a solution as utopian as it is indispensable—a joint coordinating group between the different Commissioners and their Chefs de Cabinet is urgently required.

It is the thankless task of the EC to be saddled with economic activities that are in trouble: first coal and steel, then agriculture, and—increasingly—other weak sectors. It was all but excluded from the advanced industry of the sixties, nuclear energy, and risks the same fate for new activities in the eighties. Yet the rhetoric that led to the establishment of the Directorate General for Industrial Affairs in the mid-sixties has now become nothing less than obvious: divided, Europe will be unable to maintain its place in the world markets for advanced goods. The British experience of very high expenditure on advanced industry for decades, always insufficient to match the financial and marketing resources of larger competitors, could well be generalized for countries like France and Germany, which still feel confident that they can go it alone.

Notes

1. See *The Case for Positive Adjustment Policies:* A Compendium of OECD Documents (Paris, 1979).

2. Robert Bacon and Walter Eltis, *Britain's Economic Problem: Too Few Producers* (London: Macmillan & Co., 1976).

3. "Policies for Adjustment: Some General Orientations," in *The Case for Positive Adjustment Policies,* op. cit.

4. *Ibid.,* p. 4.

5. *Ibid.,* p. 3.

6. OECD, *Facing the Future,* Interfutures Report, 1979.

7. UN/ECE, *Structure and Change in European Industry* (UN, 1977). Some of the principal findings of this report are summarized in Chapter 1 above.

8. The "march of the forty thousand" in Turin in October 1980, which forced the unions to call off a strike against FIAT, is a case in point. The strike was in pursuit of objectives that would have bankrupted the company. The episode also illustrates the limits of Positive Adjustment in a given social setting. The increase in FIAT's productivity of some 15 percent resulting from the settlement did not suffice to jack it up to the Japanese levels, which were twice as high.

9. *Industrial Policy in the Community,* Memorandum from the Commission to the Council, Commission of the EC, Brussels, 1970. A Directorate General for Industrial Affairs was created in 1965.

10. See, for instance, the list of most-important cases cited in H. Smit and Peter Herzog, *The Law of the European Community: A Commentary on the EEC Treaty,* vol. 3 (New York: Matthew Bender & Co., 1976), pp. 389–91.

11. The Directive concerning Public Works was published in the *Official Journal* 15.8.1971; that on Public Purchasing on 15.1.1977.

9 Industrial Policy and the International Economy

JOHN PINDER

My coauthors have sketched a vast panorama of industrial problems in the international economy and of the policies through which the leading industrial powers have tried to grapple with them. Now it falls to me to draw some conclusions.[1]

Economic Adjustment and Industrial Policies

The foregoing chapters abundantly demonstrate the difficulties that lead to the adoption of industrial policies. Saunders has shown how the developing countries have been catching up in the various sectors of industrial production, as well as converging toward the advanced industrial countries in the structure of their production and trade, and how trade among the industrialized countries has become ever more intense. While this gives the opportunity for greater welfare all round, it has also confronted us with more problems. For both the costs of economic adjustment and the social resistance to it have increased, and the pressure for adjustment comes from a process of industrial change that will continue for decades and perhaps centuries to come.

The chapters by Woolcock and Edwards have singled out some industrial sectors as examples of the difficulties. Textiles and clothing firms in the industrial countries have been weakened by the pressure from newer producers to the point where protection has become general and almost all governments have had to provide aid for adjustment. Low use of capacity, heavy losses, and large lay-offs in steel, shipbuilding, and synthetic fibers have contributed to slow growth and high unemployment in the advanced industrial economies, which in turn make the ills in these sectors harder to cure. In aerospace, the huge costs of development have made government aid inevitable.

Although the market pressures are increasingly international, the political authorities which make industrial policies to deal with them remain predominantly national. The subsequent chapters showed how industrial policies have been developed in response to these pressures in the major advanced industrial countries. Japan comes first, with the most-consistent and complete system of industrial policy. Hosomi and Okumura show how, in the earlier postwar period, the government played a powerful part in guiding industry toward modernization and rationalization, behind a high protective wall but with the clear aim of achieving international competitiveness. In the 1960s, as many sectors became competitive, the protection was reduced and the government fell back into a supporting role, intervening where there was a particular need, as for financing advanced research and development or authorizing recession cartels. In the rougher economic conditions of the 1970s this trend continued, but with more emphasis on positive adjustment away from sectors in which there is chronic overcapacity or the competition of newly industrializing countries cannot be matched; and the critical need for energy conservation may lead to a new expansion of industrial policy in the 1980s.

Japan's industrial policy is relatively consistent and complete because the Japanese have always regarded it as a practical remedy, to be applied wherever market forces alone do not seem likely to ensure industrial development. The Americans, on the contrary, have regarded it as foreign to a liberal economy, so that measures which elsewhere would be seen as a part of industrial policy have been scattered among a number of other labels. Not that such measures have been few or unimportant, either historically or recently. Protection after the foundation of the United States was designed to foster industrial development. The same could be said of federal policies toward transport and natural resources in the nineteenth century. The antitrust acts were designed to safeguard the competitive system. More recently, policies for various sectors such as energy, shipping, agriculture, some raw materials, and defense can be seen as aspects of industrial policy; and there has been recourse to new measures of protection for textiles, for steel, and for a number of products under Orderly Marketing Arrangements. The accumulation of such measures in response to mounting economic difficulties led, as Diebold recounts, to a growth of American interest in industrial policy.

Diebold also shows how Canadian interest in industrial policy has long been intense. The Canadians have been fairly free of American inhibitions about the subject. Their problem, foreshadowing that of several newly industrializing countries, has been to strike a suitable balance between primary and secondary production, to promote competitive industries from a small domestic market, and to control foreign investment without frightening it off. With rising levels of technology and growing international interdependence, these concerns, and hence the importance of Canadian industrial policy, can only be expected to increase.

In Western Europe, with Britain as a significant exception, the Americans' historic bias against industrial policy is largely absent. Liberalization was so successful in the 1950s and 1960s that industrial policy was eclipsed as an issue by the rise of the market forces. But in the 1970s industrial policy returned to prominence, in the many guises determined by differing national conditions and traditions, together with a new level of policy-making in the European Community. As Hager explains, industrial policy in Europe may be evaluated not just in terms of economic efficiency or of the relationship between a particular interest and the general interest, but as one means of securing social peace in a society that has been deeply divided by class. As long as jobs and working conditions are under pressure from international economic forces—and Hager argues that this may be for a long time—industrial policy will be supported by this compelling additional motive.

The Danger of International Disintegration

Some people deplore this intrusion of industrial policy in the advanced market economies. Others, including this writer, regard it as a necessary response to the imperfections of markets and the requirements of modern society, even if most countries are still at an early stage on the curve of learning to practice industrial policy efficiently. On either view, the growth of national industrial policies in an international economy is dangerous for the international system. For these national policies could turn the tide of rising economic interdependence and integration, which has accompanied three decades of rising prosperity, into a current of separation and disintegration, with incalcuable political as well as economic consequences.

One evidence of this is the revival of directly protective measures. The Multi-Fibre Arrangement, nearly two decades after its origin in a temporary restriction of imports of cotton textiles, shows no sign of withering away; on the contrary, it is more likely to be followed by similar arrangements for other hard-pressed industrial sectors. The use of Orderly Marketing Arrangements (and of their informal equivalents, such as the limit on French imports of Japanese cars), which restrict imports from Japan and the newly industrializing countries, has not been declining but gathering strength. The protection of steel markets in the United States and the European Community may be regarded, at least to some extent, as a systematic application of the principle of the antidumping duty, since its main purpose is to prevent prices from falling below the costs of the efficient Japanese producers. But double-pricing is so prevalent in the oligopolistic markets of the contemporary economy that the systematic prevention of dumping, if it extends far beyond the steel industry, could lead to a proliferation of regulations applied at national frontiers, and hence to national protection.

The maintenance of open markets has also been threatened by the spread of aggressive dumping, which goes beyond the norms of oligopolistic practice; and Edwards's study of shipbuilding (Chapter 4) shows how the parlous state of the shipbuilding industry has caused governments to vie with each other in dumping by means of public subsidies.

Textiles, steel, and shipbuilding are only prominent examples of sectors subjected to pressures that lead to protection or sometimes to aggressive dumping. Footwear, synthetic fibers, and cars are not far behind, and many others can be added to the list. Protection and aggression are not always easily recognizable, or even intended, as such. They can take many forms of industrial policy beyond the classic modes of import restrictions and export subsidies. The separation of markets can be occasioned by national measures of industrial policy, such as recession cartels which, in the absence of an international industrial policy, may seem inescapable to many national governments.

The danger of a vicious escalation of protection, aggression, and retaliation undermining the system of open economies is clear to most governments of the advanced industrial countries. The peace and prosperity of the 1950s and 1960s, when this system was developed, have driven home the lesson that the autarky of the 1930s should be avoided. A number of international arrangements have been made to this end. The Tokyo Round was completed with substantial tariff cuts and new procedures for dealing with trade distorting subsidies and discrimination in public purchasing. In the OECD, there have been the repeated and largely successful trade pledges, the agreement on Orientations for adjustment policies,[2] and the establishment of a steel committee which aims to influence national steel policies that may damage other countries (see p. 80 above).

Yet it may be feared that such measures are not enough. The pressures on the major industrialized economies are great and may intensify. The countries of the European Community feel themselves to be open markets with far higher rates of import of manufactures than Japan or the United States. Governments may fear that the cohesion of their societies or of the Community will be at risk without protection of hard-pressed sectors or industrial policies with equivalent effect. The Japanese are acutely conscious of their vulnerability if imports of energy products were to be interrupted, and might feel obliged to pursue trade policies that others would feel to be aggressive if this seemed necessary in order to secure Japan's supplies. The Americans, after two decades of economic supremacy, lost ground in the international economy and increasingly tended to ask whether the international system works to the benefit of themselves as well as others. Pressures that relate to trade (and Americans, like Europeans, are inclined to believe that they have the most-open market), the dollar, or multinational companies can reinforce such doubts during a period of economic difficulties, and this could be aggravated by any upsets in relation to the Americans' overriding security responsibilities.

While these major economies have shown a degree of robustness in their ability to absorb shocks and yet maintain their open trading postures, each of them requires a measure of reciprocity from the trading partners if this posture is to remain unchanged. But partners might not provide what seems to be fair reciprocity if their own essential interests appear to them to be threatened. There is a significant danger that, with such interests under pressure, one or two substantial countries could break ranks and become sharply more protective, particularly if they are subject to economic weakness (e.g., Britain), a nationalist or protectionist tradition (France), or strong domestic political pressures (the United States); and this could lead, through a chain reaction, to disintegration of the international economy into a set of hostile economic leviathans, armed against each other with all the weapons of trade and industrial policy.

Even if fears of an economic Armageddon may seem exaggerated, the danger of an incremental return to protectionism is widely recognized. If it is true that the structure of the modern economy requires a growing measure of industrial policy, this danger will remain through good as well as bad conjunctures, and the international system will have to be adapted to deal with it. But there can be no doubt of the danger when the conjuncture is as bad as in the early 1980s. High unemployment and low growth greatly enhance the social and political pressures for protective industrial policies. The internationally received opinion, enshrined in the OECD guidelines, that there should be policies of positive adjustment for shifting resources out of uncompetitive activities, invites the question: "Shifting them into what?" It is a serious question that deserves a serious answer.

Unemployment and Positive Industrial Policies

The orthodox answer to the question of unemployment has been given in terms of macroeconomic policy. But with few exceptions, macroeconomic policy in Western countries has allowed high rates of unemployment, usually 5 percent or more, for most of the last decade; and there is no clear prospect that inflation will be controlled for any length of time without monetary policies that limit economic activity so as to keep unemployment at such high rates — which, among other costs, greatly enhances the danger to the international trading system.

If we cannot be confident that macroeconomic policy will bring full employment, we clearly have to consider the employment effects of positive adjustment policies that can make unemployment worse. We should surely go further and ask whether industrial policy can play a part in the promotion of new economic activities and jobs: whether there can be a job-creating or "positive industrial policy" as a counterpart to the job-destroying element of "positive adjustment."

The economic rationale for such a policy is that the rewards of creating new activities and new jobs may have come to be insufficient in relation to the costs and difficulties for the entrepreneur who creates them, to the point where too few activities are started to replace those that are wound up. In Marshall's metaphor, there are not enough saplings to replace the old trees that fall, so the wood in the forest becomes less. This possibility hardly occurred to the British classical economists, because economic activity had been self-generated in the British industrial revolution. Hamilton and List, in countries with fewer saplings, took a different view; and protective and financial instruments were used to foster industrial development in the United States, on the continent of Europe, and later in Japan. But the dominance of Anglo-Saxon economics and the long boom of the 1950s and 1960s seems to have weakened the impulse to use public policy to promote new industrial activities. Meanwhile, the costs of skills and equipment needed to start new activities have increased; the efforts required to deal with legal, administrative, and social complexities have escalated; and since the 1970s the sluggish demand, the low rate of profit, and the economic and political uncertainties have blunted the incentive to make the efforts and incur the costs.

If this is plausible, then there is a need for policies to reduce the market imperfections that impede the starting of new activities, as well as to create the macroeconomic conditions that encourge them. A number of indications as to how this can be done may be drawn from the chapters on industrial policies in Japan, North America, and Western Europe.

The cost of training for skills has increasingly been met by the public purse under the manpower policies that have become normal in Western Europe, of which the German and Swedish policies offer the foremost examples. In Japan the big companies are responsible for much of the training that in Europe is government-financed; but the excellence of general education provides an essential basis, and the higher education for large numbers of managerial and professional people is also provided by the state. Whereas in the United States the public sector makes a relatively small contribution to the provision of skills, the Europeans instead have to complete a process that is already well under way. Perhaps education for management is less developed in Europe, however; and education for entrepreneurship, in smaller as well as larger firms, might benefit from much closer consideration. In Japan, the need may be rather for a growth of public provision for manpower policy, to cope with structural changes that go beyond the scope of most individual firms, particularly in sectors where the firms are not big.

The cost of research and development in high technology sectors is a focus for industrial policy in most of our countries. Yet in a number of countries, including Britain, Canada, and the United States, expenditure on research and development has been falling and government aid for it has been cut. This can hardly help such industrialized countries to meet the challenge of the newly industrializing, even if there is a case for distributing the effort more widely through the economy. But research and development at lower levels of technology is less considered, and often less favorably treated by tax and subsidy, than other, less-creative forms of investment. General investment incentives are widely applied, especially in the less-prosperous regions; but they are not always seen, along with public investment in infrastructure, as being among the essential instruments of an employment-creating policy.

The regulations to protect the environment, working conditions, and other social goods all have their particular justification, but they result in a social ill if their combined effect is to hamper the creation of sufficient jobs. It has been strongly argued (p. 243 above; see also pp. 177–78) that the accretion of such regulations has acted as a sort of antiindustrial policy. While most regulations doubtless reflect the real needs of modern society, they should certainly be made with the effects on industry and employment in mind, so that the damage to economic activity is limited to the minimum necessary, and industry is compensated where damage may be inevitable. Partly this is a matter of causing officials, politicians, and lawyers to be generally more sensitive to industrial needs, as the economic impact statements required under American laws are designed to do. In Japan, where official sensitivity to industrial needs is well established, the growth of social legislation does not seem to have hampered industry as it has in Europe or the United States. There may be a need in all modern economies for a strong group of people responsible for industrial policy to view the creation of economic activities in the round, so that costs and obstacles are where possible minimized and where necessary offset: for a complete, positive industrial policy that would necessarily include an anti-antiindustrial policy, to identify and counter the damaging effects of other branches of policy.

Even when industrial needs are taken fully into account, the starting of new economic activities will remain a complicated business, not only because of official regulations but also because many forms of industrial production and sale are complex in themselves. To enable smaller businesses—the saplings in the forest—to be successful, there is a need for extension services such as have had a great impact on the efficiency of agriculture in the United States and elsewhere. Such services are offered under some countries' small business programs, and also by various development agencies and banks. But in most countries, a strong service of this sort is not yet seen as a normal condition for the success of new businesses or the expansion of small companies in an increasingly complex economy and society.

Profit and Investment

However much the cost of skills or equipment needed for new activities may be subsidized and the administrative obstacles overcome, a capital cost is involved, which may be expressed as a sum per workplace created, and the money has to come from somewhere. That total investment is equal to the difference between production and current consumption is a tautology in any type of economy (even if the resources available for creating workplaces can be adjusted by drawing-down stocks, reducing other investments, or borrowing from abroad). A low rate of profit, such as the advanced industrial economies have experienced in the 1970s, has a major influence on the difference between production and current consumption, and can hardly be helpful to productive investment. In such economies, moreover, where the starting of most new activities depends on an entrepreneur obtaining the necessary capital and taking the risk of losing it, activities are not likely to be started unless the entrepreneur expects to gain more than he would earn in a job without that risk or from the yield on the capital in a safer investment. When the expectations of profit are poor, as they generally will be when current rates of profit are low, markets slow, and uncertainties great, too few new activities will be started to outweigh the jobs lost through old activities being wound up.

This is all so plain and simple that readers may question whether it deserves a paragraph of print. The answer is that, ever since Ricardo, the rationale and use of profit have been at the heart of ideological conflict in Europe, so that to introduce profit into the discussion of politics or policy is to risk causing a breach of the social peace. As Hager explains, the social peace in the postwar period is an achievement that most people in Western Europe value. So they prefer not to discuss profit. The division of resources between capital and labor may be discussed rationally in the economic literature; but the need for enough profit as a condition of full employment and growth has been kept off the agenda of politics. This did not harm the European economies in the 1950s and 1960s, when profit rates were generally high enough. But it could be fatal if profits remain in the 1980s as low as they were in the 1970s, thus impeding new investment and increasing unemployment yet more, while Europeans remain afraid to discuss properly the prime condition of recovery.

Although Japanese economic policy seems to have been little affected by the clash of nineteenth century ideologies which has had so much influence on European policy and behavior, politics and profits can come into conflict in Japan, as was shown when the Japanese government froze the prices of some manufactures after the rise of oil prices in 1973, at levels which eroded the profits and financial structure of many Japanese companies. In the United States, political divergence over profits has taken the form not of socialism versus capitalism as in Europe, but of populism versus big business, of which the antitrust laws, which should counter the power of big business to make excessive profits, were one manifestation. What has not been widely realized is that the low profits of the 1970s may have been caused by new forms of imperfect competition and market power, which should also be corrected and controlled.

The weakness of investment in the 1970s has been attributed to the increase in the price of labor relative to that of capital. Economists often attribute this in turn to a change in the relative scarcities of the two factors of production, of which one depends mainly on demography and the other on savings and monetary policy. It seems to be implicitly assumed that the prices of the two factors are determined by supply and demand in perfect markets. But it is hard to believe that labor, even including its component of skill, was scarce in the 1970s with unemployment around 5 percent; and it is hard to take seriously an assumption that the price of labor is determined in a perfect market.

It is surely more realistic to take into account a substantial element of cost push, based on labor's bargaining power, which in turn is based less on labor's scarcity than on the cost of interruptions to production relative to the cost of higher pay (or other increases in labor costs), much of which can probably be passed on to the consumer in higher prices. If the whole of pay increases could be passed on in price increases, this would convert the rate of pay inflation into an equivalent rate of price inflation but leave profits intact. It is difficult to identify the limits to such a pay-price spiral, however, and governments act to check it by restrictive monetary policy or demand management. This weakens the price push and slows the rate of price inflation. If it weakened pay push and hence the rate of pay inflation by the same amount, inflation would slow while profits remained intact. But in fact this has not happened. Profits have fallen and it seems reasonable to suppose that pay push is stronger than price push, partly perhaps because it costs a consumer who resists a price increase less to postpone his purchase than it costs a manufacturer who resists a wage increase to cause the suspension of his production, and partly no doubt because in the short and the medium term it costs the manufacturing firm itself much less to reduce its profit and hence capacity for new investment than to have the factory shut down. With imperfections biasing markets in these directions, it would be surprising if profits, investment, and the creation of new jobs were not eroded; surprising, in fact, if in the 1980s unemployment does not continue to increase.

In Japan, Germany, and Austria, unemployment has been much lower than the OECD average. How can this be explained, if markets are not much less imperfect in those countries than elsewhere?

In Japan, pay push seems to be moderated by a concern for the strength of the firm, on which employees (and hence unions whose membership, in big firms, is coterminous with the firm itself) see their future to depend. The firm, for its part, has to strengthen its position by investing its surplus, if the employees are to feel that their reasonable behavior has been justified and thus be ready to repeat it in the future. The arrangement could be described as an implicit "investment contract," whereby the employees accept that the firm has a sufficient surplus and the managers ensure that it is invested to develop the firm's production.

In Germany, pay push is moderated in an oligopolistic labor market, dominated by 16 industrial unions, of which the largest, IG Metall, acts as the price leader. Since the rate of pay increase negotiated by IG Metall will determine the rate of inflation in the economy, apart from uncontrollable factors like the price of oil, and the more-controllable rate of profit, the union, with its large membership of consumers as well as producers, settles for a noninflationary increase. If the result were high profits that were not reinvested in the industry, there would be trouble in the wage round next year. It is therefore seen to be in the mutual interest that the profit stemming in part from moderation should result in mutually beneficial investment. This, again, could be called an implicit investment contract between the unions and the firms in their sectors of industry.

In Austria, where pay is determined in a national bargain in which unions, employers, and the government participate, and prices are controlled by a body in which the three parties are represented, the relationship between pay and prices is designed to ensure sufficient investment.

In each of these three countries, the behavior of unions and firms in the imperfect markets for labor and products is such as to ensure a difference between pay and prices sufficient to allow for investment and to ensure that it is generally invested. This bargain is struck, implicitly or explicitly, mainly at the level of the firm in Japan, of the sector in Germany, and of industry as a whole in Austria, depending in each case on where the principal collective bargains are made; although doubtless pay and prices are usually influenced at each level and a complete system for ensuring a surplus that is used for investment must provide, at least implicitly, for such an investment contract at each level. If the strength of pay push has any importance in the contemporary economy, it is entirely logical that such understandings or agreements must be made between those who are responsible for pay, prices, and investment, if we are to avoid the erosion of the surplus on which investment, and hence the future of employment, has to be based.

It is not for nothing that profit has been the focus of so much ideological conflict; and the form of the investment contract will reflect the balance struck by the parties to this conflict in each country. At a minimum, if workers are to moderate the use of their bargaining power, they need to be satisfied, on the basis of either previous experience or formal agreement, that enough of the surplus will in fact be invested for the benefit of the firm, sector, or country in which they work. Beyond that lie various formulae for sharing ownership of the surplus or of the industrial assets from which it is derived. The form of an effective investment contract will reflect the social system or the form of the enterprise in question, ranging from private ownership through coownership to public ownership; and whatever the social system or the form of an enterprise, the price of failure to conclude an effective contract where workers have strong bargaining power (which again can be implicit as well as explicit) will be an inadequate surplus, a stagnant firm or economy, and overt or concealed unemployment.

The rate of profit is usually excluded from a discussion of industrial policy, because it is regarded as a function of macroeconomic policy. The argument of this section is that where workers have and use bargaining power, macroeconomic policy cannot ensure an adequate rate of profit in the average firm. This has to be done by suitable bargains within the firm or the sector, or if these do not emerge from the system of collective bargaining, by means of official prices and incomes policy. Reciprocally, there has to be an assurance that the rate of investment will correspond to the rate of profit. Industrial policy will remain a repair job on a machine that cannot work properly, if such investment contracts are not made. It follows that these means of ensuring adequate profits and investment are an eessential concern of industrial policy.

Recession and Rationalization Cartels

While pay push stronger than price push can defeat any attempts to earn an adequate profit, this is not the only market imperfection that can depress profits below the level required to secure future investment and jobs. The chapter by Edwards shows how excess capacity has been accompanied by heavy losses in shipbuilding, steel, and synthetic fibers; and when oligopolistic pricing conventions fail, this will happen in any capital-intensive sector. For whatever the rate of production, a firm must pay the heavy fixed charges (which can include a large part of labor costs where law, custom, or a scarcity of skilled workers induce firms to retain workers when output falls), so that it is better to sell at prices that cover only a part of these fixed costs than to let competitors undercut one and take away too much of one's market share. Oligopolistic conventions should keep prices high enough to cover all costs and provide a surplus for investment. But firms that are particularly hard pressed during a recession can breach these conventions in order to make sales and reduce their debt; while newcomers who may have lower labor costs, new and more-efficient equipment, or insufficient knowledge of the conventions – all of which can apply to firms from newly industrializing countries – can enter the market with aggressive pricing policies. During much of the 1970s major sectors made losses or low profits because of these effects of surplus capacity; and this must have been a significant cause of the low average rate of profit in the advanced industrial economies.

The Japanese had already, in the 1960s, introduced recession cartels to maintain prices in such circumstances, directly by setting minimum prices and indirectly by allocating a production quota to each producer (and, where applicable, restricting imports). The government was involved in the arrangements in order to guard against abuse and to enforce compliance, if necessary. In this way an adequate financial structure in sectors suffering from temporary overcapacity was preserved. The Americans have not been accustomed to waive antitrust prosecution in the interests of such arrangements, although the fixing of minimum import prices for steel has introduced for that sector an element of a publicly enforced recession cartel. The European Economic Community lacks power to fix minimum prices or production quotas; but the European Coal and Steel Community, whose establishment was more influenced by French planners, does have such powers and, after informal action starting in 1975, has used some of them to maintain steel prices since 1977 (see Chapter 3's discussion of anticrisis measures).

A recession cartel is intended to tide a sector over a temporary period of overcapacity. If part of the excess capacity is structural, that is to say obsolescent or unlikely to be used again for production, a recession cartel becomes a wasteful means of keeping some unwanted capacity in being. In this case resort should be had to what the Japanese call a rationalization cartel, which provides for the removal of surplus capacity as well as for measures such as price-fixing or production quotas. The European Community has, in fact, required the steel industry in the Community to carry out some modernization and capacity reduction along with its policy of price support (see pp. 66–68). At an earlier stage the German steel industry was allowed to organize rationalization groupings to allocate orders and phase the introduction of new capacity (pp. 69–70). In other sectors, however, the Community has not managed to embody the public interest in recession or rationalization cartels, as the Japanese government has done. Edwards recounts (pp. 97–98) how the manufacturers of synthetic fibers sought the approval of the Commission of the Community for a rationalization cartel in which production would be restricted so as to maintain prices while capacity was reduced. But the Directorate General for Competition opposed the arrangement on the grounds that the benefit to consumers was not clear, and this view was upheld by the Commission against the advice of the Directorate General for Industrial Affairs. It must be doubtful, however, whether consumers benefit when the development of the sector is impeded in this way, and when the development of the economy as a whole may be retarded by the accumulated influence on other sectors of a negative view of recession and rationalization cartels. There is a strong case for concluding that the economics on which such decisions are based take insufficient account of the need for profit if welfare is to be promoted in a dynamic economy, and of the imperfection of markets in which profit is determined. If this is accepted, then the merit of measures such as rationalization cartels, which are designed to correct imperfections that reduce profits and hold up the adjustment of industry to new conditions, becomes evident. They can be seen as another form of investment contract in which prices are maintained on condition that a satisfactory investment policy is pursued; and as such, they are an important instrument of industrial policy.

International Implications of Positive Industrial Policies

Without positive industrial policies to promote new economic activities, unemployment may continue to rise and the resistance to protectionism consequently weaken. But although international economic disintegration is much more likely without such policies, they do at the same time themselves create an international problem, because many of them can act as nontariff distortions of trade that injure the exports or disrupt the domestic markets of trading partners. It is the argument of this chapter that the policies are necessary; but it must also be realized that they intensify the need for international arrangements to deal with the implications of national industrial policies.

The international arrangements to deal with microeconomic industrial policies constitute a large subject that is considered later. Here it is useful to raise an issue more closely related to macroeconomic policy: that of profits with their impact on new investment. The rate of profit is strongly influenced by the rate of interest, as is the expected rate of profit required to induce new investment. The rate of interest in each advanced industrial country is in turn strongly influenced by the rate of interest in the international capital market, and hence by the monetary policy of each major economic partner. The international system has a notoriously deflationary bias, because it is easier to sustain a surplus than a deficit in a country's balance of payments. It must be asked whether the monetary authorities of powerful countries have paid enough regard to the need for a good rate of profit in industry throughout the industrialized countries, and whether such regard would not lead more often to concerted efforts to bring down the interest rates that most affect productive investment.

Among other arrangements that affect the rate of profit, the recession and rationalization cartels also have pronounced international implications. Either they are set up on a national basis and safeguarded against disruption from outside by unilateral protection; or they are set up after negotiation, as the international steel arrangements have been; or they are constituted by a group of countries as a joint arrangement, as the European Community's recession cartel for steel has been. The latter is by far the most integrative way to deal with the problem. But it is very much the exception, proving the rule that public policy at the international level is indifferent or hostile to measures that support prices and profits in this way.

Such indifference or hostility might be justified if the need to support profits and encourage their reinvestment, in order to generate enough activity and employment, was the temporary consequence of a short-term recession. In such circumstances it would not be worthwhile to make complicated arrangements that might become unnecessarily restrictive and would be apt to outlive their usefulness. But the present period of high unemployment and low growth is more serious than that. It has lasted nearly a decade and may well last another, if new systems of policy are not devised to tackle the root causes, of which the market imperfections that create the need for such industrial policies may well be one. The more-successful major economies applied effective industrial policies during the good years of the 1950s and 1960s, as we have seen was the case in Japan, Germany, and France. With the continued rise in the economic costs of adjustment, and the lowering of the threshold of tolerated social pain, the need for industrial policies is likely to continue to increase, even after a return to full employment and faster growth. Effective industrial policy may, indeed, have become an essential condition of adequate employment and growth. For such growth implies constant adjustment to technological change, to closer interdependence among the advanced industrial economies and, last but perhaps eventually most, to the growing pressure of imports from the newly industrializing countries, whose industries Saunders shows to have been converging on those of the more advanced.

Newly Industrializing Countries, Positive Industrial Policy, and GATT

By all the measures which Saunders applies, the newly industrializing have been converging on the advanced industrial countries. Indeed, most of his measures show that the developing countries as a whole have been converging, so that the newly industrializing countries, which are their vanguard, have been doing so faster. To repeat Saunders's telling phrase, "the developing countries as a group are 'catching up' almost all round" (see p. 12). This has been reflected in the faster growth of their manufacturing output and gross domestic product (see Table 1.3; the same table shows that Eastern Europe has also grown faster). Their manufacturing structure has been converging, whether defined in the ratio of heavy to light industries (Table 1.4 and following) or of faster-growing to slower-growing sectors (pp. 12–13). They are very strong in the conventional labor-intensive sectors: their production of clothing and footwear has been growing more than three times as fast as in the advanced industrial countries (Table 1.7). But their strength has been spreading: the share of engineering products in exports from South to North rose from 8 percent in 1973 to 21 percent in 1976 (p. 29).

Although, for most of the developing countries, equality with the advanced industrial countries is still remote, industrialization is becoming a worldwide process, and it is not surprising that those who are learning to apply well-tried technologies should grow faster than those who are closer to the frontiers of knowledge. Nor should it, according to the classical economics, cause any alarm. For the newly industrializing countries should spend their export earnings buying goods from the more-industrialized (and they do; apart from OPEC they normally incur a big deficit on their trade with the advanced industrial countries). If they become too competitive over a wide range of standard manufactures, the rates of exchange between their currencies and those of the advanced industrial countries should be adjusted until each side has a comparative advantage in a sufficient number of goods to balance the trade again.

Yet many in the advanced industrial countries are alarmed. As Hager argues, the number of people who can be absorbed into industrial employment in the developing countries is enormous, so that labor is likely to remain cheap and pliant. In most of the advanced industrial countries, on the contrary, labor is dear and has, by a combination of law, custom, and collective bargains, become inflexible. With standard technologies readily transferable, this leads to the fear that the developing countries will become unbeatable in one product after another, and the more-advanced countries will be obliged to retreat into a bastion of higher technology that will not provide enough employment and export opportunities.

On a static view, the exchange rates can still be fixed at a level that will balance the trade: there is a price at which enough of the standard products from newly industrializing countries would become uncompetitive and enough from the advanced industrial would be competitive. But the effect of a long process of erosion of competitiveness, even if offset by a series of devaluations, may be to take the dynamism out of an economy. If cost push resists the cut in living standards that devaluation implies, the result is inflation accompanied by monetary policy that holds down investment (which has in fact been the consequence of changing terms of trade in the 1970s). If the economic and social costs of adjustment impede the redeployment of resources out of sectors that are under pressure and into new employment elsewhere, the result is either sectors which are unproductive and unprofitable, or resources which are unemployed—in both cases a drag on the economy (which has in fact been the case in the 1970s). The success of British industry and the classical economists in the eighteenth and early nineteenth centuries brought a protective reaction from Hamilton and List, which was justified in particular cases by the classical economists in the infant industries exception to the free trade rule, and in the twentieth century generalized again by Prebisch and others into a justification for the protection of less-developed economies. There has been no comparable development in thinking about old industries or old industrial economies, although the examples of textiles and clothing, of Scotland, Northern Ireland, Northeast France, and Wallonia, are no longer new, and although the experience of the 1970s has provoked fears that many other industries and regions, and eventually perhaps the majority of the advanced industrial countries, may be traveling on the same road.

It is not possible to know for certain whether or not these fears are justified. But if there are grounds to suppose they may be, that is more than cause enough to consider the remedies. One is protection, as in the many Orderly Marketing Arrangements and quota restrictions on imports from developing countries, regularized for textiles in the Multi-Fibre Arrangement. If an economy lacks the resilience to find new employment for people and other resources displaced from such sectors, protection seems better than unemployment; and even when new employment is found, the process of adjusting away from a major sector such as clothing may take a long time, during which protection can be justified. But if seen as more than a means of cushioning such change, protection is an admission of failure. It keeps welfare below the level it would reach if people were successfully redeployed into other employment; it could lead, if applied repeatedly, to general industrial sclerosis in the importing country; it retards economic development in the exporting country; and it can mar international political relations.

These arguments lead to the OECD's case for positive adjustment, which countenances temporary protection only if it is accompanied by measures to shift out of the protected sector any resources that cannot be made internationally competitive. The case is convincing, however, only if the shifted resources are reemployed and the economy remains in international balance at an exchange rate that does not cause macroeconomic disruption or decline; and this leads back to the argument for a positive industrial policy designed to ensure that the forces that generate new activity are sufficiently stronger than the obstacles, so that enough new jobs will be created to replace the old ones that are wound up.

A positive industrial policy was argued to be needed in order to promote the development of our own economies, apart from the pressures that come from international trade. If such a policy succeeds, however, it will at the same time enable the trade between the advanced industrial countries and the newly industrializing to expand without the fear that this may lead the former into an economic decline. For policies that help to create viable new activities will by the same token preserve our economies from the kind of stagnation suffered by those regions whose economies have been based on the great nineteenth century industries of textiles, coal, iron, and steel. We will have developed a method that enables other economies to catch up on us without damaging our own.

Except in Japan, positive industrial policy has not been developed to the point where one can be fairly confident of success, although many elements of such a policy exist in a number of countries. Until we are confident that adjustment out of hard-pressed activities will be balanced by the creation of new ones, protection of the hard-pressed activities will certainly continue. The GATT may maintain some order in the process, as it has done with the Multi-Fibre Arrangement, but it will not turn the rising tide of protection.

If macroeconomic policy alone returns us to full employment and economic health, the protective tide will fall and life in GATT may return to the normalcy of the 1960s. But it seems more likely that economic health will require a strong and regular dose of positive industrial policy, which will confront the regulation of our trade relations in the GATT with increasingly complex problems.

Procedures which were agreed in the GATT's Tokyo Round will help to deal with some of these problems. Both subsidies and public purchasing are important instruments of positive industrial policy, and the codes relating to them will provide a means of discussion and negotiation about complaints. This will be worthwhile, but it is doubtful whether it will be enough. The form of subsidies and decisions on public purchasing can be very complicated and their effects a matter for judgment. In order to arrive at solutions that meet common consent there must be, as Diebold puts it, "some agreement on aims and methods that not only permit structural change but encourage it, fostering economic efficiency (broadly conceived), providing international equity, and recognizing the need to allow for diversity arising from political autonomy and difference in social aspirations" (p. 197). These are things on which agreement is hard to reach, even among people with broadly similar ideas who know each other well. The number and diversity of contracting parties to the GATT militate against agreement except at a superficial level; and the number of cases to which the agreed principles would have to be applied, if the international implications of industrial policy are to be seriously tackled, would be enormous. The members of GATT will probably show restraint in the number of cases they raise, and bring forward only those on which the issue is straightforward enough to render an agreed conclusion likely. This will be useful, and will influence behavior in other cases similar to those that are raised. But it does not seem likely to measure up to the growing size of the problem. Attempts to bring a great many cases would, on the other hand, be unwise, not only because they would overload the machinery but also because agreed decisions, given the diversity of membership, would be hard to reach; the only sanction against countries which fail to comply with a decision is retaliation, which, if applied too often, would itself be a cause of disintegration.

Advanced Industrial Countries and OECD

The differences among advanced industrial countries are, almost by definition, less extreme than between them and the newly industrializing countries. The growth of trade among the advanced industrial countries is consequently of a kind to which adjustment is less difficult. The majority of their mutual exchange of manufactures consists of intraindustry trade, in which both partners export and import products of the same industrial sector. Adjustment is easier because firms on both sides often specialize more within their existing product range, while not being removed from this range altogether.

Adjustment is still a major problem, however. Trade among the advanced countries is twice as big as their trade with the developing countries and the Soviet bloc together. Within this large amount, a substantial proportion reflects big differences between the trading partners' skills, efficiency, and factor costs. At one end of the scale, some of the South European countries, while ahead of the newly industrializing, are still catching up on the main body of the advanced industrial countries. At the other end, Germany and the United States are technologically superior, while Japan is in a class of its own for efficiency, quality, and now also technology in a number of sectors. The American and European protection of steel and the list of Orderly Marketing Arrangements bear witness to the difficulty that Americans and Europeans experience in adjusting to the deep penetration into their markets of many Japanese products. European reactions to American synthetic fibers and American reactions to European steel show that the troubles do not all lie between Japan and its trading partners. The growth of the United Kingdom's textile imports from developed market economies to 25 percent of total British consumption in 1975, compared with 8 percent in 1959/60, compares with the developing countries' almost static share of 5 percent in those years (see Table 1.18). Overcapacity in industries such as steel, shipbuilding, and synthetic fibers has been largely a problem of capacity in the advanced, not the newly industrializing countries. In short, with so much interpenetration among the advanced economies, they increasingly cause and are affected by industrial policy in each other. More than in their trade with the newly industrializing, they face the choice between collective arrangements and disintegration.

The GATT codes for subsidies and public purchasing will doubtless be used by the advanced industrial countries. But, as we have seen, these and other manifestations of industrial policy are so numerous and complex that a greater mutual understanding will be needed to bring them into sufficient harmony than is likely to be attainable in the GATT. This points toward discussion of the problems among the advanced industrial countries themselves, and this has taken place within the OECD. In addition to the repeated pledges not to resort to protection against each other, the member governments have agreed on the positive adjustment Orientations and set up the Steel Committee.[3]

The Orientations have been discussed by Hager in Chapter 8. They stress the avoidance of "selective action to assist loss-making activities" and lay down criteria for such action: it should be temporary and degressive; it should be linked to plans to phase out obsolete capacity and reestablish financially viable entities; the cost should be evident; private risk capital should be associated with public funds; any assistance to individual companies should provide an incentive for better management; regional aid should be for all enterprises, not just those in difficulty; arguments about national security should not be abused in the interests of self-sufficiency. There is a warning against governments trying to "pick winners," mitigated by recognition of the case for public support of investment relating to energy, the environment and health; for incentives for long-term research and development; and for policies to ensure that small and medium-sized companies have access to venture capital and incentives to innovate, specialize and modernize.[4]

There is a strong case for rigor in government decisions about protection and assistance for sectors or firms in trouble. But it is severely weakened if the need to stimulate new activities is ignored. Yet the only contribution that the Orientations made to positive industrial policy, to set against their rigor about protection and assistance, was the injunction against picking winners, modified by the Orientations' own short list of tips. This reflects an American rather than a Japanese view of industrial policy. But in matters of industrial policy it is the Japanese who have the most valuable experience, followed by some of the Europeans, such as the Germans and the French.

This suggests that the OECD should give more time to the discussion of industrial policy, so that the experience of positive industrial policy can be exchanged to set alongside the more classical "trade policy" view reflected in the Orientations. The Triangle Paper on *Industrial Policy and the Industrial Economy* proposed that "a Working Party of the OECD type should be established for international discussion of industrial and other structural policies."[5] It also suggested "the production by industrialised countries of annual national reports on major subsidy items," mainly for national accountability but also for international discussion; "a process of annual discussions about selected aspects of industrial and other structural policies, such as the OECD has organised in the field of macroeconomic policies"; and the establishment of an institute "located near but not in the OECD," to carry out on a continuing basis the work that was done by the Interfutures project, and thus provide "better knowledge about worldwide trends in key industrial sectors."[6] The OECD has, in 1980, gone part of the way by establishing a Positive Adjustment Policy Sub-committee of its Economic Policy Committee, which is conducting discussions of selected policy fields. Such processes of research, discussion, and review should contribute to official understanding of the circumstances and attitudes of partner countries and, more fundamentally, of the nature of industrial problems and policies. But the work must be informed by a sufficient awareness of the need for positive industrial policy that goes much wider than the concept of positive adjustment as defined in the OECD Orientations. The countries with the most experience of positive industrial policy would have a particular responsibility for stimulating this awareness.

While it was, at the time of writing, too early "to assess the effects of the steel committee on national steel policies," (p. 80 above) this OECD sector committee in its initial period did nothing to discourage the idea that further, more general study of industrial policy in the OECD would be worthwhile. Woolcock points out, however, that any effect the steel committee has will be indirect. The negotiations on steel arrangements took place elsewhere. The hope is that discussions in the OECD committee will influence national policy-makers. This is certainly of value. But just as GATT may be a forum for negotiation without the consensus required if such a vast and complex issue as the international implications of industrial policy is to be satisfactorily resolved, so the OECD may be a forum for reaching consensus, without the instruments for negotiations and decisions. The subject is important enough to merit a more-complete process of analysis, decision, and implementation; and here the experience of the European Community is of particular interest.

The European Community and Industrial Policy

The interdependence of the European Community's member countries is particularly close. They export to each other, on average, one-tenth of their gross domestic product and twice that proportion of their manufacturing production. They have a correspondingly great interest in the effects of each other's industrial policies and a need for cooperative or common policies. As countries which, despite their differences, have much in common, they are well placed to reach accommodations and joint decisions. As a result of the drive for unity that followed World War II, moreover, they have established, in the Community, a system designed to facilitate cooperation and common action in institutions that are more powerful than those of other international organizations and that use a unique array of common legal, financial, and fiscal instruments.

As Hager explained in his discussion of the role of the Community (Chapter 8), these institutions and instruments were not established with the aim of making positive industrial policy. Although the European Coal and Steel Community, founded in 1952, provided for an industrial policy with respect to those two sectors, the main thrust of the European Economic Community, founded six years later, was to create a common market in which trade among the member countries would be free and undistorted. This was, in fact, similar to the aim of the GATT, although farther reaching and to be achieved by stronger methods.

Unlike the GATT, the Community, as a regional group, equipped itself with a common external tariff. This was designed as a corollary of the internal free trade, to prevent distortions in trade among the members, not as an instrument of industrial policy; and the main achievement of the common commercial policy, for which the tariff is the major instrument, has been to put the Community's weight behind the liberalization of international trade in successive GATT rounds, which would hardly have been so successful without the Community to provide an equal negotiating partner for the United States. Although this was not the intention and has not been the practice, the Community could use its commercial instruments (mainly tariffs and quotas) to pursue a policy of general protection, as the United States, Japan, and most Continental countries have done at some stage in their histories. The Community's huge exports of manufactures (again not far short of a tenth of gross community product) will long remain a powerful argument against this, however, and the more-likely role of Community tariffs and quotas in industrial policy is as a catalyst for a more-general Community industrial policy and a lever to bring the member governments' industrial policies into line wtih Community needs.

As long as trade policies are liberal, subsidies, or more precisely state aids (the Community's term, which includes other fiscal incentives), will be more important than tariffs as an instrument of industrial policy. The Treaty of Rome, which was more concerned with the removal of distortions to trade in the Common Market than with other forms of industrial policy, prohibited state aids that might distort competition, while allowing for some exceptions including those to promote economic development in areas with low income or employment, to remedy serious economic disturbances in member states, or to "facilitate the development of certain economic activities or economic areas, where such aid does not adversely affect trading conditions to an extent contrary to the common interest."[7] The Commission has the duty of identifying state aids that do or might distort competition, and if it decides that the aid is not compatible with the Common Market, the state in question must comply or be referred to the Court of Justice. Only a unanimous decision by the Council of Ministers in the state's favor can forestall the decision of the Court. Thus there is, unlike in the GATT, a highly integrative system for ensuring compliance with the Community decisions.

In the two decades of the EEC's existence the procedure has not been used very frequently, and almost always with the object of removing distortions to trade. Recently, however, the Community's powers have been used as a lever to secure positive adjustment in the member countries' steel and shipbuilding industries. Woolcock shows how the Commission's agreement to steel subsidies was made conditional on programs for restructuring the industry (p. 66); in this the Commission was strongly supported by the German government, whose agreement to steel import quotas, much wanted by other member governments, could have been withheld if the subsidies were allowed without the restructuring. The permission to grant state aids to shipbuilding has also been linked with the reduction of shipyard capacity.

Since most industrial subsidies could be said to distort competition, the Community's power to disallow them could become a very powerful instrument of control over member governments' industrial policies. As things stand at present, however, this power is limited in practice. The Commission is responsible for using it, but does not usually pick quarrels with member states, which can make life difficult for the Commission in various ways, even if it is hard for them to vote unanimously in the Council against a Commission decision on a state aid. It is also politically imprudent for the Community to go too far in exercising a power to prevent things being done and thus alienate political support, without at the same time attracting support by exercising power in a way that is more welcome. The forbidding of state subsidies is, moreover, a less-efficient way of promoting positive industrial policies than the granting of Community subsidies would be. Which leads us to the question of subsidies granted by the Community itself.

Although the state aids given by member states are much larger, the Community also provides a range of subsidies relevant to industrial policy. The Social Fund helps to finance training in the member countries. The Regional Development Fund provides some aid for the establishment of industries as well as the building of infrastructure. So does the Investment Bank, on a larger scale but charging interest rates, which tend however to be favorable to the borrower and are in some cases subsidized. The Agricultural Guidance and Guarantee Fund helps the creation of alternative employment in agricultural areas. Euratom finances research and development, some of which is applicable in industry. There is a small budget for Community research relating to data-processing. The European Coal and Steel Community, which receives a levy on the production of coal and steel in the Community, spends some of it in helping to finance restructuring of the steel industry and some in promoting new industrial employment in areas where steel workers are made redundant.

These various funds enable the Community to play a part in promoting adjustment and industrial employment, beyond its more-negative power to control the aids given by member states. But the sums that can be said to be used for industrial policy are not large, and their control is divided among a number of directorates general in the Commission, as well as the Investment Bank. The Commission has proposed the allocation of additional funds for purposes such as a scrap-and-build scheme to provide orders for shipbuilding, a larger program of research on data-processing, and an arms production board; but the member governments have not agreed. If positive industrial policy begins to receive the attention it deserves, however, the strength of the case for funds to support actions of common interest such as the scrap-and-build scheme can hardly fail to be evident. A decision on such proposals is often thwarted by difficulties relating to a single member state, and agreement is more likely if there are resources from which such states can derive some benefit.

Diebold has pointed out that antitrust legislaion is a form of industrial policy (see Chapter 6). The Community's cartel laws, based on articles 85 and 86 of the Rome Treaty, have like the American laws been used in pursuit of the liberal aim of more perfect competition. A number of significant cases have been judged by the Community Court and the judgements enforced on companies, including some major multinationals. The Community has thus shown how a dilemma facing antitrust actions against multinational companies can be resolved. Where legislation is national, disputes arise as to whether the law of the multinational's country of origin should have jurisdiction or the law of the country to which the behavior at issue relates. If there is common legislation for a group of countries to which all the countries involved belong, such disputes do not arise; and there is a law to deal with multinational cartels. This is only a partial solution, since it does not apply when countries outside the group are also involved. Since many multinationals are of American origin, this is an important qualification. As common legislation for a wider group of countries is not feasible at present (although there are the OECD and the UNCTAD investment codes), there may be a case for a formal understanding about the relationship between Community and U.S. jurisdiction.

Just as the Community's power over state aids can be used not only to prohibit them but also to allow them on condition that an agreed program of restructuring takes place, so the cartel legislation could be used to encourge industrial adjustment. Proposals to this effect were made when the Community producers of synthetic fibers sought leave to form a rationalization cartel that would reduce capacity and underpin the price level by sharing markets meanwhile. The Commission, as we have seen earlier (p. 98), turned down their request. Yet without removing the drag of excess capacity and without prices that provide a profit on which investment for the future can be based, the industry cannot develop in a way that will provide benefits for the consumer in future. Rejection of the rationalization cartel was comprehensible in terms of a static analysis, in which the ability of a sector to progress by means of research, development, and investment so as to serve the consumer in future does not enter into the calculation; and in the years when oligopolistic pricing held firm and yielded enough profit, a static analysis did little harm because in most countries the dynamism of the economy looked after itself. But with production far below capacity, prices weak, and profits low or nonexistent, the static view cuts out the opportunity of industrial development and thus ill serves both producers and consumers. Up to now, the Community's competition policy has not, like Japanese policy, been helpful to recession or rationalization cartels. This could, and following the argument of this chapter should, change in the future, and thereby strengthen the Community's positive industrial policy. Meanwhile, however, we have to look to the Community's steel sector, which comes under the different legislation of the European Coal and Steel Community, to find an example of industrial policy implemented through this kind of cartel.

The Community was endowed, in the Treaty establishing the ECSC, with some instruments of industrial policy that are not available for other sectors that fall under the EEC Treaty. The ECSC funds available for restructuring and providing new employment have been mentioned. The legislation that enabled the Community to establish a recession cartel for steel comes from articles 58, 59, and 61 of the ECSC Treaty, which provide for the regulation of prices and of production when there is a crisis in the steel market. As Woolcock shows (p. 65), the Commission managed at first to secure some measure of voluntary price maintenance, which firms were encouraged to respect by fear that compulsory minimum prices were the alternative. When the voluntary method proved ineffective, obligatory minimum prices were fixed for some key products, enforceable in Community courts through fines on companies that sell below them. Import base prices were fixed, following the example of the American import prices, at levels based on the costs of efficient Japanese producers; and the Community negotiated with external suppliers quotas which allowed them broadly to retain, but not increase, their share of the Community market. The power to fix production quotas for Community steelmakers, which is procedurally harder to introduce, had not been used before 1981 but had served as an inducement to companies to limit their output voluntarily. The combination of these measures has been used, as Woolcock explains, to maintain prices at levels that provide a return for the Community's efficient producers, without feather-bedding high-cost output; and the Community's power to control subsidies has been used, as we have seen, to ensure that restructuring takes place. Thus the steel recession cartel has limited the damage to the financial structure of efficient companies, while securing some modernization and the removal of obsolete capacity, and allowing imports to retain their market share. The Community has not only a very large export of manufactures but also a large surplus of manufactured exports over manufactured imports, which inhibits the Community from too much protection of its industry, for fear that it would come off worst from retaliation or a trade war. It has been argued, consequently, that a common industrial policy is not likely to follow the protectionist example of the common agricultural policy. The experience of the policy for steel lends support to this view.

A Positive Industrial Policy for the Community: Resources, Ideology, Institutions

The Community has, then, many of the instruments of industrial policy: powers to grant subsidies and to control the member states' aids; the instruments of trade policy, particularly tariffs and quotas; legal instruments to prohibit or regulate cartels; powers to regulate the price and production of steel; and some other instruments that we have not considered, such as control over national discrimination in public purchasing or in defining specifications. Yet the Community's use of these instruments, while effective in a number of cases, has remained far from what could be expected of a positive industrial policy, even allowing that all policies which do not affect a common interest should be conducted by the member governments, not the Community. One has only to compare the Community with Japan to realize what the Community may be losing as a result of its inadequate performance in this field.

One reason for the inadequacy of Community industrial policy is the lack of financial resources. The member governments are understandably jealous of their financial prerogatives and reluctant to transfer more substantial resources to the Community. Agreement among the member governments on many of the thorny issues of industrial policy is hard to reach. Lack of Community money makes it harder to reach than it need be. As a consequence, restructuring in industries such as shipbuilding is held up, schemes such as scrap-and-build which would bring new orders to the sector are not adopted, and three separate models of fast-breeder reactors are developed at enormous unnecessary cost. While an adequate budget for a positive industrial policy would imply more Community spending in a number of directions, it could also cut much wasteful expenditure, such as that on at least one of the reactor programs.

Money for industrial policy will not be spent well unless there is a consensus about aims and methods. Countries such as Britain, France, Germany, and Italy have very different views on such matters: less different than may appear from the views they express, perhaps, and covering a fairly wide spectrum within each country, but still different enough to be often an obstacle to agreement, particularly when the views, such as German support for free trade, coincide with interest, such as the Germans' need to prevent retaliatory protection in the markets of their powerful exporting industries. Ideological differences are also found within the Commission, where we saw that the Directorates General for Competition and for Industrial Affairs disagreed about the legitimacy of the rationalization cartel for synthetic fibers. Divergent ideologies as well as interests, and the lack of a consensus on the character of a positive industrial policy, are a second reason why the Community's industrial policy is inadequate.

A third major reason lies in the institutions in which Community decisions are taken. It is, again, understandable that member governments are jealous of their sovereignty as well as their money. But their insistence on having a wide range of national requirements accommodated in every Community decision makes the decisions weak and late, if they are taken at all. This way of doing business is incompatible with the needs of such a highly interdependent group of economies. Various official reports have been made at the request of the member governments, to recommend improvements in the Community institutions.[8] Each made sensible suggestions that the governments ignored. This is not the place to go into detail on the subject, but two observations may be worth making. First, the importance of industrial policy is not reflected in the institutions, apart from the Commission with its Directorate General for Industrial Affairs. The Council has no meeting of ministers responsible for industrial policy, and the Parliament has no committee to deal with industrial policy. This doubtless reflects, in part, ideological differences on the subject; but it is in the Community's interest to give proper attention to industrial policy, and this would be helped by a regular forum in the Council and the Parliament. Second, the incompatibility between economic interdependence and political sovereignty is something that we can and doubtless must live with for a time. But it should be said, even if it is not everywhere a popular thing to say, that a more federal way of taking decisions on important matters of common concern is increasingly essential to the economic and political health of the Community.

Economic Convergence and Wider Cooperation

Why has the European Community gone so much farther than other groups of countries to equip itself with the instruments and institutions with which it can make industrial policy? The close interdependence among the member countries, and their fear of the consequences if the autarky of the 1930s were to return, have persuaded them of the need to establish their common institutions for a variety of purposes, and to endow the institutions with common instruments which, although often intended as means only for preventing distortions to trade (the common external tariff, the cartel legislation, and the control over state aids), can in fact be used for other purposes of industrial policy. But the interdependence not only makes the capacity to decide and act together more necessary; it also makes common action more possible. For the close relationship among the member countries is associated with a degree of economic, social, and political similarity (parliamentary democracy, the mixed economy), with some experience of common institutions and with the plain fact of geographical proximity, which reduce the obstacles to reaching agreement, even if this still remains difficult. As the need for some decisions of industrial policy has become more pressing through the 1970s, the Community has been pushed by events into using some of this capacity for common action.

Events are also pushing the wider international community into a greater need for cooperation about industrial policy, particularly among the advanced industrial countries but also with the developing countries and the East Europeans.

The application of modern technology throughout most of the world and continuing techological development seem certain to cause international interdependence to continue to intensify; and this, combined with the market imperfections associated with the advance of technology, is likely to ensure that the role of industrial policy and its international implications become yet more important in the future.

The wider the net of international cooperation is cast, the harder it is to cooperate. Economic, social, and political similarities become less, there is less experience of common institutions, and distance reduces contact. The OECD countries could not, at present, adopt the institutions and instruments that are acceptable and workable in the European Community; nor could the developing countries or the East Europeans conduct with the advanced industrial countries the sort of intimate discussion, based on shared circumstances and assumptions, that is possible in the OECD. But the circumstances that constrain the degree of cooperation are not static. Economies are converging, as Saunders shows, toward more similar structures and levels. The growth of trade and other links, even if the term global village exaggerates the result, is leading toward a closer-knit world economy and, with many fits and starts, society. Strong forces are pressing toward more interdependence. Some who believed that economic convergence would be followed by political convergence have been disappointed; but this may well have been because they expected too much, too fast. The societies and politics of advanced industrial countries now have so much in common that it seems possible to envisage them working their way toward some forms of policy integration in which the European Community continues to be the pioneer. Some of the newly industrializing countries are reaching a stage where they could begin to join with the advanced industrialized countries in the kind of activities undertaken in the OECD, and to apply more fully the rules of the GATT. At least some of the other less-developed countries will continue on the line of economic convergence; and policy convergence on the part of East Europeans, although the more sanguine expectations have not been fulfilled, may well be a significant trend over the long run.

It may therefore be useful to accompany the idea of a ladder of economic convergence, which emerges from the Saunders chapter, with an idea of policy convergence, whereby countries at each stage of the economic ladder will be reaching for forms of economic policy which suit that stage of economic development and which have something in common with at least some of the other countries at a similar stage. If this is combined with a ladder of interdependence, on which countries become more interdependent as they become economically more advanced, the result will be that both the need and the capacity for cooperation on industrial policy will increase.

These ladders are not put forward as a deterministic model. They may be broken by economic events (the effect of oil prices on the less-developed countries), political trends (nationalism, religious or ideological fundamentalism) or a reversal of interdependence (autarky resulting from economic instability and unemployment). But they are suggested as desirable and possible. The world faces a double challenge: to evolve forms of economic policy, including industrial policy, that are suitable for the modern economy; and to achieve the integration of policies that should follow the growing integration of economies. Both challenges are very hard to meet; but if they are not met, it seems certain that both the economic condition of the countries that fail to meet them, and international political relationships, will remain suboptimal, to the point where that piece of economic jargon will have to be replaced by plain English words such as bad or downright disastrous. Among other needs, if the challenges are to be met, are the intellectual basis for the development of industrial policy and of international policy integration. I hope that our book will have made some contribution to this.

Notes

1. These do not, unfortunately, reflect the authors' collective wisdom. Although I have learnt much from my colleagues, they have no responsibility for what I write here. Those who are interested in a collective view can find it in John Pinder, Takashi Hosomi, and William Diebold, *Industrial Policy and the International Economy,* The Triangle Papers: 19 (New York, Paris and Tokyo: The Trilateral Commission, 1979).

2. OECD Communiqué A(78)23 of June 15, 1978.

3. Ibid.

4. "Policies for Adjustment: Some General Orientations" in *The Case for Positive Adjustment Policies:* A Compendium of OECD Documents (Paris, 1979).

5. Pinder, Hosomi, and Diebold, op. cit., p. 70.

6. Ibid.

7. Treaty establishing the European Economic Community, Article 92. This article, and the other Rome Treaty articles that concern state aids, are discussed in Chapter 8.

8. See, for example, E C Commission, Bulletin, supplement 9/73 (Vedel report); EC Commission, Bulletin, supplement 1/76 (Tindemans report); *Report on European Institutions,* presented by the Committee of Three to the European Council, October 1979 (Three Wise Men's report).

Index

The Editor and Contributors

The Director of the Policy Studies Institute in London, John Pinder is the former Director of Political and Economic Planning and the former International Director of the Economist Intelligence Unit. His many publications include books and articles on the European Community, East-West trade, and international aspects of industrial policy. He is coauthor, with William Diebold and Takashi Hosomi, of *Industrial Policy and the International Economy,* published by the Trilateral Commission.

William Diebold, Jr., is a Senior Research Fellow with the Council on Foreign Relations in New York. His areas of expertise include international trade, Western European economic integration, and foreign economic policy (he worked for the U.S. government to help create post-World War II international economic organizations), and his books include *Industrial Policy as an International Issue, The United States and the Industrial World, The Schuman Plan,* and *Trade and Payments in Western Europe.*

Geoffrey Edwards, Deputy Director of the Federal Trust for Education and Research, London, is presently involved in research projects on the North-South dialogue and on Turkey and the European Community. He is coauthor of *A Wider European Community? Issues and Problems of Further Enlargement, A Common Man's Guide to the Common Market,* and the forthcoming *The Defence of Europe,* and is a joint editor of *Federal Solutions to European Issues.*

Currently a Research Fellow at the European University Institute, Florence, Wolfgang Hager has served as Director of Studies, European Community Institute for University Studies, Brussels, as a European Secretary, the Trilateral Commission, and as Senior Fellow in international economics at the German Society for Foreign Policy, Bonn. His extensive publications in German and English include articles and books on international economic relations, foreign policy, energy, and the European Community.

Takashi Hosomi has been associated with the Ministry of Finance, Tokyo, as Director General of the Tax Bureau, as Vice Minister of Finance for International Affairs, and as special advisor to the Minister of Finance. He retired as Adviser to the Industrial Bank of Japan in 1981 to become President of the Overseas Economic Cooperation Fund, Tokyo.

Ariyoshi Okumura has been the General Manager of the Financial Planning and Industrial Research departments of the Industrial Bank of Tokyo. He has also served as a task force member of the Japan-U.S. Economic Relations Group, as a delegate to the Trilateral Commission Washington Conference in 1981, and as a member of the MITI Industrial Structural Council Committee and the Advisory Committee for Energy.

A Professorial Fellow at the Sussex European Research Centre, England, Christopher Saunders has been Director of Economic Research, UN Economic Commission for Europe, Director of the National Institute for Economic and Social Research, London, and Deputy Director of the Central Statistical Office, London. He has contributed widely to publications of the Economic Commission for Europe, the National Institute for Economic and Social Research, and the Central Statistical Office on, among other topics, European economies, international trade and industry, national accounts, pay structures, and incomes policies.

Another specialist on U.S.-European trade and economic relations, Stephen Woolcock is Research Fellow at the Royal Institute of International Affairs, London. His previous research has included the role of the newly industrializing countries and industrial policy in the European Community.